IGCSE Chemistry

Andrew Clegg

www.internationalschools.co.uk

Free online support
Useful weblinks
24 hour online ordering

Heinemann is an imprint of Pearson Education Limited, a company incorporated in England and Wales, having its registered office at Edinburgh Gate, Harlow, Essex, CM20 2JE. Registered company number: 872828

www.heinemann.co.uk
Heinemann is a registered trademark of Pearson Education Limited

Text © Pearson Education Limited 2009

First published 2009

13 12 11
10 9 8 7 6 5 4

British Library Cataloguing in Publication Data is available from the British Library on request.

ISBN 978 0435966799

Copyright notice
All rights reserved. No part of this publication may be reproduced in any form or by any means (including photocopying or storing it in any medium by electronic means and whether or not transiently or incidentally to some other use of this publication) without the written permission of the copyright owner, except in accordance with the provisions of the Copyright, Designs and Patents Act 1988 or under the terms of a licence issued by the Copyright Licensing Agency, Saffron House, 6–10 Kirby Street, London EC1N 8TS (www.cla.co.uk). Applications for the copyright owner's written permission should be addressed to the publisher.

Edited by Paul King and Saskia Besier
Designed by Tony Richardson
Typeset by Tech-Set Ltd
Original illustrations © Pearson Education Limited 2009
Illustrated by Tech-Set Ltd
Cover design by Creative Monkey
Picture research by Ginny Stroud-Lewis
Cover photo/illustration © Wellcome Images / Karen Neill / LCI
Printed in China
GCC/04

There are links to relevant websites in this book. In order to ensure that the links are up-to-date, that the links work, and that the sites are not inadvertently linked to sites that could be considered offensive, we have made the links available on the Heinemann website at www.heinemann.co.uk/hotlinks. When you access the site, the express code is 6799P.

On the CD
Past paper questions are reproduced by permission of the University of Cambridge Local Examinations Syndicate.

The University of Cambridge Local Examinations Syndicate bears no responsibility for the example answers to questions taken from its past question papers which are contained on the CD contained within this publication.

Acknowledgements

The author and publisher would like to thank the following individuals and organisations for permission to reproduce photographs:

p.1 t. © Cleveland Bridge Company, b. © Pearson Education Ltd / Trevor Clifford; p.2 t. © Pearson Education Ltd / Peter Gould, b. © Digital Vision; p.3 l. © Getty Images / Hulton Archive, r. © Alamy / Mary Evans Picture Library ; p.4 © Science Photo Library / NASA; p.5 t. © Getty Images / PhotoDisc, b. © Science Photo Library / Sinclair Stammers; p.8 © Science Photo Library / Martyn F Chillmaid; p.9 © Science Photo Library / Andrew Lambert Photography; p. 12 tl. © Art Directors and Trip, tr. © Qatar Liquefied Gas Company Ltd., b. © Alamy / AfriPics.com; p.15 © Shutterstock / Brian Weed; p.20 tl., tr., bl. © Getty Images / PhotoDisc, br. © Pearson Education Ltd / Malcolm Harris; p.21 t. © Art Directors and Trip, b. © Science Photo Library / Andrew Lambert Photography; p.28 t. © Science Photo Library / Dr Tony Brain and David Parker, b. SIL; p. 35 © Corbis / Bettmann; p.39 © British Museum; p. 43 © Ginny Stroud Lewis ; p.50 © Science Photo Library / Arnold Fisher; p.51 © Shutterstock / Travis Manley; p.52 t. © Ginny Stroud Lewis, b. © Science Photo Library / Alfred Pasieka; p.56 t. © Alamy, b. © Andrew Clegg; p.57 © Art Directors and Trip; p.58 tr. © Shutterstock / Tom Curtis, tl. © Andrew Clegg, b. © Digital Stock; p.59 © Simon Wilkie; p.61 © Alamy / avatra images; p.70 l. © Getty Images / Hulton Archive; r. © Getty Images / PhotoDisc; p.77 © Art Directors and Trip; p.78 l. © Science Photo Library / Charles D Winters, r. © Art Directors and Trip; p. 81 © Science Photo Library / Russ Mann / Agstockusa; p.84 l. © Pearson Education Ltd / Gareth Boden, r. © Science Photo Library / Arnold Fisher; p. 94 © Shutterstock / Denis Pepin; p. 97 © Science Photo Library / Jim Varney; p. 101 © Science Photo Library; p. 104 © Science Photo Library / Maximilian Stock Library; p. 107 t. © Science Photo Library / Pascal Goetgheluck, bl. © Getty Images / Hulton Archive, br. © Getty Images / Time & Life Pictures; p. 108 l. © SS Great Britain Museum, Bristol, r. © Pearson Education Ltd / John Millar; p. 109 © Science Photo Library / John W Alexanders; p. 111 © Alamy / Stock Connection Distribution; p. 112 © Alamy / Visual Arts Library (London); p. 121 © Andrew Clegg; p. 125 tl. © By courtesy of the SS Great Britain Trust, tr. © Alamy / photosublime, b. © iStockPhoto.com / Michal Kolosowski; p. 128 © Corbis / Ariel Skelley; p. 130 © The Bridgeman Art Library; p. 134 © Alamy / Jim Parkin; p. 135 t. © Getty Images / Time & Life Images, b. © Alamy / Peter Bowater; p. 136 © Alamy / Leslie Garland Picture Library; p. 137 © Pearson Education Ltd / Peter Gould; p. 138 t. © Alamy / The London Art Archive, b. © Topfoto / Fortean; p.139 © Science Photo Library / Adam Hart-Davis; p. 142 tl. © Anglo American , tr. © Alamy / William Robinson, b. © Alamy / Derry Brabbs; p. 143 © Corbis / Julia Waterlow; Eye Ubiquitous; p. 145 t. © Courtesy of the Ironbridge Gorge Museum Trust, b. © Shutterstock / Gert Johannes / Jacobus Very; p. 146 © Alamy / Photolocate; p. 152 t. © Alamy / AfriPics.com , b. © Shutterstock / Gary James Calder; p. 155 t. © akg-images / Erich Lessing, c. © Science Photo Library / Detlev Van Ravenswaay, b. © Mary Evans Picture Library; p. 156 © Alamy / Colin Hugill; p. 158 l. © NASA / JSC, c., r. © NASA; p.163 © Science Photo Library; p. 164 © Fancy / Punchstock; p. 165 l. © Science Photo Library / Adam Hart Davies, r. © iStockPhoto.com / Anka Kaczmarzyk; p.166 © Alamy / Neil Setchfield; p. 173 t. © Shutterstock / Multiart, c. © Alamy / Stock Connection, bl. © Shutterstock / David Peta, br. © Getty Images / PhotoDisc; p. 174 l. © Ginny Stroud-Lewis, r. © iStockPhoto.com / Dave White; p. 186 tl. © Shutterstock / John Rawsterne, tr. © Getty Images / PhotoDisc, bl. © Corbis / Richard du Toit; Gallo Images, br. © Ginny Stroud-Lewis; p. 196 © Alamy / Peter Horree; p. 203 © Alamy / Norbert Speicher; p.205 © Science Photo Library; p. 210 © Ginny Stroud-Lewis; p. 213 t. © iStockPhoto.com / Thomas Zenker, b. © Andrew Clegg; p.215 t. © Alamy / Alan King, b. © Shutterstock / Robert Hardholt; p.216 l. © Archiv der Max-Planck-Gesellschaft, Berlin-Dahlem, r. © BASF; p. 218 © Science Photo Library / Martin Bond; p. 220 © Shutterstock / Jim Mills; p.222 © www.saltsense.co.uk; p. 224 © Shutterstock / Semen Lixodeev; p. 225 © Ginny Stroud-Lewis; p. 226 © Shutterstock / Chad McDermott.

Every effort has been made to contact copyright holders of material reproduced in this book. Any omissions will be rectified in subsequent printings if notice is given to the publishers.

Contents

Introduction   vii

Chapter 1   What is chemistry?   1

Chapter 2   What is matter?
2.1 Solids, liquids and gases   6
2.2 Matter is made of particles   7

Chapter 3   Mixtures and substances
3.1 Solutions   13
3.2 Methods of purifying substances   14
3.3 Finding out how pure a substance is   17
3.4 How do we know when a substance is pure?   19

Chapter 4   Atoms and molecules
4.1 How small are atoms and molecules?   29
4.2 A short history of atomic theories   30
4.3 Using symbols to represent elements   32
4.4 How many protons, neutrons and electrons are there in the atom?   33
4.5 Isotopes   34
4.6 Atomic mass and molecular mass   34
4.7 A pattern of elements – the Periodic Table   35
4.8 The electronic structure of the elements   37
4.9 Radioactive isotopes   39

Chapter 5   How atoms combine
5.1 Classifying materials   44
5.2 Covalent bonds   44
5.3 Double and triple covalent bonds   47
5.4 The properties of covalent compounds   48
5.5 Ionic bonds   48
5.6 The properties of ionic compounds   50
5.7 Macromolecules   51
5.8 Metallic bonds   54

Chapter 6 The Periodic Table

6.1	Blocks of elements in the Periodic Table	57
6.2	Group I: the alkali metals	59
6.3	Group VII: the halogens	62
6.4	Group VIII: the inert gases	66
6.5	The transition metals	68
6.6	Trends across the periods	70

Chapter 7 Acids and alkalis

7.1	What are acids and what do they do?	75
7.2	A pattern in acids and alkalis – pH	77
7.3	How we use acids and alkalis	80
7.4	Oxides and pH	81
7.5	What happens when acids and bases react together?	84
7.6	Making salts	86
7.7	Identifying ions in salts	88

Chapter 8 Oxidation and reduction

8.1	Reducing metal ores	95
8.2	Oxidation of metals	95
8.3	Oxidation state	95
8.4	Another definition of oxidation and reduction	96
8.5	Electrolysis	98
8.6	Explaining electrolysis	101
8.7	Applications of electrolysis	105

Chapter 9 Metals

9.1	Why metals are so useful	107
9.2	A pattern of metals – the reactivity series	112
9.3	How readily will a metal form its positive ion?	116
9.4	How stable are metal compounds?	118
9.5	The names of some chemical compounds	120
9.6	Corrosion and its prevention	121

Chapter 10 Chemistry and energy

10.1	Conservation of energy	126
10.2	Energy changes during chemical reactions	126
10.3	Fuels	130
10.4	Sustainable fuel supplies	133
10.5	Cells and batteries	136

Chapter 11 Extracting and using metals

11.1	Mining and concentrating the ore	143
11.2	Reducing the ore to metal	144
11.3	Extraction of metals and the reactivity series	147
11.4	Making iron and steel	147
11.5	Making aluminium	149
11.6	Making zinc	150
11.7	Uses of metals	151
11.8	Alloys	153

Chapter 12 Chemistry and the environment

12.1	Our atmosphere	159
12.2	Pollution of the atmosphere	164
12.3	Water	168

Chapter 13 Fast and slow reactions

13.1	Making reactions go faster	174
13.2	Light and chemical reactions	180
13.3	Reactions that go both ways	181

Chapter 14 Organic chemistry

14.1	Carbon, a special element	187
14.2	Alkanes	189
14.3	Alkenes	191
14.4	Alcohols	194
14.5	Organic acids	197

Chapter 15 Macromolecules

15.1	Big molecules	204
15.2	Synthetic polymers	205
15.3	Natural polymers	207
15.4	Fats and oils	209

Chapter 16 Industrial chemistry

16.1	Making use of the gases of the air	213
16.2	Sulfur and the sulfuric acid industry	217
16.3	Industries based on lime	220
16.4	The alkali industry	222
16.5	The petroleum industry	225

Chapter 17 How much?

17.1	Relative atomic and molecular masses	229
17.2	The mole	231
17.3	Formulae of compounds	236
17.4	The volume of a mole of gas	240
17.5	Moles in solutions	244

Index

251

Introduction

This book includes many features that will help you during the course. Some of these features are described below.

Supplementary material Sections marked with a letter S and a line like this

indicate supplementary material. You need to cover this material only if you are taking the extended syllabus.

Did you know? The material at the start of each chapter, on a purple background, or in the 'Did you know' boxes is not specifically required by the syllabus, but is designed to widen your knowledge and deepen your understanding.

  DID YOU KNOW?

If you share your tin of cola with everybody else in the world, you would each have about
1 000 000 000 000 000 molecules to drink.

Links The links show you where the activities on the CD fit in the course.

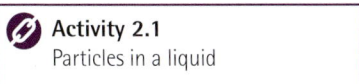 Activity 2.1
Particles in a liquid

Worked examples

The worked examples show you how a problem is solved and demonstrates the way in which your answer should be set out.

> ### WORKED EXAMPLE
>
> 12 10 g of a hydrocarbon is found to contain 8 g carbon and 2 g hydrogen. Its relative molecular mass is 30. What is its empirical formula and its molecular formula? (C = 12, H = 1)
>
> 8 g carbon combines with 2 g hydrogen
>
> Therefore 1 g carbon combines with $\frac{2}{8}$ g hydrogen
>
> Therefore 12 g carbon (1 mole) combines with $2 \times \frac{12}{8}$ g hydrogen

Questions

There are questions throughout the book to check your understanding of each unit or topic.

> ### QUESTION
>
> 6.15 What is meant by the term 'transition metals'? List their characteristic properties.
>
> 6.16 Describe how the reactivity of the transition metals changes (a) across periods and (b) down groups.

Chapter 1

What is chemistry?

Chemistry is part of all our lives. Chemists have done many things that affect the way we live. Look at these pictures; all the objects you can see are made out of mixtures of different materials. All these materials have been made by chemists.

◀ **Figure 1.1**
The Victoria Falls Bridge over the Zambezi between Zimbabwe and Zambia was built between 1905 and 1908. It is made from steel and the builders used their knowledge of the different properties of steel to design and construct it.

Websites

Go to www.heinemann.co.uk/hotlinks, insert the express code 6799P and click on 1.1.

◀ **Figure 1.2**
Can you imagine a world without plastics? Many older people can because all these materials were invented by chemists in the last 60 years.

Figure 1.3
Many chemicals are very useful to us. All the items you can see here have been discovered by chemists in the last 100 years.

Figure 1.4
Fuels allow us to travel further and faster than ever before. Petrol and diesel were developed by chemists from crude oil.

 DID YOU KNOW?

Modern chemistry was first developed by Arabic chemists, between 1200 and 600 years ago. They developed ways of extracting metals. They made acids and alkalis and studied their reactions. The chemists were good at making perfumes and invented fractional distillation to extract them from plants (see pages 196 and 227). Perhaps the 'experimental method' was the most important thing they gave to chemistry; studying through practical experiments. Many modern pieces of science equipment were first invented by Arabic scientists.

Here are some more ways that chemists have influenced the way we live.
- When we are ill we use medicines developed by chemists to help us get better.
- Chemists have helped to make food safe to eat.
- Chemists have developed ways of making water clean and safe to drink and of purifying sewage so that the water can be re-used.
- Chemists have discovered and developed many different materials that are part of our daily lives. Think of paints, glues, cleaning materials, insecticides, fertilisers, and more. Where did life come from?

What is chemistry?

- Chemists working with metals, called metallurgists, have developed all the different kinds of metals we use in our daily lives and invented the processes we use to extract them from their ores.
- Chemists have invented all the different materials that modern buildings are made from.
- Chemists have invented explosives. These have been used to help us get useful materials out of the ground but they have also been used to make ammunition and bombs, which have killed or injured millions.
- Chemists have even made artificial diamonds!

You can probably think of many more things that chemists have done that affect your life.

◀ **Figures 1.5 and 1.6**
Two famous chemists. Marie Curie (left) was awarded two Nobel Prizes, one for chemistry and one for physics, for the work she did on radioactivity. Dorothy Hodgkin (right) received the 1964 prize for using X-rays to work out the structure of two complex and important biological molecules, insulin and vitamin B12.

Chemistry is the study of matter. Chemists try to find out the answer to important questions like these:
- What are substances made of?
- Why do substances behave in the way they do?
- How can we change one kind of matter into another?
- Can we discover any patterns in the way some substances behave which will allow us to predict how other substances might behave?

Chemists can then go on to ask useful questions like these:
- How can we obtain useful materials from the earth and from living things?
- How can we make new substances that are useful to us?

This book will give you the answers to some of these questions. It will help you understand chemistry and the benefits it brings us. It will also help you to understand the problems that have been caused by chemistry, when we destroy the natural environment in order to get the chemicals we need and when we pollute air and water with waste chemicals we want to get rid of.

 DID YOU KNOW?

The chemist who invented dynamite, an explosive used for quarrying, was a Swede called Alfred Nobel. The invention earned him a large fortune. In his will he left the money (the equivalent of 100 million dollars today) to the Swedish Academy of Sciences to invest. He instructed them to use the money earned by the investment to give prizes each year to scientists who make major discoveries. These are called the Nobel Prizes. Each prize is now worth over a million US dollars.

3

Chapter 2

What is matter?

Figure 2.1
Our Sun is a ball of glowing hydrogen and helium gas. At the bottom left you can see a solar **prominence**. The Sun ejects a massive plume of gas into space. The plume is about 100 times the size of the Earth.

Websites

Go to www.heinemann.co.uk/hotlinks, insert the express code 6799P and click on 2.1.

DID YOU KNOW?

You can see the Orion Nebula overhead at night from October to March. The constellation of Orion is easy to find because it has three bright stars in a straight line quite close to each other. This is Orion's Belt (Orion was a hunter in Greek folklore). Hanging from his belt at right angles you can see three more stars that make up his sword. The middle one you can see looks a bit blurred. This is because it is not a star but a nebula, a massive cloud of glowing hydrogen gas about 10 000 000 000 000 000 km in diameter. (For comparison, the distance from here to the Sun is about 150 000 000 kilometres.)

What is the Universe made of? Is all the matter in the Universe the same? What do we know about what the objects in these pictures are made of? We know what the Moon is made of because American astronauts have been there and brought some moon rock back here.

We know that the Sun is made mainly out of two substances, the gases hydrogen and helium. We know that the Orion Nebula is made almost entirely of the gas hydrogen, glowing very hot. We know what these are made of because of the kind of light that is given off; scientists can look at them and they can tell that the light comes from very hot hydrogen and helium.

What is matter?

◀ **Figure 2.2**
The Moon is made of the same material as the Earth. It is the smaller remains of a gigantic collision between two planets close to each other, one of which was the early Earth, about four thousand million years ago. This collision made Earth bigger than it was before the collision, big enough to have a large enough gravity to hold on to its atmosphere. The Moon is too small – all the atmosphere and water it once had escaped into space long ago. The distance from the Earth to the Moon is about one third of the diameter of the Sun.

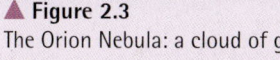

We know what meteorites are made of and we know that this matter came originally from the middle of an exploding star.

What about matter in the Universe that does not give off light? We cannot see this matter. What is that made of? How do we even know it is there?

In this chapter we will study just the matter that is around us here on Earth.

▲ **Figure 2.3**
The Orion Nebula: a cloud of glowing hydrogen about ten thousand million million kilometres across.

Figure 2.4 ▶
These meteorites were once part of the centre of a distant sun that exploded long ago. They are all part of the same metal object that exploded as it fell to Earth during prehistoric times, in what is now the small town of Gibeon, Namibia. They are made up of 90% iron, 8% nickel, with 2% other metals, mainly cobalt.

Websites
Go to www.heinemann.co.uk/hotlinks, insert the express code 6799P and click on 2.2.

5

2.1 Solids, liquids and gases

There are three kinds of matter around us; solids, liquids and gases. We call these the three states of matter. You already know the main properties of these states of matter but here is a table to remind you.

▼ Table 2.1
Properties of solids, liquids and gases.

Property	Solid	Liquid	Gas
What do they feel like when you touch them?	You can touch solids but you cannot put your hand into them. They do not change shape.	You can put your hand into them and move it around. Liquids take the shape of the container that holds them.	You can put your hand into them and move it around easily. You can only feel gases when they blow against your skin. Gases do not have a shape, they expand throughout the container that holds them.
What happens when you heat them?	They expand slightly. With more heating they melt into a liquid.	They expand slightly. With more heating they boil into a gas.	They expand a lot.
What happens when you cool them?	They contract slightly.	They contract slightly. With more cooling they freeze into a solid.	They contract a lot. With more cooling they condense into a liquid.
What happens if you compress them?	They are not easily compressible.	They are not easily compressible.	They are easily compressible.
How dense are they?	The density of most solids varies between about 0.5 g/cm³ to around 20 g/cm³	The density of most liquids at room temperature varies around 1 g/cm³ but there are some notable exceptions such as mercury.	The density of most gases at room temperature and pressure is small, less than a thousandth of a typical liquid.

The diagram below summarises the effect of heating and cooling the three states of matter.

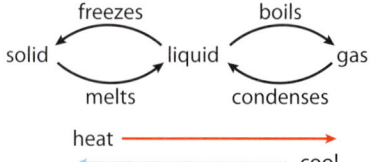

▶ Figure 2.5
The effects of heating and cooling states of matter.

If you put a small amount of iodine in a gas jar with a lid on it and leave it for a few days, you will notice that the iodine gradually disappears but you will not see any liquid iodine (but take care, do not remove the lid, as it is rather poisonous). The solid iodine changes directly into gaseous iodine without forming a liquid. This process is called **sublimation**; the iodine **sublimes**. Solid carbon dioxide is another substance that sublimes when it is heated; it changes directly to gaseous carbon dioxide at −78°C.

What is matter?

The word sublimation describes the change from solid directly to gas in both directions, both from solid to gas or from gas to solid. The white powdery 'hoar' frost that you can sometimes see on a cold morning (and also in your fridge ice-box) is caused by water vapour subliming directly to ice.

2.2 Matter is made of particles

A Greek poet and philosopher called Democritus, who lived at the time of Pythagoras over 2500 years ago, reasoned that matter was made out of particles. He imagined cutting a piece of matter in half, then cutting a half piece in half and so on. He reasoned that it was not theoretically possible to continue dividing a matter in half for ever and that there would come a time when each of the halves was one particle of matter, which could not be cut further. He called such a particle an 'atomos' which means 'something that cannot be divided'.

We now have much **evidence** that all matter is made of tiny particles. Scientists look for evidence and make **theories** that explain the evidence. A good theory is one that can explain evidence from many different observations and the 'kinetic particle theory' is one of these. You will learn in this chapter of many observations that can be explained by the particle theory.

The kinetic particle theory suggests that all matter is made of tiny particles and that these particles have energy. This energy causes them to move. The word 'kinetic' means 'moving'.

The particles in a solid are arranged in a regular way in rows. They cannot move around because they are held together by strong forces of attraction. They can move by vibrating.

When a solid is heated, the particles vibrate faster. To do this they need a little more space and so they have to move slightly further apart. This explains why solids **expand** slightly when they are heated.

When enough energy is given to particles in a solid they can move out of their fixed positions and move round each other. This happens when the solid **melts**. In the liquid that is formed, the particles are still as close to each other as in the solid. They have enough energy to allow the particles to move around but they do not have sufficient energy to overcome the forces that hold them next to each other. So, although they can move, they still touch each other as they did in the solid.

If more energy is given to the particles, they move and vibrate faster and faster until they have enough energy to overcome the forces holding them together. The particles then can escape from the liquid and move around quickly and independently. This is what happens when liquids **boil**.

When gas particles cool, the opposite processes happen. The gas particles move more and more slowly until they do not have enough energy to overcome the attractive forces that keep them stuck together when they hit each other. At this point the gas **condenses** to a liquid. As the liquid particles get cooler, they move more and more slowly until they are

> **DID YOU KNOW?**
> Substances sublime because the energy needed to change them from solid to liquid is more than the energy needed to change them from liquid to gas. This is very rare. It means that the boiling points of such substances are actually lower than their melting points!

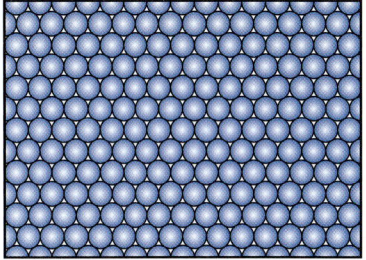

▲ **Figure 2.6**
In a solid the particles are close together but they cannot move around. They can, however, vibrate.

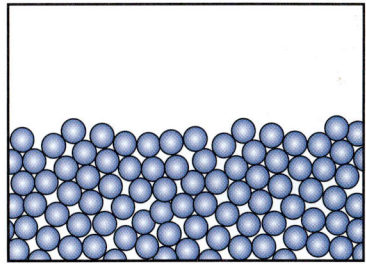

▲ **Figure 2.7**
In a liquid, the particles are still close together but they can move around randomly. They also vibrate.

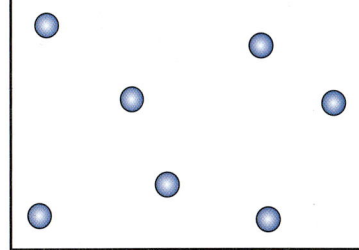

▲ **Figure 2.8**
In a gas the particles are far apart and do not touch each other. They move rapidly and randomly. They also vibrate.

unable to move at all. They all fall in line with each other when they stop moving. When this occurs the liquid **freezes** or **solidifies**.

These processes are shown in the diagrams below.

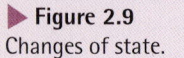
Figure 2.9
Changes of state.

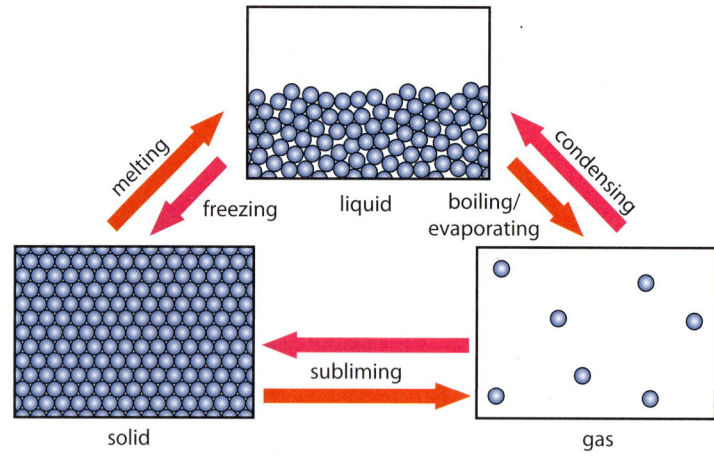

Diffusion

Activity 2.1
Particles in a liquid

More evidence for the existence of particles is shown in the observations below. You could try these investigations. Can you think of a different theory of matter that can explain all these results better than the kinetic particle theory?

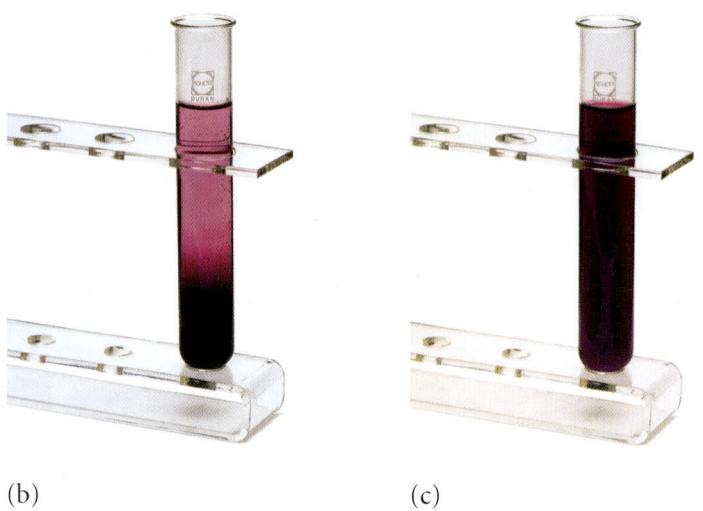

(a) (b) (c)

▲ Figure 2.10
Three test tubes of water with a crystal of potassium manganate(VII) in them: (a) when crystal is just in, (b) after a few minutes, and (c) after a day.

The pictures above show a test tube of water with a crystal of potassium manganate(VII) at the bottom. Potassium manganate(VII) is also known as potassium permanganate and is a solid that dissolves in water to give a deep purple solution. The second picture was taken a few minutes after the first one and the third picture after a day. You can see that the purple potassium manganate(VII) gradually spreads through the liquid. This process is called **diffusion**.

What is matter?

But how does it do it? We can explain this using particles. The purple particles of potassium manganate(VII) in photograph (a) are almost all in the solid crystal, in lines next to each other. In photograph (b) some of these particles have broken away from the crystal and they have diffused into the liquid. They move between the particles of water. By the next day, all the particles have moved into the water, forming a solution of potassium manganate(VII). The kinetic particle theory can be used to explain diffusion.

◀ **Figure 2.11**
The picture on the left shows bromine beginning to diffuse through the air in the gas jars. The picture on the right, taken two hours later, shows bromine gas diffused evenly through the air in the jars

 **Activity 2.2**
Particles in a gas

Look at these pictures of two gas jars. In the first picture a few drops of the liquid bromine have been put in the bottom of the jar. Bromine is a brown liquid that easily **vaporises** into a gas; you can see some of the gas just above the liquid. The second picture was taken about 15 minutes later and you can see that the gas has diffused throughout both jars. The particles of the bromine gas have moved between the gas particles of the air in the gas jar. This is another example of diffusion, which can be explained by the kinetic particle theory.

You will note that the particles of bromine moving in the air move much faster than the potassium manganate(VII) particles moving in water. This is because the gas particles in air are further apart than the water particles and it is easier for the other particles to move in between them.

If you put a filter paper between the two jars in the bromine experiment you will find that it does not slow down the bromine diffusion. This shows that the bromine particles are not stopped by the paper. The bromine particles are much smaller than the holes in the filter paper.

The rate of diffusion of a gas depends on how heavy its particles are. Small, light particles like hydrogen move much faster than larger, heavier particles like carbon dioxide. Hydrogen can diffuse through air much faster than carbon dioxide.

The Brownian movement: a mystery explained by the particle theory

Throughout the seventeenth and eighteenth centuries, scientists had reported the strange random movements of tiny particles like pollen in water. Some thought that these particles were moving because they were alive, but a botanist called Robert Brown showed in the 1820s that charcoal dust also moved in the same way. Brown could not think of an explanation for this movement, which became known then as the 'Brownian movement'. It was only explained eighty years later by the kinetic particle theory. The great physicist Albert Einstein was one of the scientists who explained it.

You can see the Brownian movement using a 'smoke cell' and a microscope. The smoke cell is a short plastic or glass tube that is illuminated by a bright light from the side. The bottom is sealed. The smoke is made by burning a bit of string and allowing some of the smoke to go into the cell. The cell is covered by a microscope coverslip and is put under the microscope. This is shown in the diagram.

What makes the smoke particles move? The smoke particles are small pieces of carbon floating in the air. Although they are small, they are made up of millions of particles of carbon. All the time they are being knocked around by the air particles around them. The air particles are far too small to see under the microscope. But what we can see is how the much larger smoke particles are being made to move as they are knocked around in all directions by the invisible air particles hitting them.

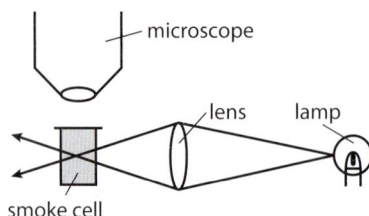

▶ Figure 2.12
Brownian motion.

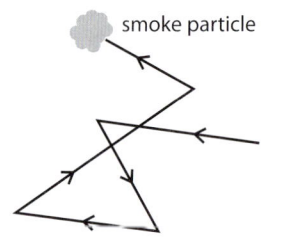

▲ Figure 2.13
Random movement of a particle due to Brownian motion.

 QUESTIONS

2.1 Use the theory that matter is made of particles to explain the following observations.
   a) An inflated balloon always goes down in a few days.
   b) Solids have fixed shapes.
   c) A closed syringe full of air can easily be compressed but if it is filled with water the plunger cannot be pushed down.
   d) Liquids stay at the bottom of the containers they are put in.

2.2 Explain the following processes by describing what happens to the particles of matter in each case.
   a) Clothes drying on a line.
   b) Sugar dissolving in a cup of coffee.
   c) Frost forming on a cold night.

2.3 A gas tap in a laboratory is turned on. Explain, in terms of particles:
   a) why only the people very near the tap smell the gas immediately
   b) why everyone in the laboratory can smell the gas within a few minutes.

What is matter?

 SKILLS QUESTION

2.4 Hydrogen chloride is a colourless gas that is given off by concentrated hydrochloric acid. Ammonia is a colourless gas that is given off by concentrated ammonia solution. When the two gases meet they react to make ammonium chloride, which is a white powder. Hydrogen chloride particles are larger and heavier than ammonia particles.

Predict roughly where you might expect to see a ring of white powder forming in the tube below, giving reasons for your prediction.

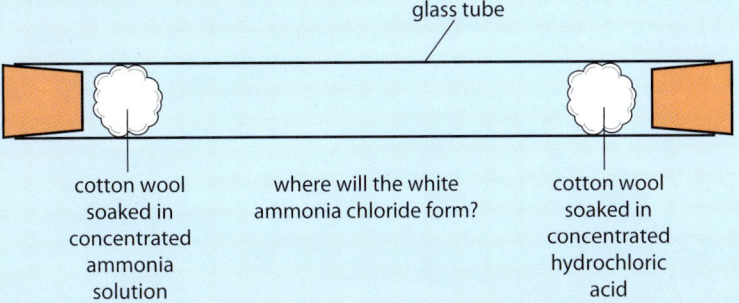

◀ **Figure 2.14**
Diffusion tube.

Summary

Now that you have completed this chapter, you should be able to:

- distinguish between the three kinds of matter: solids, liquids and gases
- know how solids, liquids and gases behave when they are heated or compressed
- know the meaning of the terms melting, boiling, condensing, freezing and subliming
- know that matter is made up of particles and be able to explain the difference in the structure and movement of the particles in solids, liquids and gases
- explain diffusion in liquids and gases in terms of the movement of particles
- S explain why the rate of diffusion depends on the mass of the particles; small particles diffusing faster than large ones.

Chapter 3
Mixtures and pure substances

▲ **Figure 3.1**
Engine oil and cooking salt.

▶ **Figure 3.2**
A modern oil refinery.

◀ **Figure 3.3**
Salt purification by crystallisation (page 15) from sea water at Walvis Bay, Namibia.

Have you ever thought where all the chemicals that you use each day come from? Figure 3.1 shows two common materials, some engine oil and cooking salt. These substances are made in very large amounts all over the world. The engine oil came out of the ground and the salt came from the sea. Figure 3.2 shows an oil refinery that converts crude oil into

Mixtures and pure substances

many refined products, including engine oil. Figure 3.3 shows crude salt made from seawater at Walvis Bay in Namibia. What are the processes that we use to make useful substances like these from crude substances that we get out of the ground or the sea?

All substances are either pure substances or mixtures. Almost all naturally occurring substances are mixtures. To make useful materials from them it is necessary to separate these mixtures into their pure components. After we have separated a mixture we need to know whether the substance we have obtained is indeed pure. This section is about ways of separating mixtures and ways of telling whether or not the products are pure substances.

3.1 Solutions

Try shaking some sand with water in a plastic bottle. Then try the same with salt instead of sand. You will notice that the salt **dissolves** in the water but the sand does not. The salt is **soluble** in water but the sand is **insoluble**. Water is a liquid that is a very good **solvent**. Many substances will dissolve in water.

Some substances dissolve in water better than others. If you keep trying to dissolve more and more of a solid in water, you will find that eventually no more will dissolve. We call this a **saturated solution**. We can measure the **solubility** of a substance in water. We measure the maximum amount of a substance that will dissolve in 100 g water. Table 3.1 shows the solubility in water of a number of common substances.

Substance	Solubility (g per 100 g water)
Sodium chloride (table salt)	35.9
Calcium carbonate (limestone)	0.04 (this is so small that we call this substance 'insoluble')
Sodium hydrogen carbonate (baking soda)	7.8
Sugar	203

◀ Table 3.1
Solubility of some common substances in water (measured at 25 °C).

As you can see from the table, solubilities of substances in water vary widely. Solubilities vary with temperature. Most substances dissolve better in hot water than cold water. This is why we usually use hot water for washing things.

Water is a good solvent for many substances but it will not dissolve substances like fat and butter. They will dissolve in other liquids such as petrol and paraffin. Petrol and paraffin, however, do not dissolve substances like salt and baking soda, which dissolve in water. Later in this book you will discover the reason for this.

Can you explain, using the kinetic particle theory, how a substance dissolves?

3.2 Methods of purifying substances

Most mixtures contain one useful substance and a number of impurities. We want to obtain the useful substance in a pure form. There are many ways we might be able to do this. The way we choose makes use of a difference between the pure substance and the impurities. It is useful to classify mixtures into four categories to help us think about these differences; these are mixtures of:
- solids and liquids (such as sea water)
- two or more solids (such as a metal ore)
- two or more liquids (such as crude oil)
- two or more gases (such as air).

We can classify this group still further. The solid we want to get in a pure form might be soluble or it might be insoluble.

Separating an insoluble solid from a liquid

If the solid is insoluble then **filtering** is the usual separation method. An example might be sand from the seashore that we need for building. The sand will contain salt, which weakens the cement. The sand can be mixed with water and filtered. The salt dissolves in the water but the sand does not. Most of the salt will be taken away in the water. Figure 3.4 shows this on a small scale.

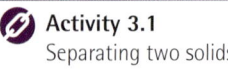

▶ Figure 3.4
Purifying sand contaminated with salt.

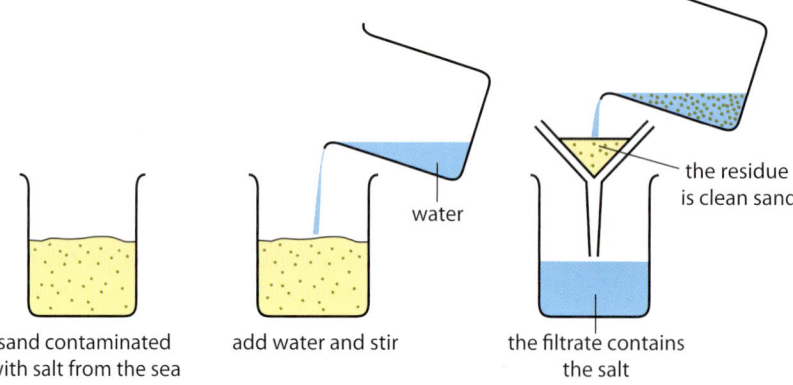

sand contaminated with salt from the sea   add water and stir   the filtrate contains the salt   the residue is clean sand   water

Activity 3.1
Separating two solids

The sand can be cleaned further by pouring water through the sand residue on the filter paper.

KEY TERMS

Some useful words

Solution – the clear liquid formed when a solid dissolves in liquid
Solute – the solid that dissolves in a liquid to form a solution
Solvent – the liquid that dissolves the solid in a solution
Soluble solid – a solid that will dissolve in a liquid to form a solution
Insoluble solid – a solid that will not dissolve in a liquid
Filtrate – the clear solution that passes through a filter paper
Residue – the insoluble solid that remains on the filter paper

Mixtures and pure substances

Separating a pure solid from a solution

If the solid is soluble then the liquid must be **evaporated**. This can be done by heating the solution or by just leaving it in sunlight. This will leave the solid solute behind.

A useful way of making sure that a soluble solid is obtained in a pure form is to evaporate off most of the liquid and then leave the solid to form crystals. The liquid above the crystals will contain any soluble impurities and can be poured off. This process, called **crystallisation**, is used in the pharmaceutical industry for making drugs which must be very pure. It is also used in making salt from seawater. The salt at Walvis Bay in Figure 3.3 was produced by using the sun to evaporate most of the water from seawater and then the salt is allowed to crystallise in large lagoons.

▲ **Figure 3.5**
We can often buy 'sea salt' crystals for cooking. This salt has been allowed to crystallise slowly from seawater and the crystals are quite big.

Separating a pure liquid from a solution

If the liquid, rather than the solid, is required, a process called **distillation** is used. The liquid is evaporated and the vapour is then condensed to give a pure liquid. This is shown in Figure 3.6.

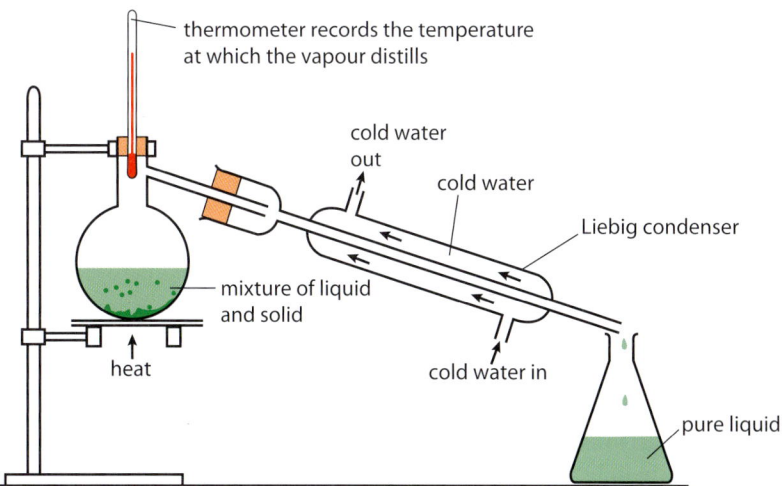

◀ **Figure 3.6**
Distillation is a method of obtaining pure water from impure water.

The special equipment for condensing the vapour shown in Figure 3.6 is called a Liebig condenser, after the nineteenth century German chemist who invented it.

Separating a solid from a mixture of solids

These mixtures can often be separated by the methods described above if one of the solids is soluble. This is often used in industry; salt is a very important raw material for the chemical industry and it is often found in the form of rock salt. The rock salt was formed millions of years ago when a sea dried up. In rock salt, there is often a lot of sand.

> **DID YOU KNOW?**
>
> Justus Liebig not only invented the Liebig condenser, he also invented and patented the Oxo cube.

 **SKILLS QUESTION**

3.1 Plan an investigation to obtain pure sugar from a mixture of sugar and glass. Use the ideas for filtration and crystallisation that you have met above.

15

Separating solid mixtures is an important part of the waste recycling industry, which is growing rapidly all over the world. When metal objects are recycled, it is often difficult to separate one metal from another. There is an easy way to separate iron from 'non-ferrous' metals and that is to use a large **electromagnet.** This lifts all objects containing iron and leaves behind non-ferrous objects.

Separating a pure liquid from a mixture of liquids

The usual way to separate mixtures of liquids makes use of the fact that they will almost certainly have different boiling points. Distillation can then be used to separate the liquids. This is used widely in the drinks industry to make spirits.

Distillation, however, does not separate two particular liquids very well. The mixture distilled in the drinks industry contains these two liquids, ethanol (alcohol, boiling point 78 °C) and water (boiling point 100 °C).

If a mixture of ethanol and water is distilled, the liquid that condenses will not be pure ethanol. It will also contain some water. It can be distilled again and then the proportion of ethanol will be greater. Each time the product is re-distilled, purer ethanol is obtained. There is a process that does a lot of re-distillations in one operation and it is called fractional distillation or **fractionation**.

Fractional distillation requires a tall column above the distillation flask. This column has barriers inside, which do not block it but allow the vapour to rise and the liquid to flow downwards slowly. The liquid is continuously condensed and re-distilled as it rises up the column. The hottest part of the column is at the bottom near the heated distillation vessel. The coolest part of the column is at the top. Figure 3.7 shows a laboratory **fractionating column** being used to obtain ethanol from a mixture of ethanol and water. In this column the barrier to the flow is provided by small pieces of glass that are packed into the column.

Fractional distillation is used in the oil industry and this will be studied in Chapter 14.

▼ **Figure 3.7**
Separating a mixture of liquids with different boiling points by fractional distillation.

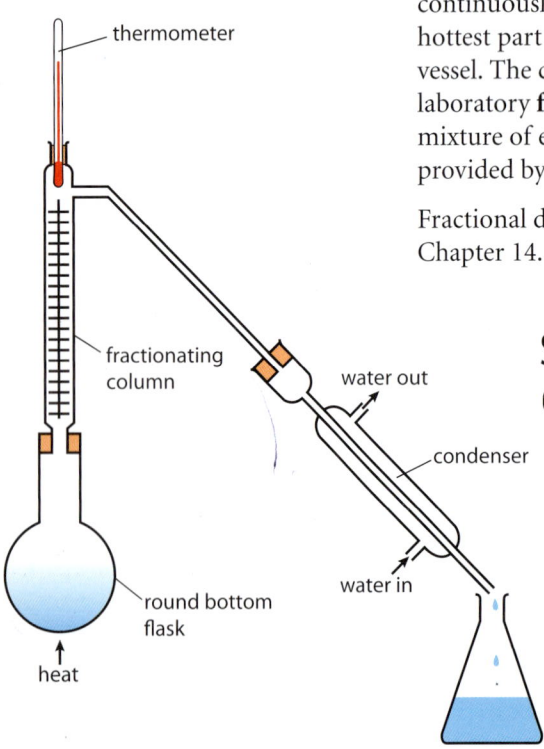

Separating a pure gas from a mixture of gases

Fractional distillation can also be used to separate a mixture of two or more gases. First, however, the gases must be cooled until they turn into a liquid. The fractional distillation of liquid air is described in Chapter 12.

Another method often used to remove a gaseous impurity from another gas is to pass the mixture through a solid chemical that will react with the impurity. This is how gas masks work. This method is also used to remove sulfur dioxide from the gases produced by large coal-burning power stations. Sulfur dioxide is a serious air pollutant in some parts of the world, particularly northern Europe. The gases in the chimney are passed though calcium oxide granules. As you will learn in Chapter 12, this will react with the acidic sulfur dioxide.

3.3 Finding out how pure a substance is

We often want to know how pure a substance is. We also often want to know how many substances there are in a mixture and what they are. To do this we use a technique called **chromatography**. There are many different kinds of chromatography; the easiest one to use is **paper chromatography**. Figure 3.8 shows how this is used to show what dyes are present in water-soluble inks.

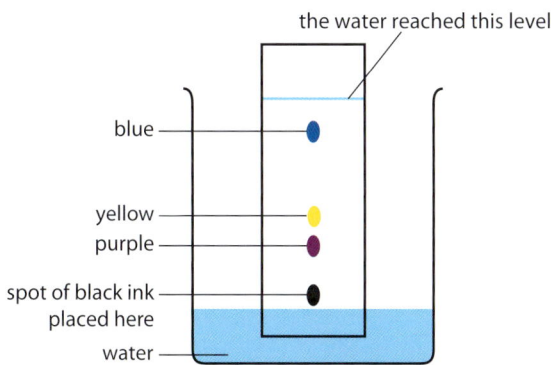

◀ Figure 3.8
The chromatography paper on the left shows that the black ink is made of a mixture of three dyes.

A small dot of the ink is made on some filter paper (or special chromatography paper) and it is suspended in water (or another suitable solvent). The water rises up the paper and, as it rises, takes the ink with it.

You will notice that some dyes rise up the paper more easily than others. The technique will separate a mixture of dyes. It can tell us whether a dye is a pure substance or not. The technique works because of the different strength of the forces holding the different dyes to the paper. When these are weak, the dye will move easily. The paper at the end of the experiment is called a **chromatogram**.

There are many other kinds of chromatography. One useful one uses a column of pure sand (silica) in a glass tube, instead of the paper, and the liquid runs down instead of up. This is called **column chromatography**.

 Activity 3.2
Do inks contain a single dye or a mixture?

What are Rf values?

The chromatography paper holds back (or **retains**) some compounds in a mixture more than others. We call this variable the **retention factor** or **Rf value** of the chemical. The retention factor, or Rf, is defined as the distance travelled by the compound divided by the distance travelled by the solvent.

$$Rf = \frac{\text{distance travelled by the compound}}{\text{distance travelled by the solvent front}}$$

 Activity 3.3
Investigating the dyes in sweets

For example, if a compound travels 2.1 cm and the solvent front travels 2.8 cm, the Rf value is 0.75.

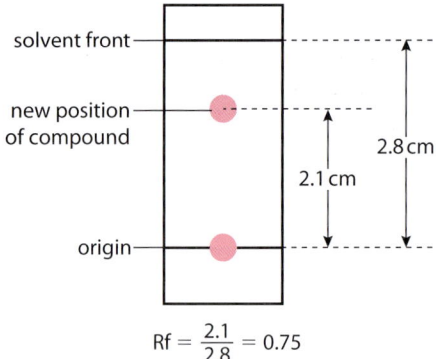

The Rf value of a compound in any chromatogram will depend on the experiment; it will change if the experimental conditions change.

Look at the chromatogram in Figure 3.8. Can you work out the approximate Rf values for the dyes in the three inks?

Chromatography can also be used to tell us about the purity of colourless substances. There are two common ways of doing this. The first is to use a **locating agent**. This is a substance that is sprayed onto the paper after the experiment and which reacts with the colourless spots to make a coloured substance.

The second way is to use paper (or silica) that has been treated with a substance that fluoresces when ultraviolet light shines on it. The spots cover up this substance and so they can be seen as dark patches under an ultraviolet light.

Chromatography is a very important technique with many uses. Its main use is to tell us what substances might be present in a mixture. We call this process **analysis.** We use chromatography to **analyse** the mixture to try and find out what it contains.

This list gives some examples of the use of chromatography for analysis:
- to analyse polluted air and water
- in hospital laboratories to analyse medical samples such as blood and urine
- to check the purity of foods and drinks when they are manufactured
- to find out whether drugs are pure and safe
- to help solve crimes by analysing blood stains and other substances that might be found where a crime has been committed.

An example of the use of a **chromatographic analysis** with a locating agent is the analysis of complex substances called proteins. These are made of simple substances called amino acids. Proteins can be broken down into amino acids and the solution is then analysed using paper chromatography. The amino acids cannot be seen until the paper is sprayed with a locating agent and then heated. The different amino acids travel different distances up the paper. The result can tell us which amino acids are present in the protein.

Wherever there is a chemistry laboratory, you will almost always find some chromatography being done.

Mixtures and pure substances

 SKILLS QUESTION

3.2 Design an experiment to investigate the purity of dyes used to colour sweets such as Smarties®.

DID YOU KNOW?

An interesting kind of chromatography is called electrophoresis. In this, an electric potential difference is made on the paper by attaching the top and the bottom of the paper to a DC voltage source. This creates a 'potential gradient' on the paper and different molecules are pulled at different rates along the gradient. This is widely used as part of DNA analysis techniques in forensic science and the study of genes.

 Activity 3.4
What is the melting point of ice?

3.4 How do we know when a substance is pure?

One way of telling if a substance is pure is to look at its chromatogram. But we cannot make chromatograms for many substances. How do we know, for example, if water is pure?

If you put some crushed melting ice in a beaker and take its temperature with a thermometer you will expect the temperature to be 0 °C. This is the temperature of all melting ice.

If you add salt to the ice, you will find that the temperature goes down. This is because the melting point of salt water is below zero. You may also have noticed that the salt water ice melted over a range of temperatures while the pure ice melted at exactly 0 °C.

There are two important observations here.
- Pure substances melt (and boil) at a temperature that is always the same for a particular substance. Pure water always boils at 100 °C (at 1 atmosphere pressure) whereas pure alcohol (ethanol) always boils at 78 °C.
- If there is an impurity in a liquid, its boiling point is raised slightly and its freezing point is lowered and neither of the points is sharp. So salty water will freeze over a range of temperatures a little below 0 °C and it will boil over a range of temperatures just above 100 °C.

We can therefore use the melting and boiling point of a pure substance to tell us:
- whether the substance is indeed pure
- what the substance might be.

DID YOU KNOW?

The American spacecraft called Viking that landed on Mars in the early 1980s carried many instruments with it. One of them was a device which automatically analysed samples of the Martian soil by chromatography.

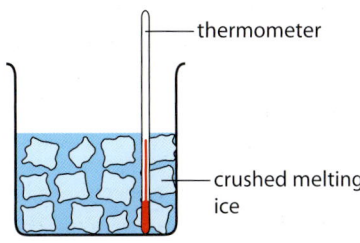

◀ **Figure 3.9**
The temperature of this melting ice is 0 °C. But what will happen to the temperature if you add salt?

19

What are pure substances made of?

In the last section you found out about the different methods chemists use to make pure, useful substances out of the mixtures we find around about us. These methods are called **physical** methods of purification. The pure substances produced by these methods have sharp melting and boiling points, and chromatography – if it is possible – will show that they only produce one spot on chromatography paper. Some of these pure substances are **elements** but most of them will be **compounds**.

All the **physical processes** for separating mixtures have one thing in common; they can easily be reversed. In order to understand the difference between elements and compounds it is necessary to study **chemical processes**. Most chemical processes cannot easily be reversed.

These pictures (Figures 3.10 to 3.12) are all examples of chemical processes, or **chemical reactions**.

KEY TERMS

Compounds are substances that are formed when two or more elements combine chemically.

▼ **Figure 3.10**
Examples of chemical reactions.

Can you imagine any of these chemical processes going backwards? Can you imagine food uncooking itself so that you get raw potatoes out of mashed potatoes? Can you imagine rusted iron turning back into shiny metal or a plant leaf ungrowing?

Mixtures and pure substances

When these chemical reactions happen, new substances are made from the original substances. We call the original substances the **reactants** and the new substances the **products** of the reaction. Think about the reactants and products in the previous reactions.

When the candle in Figure 3.11 burns, the candle wax is one of the reactants. One of the products of the burning is water. You can see condensation on the inside of the beaker. This is an example of a chemical reaction. The oxygen in the air takes part in the reaction and the reaction stops when the oxygen in the air is used up. This is why the candle under the jar does not continue burning until the wax is used up. It goes out after a short time.

The burning reaction is **irreversible**. Can you imagine candle wax being formed from the gases produced by the candle?

As well as being irreversible, the chemical reactions you have studied in this section involve an **energy change**. Chemical energy in the candle wax and the firewood was changed into heat energy and light energy during the reaction. Heat is even given off by rusting but it happens so slowly we do not notice it. During chemical reactions there is always an energy change. In most chemical reactions energy is produced but in a few reactions it is taken in.

▲ Figure 3.11
Candle burning under an inverted beaker.

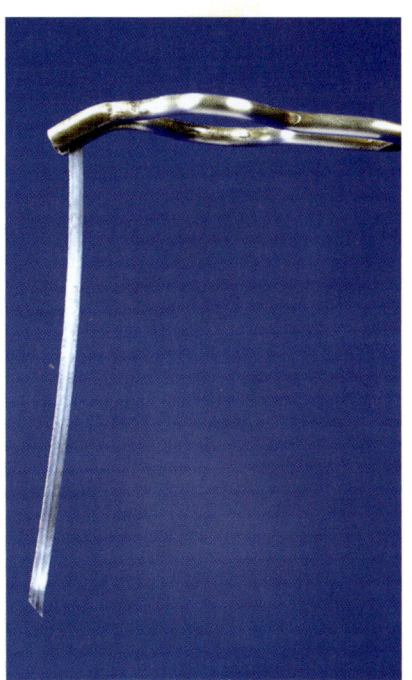

Figure 3.12 shows magnesium burning. Magnesium is a pure metal. It burns in the air. When it burns it combines with oxygen in the air (you will find out more about this in Chapter 9). The white powder that is formed is called magnesium oxide. Magnesium, oxygen and magnesium oxide are all pure substances. Magnesium and oxygen are examples of elements. When they combine during burning they form magnesium oxide, which is a compound.

▲ Figure 3.12
The magnesium (left) combines with oxygen in the air when it burns (centre) to give white magnesium oxide (right).

21

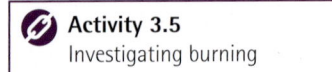

Activity 3.5
Investigating burning

Water is also a compound. It is made of the elements hydrogen and oxygen. Candle wax is mainly one compound. When the candle burns in the air, water is formed and this means that one of the elements that candle wax is made from must be hydrogen. The water is formed when this hydrogen combines with the oxygen of the air. The other element present in the candle wax is carbon and when the wax burns, this element also combines with oxygen in the air to form a compound, carbon dioxide. When the candle wax burns, the candle wax compound is breaking up and the elements in it are combining with oxygen.

So we can summarise all this as follows.
- All matter is made from chemical elements.
- These elements are often joined together to form compounds.
- Most matter around us is made up of mixtures of different compounds and sometimes also some elements.
- Mixtures can be separated into pure substances, which may be compounds or elements.
- Mixtures can be separated by physical techniques. These processes are easily reversed.
- Elements can be turned into compounds by chemical methods that are not easily reversed.

Chemical changes happen when substances change into other substances and:
- a change of energy is involved
- the process is irreversible
- the products are different from the substances used.

So:
- melting and boiling are examples of **physical changes**; but
- burning and cooking are examples of **chemical changes**.

Elements

We can **classify** elements as solid elements, liquid elements and gaseous elements (at room temperature). There are many gaseous elements but there are only two liquid ones, mercury and bromine.

We can also classify elements into two groups, **metals** and **non-metals**. All the metals except mercury are solids. Altogether there are 92 natural elements and most of these are metals. The material that makes up the Earth's crust and its atmosphere is made mainly from non-metals. We say that non-metals are more **abundant** in the Earth's crust than metals.

The tables that follow give some information about a number of common elements and compounds.

 DID YOU KNOW?

Most of the matter that we know about in the Universe consists of just two elements. About 75% of the matter in the Universe is the element hydrogen and 25% is helium. All the other elements together make up just a very tiny fraction of one percent. Our planet therefore is very different from most of the rest of the Universe.

Mixtures and pure substances

▼ Table 3.2 Data on common elements.
The state at room temperature is shown by 's', 'l' or 'g'. The abbreviation 'sub' indicates that the element sublimes. The densities of gases are at 15 °C.

Element	Symbol	Atomic number	Relative atomic mass	State	Melting point (°C)	Boiling point (°C)	Density (g/cm³)
Aluminium	Al	13	27	s	660	2350	2.0
Argon	Ar	18	40	g	−189	−186	0.00166
Barium	Ba	56	137	s	710	1640	3.59
Beryllium	Be	4	9	s	1285	2470	1.85
Boron	B	5	11	s	2030	3700	2.47
Bromine	Br	35	80	l	−7	59	3.12
Calcium	Ca	20	40	g	840	1490	1.53
Carbon (diamond)	C	6	12	s	3550	4827	3.53
Carbon (graphite)	C	6	12	s	3720 (sub)	–	2.25
Chlorine	Cl	17	35.5	s	−101	−34	0.00299
Chromium	Cr	24	52	g	1860	2600	7.19
Cobalt	Co	27	59	s	1494	2900	8.80
Copper	Cu	29	64	s	1084	2580	8.93
Fluorine	F	9	19	s	−220	−188	0.00158
Gallium	Ga	31	70	g	30	2070	5.91
Germanium	Ge	32	73	s	959	2850	5.32
Gold	Au	79	197	s	1064	2850	19.28
Helium	He	2	4	s	−270	−269	0.00017
Hydrogen	H	1	1	g	−259	−253	0.00008
Iodine	I	53	127	g	114	184	4.95
Iron	Fe	26	56	s	1540	2760	7.87
Krypton	Kr	36	84	s	−157	−153	10.00346
Lead	Pb	82	207	g	327	1760	11.34
Lithium	Li	3	7	s	180	1360	0.53
Magnesium	Mg	12	24	s	650	1100	1.74
Manganese	Mn	25	55	s	1250	2120	07.47
Mercury	Hg	80	201	s	−39	357	13.55
Neon	Ne	10	20	l	−249	−246	0.00084
Nickel	Ni	28	59	g	1455	2150	8.91
Nitrogen	N	7	14	s	−210	−196	0.00117
Oxygen	O	8	16	g	−219	−183	0.00133
Phosphorus (white)	P	15	31	g	44	280	1.82
Platinum	Pt	78	195	s	1772	3720	21.45
Potassium	K	19	39	s	63	777	0.86
Silicon	Si	14	28	s	1410	2620	2.33
Silver	Ag	47	108	s	962	2160	10.50
Sodium	Na	11	23	s	98	900	0.97
Sulfur (monoclinic)	S	16	32	s	115	445	1.96
Sulfur (orthorhombic)	S	16	32	s	–	–	2.07
Tin	Sn	50	119	s	232	2720	7.28
Uranium	U	92	238	s	1135	4000	19.05
Xenon	Xe	54	131	g	−112	−108	0.0055
Zinc	Zn	30	65	s	420	913	7.14

Table 3.3 Data on common compounds.

The state at room temperature is shown by 's', 'l' or 'g'. The solubility of each compound in water at room temperature is broadly classified as 'i' (insoluble), 'sps' (sparingly soluble), 's' (soluble) or 'vs' (very soluble). The abbreviation 'r' indicates that the compound reacts with water. Some compounds can have hydrated forms. This is shown by 'h'. These forms will usually dehydrate before the melting point. The abbreviation 'dec' means that the compound decomposes on heating; the abbreviation 'sub' means that it sublimes. Unless stated otherwise, all the compounds are white or colourless.

Compound	Formula	State	Melting point (°C)	Boiling point (°C)	Solubility	Notes
Aluminium chloride	$AlCl_3$	s	sub	–	r	
Aluminium oxide	Al_2O_3	s	2015	2980	i	
Ammonium chloride	NH_4Cl	s	sub	–	s	
Barium chloride	$BaCl_2$	s	963	1560	s	h
Barium sulfate	$BaSO_4$	s	1580	–	i	
Calcium carbonate	$CaCO_3$	s	dec	–	i	
Calcium chloride	$CaCl_2$	s	782	2000	s	h
Calcium hydroxide	$Ca(OH)_2$	s	dec	–	sps	
Calcium nitrate	$Ca(NO_3)_2$	s	561	dec	vs	h
Calcium oxide	CaO	s	2600	3000	r	
Carbon monoxide	CO	g	−205	−191	i	
Carbon dioxide	CO_2	g	sub	–	sps	
Chromium(III) oxide	Cr_2O_3	s	2435	4000	i	green
Cobalt(II) chloride	$CoCl_2$	s	730	1050	s	h, red
Copper(II) chloride	$CuCl_2$	s	620	dec	s	h, green
Copper(II) nitrate	$Cu(NO_3)_2$	s	114	dec	vs	h, green
Copper(I) oxide	Cu_2O	s	1235	–	i	red
Copper(II) oxide	CuO	s	1326	–	i	black
Copper(II) sulfate	$CuSO_4$	s	dec	–	s	h, blue
Hydrogen bromide	HBr	g	−87	−67	vs	
Hydrogen chloride	HCl	g	−114	−85	vs	
Hydrogen fluoride	HF	g	−93	20	s	
Hydrogen iodide	HI	g	−51	−35	s	
Hydrogen oxide (water)	H_2O	l	0	100		
Hydrogen peroxide	H_2O_2	l	0	150	vs	
Hydrogen sulfide	H_2S	g	−85	−60	sps	
Iron(II) chloride	$FeCl_2$	s	677	sub	s	yellow-green
Iron(III) chloride	$FeCl_3$	s	307	dec	s	h, orange
Iron(III) oxide	Fe_2O_3	s	1565	–	i	red
Iron(II) sulfate	$FeSO_4$	s	dec	–	s	pale green
Iron(II) sulfide	FeS	s	1196	dec	i	black
Lead(II) bromide	$PbBr_2$	s	370	94	i	
Lead(II) chloride	$PbCl_2$	s	501	950	sps	
Lead(II) nitrate	$Pb(NO_3)_2$	s	dec	–	s	
Lead(II) oxide	PbO	s	886	1472	i	yellow
Lead(IV) oxide	PbO_2	s	dec	–	i	brown
Magnesium chloride	$MgCl_2$	s	714	1418	s	h
Magnesium nitrate	$Mg(NO_3)_2$	s	89	–	vs	h
Magnesium oxide	MgO	s	2800	3600	i	
Manganese(IV) oxide	MnO_2	s	dec	–	i	black
Mercury(II) chloride	$HgCl_2$	s	276	302	sps	
Mercury(II) oxide	HgO	s	dec	–	i	red
Nitric acid	HNO_3	l	−42	83	vs	
Nitrogen hydride (ammonia)	NH_3	g	−78	−34	vs	
Nitrogen monoxide	NO	g	−163	−151	sps	

Mixtures and pure substances

Compound	Formula	State	Melting point (°C)	Boiling point (°C)	Solubility	Notes
Nitrogen dioxide	NO_2	g	−11	21	s	brown
Phosphorus trichloride	PCl_3	l	−112	76	r	
Phosphorus pentachloride	PCl_5	s	dec	–	r	
Phosphorus pentoxide	P_4O_{10}	s	sub	–	r	
Potassium bromide	KBr	s	730	1435	s	
Potassium chloride	KCl	s	776	1500	s	
Potassium hydroxide	KOH	s	360	1322	vs	
Potassium iodide	KI	s	686	1330	vs	
Potassium manganate(VII)	$KMnO_4$	s	dec	–	s	purple
Potassium nitrate	KNO_3	s	334	dec	vs	
Silicon dioxide (quartz)	SiO_2	s	1610	2230	i	
Silver bromide	AgBr	s	432	dec	i	cream
Silver chloride	AgCl	s	455	1550	i	
Silver iodide	AgI	s	558	1506	i	yellow
Silver nitrate	$AgNO_3$	s	212	dec	vs	
Sodium carbonate	Na_2CO_3	s	755	1390	s	h
Sodium bromide	NaBr	s	851	dec	s	
Sodium chloride	NaCl	s	808	1465	s	
Sodium hydroxide	NaOH	s	318	1930	s	
Sodium nitrate	$NaNO_3$	s	307	dec	s	
Sodium oxide	Na_2O	s	sub	–	r	h
Sodium sulfate	Na_2SO_4	s	890	–	s	
Sulfur dioxide	SO_2	g	−75	−10	vs	
Sulfur trioxide	SO_3	l	−17	43	r	
Sulfuric acid	H_2SO_4	l	10	330	vs	
Zinc chloride	$ZnCl_2$	s	283	732	vs	
Zinc oxide	ZnO	s	1975	–	i	h
Zinc sulfate	$ZnSO_4$	s	740	dec	vs	

QUESTIONS

3.3 How would you separate the substance named in each of the following mixtures?
   a) pure ethanol (alcohol) from beer
   b) iron filings from a mixture of metal filings
   c) water from tea

3.4 Look at the chromatogram in Figure 3.13. What does it tell you about the three colours? Do any of the colours contain the same dye?

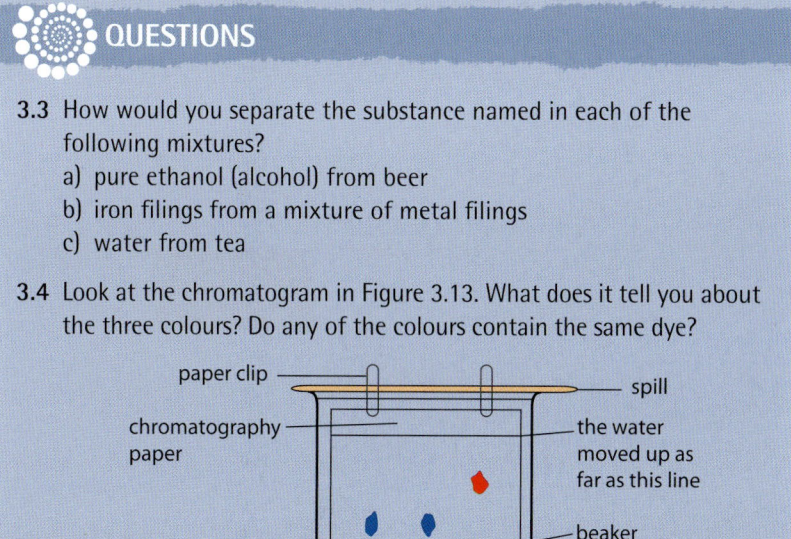

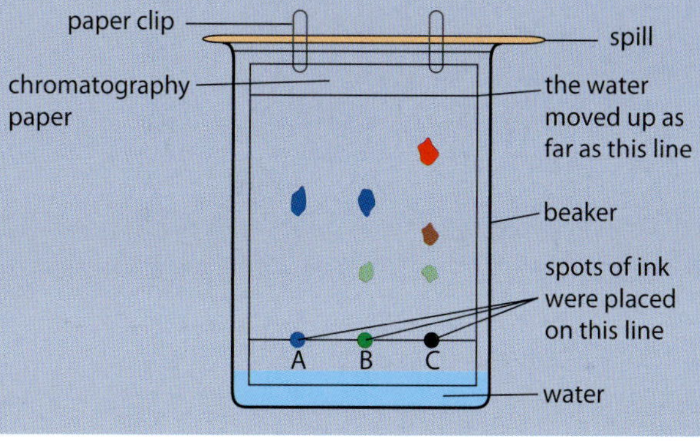

◀ Figure 3.13
A chromatogram of three coloured inks.

▶ **Table 3.4**
The change of solubility with temperature for three substances.

3.5 Table 3.4 shows how the solubility of three substances in water varies with temperature.

Temperature (°C)	10	20	30	40	50	60	70	80
Solubility of sodium chloride (g/100 g water)	36	36	36	37	37	38	38	39
Sodium carbonate (g/100 g water)	13	22	40	49	49	46	45	44
Potassium nitrate (g/100 g water)	20	32	64	81	110	121	133	169

a) Plot a graph showing how the solubility of the three substances varies with temperature. Use the same axes for all three graphs.

b) Describe how the solubility of each substance changes with temperature.

c) Which substance is the most soluble substance at:
   (i) 15 °C ?
   (ii) 55 °C?

d) At what temperature are the solubilities of sodium chloride and potassium nitrate the same?

3.6 Using the data from Table 3.2 write a total of at least 10 elements in this table so that there is at least one element in every space in the table.

	Non-metals	Metals
Solid		
Liquid		
Gas		

3.7 Classify the following substances as metallic element, non-metallic element, mixture or compound.

　　　　　seawater
　　　　　pure water
　　　　　air
　　　　　nitrogen
　　　　　gold
　　　　　brass
　　　　　ethanol
　　　　　paper

Summary

Now that you have completed this chapter, you should be able to:

- explain how soluble solids dissolve in a solvent to form a solution
- know that water is a very good solvent and that many substances will dissolve in it
- define solubility and understand that a saturated solution is a solution in which no more solid and will dissolve
- explain the use of filtration, distillation and fractional destination in separating mixtures
- explain the use of chromatography to show us what substances are present in a mixture and how chromatography can also be used on a larger scale to separate the components of a mixture
- know that pure substances melt (and boil) at a sharp temperature that is always the same for a particular substance
- know what happens to the boiling and melting points of a substance when some impurities are present
- distinguish between physical and chemical changes and understand that physical changes are usually reversible but chemical changes are not
- recognise that all matter is made of chemical elements which are often joined together chemically to form compounds
- classify elements as solids, liquids and gases, metals and non-metals.

Chapter 4

Atoms and molecules

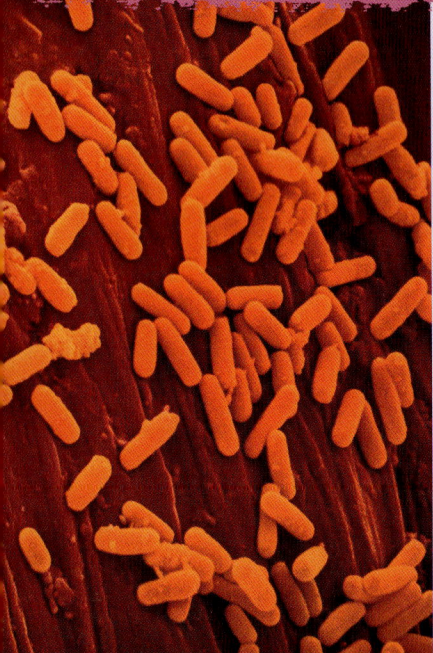

Do you know the diameter of one of your hairs? You can see it quite clearly under a microscope. The diameter will depend on who you are. Some people have thin hair that is only about 20 micrometres in diameter. Other people's hair can be nearly 10 times as thick as this. The bacteria on the tip of the pin in Figure 4.1 are smaller; they are 2 or 3 micrometres long. The gap between a computer hard drive and the head that reads it is one fiftieth the size of these bacteria; about one tenth of a micrometre. But all these are big compared with the size of **atoms**, which is what all matter is made of.

◀ **Figure 4.1**
A microscope using light allows us to see things as small as these bacteria on a pinhead. These are magnified ten thousand times. However, it is not possible for us to see atoms using a light microscope.

KEY TERMS

There are	
100 centimetres (cm)	
1 000 millimetres (mm)	
1 000 000 micrometres (μm)	in 1 metre
1 000 000 000 nanometres (nm)	
1 000 000 000 000 picometres (pm)	

▼ **Figure 4.2**
SIL stands for 'semiconductor interface laboratory' which is the laboratory in the university of Swansea, Wales, which made this.

The diameter of your hair is about 1 million times the diameter of the carbon atoms that it is mainly made of. All atoms are smaller than 1 nanometre. The largest atom is the caesium atom (caesium is a very reactive metal) and it has a diameter of 300 picometres or 0.3 nanometres. If you imagine an apple magnified to the size of the Earth, then the atoms in this big apple would be approximately the size of the original apple.

But we can now 'see' atoms. We cannot see them with an ordinary microscope that uses light but we can use a device called a scanning tunnelling microscope (STM). We can also use this for making things that are the size of just a few atoms.

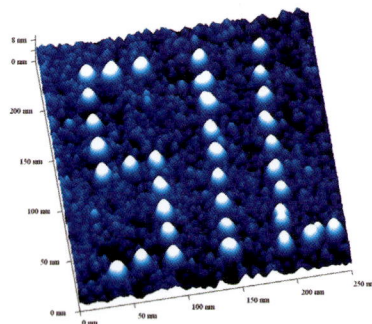

◀ **Figure 4.2**
Nanowriting – each of these dots is just a few nanometres in diameter.

Atoms and Molecules

The picture in Figure 4.2 shows some 'nanowriting' done using an STM at Swansea University in Wales. 'SIL' is the name of the laboratory – the Semiconductor Interface Laboratory. The substance used was tin dioxide and each of the white dots are about 25nm in diameter and made out of a few thousand atoms that have been changed using the STM. The colours are 'false' to allow us to see what has happened; tin dioxide is not really blue and white.

4.1 How small are atoms and molecules?

You know from Chapter 2 that if you add a small crystal of potassium manganate(VII) to water you get a deep purple solution. If you then throw away half the solution and top it up with water it will still be quite deep purple. How many times do you think you could do this before you could no longer see that the liquid was a slight purple colour? Try it. What is the largest volume of water that one small crystal of potassium manganate(VII) will make a pink colour? It is clear that the individual particles of potassium manganate(VII) must be extremely small.

In Chapter 2 you also studied how matter is made out of particles. The smallest of these particles is called an **atom**. Most particles, however, are made out of two or more atoms combined together. These are called **molecules**. All the molecules of a particular pure substance are identical and they are different from the molecules of any other substance.

It is possible to carry out a simple investigation that gives us a rough idea of how small the particles actually are. What we do is to try and measure the thickness of a thin layer of oil on top of water. This layer cannot be less than one molecule thick so if we can measure it we will know that a single molecule must be smaller than this thickness.

At some time you must have seen a thin layer of oil on the top of water; it often appears to be coloured like a rainbow. The diagrams show how to make a layer of oil on top of water using just a single tiny drop of oil. The oil drop is on the end of a wire and if you look at it through a magnifying glass next to a ruler you can get a good idea of how big the drop is.

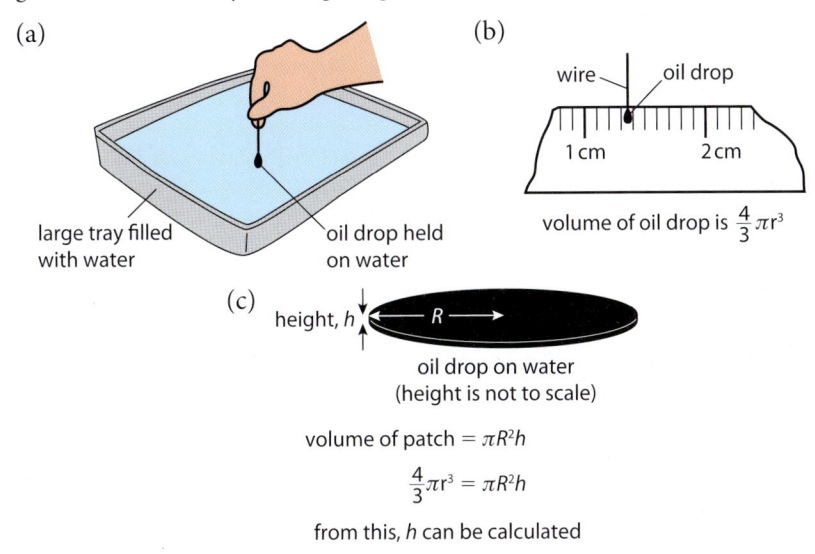

DID YOU KNOW?

If you share your tin of cola with everybody else in the world, you would each have about 1 000 000 000 000 000 molecules to drink.

Activity 4.1
Estimating particle size

(a) large tray filled with water — oil drop held on water

(b) wire, oil drop
1 cm   2 cm
volume of oil drop is $\frac{4}{3}\pi r^3$

(c) height, h ← R →
oil drop on water
(height is not to scale)

volume of patch = $\pi R^2 h$

$$\frac{4}{3}\pi r^3 = \pi R^2 h$$

from this, h can be calculated

Figure 4.3
Oil drop experiment.
(a) Putting the oil onto the water.
(b) Measuring the approximate diameter of the drop.
(c) Estimating the size of the oil drop on the water.

> **DID YOU KNOW?**
>
> If you throw a bucketful of water into the South Atlantic Ocean in Argentina and then travel across the Atlantic to South Africa and take out a bucket full of the South Atlantic Ocean there, there will probably be some of the molecules from your Argentinean bucketful in your South African bucket. This is because there are many more molecules of water in a bucketful than there are bucketfuls of water in the South Atlantic Ocean.

When the drop touches the surface of the water it, will spread out into a very thin layer. Its volume will not change, just its shape. So if we know the volume of the original drop (remember its volume is $\frac{4}{3}\pi r^3$) and we measure the area of the oil patch on the water, we can calculate the height of the patch using this volume equation.

$$\text{volume of oil} = \text{area of oil patch} \times \text{height of oil patch}$$

The patch must be at least one particle high. In fact it is probably many tens or even hundreds of particles high. So we know that the molecules in the oil must be many times smaller than the height of the oil layer.

The thickness of an oil layer is usually around 0.000 001 mm. We can therefore say that the diameter of an oil molecule must be less than 0.000 001 mm. How many molecules would you need to make a row of them (touching each other) that is 1 mm long?

4.2 A short history of atomic theories

Scientists think up theories that explain all the observations they make. They often call these theories 'models' of what really happens in nature. You have already studied the particle theory, which explains observations like diffusion and the Brownian motion.

When scientists make any observation that cannot be explained by the theory, the theory must be modified so that it does explain it. If this cannot be done, the theory has to be thrown out and a completely new one thought up. Over the last few thousand years there have been many atomic theories. Each one can explain more observations than the one before it. The most important theories are summarised in Table 4.1.

▼ Table 4.1 Atomic theories

Scientist	Year	Description of the model	
Democritus	about 500 years BCE*	Matter was made of tiny solid particles. They could not be made from nothing and could not be destroyed. Different substances had atoms of different shapes and sizes.	
John Dalton	1803	The first atomic theory that was based on experiment. Dalton proposed that matter consists of tiny particles called atoms that are solid and cannot be split. Different substances were made of atoms of different sizes. Atoms join together to form larger particles.	
John Joseph Thomson	1897	Thomson discoverd the electron in 1897 when he heated certain metals in a vacuum. He found that it had a negative charge and that it was much smaller than an atom. He proposed that atoms were made up of positively charged matter with electrons scatterd evenly through it. Thomson is widely thought of as the father of modern atomic physics and he received the 1906 Nobel Prize for physics. His research team in Cambridge were awarded another 6 prizes between them.	

Atoms and molecules

Ernest Rutherford	1911	Ernest Rutherford was a New Zealander who worked at Manchester University. He bombarded a very thin piece of gold with a stream of newly-discovered alpha-particles which were positively charged. Astonishingly almost all of them went through the gold as though it was not there! A few however, were reflected back. The theory had to be rethought; atoms could not be solid things. Rutherford said that atoms were mainly space. He proposed that an atom must consist of a tiny positive dense nucleus surrounded by space contaning electrons. He proposed that these nuclei were made up of positive particles which he called protons. Rutherford won the Nobel Prize for physics in 1908.
Niels Bohr	1913	Bohr proposed that electrons circulated around the nucleus in definite orbits like the planets went round the sun. The electrons in orbits (the name 'shell' is used instead of 'orbit') far away from the nucleus could be removed from the atom more easily than the ones near the nucleus. This idea explained how and why atoms joined together in molecules, as you will see below.
James Chadwick	1932	The nucleus consists of protons with a positive charge and neutrons which have no charge.
Many scientists	Since 1932	The atomic theory has been refined much since 1932. Much of the work has used mathematics to work out how the particles move. Many other particles have been discovered. An important idea is that particles like the proton and the neutron are each made from three smaller particles called *quarks*. There are six different kinds of quarks.

*BCE stands for 'Before Current Era' and is the same as the old 'BC' meaning 'Before Christ'. 'CE' (Current Era) is used in the book instead of 'AD' (Anno Domini).

Bohr's atomic theory

The 'Bohr atom' consists of a very small dense nucleus containing protons (and also, as Chadwick discovered, neutrons). This is surrounded by electrons orbiting in 'shells' at different distances from the nucleus.

The mass of the atom is concentrated in the particles in the nucleus and the electrons are very light and small. Atoms of the same element always have the same number of protons. Atoms of different elements have different numbers of protons.

The protons are positively charged and the electrons negatively charged. The number of protons is always the same as the number of electrons, because the atom overall is electrically neutral.

Bohr's theory is a very good one. It explains Rutherford's observation that atoms do not stop small particles. It explains Thomson's observation that a metal can give off electrons when it is heated in a vacuum. And it helps us explain how and why atoms combine as you will find out in Chapter 5.

Websites

Go to www.heinemann.co.uk/hotlinks, insert the express code 6799P and click on 4.1.

DID YOU KNOW?

Modern atomic theory is very complex. One prediction that the theory makes is the existence of a particle called the *Higgs boson* that is essential to the explanation of what mass actually is. The problem is that (at the time of writing this book, 2008) this particle has never been detected. Scientists have set up a huge experiment in a big expensive machine called a Large Hadron Collider deep in a 27 km diameter circular tunnel deep under the Alps in Switzerland. This experiment will be started in 2009 or so. If the Higgs boson is detected it will confirm the modern theory of mass and matter. If it is not, we may have to think again.

4.3 Using symbols to represent elements

Dalton's idea of symbols to represent elements is very useful. It allows us to understand clearly how the atoms join together. These days we no longer use symbols but a form of shorthand to represent the elements. Each element is represented by one or two letters. These letters usually come from the modern English name of the element (Ca for calcium, Mg for magnesium). However, some of the elements have been known for a long time and the shorthand comes from the ancient Latin name (iron is Fe from *Ferrum*, gold is Au from *Aureum*). Table 4.2 shows the shorthand symbols for some common elements.

▶ Table 4.2 Symbols of some common elements.

Element	Symbol	Element	Symbol	Element	Symbol
Aluminium	Al	Helium	He	Oxygen	O
Argon	Ar	Hydrogen	H	Phosphorus	P
Bromine	Br	Iodine	I	Potassium	K
Calcium	Ca	Iron	Fe	Silicon	Si
Carbon	C	Lead	Pb	Silver	Ag
Chlorine	Cl	Magnesium	Mg	Sodium	Na
Chromium	Cr	Mercury	Hg	Sulfur	S
Cobalt	Co	Neon	Ne	Tin	Sn
Copper	Cu	Nickel	Ni	Uranium	U
Gold	Au	Nitrogen	N	Zinc	Zn

The symbols allow us, like Dalton, to write shorthand formulae for molecules formed when atoms combine together. The small number to the right of the symbol tells us how many atoms of that element there are in the molecule of the compound. Table 4.3 shows how this works.

▶ Table 4.3 The numbers of atoms in compounds.

Name	Formula	Number of each atom in the molecule
Water	H_2O	2 atoms of hydrogen, 1 atom of oxygen
Carbon dioxide	CO_2	1 atom of carbon, 2 atoms of oxygen
Glucose	$C_6H_{12}O_6$	6 atoms of carbon, 12 atoms of hydrogen, 6 atoms of oxygen
Sulfuric acid	H_2SO_4	2 atoms of hydrogen, 1 atom of sulfur, 4 atoms of oxygen

4.4 How many protons, neutrons and electrons are there in the atom?

Table 4.4 summarises our picture of the atom. The atom consists of three particles: the proton, the neutron and the electron.

Particle	Where in the atom	Relative mass	Charge
Proton	Nucleus	1	+1
Neutron	Nucleus	1	None
Electron	Orbiting the nucleus	about $\frac{1}{2000}$	−1

Table 4.4 Summary of the properties of protons, neutrons and electrons.

The mass of the particles is not given in the usual mass units, kilograms. This is because one proton has a mass of approximately 0.000 000 000 000 000 000 000 000 006 kg, which is a rather inconvenient number to use! Instead we take the mass of the proton as our unit of mass. We call the mass of the proton one **atomic mass unit** (amu). The neutron has the same mass as the proton but the electron is much lighter, almost $\frac{1}{2000}$ amu.

Table 4.5 shows some details about the six lightest elements. The masses are in amu. If an atom has a relative mass of 12 it means that it has a mass that is 12 times the mass of the proton.

Notice that the number of protons is always equal to the number of electrons. This is because the charges on the atom must balance, as the atom itself has no overall charge. Notice also that the total relative mass of the atom is equal to the number of protons plus the number of neutrons. We ignore the very small mass caused by the electrons.

Elements	Symbol	Number of particles			Relative mass
		Protons	Neutrons	Electrons	
Hydrogen	H	1	0	1	1
Helium	He	2	2	2	4
Lithium	Li	3	4	3	7
Beryllium	Be	4	5	4	9
Boron	B	5	6	5	11
Carbon	C	6	6	6	12

Table 4.5 Some data about the first six elements.

We call the number of protons the **proton number** or sometimes the **atomic number**. It is often represented by the capital letter **Z**.

We call the relative mass of the atom the **nucleon number**, or sometimes the **mass number**. This is often represented by the capital letter **A**.

4.5 Isotopes

Table 4.6 shows some details of two atoms. They both have the same proton number and therefore they must be atoms of the same element, chlorine.

▶ Table 4.6
Atomic details of chlorine isotopes.

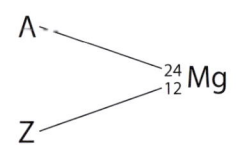

Protons	Neutrons	Electrons	Relative mass
17	18	17	35
17	20	17	37

Note that the two atoms of chlorine differ only in the number of neutrons. One atom has 18 and the other has 20 neutrons. Both are atoms of chlorine and they have exactly the same chemical properties. Atoms of the same element that have different numbers of neutrons are called **isotopes.**

About 75% of all chlorine atoms are the lighter isotope (called chlorine-35) and the remaining 25% are atoms of the chlorine-37 isotope. This means that the average relative mass of chlorine is 35.5 amu.

All elements occur naturally in the form of two or more isotopes. For most elements, one isotope is much more common than the other.

We can write the element symbol to show the nucleon number (A) and the proton number (Z) in the shorthand symbol for the element. How this is done is shown in Figure 4.4.

4.6 Atomic mass and molecular mass

It was Dalton who first realised that atoms of different elements had different masses. He realised that hydrogen was the lightest and he gave it a mass of 1. He called this the 'atomic weight'. We now call it the **relative atomic mass**. All the other atoms are heavier than hydrogen. Carbon, for example, has a relative atomic mass of 12.

These numbers for hydrogen and carbon are the same as the nucleon number for the common isotopes of these elements (shown in Table 4.5). But this is not so for many elements because they exist naturally in the form of several isotopes. Each isotope has a different nucleon number and the relative atomic mass is the average of all the nucleon numbers of all the atoms in the sample of the element. Because of this, the relative atomic mass of most elements is not exactly a whole number. Chlorine has a relative atomic mass of 35.5. This is because chlorine consists of a mixture of the two isotopes, chlorine-35 and chlorine-37.

If the relative atomic mass of hydrogen is 1 and that of oxygen is 16, then we can easily calculate the **relative molecular mass** of the compound water, as long as we know how many atoms of hydrogen and oxygen there are in a molecule of water.

The molecule of water (H_2O) contains two atoms of hydrogen and one of oxygen. Water therefore has a relative molecular mass of $1 + 1 + 16 = 18$.

▲ Figure 4.4
The symbol of magnesium showing the nucleon number (A) and the proton number (Z). The two isotopes of chlorine can therefore be represented as $^{35}_{17}Cl$ and $^{37}_{17}Cl$.

4.7 A pattern of elements – the Periodic Table

Before scientists can think up useful scientific theories to help us understand the universe around us, they have to make a lot of observations and collect data. This was what many chemists were busy doing a hundred and fifty years ago; they collected a lot of information about the properties of elements and the kind of compounds they made when they joined together.

By around a hundred and fifty years ago scientists had discovered many elements and had also been able to calculate their atomic masses (even though they only had a very simple idea of what an atom was like). Then some chemists began to look for patterns in all the data. It was from the patterns they found that they could devise the theories that explained the observations they had made.

A German chemist called Johann Döbereiner was the first to find a pattern. He realised that many elements could be grouped together in threes. The elements in each group were very similar. Lithium, sodium and potassium formed one group; they were all very reactive metals. Chlorine, bromine and iodine formed another group, this time of reactive non-metals. One group that had been known of for a long time was copper, silver, and gold.

In 1864 an Englishman called John Newlands realised that if he arranged the elements in a list in order of their relative atomic masses, each element was often very similar to the one eight places above it.

Later still, in 1869, the Russian, Dmitri Mendeleev, took all these ideas and produced his famous *Periodic Classification of the Elements*. This combined the ideas of Döbereiner and Newlands and it has proved to be very useful. It has helped us to understand much more about the elements that matter in the universe is made out of. The modern Periodic Table is based on Mendeleev's original one.

> **DID YOU KNOW?**
>
> It is interesting that many of the scientists were not studying chemicals because they really wanted to find out about them; they were really looking for ways of turning cheap metals into gold and so getting rich quickly! None of them got rich but we learnt a lot of chemistry from them. These scientists were called alchemists.

◀ **Figure 4.5**
Dmitri Mendeleev, 1834–1907, produced his well-known Periodic Table of the elements in 1869.

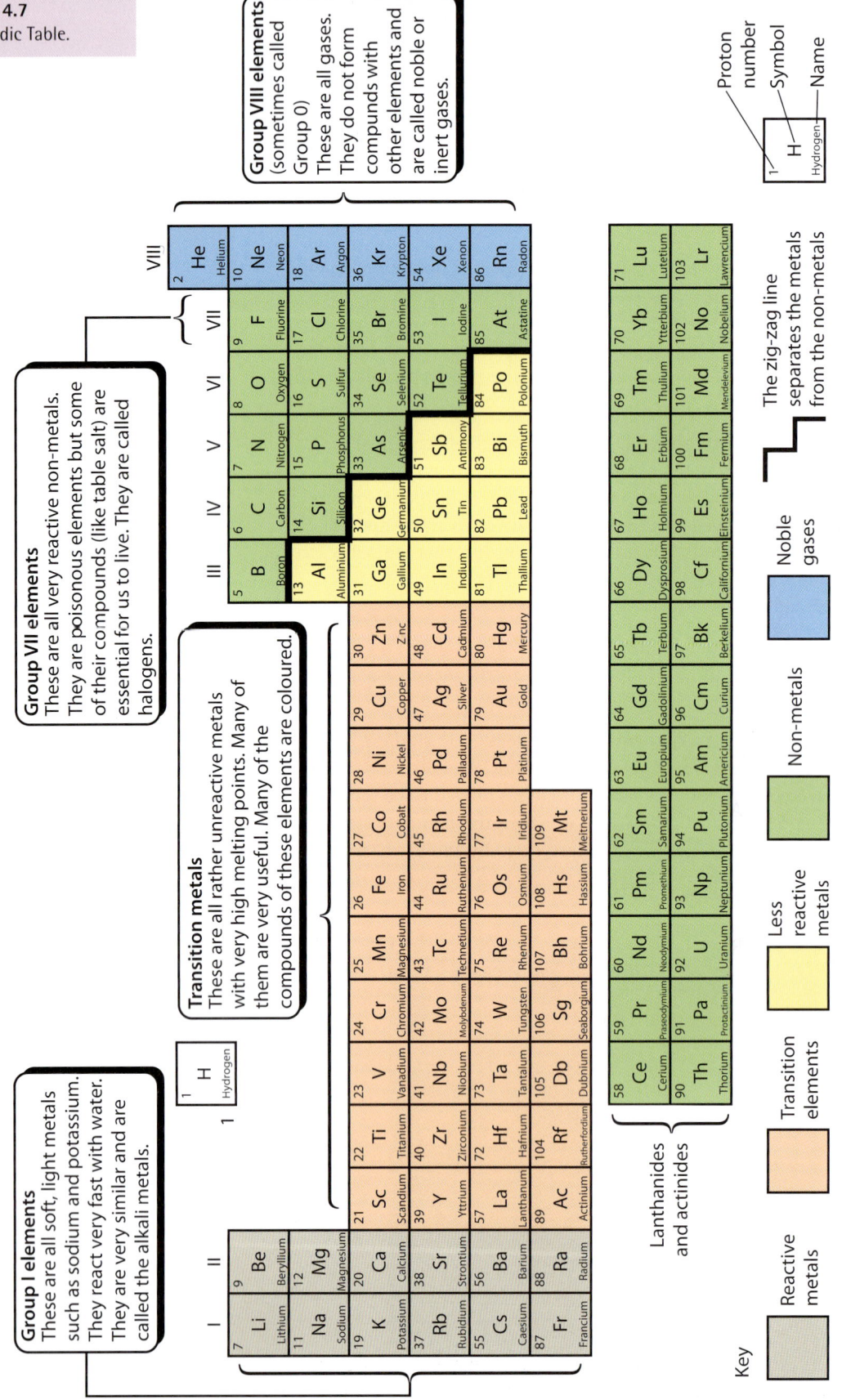

▶ **Table 4.7**
The Periodic Table.

Group I elements
These are all soft, light metals such as sodium and potassium. They react very fast with water. They are very similar and are called the alkali metals.

Group VII elements
These are all very reactive non-metals. They are poisonous elements but some of their compounds (like table salt) are essential for us to live. They are called halogens.

Group VIII elements
(sometimes called Group 0)
These are all gases. They do not form compounds with other elements and are called noble or inert gases.

Transition metals
These are all rather unreactive metals with very high melting points. Many of them are very useful. Many of the compounds of these elements are coloured.

		Proton number — Symbol — Name
		1 H Hydrogen

The zig-zag line separates the metals from the non-metals

Key

- Reactive metals
- Transition elements
- Less reactive metals
- Non-metals
- Noble gases

I	II												III	IV	V	VI	VII	VIII
																		2 He Helium
3 Li Lithium	4 Be Beryllium												5 B Boron	6 C Carbon	7 N Nitrogen	8 O Oxygen	9 F Fluorine	10 Ne Neon
11 Na Sodium	12 Mg Magnesium												13 Al Aluminium	14 Si Silicon	15 P Phosphorus	16 S Sulfur	17 Cl Chlorine	18 Ar Argon
19 K Potassium	20 Ca Calcium	21 Sc Scandium	22 Ti Titanium	23 V Vanadium	24 Cr Chromium	25 Mn Manganese	26 Fe Iron	27 Co Cobalt	28 Ni Nickel	29 Cu Copper	30 Zn Zinc		31 Ga Gallium	32 Ge Germanium	33 As Arsenic	34 Se Selenium	35 Br Bromine	36 Kr Krypton
37 Rb Rubidium	38 Sr Strontium	39 Y Yttrium	40 Zr Zirconium	41 Nb Niobium	42 Mo Molybdenum	43 Tc Technetium	44 Ru Ruthenium	45 Rh Rhodium	46 Pd Palladium	47 Ag Silver	48 Cd Cadmium		49 In Indium	50 Sn Tin	51 Sb Antimony	52 Te Tellurium	53 I Iodine	54 Xe Xenon
55 Cs Caesium	56 Ba Barium	57 La Lanthanum	72 Hf Hafnium	73 Ta Tantalum	74 W Tungsten	75 Re Rhenium	76 Os Osmium	77 Ir Iridium	78 Pt Platinum	79 Au Gold	80 Hg Mercury		81 Tl Thallium	82 Pb Lead	83 Bi Bismuth	84 Po Polonium	85 At Astatine	86 Rn Radon
87 Fr Francium	88 Ra Radium	89 Ac Actinium	104 Rf Rutherfordium	105 Db Dubnium	106 Sg Seaborgium	107 Bh Bohrium	108 Hs Hassium	109 Mt Meitnerium										

Lanthanides and actinides

58 Ce Cerium	59 Pr Praseodymium	60 Nd Neodymium	61 Pm Promethium	62 Sm Samarium	63 Eu Europium	64 Gd Gadolinium	65 Tb Terbium	66 Dy Dysprosium	67 Ho Holmium	68 Er Erbium	69 Tm Thulium	70 Yb Ytterbium	71 Lu Lutetium
90 Th Thorium	91 Pa Protactinium	92 U Uranium	93 Np Neptunium	94 Pu Plutonium	95 Am Americium	96 Cm Curium	97 Bk Berkelium	98 Cf Californium	99 Es Einsteinium	100 Fm Fermium	101 Md Mendelevium	102 No Nobelium	103 Lr Lawrencium

Atoms and molecules

The modern periodic table has eight columns of elements called **groups**. The elements in each group are all chemically similar. The elements are numbered horizontally in lines called **periods**.

The number next to the element is the **nucleon number** of the element.

In between Groups 2 and 3, starting in Period 4, there is a group of elements called the **transition elements**. In Periods 6 and 7 there are an additional 14 transition metals. These are called the **lanthanides** (or rare earth elements) in Period 6 and the **actinides** in Period 7.

Good scientific theories allow scientists to make **predictions**. One reason why Mendeleev's classification of the elements was so successful was that he realised that some of the elements had not yet been discovered and so he left gaps for them. He was able to **predict** many of the properties of the ones that had not been discovered. One of the undiscovered ones was the element germanium, the third element in Period 4. Mendeleev called this 'eka-silicon' ('eka' is Greek for 'like') because he predicted that it would have properties very like silicon. This element was discovered 15 years later. Table 4.8 shows how close Mendeleev was in his predictions.

Property	Mendeleev's predictions in 1871 of the properties of eka-silicon	Properties of the element germanium discovered in 1886
Appearance	Grey metal	Grey metal
Melting point	About 800 °C	958 °C
Density	About 5.5 g/cm^3	About 5.47 g/cm^3
Relative atomic mass	73.4	72.6
Reaction with oxygen	Reacts to form an oxide with formula MO_2 which will have a density of 4.7 g/cm^3.	Reacts to form the oxide GeO_2 which has a density of 4.7 g/cm^3.

◀ Table 4.8 Comparing the properties of germanium with Mendeleev's predictions.

4.8 The electronic structure of the elements

Mendeleev's Periodic Table is very important in chemistry. He first made it by placing elements that had similar properties in the same columns. But for a long time nobody knew why the table was the shape it was. It was only when Niels Bohr developed his modern atomic theory that the shape could be explained.

Bohr realised that the electrons circulating around the nucleus were not all the same. Some had more energy than others. The ones with most

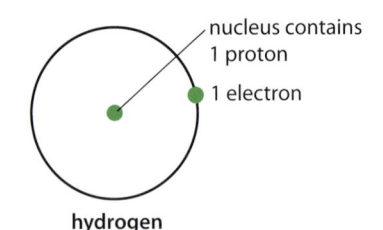

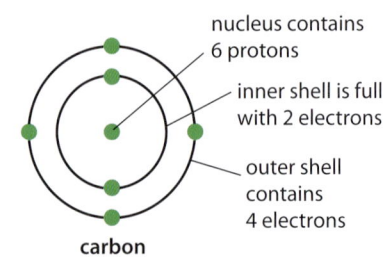

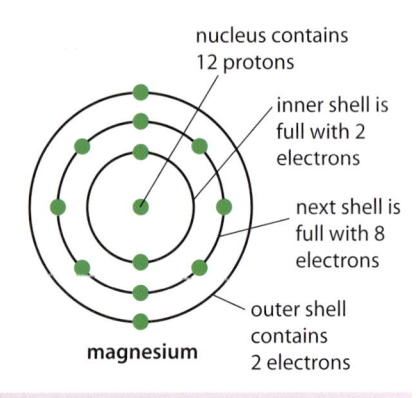

hydrogen
- nucleus contains 1 proton
- 1 electron

carbon
- nucleus contains 6 protons
- inner shell is full with 2 electrons
- outer shell contains 4 electrons

magnesium
- nucleus contains 12 protons
- inner shell is full with 2 electrons
- next shell is full with 8 electrons
- outer shell contains 2 electrons

▲ **Figure 4.6**
Electronic structures of H, C and Mg with explanations.

energy are to be found furthest from the nucleus, just as an object far from the centre of the Earth has more gravitational potential energy than an identical object nearer to it.

Bohr suggested that the electrons in an atom are to be found in orbits (called shells) around the nucleus. But these shells could not contain more than a small number of electrons each.

The electron shell nearest to the nucleus is full when it contains two electrons. The next shell can hold up to eight electrons before it is full. This shell contains electrons with more energy than the first shell. The third shell can also contain up to eight electrons. Electrons only exist in outer shells if the inner ones are full.

Figure 4.6 shows how Bohr's idea works; it shows the structure of the atoms of hydrogen, carbon and magnesium.

If you draw the structures of the first 20 elements and arrange them in a table so that the elements with the same number of electrons in their outer shell are lined up vertically, it is easy to see how Bohr's ideas explain the shape of Mendeleev's table proposed almost fifty years earlier.

In the Periodic Table, the first period contains only two elements, hydrogen (H) and helium (He). The other periods contain elements divided into eight groups and each group contains elements with similar properties. These groups are always numbered with Roman numerals from I to VIII as shown.

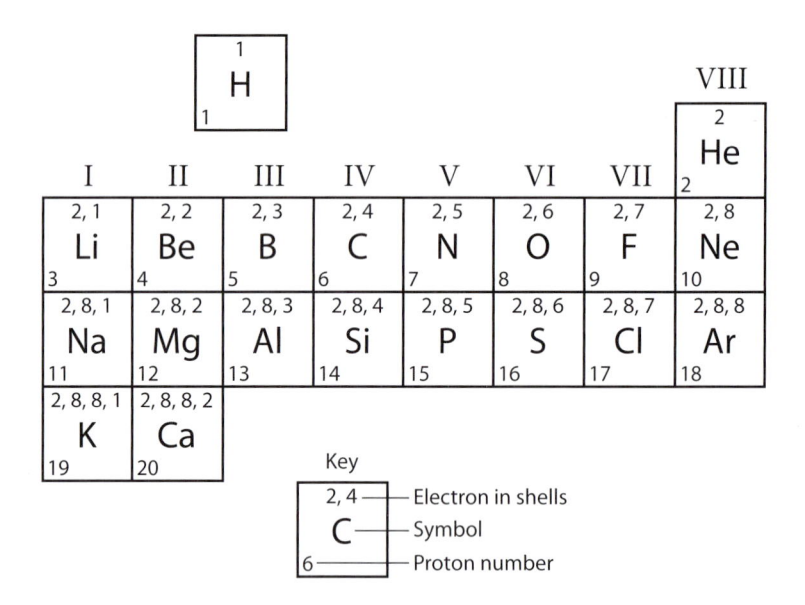

I	II	III	IV	V	VI	VII	VIII
			1 H 1				2 He 2
2,1 Li 3	2,2 Be 4	2,3 B 5	2,4 C 6	2,5 N 7	2,6 O 8	2,7 F 9	2,8 Ne 10
2,8,1 Na 11	2,8,2 Mg 12	2,8,3 Al 13	2,8,4 Si 14	2,8,5 P 15	2,8,6 S 16	2,8,7 Cl 17	2,8,8 Ar 18
2,8,8,1 K 19	2,8,8,2 Ca 20						

Key:
- 2, 4 — Electron in shells
- C — Symbol
- 6 — Proton number

▶ **Table 4.9**
The number of electrons in shells of the first 20 elements.

The following important points can be seen from Table 4.9.
- Each shell is gradually filled across each period until Group VIII is reached when the shell is full. The next shell is then filled across the period below.
- Every element in any particular Group has the same number of electrons in the outer shell. This number is the same as the Group number.
- Elements in Group VIII are a family of elements called the inert gases, which do not react with other elements. They have full outer shells.

Atoms and molecules

The fourth period of the Periodic Table is more complicated. It contains not eight elements but 18. Between Group II and Group III, there are an extra ten elements which are all metals with similar properties called the transition elements. Bohr's atomic structure is also rather more complicated for these elements. After element 20, the next 10 electrons do not go into the outer shell. Instead they go into the third shell and the number that this shell can hold increases from 8 to 18 electrons. Because of this, the number of electrons in the outer shell of the transition elements stays the same at two, like calcium.

Why are these electronic structures important? They affect the way that the elements react and this will be described in the next chapter.

4.9 Radioactive isotopes

◀ **Figure 4.7**
This is the preserved body of Lindow Man, in the British Museum. It was found in a peat marsh at Lindow in Cheshire, England. The archaeologists who dug him up called him 'Pete Marsh'.

The scientists in the British Museum say that Lindow Man was brutally murdered and pushed into the marsh sometime in the 120 years between 2BCE and 119 CE. How do they know this date so accurately? The answer is that they used a technique called **radiocarbon dating** to tell them when the cereal grains and mistletoe pollen that were part of his last meal were alive and growing. Carbon-14 dating uses the idea of **radioactivity**.

About 100 years ago a French scientist called Henri Becquerel made a chance discovery. He had some photographic plates carefully wrapped so that light could not spoil them. He stored them near a sample of the element uranium that had recently been purified. When the plates were developed they were black, just as if some light had reached them. Becquerel suggested that some kind of invisible radiation must have been given off by the uranium and had passed through the wrapping round the plates.

Pierre and Marie Curie, two other scientists who investigated this further, called the effect radioactivity.

We now know that when an isotope of an element is radioactive it has an unstable nucleus. The nucleus breaks down spontaneously (this means by itself, without help from anything else), giving off the **radiation** that

DID YOU KNOW?

Marie Curie won two Nobel Prizes. She worked at the Sorbonne in Paris and was awarded the prize for physics in 1903 for her work with Becquerel on radioactivity. In 1911 her discovery of the radioactive elements radium and polonium (called after her native land, Poland) resulted in the prize for chemistry. She is still the only person to win the prize in two different sciences. Her elder daughter, Irene Joliot-Curie, won the Nobel Prize for chemistry in 1935 for discovering that aluminium could be radioactive.

affected Becquerel's plates, and forming a new element with a different number of protons and neutrons. Only a few isotopes are radioactive. The best-known ones are isotopes of the heavier elements such as uranium (92 protons and 146 neutrons) but there are radioactive isotopes of almost every element. They usually occur naturally in very small amounts. There is even a radioactive isotope of hydrogen; it has one proton and two neutrons in the nucleus and it has a special name, **tritium**.

The radiation given off by isotopes is dangerous (it killed Marie Curie who did not realise it was dangerous). For this reason, isotopes must be handled and stored with great care. However, radioactive isotopes can also be very useful. Table 4.10 shows some examples of this. The isotopes are used in medicine, in measuring devices and in nuclear power stations.

▶ Table 4.10
Some uses of radioactive isotopes.

Isotope	Use
Uranium-235 and uranium-238	Nuclear power stations. A lot of energy is given off when they decompose. This can be used to heat water to make steam which is used to drive turbines and make electricity.
Iodine-131 and others	These have medical uses. They are carried round the body in fluids such as the blood and they can be used to show when organs are not functioning correctly. These are called tracers. Other isotopes can be used to treat cancer.
Caesium-137	This is used to tell whether a drink can is full as it comes off the production line. An empty can lets more radiation through than a full one and it can be detected. Isotopes like this can also be used as tracers in industry; a small amount can be put into gas, for example, to detect leaks. A Geiger counter is a device for detecting radiation and this can be used to find the leak.
Americium-241	This is used in common smoke detectors. The radiation it produces in the air allows a very small current to travel between two plates. When smoke gets between these plates the current is reduced and this can be used to trigger an alarm. This isotope is also used for measuring and controlling the exact thickness of things like glass and paper when they are produced.

So how did they use radioactivity for finding out when 'Pete Marsh' was alive? Carbon-14 is a radioactive isotope of carbon. It is made in the atmosphere when high-energy particles from the Sun hit nitrogen-14 in the atmosphere. A fast neutron from the Sun hits an atom of nitrogen and replaces one of its protons. This means that it is changed into an atom of carbon-14. This is called a **nuclear reaction**. The carbon-14 isotope then forms carbon dioxide by reacting with the oxygen in the air. This is then taken up by plants and the plants are eaten by animals. This carbon-14 in plants and animals is radioactive and over many centuries it gradually changes back into nitrogen. So archaeologists can tell when Pete Marsh was alive by looking at how much carbon-14 was left in his last meal.

QUESTIONS

4.1 Complete Table 4.11 showing the atomic structures of four elements.

Element	Number of protons	Number of neutrons	Number of electrons	Nucleon number
Oxygen			8	16
Sodium	11	12		
Argon	18			40
Iron		30	26	

◀ Table 4.11

4.2 Write down how many protons and neutrons there are in the nuclei of the following isotopes?

$^{12}_{6}C$

$^{56}_{26}Fe$

$^{64}_{29}Cu$

$^{235}_{92}U$

$^{238}_{92}U$

4.3 Using the relative atomic masses given in Table 3.2 to calculate the relative molecular masses of the following compounds.
ammonia (NH_3)
carbon dioxide (CO_2)
copper sulfate ($CuSO_4$)
glucose ($C_6H_{12}O_6$)

4.4 The three isotopes of carbon are carbon-12, carbon-13 and carbon-14. Draw symbols for them showing their mass and nucleon numbers. Explain how carbon-14 can help us determine the date of archaeological remains.

4.5 Fluorine atoms have a mass number of 19.
  a) Explain what is meant by 'mass number'.
  b) State the atomic number of fluorine (use the periodic table).
  c) Draw the full electronic structure of a fluorine atom.

4.6 State the number of electrons in the outer shell of the following elements. Use the periodic table to help you.
  a) bromine
  b) tin
  c) aluminium
  d) rubidium

Summary

Now that you have completed this chapter, you should be able to:

- explain how all matter is made up of tiny particles called atoms which cannot be made or destroyed
- understand that atoms of the same elements are all the same and that atoms of different elements are different from each other
- explain that atoms can join together to form larger particles
- describe the structure of atoms in terms of a small positive nucleus with electrons orbiting around it
- describe the mass and charge of protons, neutrons and electrons
- know that all the atoms of a particular element have the same number of protons which is called proton number of the element
- know the meaning of the nucleon number of the element and explain isotopes in terms of nucleon numbers
- know that some isotopes are radioactive and know what this means and why they can be both dangerous and useful
- describe how electrons occur in shells around the nucleus and how different shells can contain different numbers of electrons
- arrange elements according to their properties and electronic structure in the Periodic Table.

Chapter 5

How atoms combine

Figure 5.1
Look at these different objects; some are natural, some synthetic. They are all made up of materials with a wide range of different properties.

Think about all the materials that you can see in the pictures. Some are solids while others are liquids and also there are gases. The solids are hard, soft, rigid, flexible, warm or cold to touch, strong or weak, easily broken or unbreakable; how many more words can you think of to describe them?

What makes these materials like they are? Why are some liquid and others solid? Why do some break easily when you hit them with a hammer but others do not? Why do some dissolve easily in water but others do not?

In this chapter you will find answers to many of these observations. You will learn that many of the observations can be explained by four simple theories about how atoms join together. It is because these theories can explain so much of the **evidence** that scientists think they are very good theories.

5.1 Classifying materials

If we want to know how a radio works, we need to study the parts inside it and the way these parts are put together. Similarly, if we want to understand the properties of chemical compounds, we must know something about how the atoms in them are arranged. We call this the **structure** of the compound. So we should first look at the properties of different materials and then see if we can explain them by their **atomic** and **molecular structure**.

Look at the materials in Figure 5.1 and try to classify some of them according to some of their properties. Properties you could use are: hardness, electrical conductivity, solubility, whether the substance shatters when struck with a hammer (brittleness), melting and boiling points. Table 5.1 shows some possible results of your observations; you could add more.

> **Activity 5.1**
> Classifying materials

▼ **Table 5.1**
Physical properties of some common materials.

Object	Brittle	Conducts electricity	Dissolves easily in water	Does it melt easily (if you put it on an electric stove)?	Rigid or flexible
Car body	No	Yes	No	No	Rigid
Glass window	Yes	No	No	No	Rigid
Plastic bag	No	No	No	Yes	Flexible
Salt crystals	Yes	No	Yes	No	Rigid
Rubber band	No	No	No	Yes	Flexible
Pottery cup	Yes	No	No	No	Rigid
Newspaper	No	No	No	No	Flexible

We can explain many of these observations if we know something about how the atoms are held together in the compounds. Four types of bond will be studied. They have special names as follows:
- covalent bonds
- ionic bonds
- bonds in macromolecules
- metallic bonds.

5.2 Covalent bonds

Look again at the Periodic Table (Table 4.7). The elements in Group VIII are all the inert gases. They are called 'inert' because they do not take part in any chemical reactions. Look carefully at helium and compare it with hydrogen. The only difference in the arrangement of electrons is that hydrogen has one electron in its shell and helium has two. It is the full shell of electrons that makes helium unreactive.

How atoms combine

A full shell is a stable arrangement of electrons. You will see that this is a very important idea for understanding why atoms combine. By combining with other atoms they are able to achieve this stable arrangement of electrons.

Hydrogen gas does not consist of individual hydrogen atoms. The atoms have joined together into hydrogen **molecules** and each molecule consists of two atoms of hydrogen. Pairing like this allows the atoms to share electrons so that each atom has two in its shell. The shell is full with two electrons and a full shell is a stable arrangement of electrons (Figure 5.2).

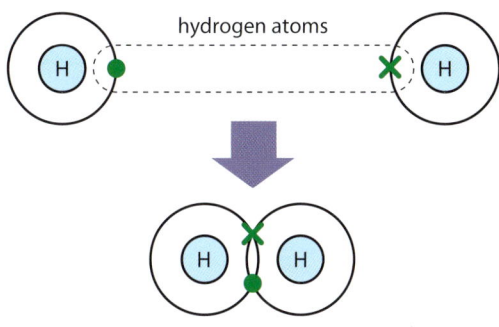

Figure 5.2
Covalent bonds in a hydrogen molecule.

Group VII elements in the Periodic Table are called the **halogens** (Greek − *halo* = 'salt' and *gen* = 'forming'). They are all elements that need only one extra electron to fill their outer shells. Like hydrogen, they can do this by sharing electrons. Figure 5.3 shows how two chlorine atoms join together to form a chlorine molecule.

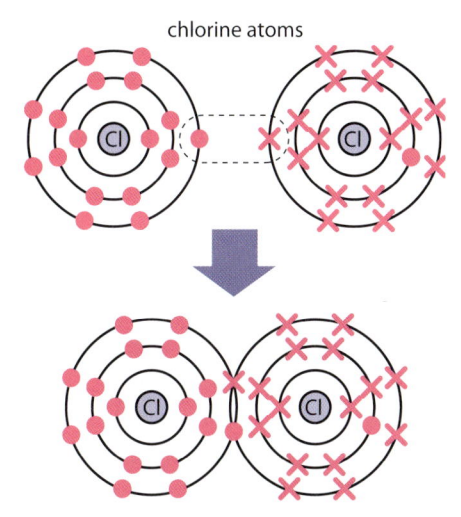

Figure 5.3
Covalent bonds in a chlorine molecule.

In both these figures, the electrons in one atom are represented by dots and those in the other, by crosses. You can see how a dot from one atom and a cross from the other atom are shared in the molecule that is formed. We call this kind of bond, where electrons are shared, a **covalent bond**.

Atoms of different elements can combine in the same way. Oxygen has six electrons in its outer shell. It needs two more to fill it. Figure 5.4 shows how two atoms of hydrogen combine with one atom of oxygen by sharing electrons so that all three atoms have full outer shells.

Figure 5.4 Covalent bonds in a water molecule.

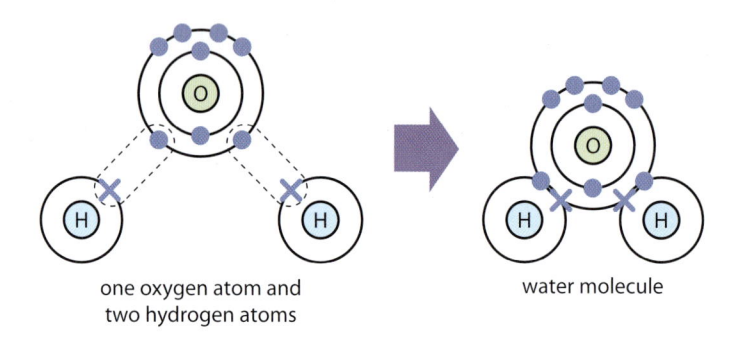

one oxygen atom and two hydrogen atoms → water molecule

Carbon is in Group IV of the Periodic Table. It has four electrons in the outer shell and therefore needs another four to fill the shell. Figure 5.5 shows how this can happen if it combines with four hydrogen atoms.

Figure 5.5 Covalent bonds in a methane molecule.

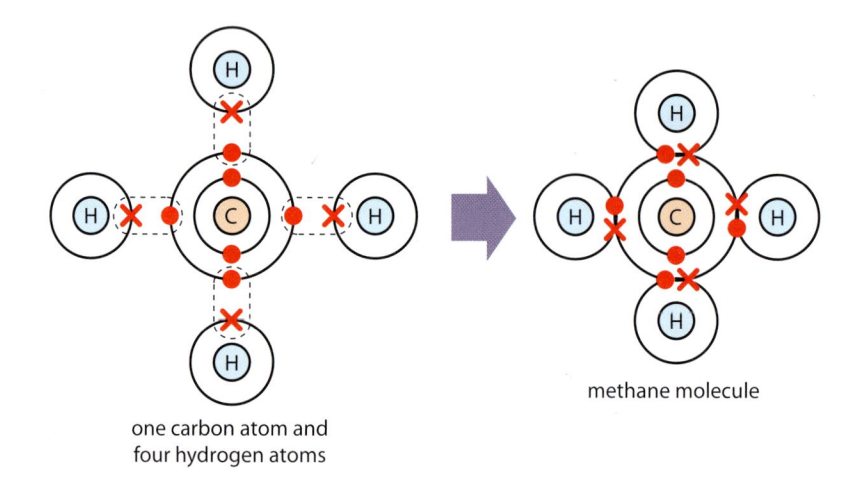

one carbon atom and four hydrogen atoms → methane molecule

The formulae for all these covalent compounds are shown in Table 5.2. The box also shows the **structural formulae** of these compounds.

Table 5.2 Formulae and structures of covalent compounds.

Compound	Formula	Structural formula
Hydrogen	H_2	H — H
Chlorine	Cl_2	Cl — Cl
Water	H_2O	H–O–H
Methane	CH_4	H–C(H)(H)–H

The formulae tell us how many atoms of each element join together to form a molecule of the compound. The formula H_2O tells us that each molecule of water contains two atoms of hydrogen joined to one of oxygen. The column on the right shows the structural formula of the compound. The bonds between the atoms are shown by lines. Each bond is made from a pair of electrons shared between the two atoms.

5.3 Double and triple covalent bonds

Like hydrogen, oxygen gas also consists of molecules and not atoms. Also like hydrogen, each molecule of oxygen contains two atoms. But oxygen has six electrons in its outer shell and so it needs two extra electrons, not one, to fill it. It can do this by sharing two electrons with another atom of oxygen. Figure 5.6 shows how this happens.

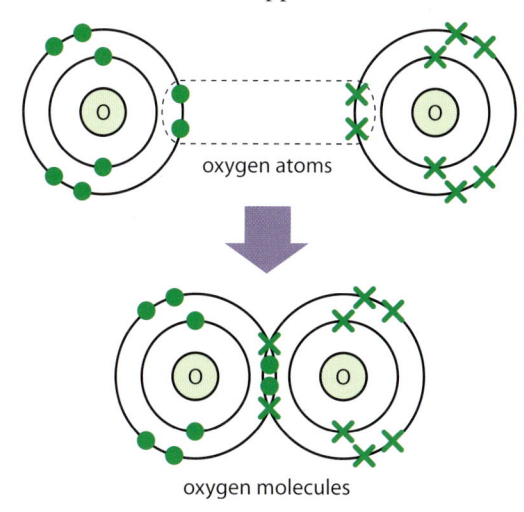

oxygen atoms

oxygen molecules

◀ **Figure 5.6**
Covalent bonds in an oxygen molecule.

In this molecule, two pairs of electrons are shared. We call this a **double bond**. We draw it with two lines like this: O=O

◀ **Figure 5.7**
Structural formula of oxygen.

Another common molecule containing double bonds is carbon dioxide. In this case the carbon needs four extra electrons and can gain them by forming double bonds with two oxygen atoms.

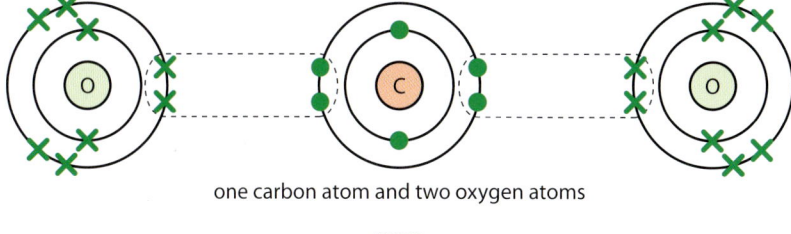

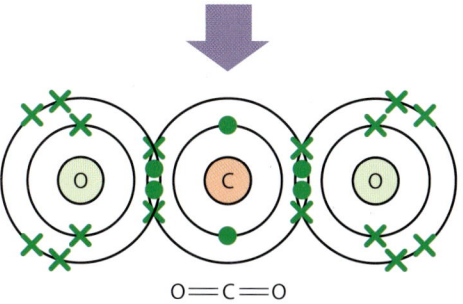

one carbon atom and two oxygen atoms

O=C=O

carbon dioxide molecule

◀ **Figure 5.8**
Structural and electronic formula of carbon dioxide.

Some compounds have triple covalent bonds. In these bonds, six electrons are shared. A common one is the nitrogen molecule in which two atoms of nitrogen join to form the molecule N_2. This is shown in Table 5.3.

There are many millions of covalent compounds in nature. Most of them are compounds containing carbon and you will meet some of them in

Chapter 14. The table also shows the electronic structures and the structural formulae of some of them.

Name	Formula	Structural formula	Description
Nitrogen	N_2	$N\equiv N$	Colourless gas
Ethene	C_2H_4	H₂C=CH₂	Colourless, flammable gas
Methanol	CH_3OH	H–C(H)(H)–O–H	Colourless, flammable liquid
Ethanol	C_2H_5OH	H–C(H)(H)–C(H)(H)–O–H	Colourless, flammable liquid

▶ Table 5.3
The structures of nitrogen, ethene, methanol and ethanol (alcohol).

5.4 The properties of covalent compounds

Look back at all the covalent compounds mentioned in the last two sections. What do they all look or feel like? You will see that almost all of them are gases. A few, like water, are liquids. Some of the compounds shown in Table 5.3 are also liquids.

There are some covalent compounds that are solids. A good example is candle wax. Its chemical name is eicosane and it has a formula $C_{20}H_{42}$. You know that if you put candle wax in hot water it will melt; so we say that eicosane is a **low melting point solid**.

We can make a general rule from these observations. Covalent compounds are gases, liquids or low melting point solids.

The reason for this is that covalent molecules are small. They are small particles that are not joined together with any strong bonds. This means that they do not need much energy to pull them apart. So they have low melting points and quite low boiling points.

5.5 Ionic bonds

Look back at the properties of materials at the beginning of this chapter. You will see that some substances easily shatter when you hit them with a hammer. These are substances that are **crystalline**. They form small shiny crystals with straight sides. Examples include salt, many rocks and minerals, and some precious stones. These substances have an **ionic** structure. A typical ionic compound is table salt, which has the chemical name **sodium chloride**. It is made of two elements, sodium and chlorine.

Figure 5.9 shows the electronic structures of the two atoms, sodium and chlorine. Note that sodium, being in Group I, has one electron in its outer shell. Chlorine (Group VII) has seven electrons in its outer shell.

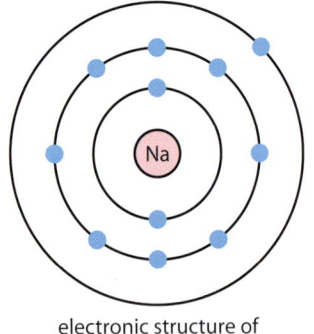

electronic structure of a sodium atom

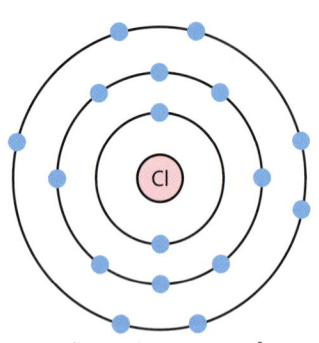

electronic structure of a chlorine atom

▲ Figure 5.9
Structures of sodium and chlorine atoms.

The chlorine atom could fill its outer shell if it could *gain* an extra electron. The sodium atom could achieve a full outer shell if it could *lose* the one outer electron. Can you guess what happens when they combine? The sodium gives up its single outer electron to the chlorine. Both atoms then have a stable, full, outer shell.

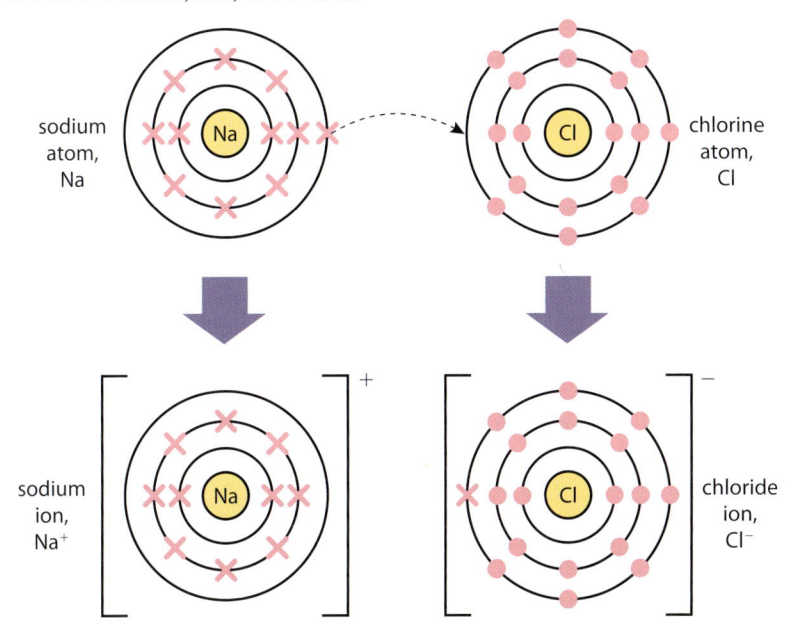

◀ **Figure 5.10**
The transfer of an electron from a sodium atom to a chlorine atom.

The chlorine atom gains one electron. Because the electron has a negative charge, the chlorine atom will gain this negative charge. This negatively charged chlorine atom is called a chlor**ide ion**. The sodium atom loses an electron. This will leave the atom with one more proton than it has electrons and so it will have a positive charge. This is called a sodium **ion.** We have a shorthand way of writing ions that shows the symbol and the charge.

The sodium ion is written as **Na⁺**.

The chloride ion is written as **Cl⁻**.

Ions with more than one charge

Magnesium is a metal in Group II of the Periodic Table. It has two electrons in its outer shell. Magnesium can form a positive ion by losing two electrons. The magnesium ion will have two positive charges (Mg^{++} or Mg^{2+}).

Oxygen is in Group VI. It has six electrons in its outer shell. It can form an **oxide ion** by gaining two electrons. The oxide ion will have two negative charges (O^{--} or O^{2-}).

Any element that has a small number of electrons in its outer shell can lose them to form a positive ion. Elements with small numbers of atoms in their outer shell are found on the left of the Periodic Table in Groups I and II and the transition elements.

Elements that form negative ions are those whose outer shells are almost full. These are found on the right of the Periodic Table and therefore they are non-metals. However, elements in the middle of the Periodic Table are also non-metals and these do not readily form negative ions.

Ionic compounds, therefore, are formed between metals (found on the left or centre of the Periodic Table) and non-metals (found on the right of the Periodic Table).

5.6 The properties of ionic compounds

Positive and negative ions are held together by electrostatic forces. You will remember from physics that opposite electrostatic charges attract each other. When ions are attracted to each other they form **ionic crystals**.

Ionic crystals

The ions are not held together just in pairs. They form what are called 'giant structures' with millions of ions arranged in rows in three dimensions with opposite charges next to each other. Figure 5.11 shows the arrangement of sodium and chloride ions in sodium chloride (common salt). The small spheres represent the sodium ions, which are smaller than the chloride ions. (Can you think why? – look at the electronic structures.)

Each salt crystal in a salt bowl is a single structure. It is a giant ionic structure made of sodium and chloride ions next to each other in a **crystal lattice**. A salt crystal as small as one cubic millimetre is a giant structure made of more than 10 million million million ions!

▲ **Figure 5.11**
Model showing how sodium ions and chloride ions are arranged in a crystal of sodium chloride. The smaller spheres represent the sodium ions.

▶ **Figure 5.12**
Crystals of table salt are all cubes.

Because of this arrangement of the ions in rows, ionic compounds are crystalline. They form regular shaped crystals and the shape depends on the arrangement of the ions. Table salt, sodium chloride, forms crystals that are tiny cubes.

Crystalline solids can be cleaved

One property of crystals is that they can easily be **cleaved**. This means that they can easily be split to form smaller crystals that have smooth parallel sides. This can be easily done with a knife blade if you hold it parallel to one of the edges of the crystal and give it a sharp tap. Figure 5.13 shows a model of this, using polystyrene balls loosely glued together to represent the crystal ions.

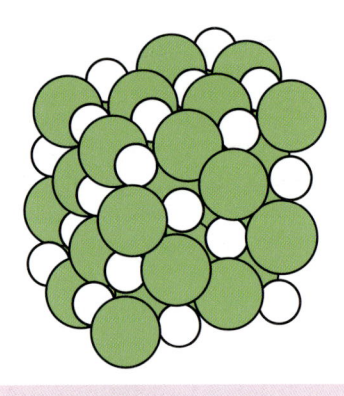

Figure 5.13
Model of cleaving a crystal.

Because crystals can be cleaved in this regular way and the cleaved crystal has a perfectly flat and smooth surface, some natural ionic crystals are valued as gemstones.

The laws of electrostatics determine how strong an ionic bond is. A bond will be strong when the number of charges on the ion is high. The bond will also be strong when the two ions are close together. This means that small ions form stronger bonds than large ones. So, in general, the strongest bonds are formed between small ions with several charges. Magnesium oxide, for example, contains very strong ionic bonds

Crystalline solids can be crushed.

If you hit salt crystals with a hammer, they can easily be crushed into a powder. The powder is made of much smaller crystals that still have straight sides. When you crush crystals you break them along the rows of ions.

Some crystalline solids will dissolve in water.

What happens when salt dissolves in water? The crystal lattice breaks down as water molecules move between the ions. The ions move away from each other and move freely in the water. The **ionic solution** conducts electricity because the ions can carry the electrical charge through it; you will learn more about this in Chapter 8.

Figure 5.14
The smooth surfaces and straight edges of these gemstones are a result of the regular arrangement of the ions in the crystals.

5.7 Macromolecules

You have seen that compounds (such as water) and gases (such as hydrogen and oxygen) are made up of particles that are small molecules. These molecules are made of only a few atoms joined together with covalent bonds. There are some substances that consist of very large numbers of atoms joined together in this way. These substances are called **macromolecules**.

Polymers

One class of macromolecules that you will meet again in Chapter 15 are called **polymers**. These are very common and there are natural ones (like the chemicals that make up our skin or wood) and man-made ones (like nylon, polythene and other plastics). Polymers are large molecules that are made up of a small group of atoms that is repeated many times, like bricks making up a house.

DID YOU KNOW?

Because ionic bonds are usually very strong, ionic compounds have quite high melting points. Table salt, for example, melts at around 800°C. The temperature of the combustion chambers of jet airliners is, however, much higher than this, usually about 1300°C. This means that if they fly through clouds of ash from volcanoes, their engines can stop because the ash is often made of ionic compounds which melt and clog the engines. It is not easy to tell whether it is safe to fly through volcanic ash.

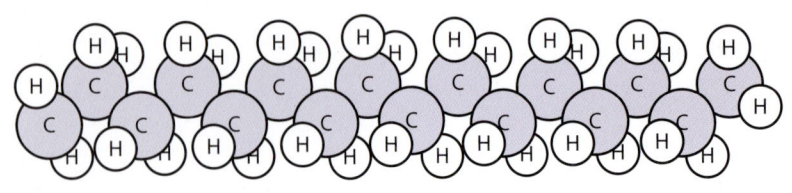

(a)

Carbon allotropes

Another example of a macromolecule is the element carbon. Carbon exists in two common forms, graphite and diamond. Each form has a different structure. We call these two different structures of carbon, **allotropes** of carbon. Other elements, such as sulfur and tin, also show **allotropy**.

The two forms of carbon are very different from each other. Diamond is the hardest natural substance known; graphite is very soft. Both forms occur naturally. Diamonds occur in certain kinds of rock that have been under very high pressure, when the rock was very hot and molten. Under these conditions the diamond crystals form.

Since diamond is so hard, it has many uses. Diamond-tipped saws are used for cutting rocks, and diamond-tipped drills for drilling through rocks. Glass engravers use diamond-tipped pencils to do their work.

Graphite is so soft it will mark paper and is mixed with clay to make pencil 'lead'. It has a very slippery surface and is used in 'graphited' lubricating oils. It has one unusual property for a non-metal; it conducts electricity. Because of this, it is used in dry cells and in electric furnaces for smelting iron and aluminium (see Chapter 11).

We can explain these differences in properties of diamond and graphite very easily if we look at the structures.

(b)

▲ **Figure 5.15**
(a) Structure of polythene made of repeating CH_2—CH_2 units.
(b) Polythene carrier bag.

◀ **Figure 5.16**
Structures of diamond and graphite.

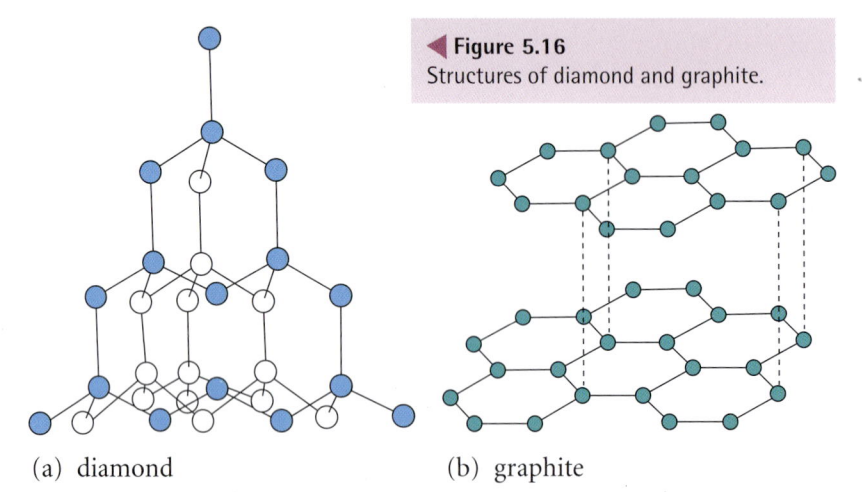

(a) diamond   (b) graphite

In diamond, each carbon atom forms four bonds in different directions. Each bond joins onto another similar carbon atom. This structure is an endless one; only part is shown here. Each carbon atom has four bonds but only a few atoms are shown here with all four of their bonds.

There is no such thing as a single molecule like there is a molecule of water or oxygen. The whole diamond crystal is one large molecule! Because the bonds are very strong and act in all directions, diamond is very hard.

▲ **Figure 5.17**
As the atoms of carbon in diamond are arranged symmetrically in a regular pattern, diamonds can be cut along the planes of carbon atoms to form symmetrical facets like this one. This is one single molecule.

How atoms combine

The structure of graphite is very different. Each carbon is joined to two others in six-sided rings that look rather like chicken wire. This structure is then repeated in layers. The bonds holding the atoms within each layer are strong. They are normal covalent bonds. The bonds holding the layers together are much weaker. Because of this, the layers can easily slide over each other or break apart. This is why graphite can mark paper; little bits of it easily flake off.

One very important point to remember is that, chemically, graphite and diamond are identical. They both have the same chemical properties. It is easy to make carbon dioxide by burning graphite in air. You can also make carbon dioxide by burning diamonds (but it is rather an expensive way of making the gas!).

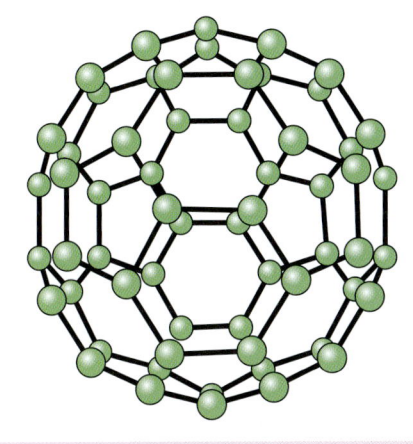

▲ Figure 5.18 C_{60} fullerene, a third allotrope of carbon.

Sand

Sand is a macromolecule. It is silicon dioxide, SiO_2, and it has the structure shown in Figure 5.19. Compare this structure with the structure of diamond; they are very similar except that silicon dioxide has an oxygen atom in between each pair of silicon atoms. This structure is an endless one. Only part of the structure is shown here; each silicon atom has four bonds but only four silicon atoms are shown here with *all* their bonds.

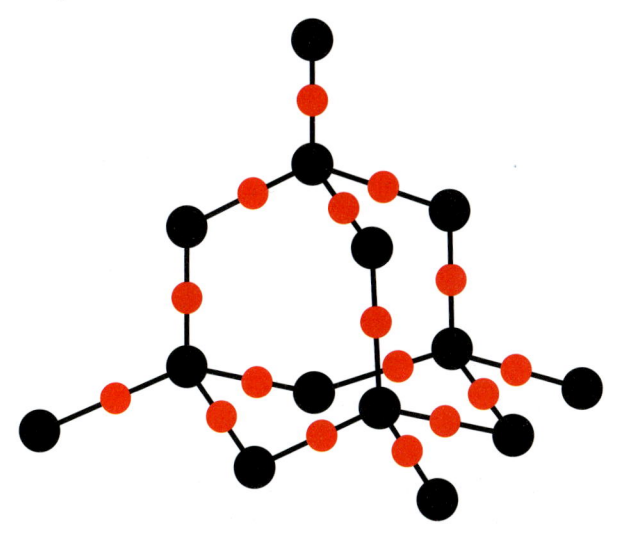

DID YOU KNOW?

The largest diamond in the world was found in South Africa in 1905. It is called the Cullinan diamond and is now part of the British Crown Jewels kept in the Tower of London. It weighs 620 g. The diamond is one single molecule made of about 30 000 0 00 000 000 000 000 000 000 atoms of carbon.

DID YOU KNOW?

There is a third form of carbon, which has only been discovered quite recently. In this form the atoms are joined together like graphite. They are not joined in a flat sheet, however, but in a sphere that looks rather like a football and has 60 carbon atoms in it. This form of carbon is called a **fullerene** after the modern American architect called Buckminster Fuller who designed buildings shaped like this. Some chemists don't call these macromolecules fullerenes; they prefer to call them 'buckyballs'. Scientists have also made a tube form of fullerene that they call carbon nanotubes because they are only a few nanometres in diameter. They are also known as 'buckytubes'.

◀ Figure 5.19
The structure of silicon dioxide. The black atoms are silicon and the red ones are oxygen. Compare this with the structure of of diamond in Figure 5.16.

> **DID YOU KNOW?**
>
> Quartz macromolecules have an interesting electrical property. They vibrate very fast at a regular rate when a small electrical current is passed though them. This vibration of the crystal is used to control most of our clocks and watches. Such clocks keep very accurate time.

Silicon dioxide is very common. Sand, quartz and flint are all forms of silicon dioxide. They are all very hard substances; sand is used to make sandpaper, and flint was used by people to make sharp tools before they learnt how to make metal tools.

The reason why silicon dioxide is hard is because of its diamond-like structure, which is very strong.

5.8 Metallic bonds

You will learn in Chapter 9 of a rather different kind of bond called the **metallic bond**. This is the bond that holds the atoms together in a metal. You will see that if you understand what this bond is like, you can explain many important properties of metals, such as their good electrical and heat conductivity.

QUESTIONS

5.1 Classify the following compounds as covalent or ionic.
NaBr
$MgCl_2$
PH_3
$FeCl_3$
H_2S
CuO

5.2 Show, using diagrams, how the elements lithium and bromine can combine to form an ionic compound.

5.3 Draw the electronic structure of ammonia (NH_3), hydrogen chloride (HCl) and silicon tetrachloride ($SiCl_4$). Draw the structural formulae of these compounds.

5.4 Sulfur is in Group VII in the Periodic Table. State how many electrons there are in its outer shell. Draw the structure of the compound formed between hydrogen and sulfur (called hydrogen sulfide).

5.5 State the formula of the compound formed between carbon and chlorine. Give a reason for your answer.

5.6 Boron and aluminium are both elements in Group III. Normally elements that are close to each other have similar properties but in this case they are rather different. For example, boron trifluoride (BF_3) is covalent but aluminium trifluoride (AlF_3) is ionic.
  a) Use 'dot and cross' diagrams to show how aluminium and fluorine combine to form an ionic compound.
  b) Draw 'dot and cross' diagrams to show the structure of covalent boron trifluoride. Do all the atoms in your structure have full outer shells? Explain why boron trifluoride often reacts easily with atoms of molecules that have two 'spare' electrons that they can share.

Summary

Now that you have completed this chapter, you should be able to:

- recognise that materials around us may be natural or synthetic and that materials have different properties which depend on how the atoms are joined together to form the compounds that make up the materials
- list the four kinds of bonds that are formed by atoms; covalent bonds, ionic bonds, bonds in macromolecules and metallic bonds
- explain how single covalent bonds are formed and draw structures of these bonds
- explain how double and triple covalent bonds are formed
- explain, using drawings, how ionic bonds are formed, and how these bonds results in crystal structures
- explain the importance in bonding of a full outer electron shell
- show how the type of bonding can explain the properties of ionic and covalent compounds
- give examples of macromolecules that have a covalent structure that continues indefinitely
- explain how these structures give rise to properties such as hardness and high melting points.

Chapter 6

The Periodic Table

Look at the Periodic Table (Table 4.7). Can you guess where on the table the following two elements are?

The first element is a metal that is very dense; a piece the size of a matchbox weighs about a kilogram. It is rather expensive; the matchbox-sized piece would cost about $20 000 (at 2008 prices). It is shiny and does not tarnish. It used to be used as needles for playing the old nineteenth century wax phonographs. These were wax cylinders with a groove cut in them by the sound vibration. When a needle follows the groove it vibrates, reproducing the original sound. The needles made of this element were very hard and did not do much damage to the wax groove.

▼ Figure 6.1
Phonograph needles used to be made of osmium, but were later changed to steel, as shown below.

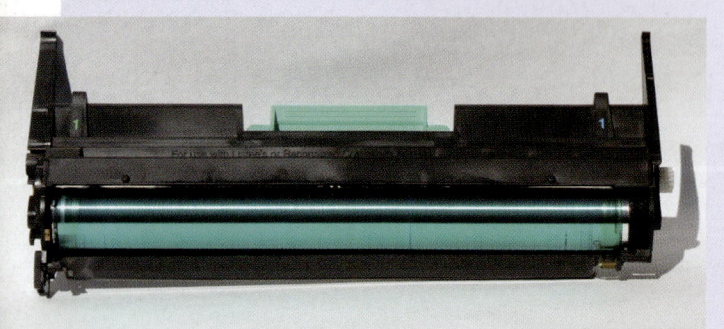

The second element is a solid non-metal which melts at 220 °C. Its density is about 5 g/cm^3 so it will sink in water. You can find it in old radio sets made before the 1960s, before the diode was invented. Devices containing this element were used instead of diodes. These days it has one very common use, which is shown in the photograph. This is a cylinder from a photocopier. Because it is a non-metal it can be charged electrostatically. This is done by shining a laser light on to it; the charged bit then picks up toner, which is then melted onto the paper.

The dense, hard, shiny, rare metal is a **transition metal.** The solid non-metal is on the right of the Periodic Table. Were you correct? The first one is **osmium** and the second is **selenium**. What this shows you is that Mendeleev's Periodic Table is a very convenient way of classifying elements. And if you know where an element is on the Periodic Table, you can predict quite a lot about it. This chapter will help you to do this better.

◀ Figure 6.2
Photocopier drum.

6.1 Blocks of elements in the Periodic Table

In this chapter you will often want to refer to the Periodic Table (Table 4.7). This is a modern form of the Periodic Table and it shows the blocks of elements with similar properties.

These blocks are:
- Groups I and II on the left, which are called the **alkali metals**
- the transition metals between Groups II and III
- the group of metals on the right of the transition metals. They are less reactive metals and display some of the properties of the non-metals
- the group of non-metals to the right of the Periodic Table. Notice that there is a stepped line that separates the metals from the non-metals.
- the rare earth elements, or lanthanides and actinides, are a group of very similar metals between Group II and the transition elements.

Within these blocks in the Periodic Table, it is possible to see trends in both the physical and chemical properties. It is this that makes the Periodic Table so useful because it allows us to predict the properties of elements we have not seen. One very important trend across the whole table is the change from metals to non-metals moving from left to right. This does not happen suddenly at the black stepped line but is gradual. The metal elements near the line show some non-metal characteristics and non-metals near the line show some metallic characteristics.

Groups I and II: the alkali metals and alkali earth metals

This block on the left of the Periodic Table contains reactive metals, which form colourless ionic compounds, most of which are soluble in water. These metals become more reactive as you go down the groups and less reactive along the periods from left to right.

Group I is called the alkali metals because, as you will find out in the next chapter, they form oxides that make an alkaline solution when they dissolve in water. Group II metals also make oxides that are alkaline. The word 'earth' in their name goes back as far as Greek times when 'earthy' substances were substances that were insoluble (like earth) and did not change if you heated them. Many compounds of the Group II metals have these properties.

These metals are all very light, which makes them useful for things where heaviness is a problem, such as in aircraft and space technology. The Group I metals are so light they float on water and they are so soft they can be cut with a knife.

The transition metals

This block of elements contains hard, strong, dense metals that have many important uses. Many are common and many have been known since ancient times. They often form coloured compounds. The metals become less reactive from left to right, like the Group I and II metals. However their reactivity *decreases* from top to bottom, which is the opposite of the

DID YOU KNOW?

Tin is a well-known metal that is next to the metal/non-metal border. It is shiny and conducts electricity. It is used to coat the inside of steel food tins. But there is also a form of tin that is a grey powder which is not at all shiny and will not conduct electricity. You will remember from carbon that two forms of the same element that have different structures and properties are called allotropes.

▼ Figure 6.3
Group I metals like sodium can be cut easily.

alkali metals. This means that the least reactive metals, such as gold, are found at the bottom right of this group.

▼ **Figure 6.5**
Silicon is an important non-metal. It is made in large, extremely pure crystals that are then sliced into thin 'wafers'. These are then used to make the electronic components found in everything from watches to computers. The protective clothing is worn, not to protect the technician, but to make sure that the pure silicon wafer is not contaminated with impurities from the human body.

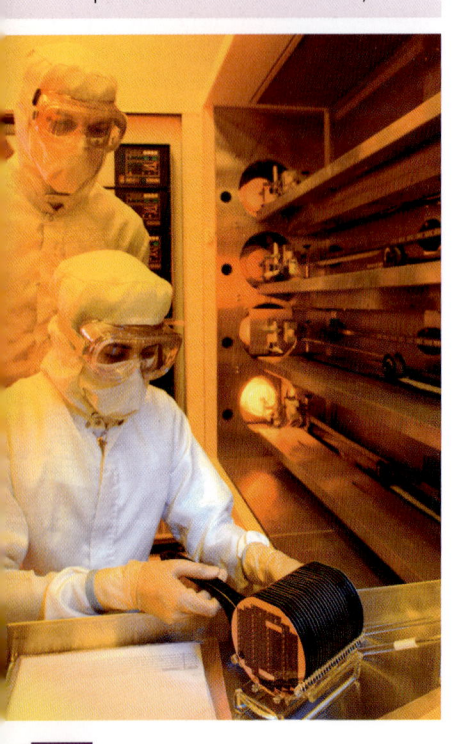

▲ **Figure 6.4**
The first bridge to be made of iron. This bridge crosses the river Severn at a place called Ironbridge in England. This was where iron was made in large quantities for the first time. An interesting feature of this bridge is the way the bits are joined together; they use woodworking joints (above left) because at this time nobody had developed the skills needed for working on large metal structures.

Group III and IV metals

This block of metals is next to the group of non-metals. Except for aluminium, their metallic properties such as electrical conductivity and heat conductivity are not as good as the transition metals and they also show some non-metallic properties. Lead is typical; it is unreactive and easy to make into useful objects. It has been known for a long time and was commonly used for water pipes and drainpipes until it was discovered that it is poisonous and damages brain cells.

The non-metals

Elements in this block vary a lot in their properties. Some are gases, one is a liquid and some are solids at room temperature. There is only one thing common to all of them; they are not metals! They form covalent compounds with each other and the ones on the right form ionic compounds with metals.

Group VIII, the inert (or noble) gases, is a special group of non-metals. Their most interesting property is that they do not react at all with other elements (because their outer shells are all full).

The lanthanides and actinides

These are really a sub-group of the transition elements. They are all very similar and are rare. The most important one is uranium, which is used mainly to make fuel rods for nuclear power stations.

6.2 Group I: the alkali metals

Table 6.1 shows some properties of the elements in Group I. We use the Periodic Table to help us see **trends** in properties of elements; you can see three trends in the table. You can see them more clearly if you plot line graphs of the proton number (*x*-axis) of the element against the property.

▼ Table 6.1
Some physical properties of Group I.

Proton number	Element	Melting point (°C)	Boiling point (°C)	Density (g/cm^3)
3	Lithium	180	1330	0.53
11	Sodium	98	890	0.97
19	Potassium	64	774	0.86
37	Rubidium	39	688	1.53
55	Caesium	29	690	1.90

The Group I elements are all soft metals, easily cut with a knife. Their melting and boiling points decrease as you look down the group. Caesium is classified as a solid but in many countries it will be a liquid much of the time. Most of the metals have densities less than 1 g/cm^3 which means they float on water.

The alkali metals are all reactive. They react with non-metals such as oxygen and chlorine and they react with water. Because they react very rapidly with oxygen and with water, they have to be stored under heavy paraffin to prevent them coming into contact with the oxygen and water in the air.

Group I elements become more reactive as you move down the group.

DID YOU KNOW?

All the elements with a proton number greater than uranium (92) are synthetic. They have been made in nuclear physics laboratories in small amounts by bombarding uranium and other heavy nuclei with nuclei of light atoms such as carbon. Some, like americium, are made commercially and have uses (see Table 4.10).

▲ Figure 6.6
The Rössing uranium open pit in Namibia. Uranium usually makes up much less than 1% of the minerals that contain it. This means that huge quantities of rock have to be quarried to provide small quantities of the purified oxide of uranium called 'yellowcake'.

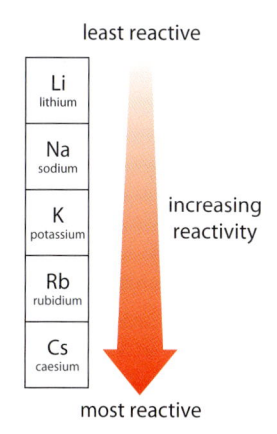

▲ Figure 6.7
Group 1 elements become more reactive as you go further down the group.

The reactions of alkali metals are shown here.

	Reaction and observations	Explanation
	A small piece of an alkali metal is put in some water in a beaker. The metal melts into a ball, skids around on the water surface and sometimes a flame is seen. The ball gets smaller and eventually is used up. The water becomes alkaline.	The metal reacts with water to form the metal hydroxide and hydrogen gas. lithium + water → lithium hydroxide + hydrogen $2Li(s) + 2H_2O(l) \rightarrow 2LiOH(aq) + H_2(g)$ The equations for using sodium or potassium are similar but with the different metal symbols, Na or K.
	If the alkali metal is made to sink by wrapping it in a piece of steel or copper gauze, bubbles of gas are produced and can be collected and tested.	The gas produced is hydrogen. You can see from the equation above that it is produced from the water, which is split up by the metal. How do you know that the gas is hydrogen? It can be tested. If it is mixed with air and ignited it explodes. This is described in Chapter 9.
	The metal is heated until it ignites. Then it burns strongly in air. Flame colour: lithium: red sodium: yellow potassium: lilac	The metal burns brightly in air. In pure oxygen it burns very brightly. A white solid is left behind. This is the oxide of the metal. sodium + oxygen → sodium oxide $4Na(s) + O_2(g) \rightarrow 2Na_2O(s)$ The equations for lithium and potassium are similar.

Activity 6.1
The properties of alkali metals

The reaction of an alkali metal like sodium with water is interesting. The metal floats because it has a density less than the density of water (1 g/cm³). When it reacts with the water, enough heat is produced to melt the metal. If the metal can be made to sink, the hydrogen gas produced by the reaction can easily be seen.

When the metal stays on the surface, the hydrogen gas is made where the metal touches the water underneath it. This causes the metal to move over the surface of the water floating on a cushion of gas – the hydrogen and the steam produced.

The metal hydroxide, that is formed by the reaction with water, is soluble.

It dissolves in the water making the water alkaline. When red litmus paper is dipped in the water it turns blue because the water is alkaline. You will read more about this in Chapter 9.

Group I compounds are all ionic. The ion formed by all the elements in the group has one positive charge and so the formulae of the compounds are all very similar. All Group I compounds are colourless crystalline solids which are soluble in water. The most common Group I compound is sodium chloride. This is well known as the salt we put on our food but it is also an important raw material for the 'alkali industry', the chemical industry that makes basic chemicals for common products such as soaps, detergents and glass.

> **Activity 6.2**
> Reaction of a Group I metal with water

▼ **Figure 6.8**
Walvis Bay in Namibia is a good place to produce salt from seawater. It is warm, sunny and it is on the coast of the Namib Desert where it never rains. This salt has been made by the evaporation of seawater by the sun. The salt is used in the southern African alkali industry.

Explaining the trend in reactivity in Group I

Why are the larger atoms in Group I more reactive than the smaller ones placed higher in the group? You can see from Figure 6.9 that the outer electron in potassium is further away from the nucleus than the outer electron in lithium. This means that the electrostatic force of attraction by the nucleus on the outer electron is less in potassium than it is in lithium. Because the outer electron in potassium is more easily removed, potassium is more reactive than lithium.

DID YOU KNOW?

If you add a lump of caesium to water in a glass trough, the reaction is so vigorous that the trough will shatter into small pieces.

▶ **Figure 6.9**
Electronic structure of lithium and potassium atoms.

The outer electron is lost during a reaction.

This outer electron is further away from the nucleus and is easier to lose during a reaction.

lithium
2, 1

potassium
2, 8, 8, 1

6.3 Group VII: the halogens

The **halogens** are the elements in Group VII. They are called halogens because 'halo' comes from the Greek word meaning 'salt' and '-gen' means 'forming'. So the word means 'salt forming'. They are all non-metals and they react with metals to form compounds called **salts**. In chemistry the word 'salt' describes many similar compounds, not just the one we know well and use in cooking and which this book will call 'table salt'.

Table 6.2 shows some of the physical properties of the common halogens. Fluorine and chlorine are gases, bromine is a liquid and iodine is a solid. They are all coloured and the colour becomes deeper down the group.

Activity 6.3
Preparation and reactions of chlorine

▶ **Table 6.2**
Trends in some physical properties of the halogens.

Proton number	Element	Melting point (°C)	Boiling point (°C)	State at room temperature	Colour
9	Fluorine	−220	−188	Gas	Yellow
17	Chlorine	−101	−35	Gas	Green
35	Bromine	−7	59	Liquid	Deep red
53	iodine	114	184	Solid	Purple/black

The elements are all poisonous but many of their compounds are essential to life. We all need table salt. This is why athletes that sweat a lot have to take table salt tablets; without these they could get severe muscle cramps.

The halogens are poisonous to us if we take in too much of them. Chlorine has been used in warfare to poison soldiers. It is a very unpleasant way of dying and the use of chlorine in warfare has been forbidden by international law. But we make use of chlorine to poison bacteria that may be harmful to us. We dissolve chlorine in drinking water and in swimming pools to kill bacteria but we do not use enough to damage us. We use iodine (dissolved in alcohol) to kill bacteria in cuts and wounds but it is not enough to harm us.

DID YOU KNOW?

In some parts of the world the water supply contains small amounts of fluorine compounds. It was found that in these areas people did not suffer much from tooth decay. This is because compounds of fluorine protect teeth from decay. This is why many types of toothpaste contain fluorine compounds. It is also why, in some countries, a small amount of a fluorine compound – such as sodium fluoride – is added to drinking water.

Some reactions between halogens and metals are shown here

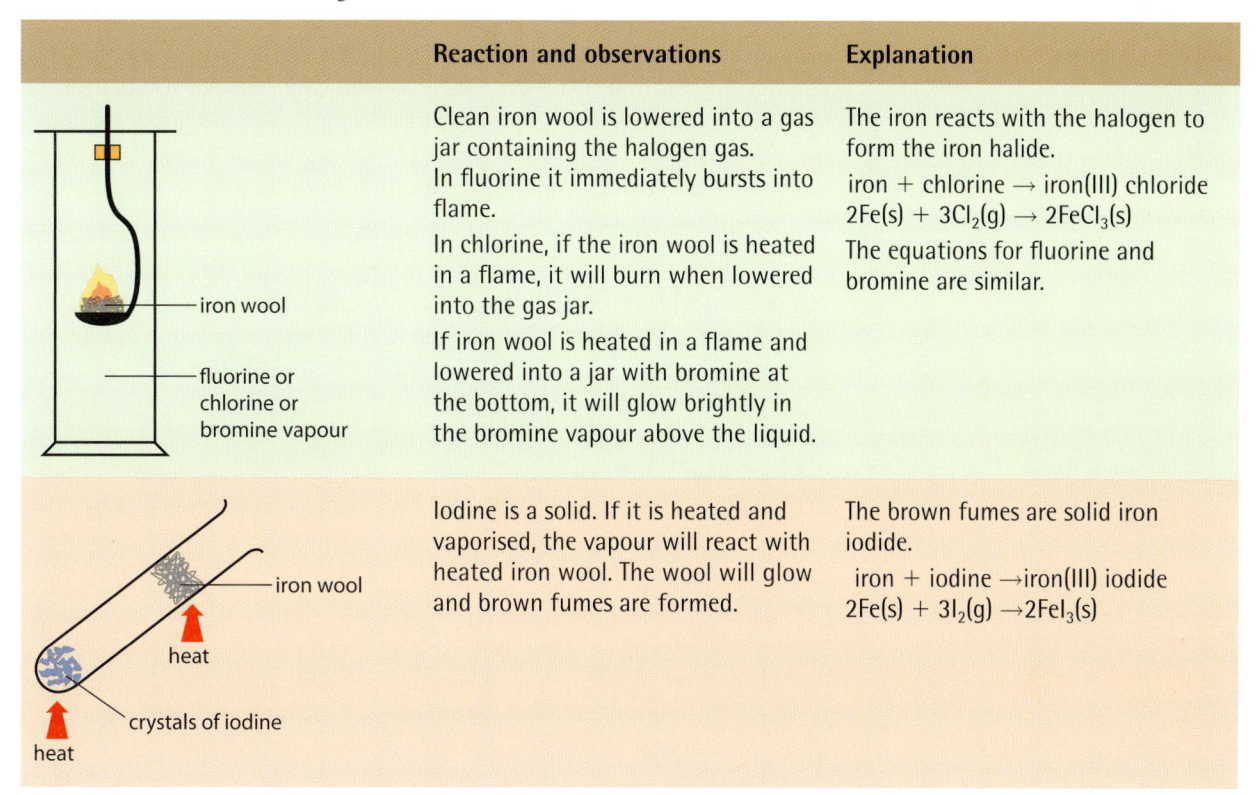

	Reaction and observations	Explanation
(diagram: iron wool lowered into gas jar with fluorine or chlorine or bromine vapour)	Clean iron wool is lowered into a gas jar containing the halogen gas. In fluorine it immediately bursts into flame. In chlorine, if the iron wool is heated in a flame, it will burn when lowered into the gas jar. If iron wool is heated in a flame and lowered into a jar with bromine at the bottom, it will glow brightly in the bromine vapour above the liquid.	The iron reacts with the halogen to form the iron halide. iron + chlorine → iron(III) chloride $2Fe(s) + 3Cl_2(g) \rightarrow 2FeCl_3(s)$ The equations for fluorine and bromine are similar.
(diagram: test tube with crystals of iodine being heated, iron wool in tube)	Iodine is a solid. If it is heated and vaporised, the vapour will react with heated iron wool. The wool will glow and brown fumes are formed.	The brown fumes are solid iron iodide. iron + iodine → iron(III) iodide $2Fe(s) + 3I_2(g) \rightarrow 2FeI_3(s)$

These reactions show how the reactivity of the halogens changes down the group. Fluorine, at the top of the group, is the most reactive and reactivity decreases moving down the group.

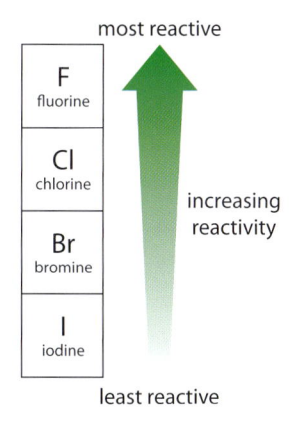

(Figure showing F, Cl, Br, I with arrow indicating increasing reactivity upward; most reactive at top, least reactive at bottom)

◀ Figure 6.10
The reactivity trend found in Group VII.

Activity 6.4
A reaction of iodine

Activity 6.5
Reactivity of halogens

Group VII compounds

As you learnt in Chapter 5, Group VII elements form:
- ionic compounds with metals
- covalent compounds with non-metals.

The ionic compounds with metals are hard crystalline substances. They contain the negative ions such as chloride (Cl^-) or iodide (I^-). A typical one is sodium chloride, table salt. We call the Group VII elements the halogens and we call their ions, the **halide ions**.

Most halides are soluble. This is why the main source of the halogens is seawater. Over millions of years the rain has washed the soluble halides out of rocks and into the seas (which is why seawater is salty). We obtain chlorine and bromine from deposits of salt left when ancient seas dry up. We often get iodine from seaweed. The seaweed takes in iodide compounds from the seawater and we can recover it by harvesting the seaweed, drying it, burning it and getting the iodide compounds from the ash.

Some halides are insoluble. These are the halides of some of the transition metals. These can be used as tests for the halide ions; a white precipitate of silver chloride is formed when silver ions are added to chloride ions; and yellow lead iodide is formed when iodide ions are added to a solution containing lead ions. These tests are summarised in Table 6.3.

▶ Table 6.3
Testing a solution for chloride and iodide ions.

Ion	Test	Test result
Chloride	Add some dilute nitric acid to the solution of chloride ions. Then add a few drops of silver nitrate solution.	If the chloride ion is present a white precipitate of insoluble silver chloride will form.
Iodide	Add some dilute nitric acid to the solution of iodide ions. Then add a few drops of lead nitrate solution.	If the iodide ion is present a yellow precipitate of insoluble lead iodide will form.

The compounds between halogens and hydrogen

The halogens form covalent compounds with hydrogen. These are all gases with a very unpleasant choking smell. They have a very important property; they are very soluble in water and the product is an acid. **Hydrogen chloride**, for example, is a gas that is very soluble in water to give **hydrochloric acid.** These hydrogen halides are all covalent gases but when they mix with water, halide ions are formed in the water. This is summarised in Table 6.4. You will learn more of the properties of these very useful acids in the next chapter.

▶ Table 6.4
The hydrogen halides.

Covalent gases		Product when the gas reacts with water	
Hydrogen chloride	HCl	Hydrochloric acid	$H^+ Cl^-$ (aq)
Hydrogen bromide	HBr	Hydrobromic acid	$H^+ Br^-$ (aq)
Hydrogen iodide	HI	Hydroiodic acid	$H^+ I^-$ (aq)

The trend in the reactivity of the halogens

Chlorine is more reactive than bromine or iodine. What do you think might happen if you add some chlorine to a solution of sodium bromide (which contains bromide ions) or sodium iodide (which contains iodide ions)?

The Periodic Table

	Reaction and observations	Explanation
chlorine water / sodium bromide solution	Chlorine gas is slightly soluble in water to form 'chlorine water'. A dilute solution of household bleach is mainly chlorine water. A drop of this can be added to solutions of sodium bromide and sodium iodide as shown. The bromide solution turns brown. If a drop of starch solution is added, no change is seen. The iodide solution turns a darker brown and turns black if a drop of starch solution is added.	If chlorine is added to a solution containing bromide ions, the chlorine atoms change into ions and the bromide ions change into bromine atoms. The same thing happens if chlorine solution is added to iodide ions. The starch tells us when iodine is present. Iodine turns starch black or purple (this is the well-known food test for starch).
	Bromine solution (bromine water) can be made by shaking up a tiny drop of bromine in water. A drop of bromine water can be added to solutions of sodium chloride or sodium iodide using the same apparatus as above. The sodium chloride solution is stained brown by the bromine. The sodium iodide solution turns a darker brown and turns black when a drop of starch is added.	There is no reaction between the bromine and the chloride ion. We can see that the brown bromine is not changed. If bromine solution is added to iodide ions, iodine is formed. The starch tells us when iodine is present. Iodine turns starch black or purple (this is the well-known food test for starch).

We can write equations for these reactions.

  chlorine + sodium chloride → no reaction
  chlorine + sodium bromide → sodium chloride + bromine
  chlorine + sodium iodide → sodium chloride + iodine
  bromine + sodium chloride → no reaction
  bromine + sodium bromide → no reaction
  bromine + sodium iodide → sodium bromide + iodine

The results of the reaction between halogens and other halide ions can be summarised in this table.

Halogen \ Halide	Chloride	Bromide	Iodide
Chlorine		✓	✓
Bromine	✗		✓
Iodine	✗	✗	

✓ = Reaction   ✗ = No reaction

The results table and the equations show us that there is a reaction only if the halogen used is higher in the group than the halide ion. This is because the halogens higher in the group are more reactive than the halogens lower in the group.

We call this kind of reaction a **displacement reaction**. We say that a more reactive halogen can **displace** a less reactive one from its salt. In the second equation above, chlorine is displacing bromine from sodium bromide solution.

Explaining the trend in reactivity in Group VII

Why are the larger atoms in Group VII less reactive than the smaller ones found higher in the group? You can see from Figure 6.11 that the outer electrons in bromine are further away from the nucleus than the outer electrons in fluorine. This means that the electrostatic force of attraction by the nucleus on the additional electron needed to make a full shell is greater in fluorine than it is in bromine. Because this attraction is stronger, fluorine forms a fluoride ion more readily than bromine forms a bromide ion.

▶ Figure 6.11
Models of fluorine and bromine atoms.

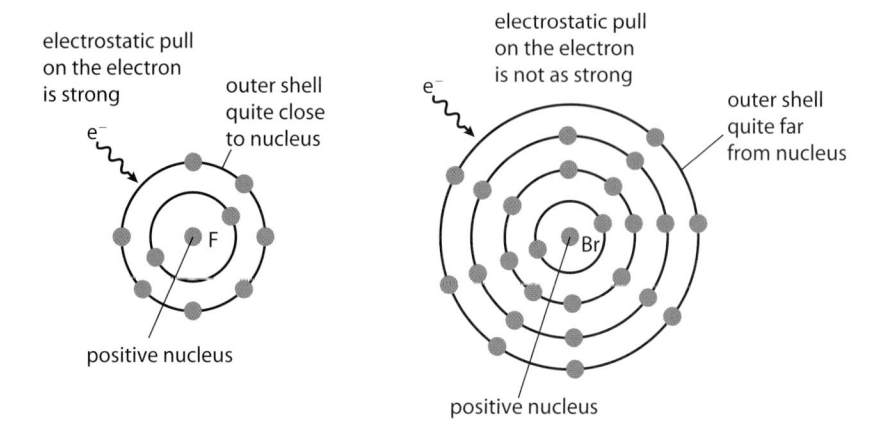

6.4 Group VIII: the inert gases

The most interesting thing about the **inert** gases is that they are chemically not very interesting. The do not react with anything. We say they are inert.

They are sometimes called the 'noble gases'. They are called this because the metals that do not tarnish – like gold and silver – were called the *noble metals*. The ones that easily rust or corrode were called *base metals*. 'Noble' and 'base' mean the opposite of each other and the words were once applied to people as well as metals!

You saw in Chapter 4 that the reason for the unreactivity of the inert gases is that they have a full outer shell of electrons and therefore do not need to combine with other elements in order to achieve this.

Table 6.5 shows the trends in some physical properties of these gases. You can see from the table that the melting and boiling points and the density increase down the group. As you go down the group, the atoms get bigger and so it is not surprising that the density increases. As the atoms get bigger, they will require more energy to make them move and so you would expect an increase in melting and boiling points.

The Periodic Table

Proton number	Element	Melting point (°C)	Boiling point (°C)	Density (g/dm³)
2	Helium	−270	−209	0.17
10	Neon	−249	−246	0.84
18	Argon	−189	−186	1.66
36	Krypton	−157	−152	3.46
54	Xenon	−112	−108	5.5

▲ Table 6.5
Trends in some physical properties of the inert gases.

Uses of the inert gases

Because they are unreactive, many of the inert gases are very useful. Table 6.6 shows some of their uses and the reasons for them.

DID YOU KNOW?

Liquid helium has some properties that are very strange indeed. It is a superfluid. This means that a beaker of it will empty itself onto the desk because the liquid will flow up the inside and down the outside of the beaker in a layer one atom thick. It also has infinite thermal conductivity. This means that if one side is heated up all the liquid is immediately heated also. These strange properties can only be explained well by a very modern theory called gauge theory.

Gas	Uses	Reason
Helium	Filling airships and balloons	Very low density, not flammable.
Helium	Mixing with oxygen to form a gas for divers to breathe	If a diver breathes normal air, nitrogen dissolves in the blood and can cause a dangerous problem called 'nitrogen narcosis' in which the diver has symptoms similar to drunkenness.
Neon	Fluorescent lights	When an electric current is passed through neon, it gives off of a bright light. The advertising signs in our towns are filled with neon.
Argon	Filling light bulbs	It is unreactive and so the filament does not burn away.
Xenon	Fluorescent lights	This works like neon but the light is very bright and much like daylight. Xenon lights are used in car headlights, but only in more expensive cars because xenon is expensive. Xenon strobe lights are used in discos.

◀ Table 6.6
Some uses for inert gases.

DID YOU KNOW?

Radon is an inert gas that is radioactive. It is slowly given off by certain rocks such as granite. Houses built on granite can build up dangerous levels of radon in the rooms if they are not well ventilated. If too much radon is breathed in, it can cause lung cancer.

6.5 The transition metals

The transition metals are found in the centre block of the Periodic Table. Although they are not all in the same group like the halogens or the alkali metals, they all have similar properties and so it is useful to study them together.

Table 6.7 shows trends in some of the physical properties of the first row of transition elements. The trends here are not as clear as those down Groups I and VII but some can still be seen. Perhaps the most important one is that, except for zinc, these metals are all very similar.

Proton number	Element	Melting point (°C)	Boiling point (°C)	Density (g/cm^3)
21	Scandium	1540	2730	3.0
22	Titanium	1674	3260	4.5
23	Vanadium	1900	3000	6.0
24	Chromium	1890	2482	7.2
25	Manganese	1240	2100	7.2
26	Iron	1535	3000	7.9
27	Cobalt	1492	2900	8.9
28	Nickel	1453	2730	8.9
29	Copper	1083	2595	8.9
30	Zinc	420	907	7.1

▲ Table 6.7
Trends in properties of the first row of transition metals.

These metals are much denser than other elements you have studied. The graph below (Figure 6.12) shows this clearly. It also shows how density is a **periodic property** of elements. What this means is that there is a pattern of densities increasing and then decreasing across each period. This pattern is then repeated across the next period.

▶ Figure 6.12
Graph of density against proton number.

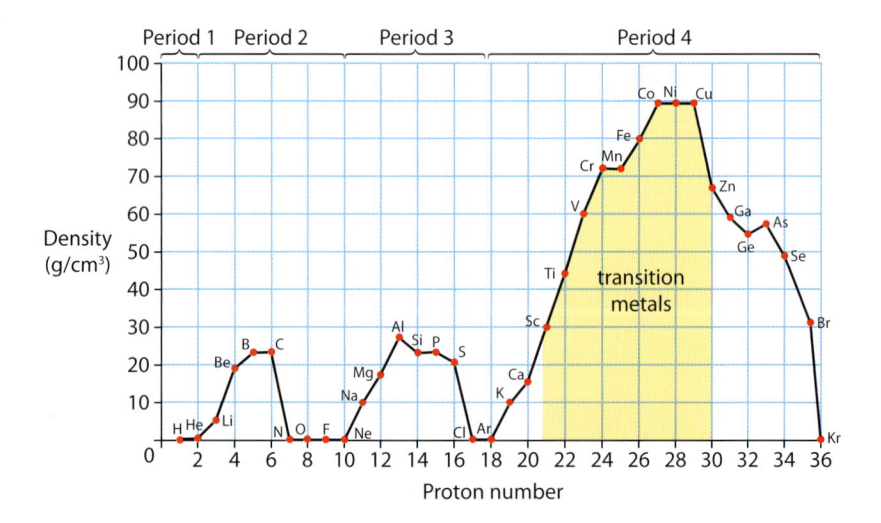

68

Other physical properties such as melting and boiling points show a similar periodic change. Try plotting similar graphs for these using the data in Table 3.2.

Transition metals form coloured compounds. The list in Table 6.8 shows a number of well-known compounds together with the transition metal present in them and also their colour.

Name	Formula	Colour
Potassium chromate(VI)	$K_2Cr_2O_4$	Yellow
Potassium manganate(VII)	$KMnO_4$	Purple
Iron(II) chloride	$FeCl_2$	Green
Iron(III) chloride	$FeCl_3$	Orange/brown
Rust (iron)	Fe_2O_3	Brown
Copper(II) sulfate	$CuSO_4$	Blue
Khaki dye (iron)	–	Brown
Haemoglobin in blood (iron)	–	Red

◀ Table 6.8
Some coloured transition metal ions.

DID YOU KNOW?

The colour of hair is caused by the presence of transition metal compounds in the hair. Brown hair contains iron or copper compounds, blonde hair contains compounds of titanium and if you are a redhead, it is because of the presence of molybdenum compounds.

The presence of transition metal compounds in some natural crystals cause them to have attractive colours, which makes them valuable as gemstones. The colours in jewels such as sapphire, emerald and amethysts are all caused by transition metals.

Two properties of transition metals make them very useful. They are usually hard and strong and they are not easily corroded. For this reason they are very widely used and you will learn more about this in the next chapter.

One important use of many transition elements is as catalysts in industrial processes. A catalyst is a substance that speeds up a chemical reaction but is not used up itself. Most industrial processes use catalysts. Many of the catalysts are kept secret by the companies that invented them but Table 6.9 lists some industrial compounds and the catalysts that are used to make them.

DID YOU KNOW?

Vehicles contain catalysts in catalytic converters. They are placed in a section of the exhaust pipe system. They break down oxides of nitrogen and also help any unburned hydrocarbons to change into carbon dioxide and water. This makes the exhaust less poisonous. Platinum is the catalyst that is mainly used. Platinum costs twice as much as gold!

Compound	Transition metal used in the catalyst
Ammonia (for fertilisers)	Iron
Sulfuric acid	Vanadium
Nitric acid	Platinum
Margarine	Nickel
Polythene	Titanium

◀ Table 6.9
Transition metals used as industrial catalysts.

DID YOU KNOW?

Do you know what the 'rare earth' elements are and what we use them for? They are the elements cerium to lutetiun at the bottom of the periodic table (page 36). They are all metals and they are similar. They are not very rare, but they are difficult to extract, so they are expensive. They are used in many electronic devices, like mobile phones and in magnets for electric cars. If you have a self-cleaning oven, then you probably have some of the rare earth metal cerium in your home.

▶ Table 6.10
Properties of oxides across Period 3.

6.6 Trends across the periods

You can see trends across the periods of the Periodic Table as well as down the groups. Look at the graph of densities (Figure 6.12). You can see that there is a trend in densities across every period. The densities of elements at the beginning of the periods are quite low. They get bigger towards the middle of the period and then fall again towards the end.

You can see that across any period, the elements on the left are metals and the elements on the right are non-metals. Elements in the middle are sometimes called 'metalloid'. This means that they have some properties of metals and some of non-metals. Silicon (Group IV) is a good example of a metalloid.

You can also see trends in the chemical properties of the elements across the periods. Table 6.10 shows the formulae and properties of the oxides of the elements for the first period, sodium to argon. The oxides of the metals, left of the period, are solids which dissolve in water to give alkaline solutions. The oxides of the elements in the middle of the period are insoluble. The oxides of the non-metals on the right of the period dissolve in water to give acid solutions. This will be discussed further in the next chapter.

Element	Group	Formula of oxide	Properties of oxide
Sodium	I	Na_2O	White crystalline solid, soluble in water to give an alkaline solution.
Magnesium	II	MgO	White crystalline solid, slightly soluble in water to give an alkaline solution.
Aluminium	III	Al_2O_3	White crystalline solid, insoluble in water.
Silicon	IV	SiO_2	White solid with giant covalent structure, insoluble in water.
Phosphorus	V	P_2O_5	White solid with covalent structure, which reacts with water to give an acid solution.
Sulfur	VI	SO_2	Gas, soluble in water to give an acid solution.
Chlorine	VII	Cl_2O	Unstable gas that reacts with water to give an acid solution.
Argon	VIII	–	Does not form an oxide.

You can use knowledge of trends in the Periodic Table to predict the properties of elements, and their compounds, that you have not met.

QUESTIONS

6.1 Chlorine is a non-metal. It is a gas like oxygen but it has a slight green colour. It is more reactive than oxygen. Predict what will happen if you lower some burning sodium into a gas jar of chlorine. Will there be a reaction? What product will be formed?

6.2 Rubidium is below potassium in Group I. Predict what might happen if you left a small piece of rubidium in the air for a few minutes. Will there be a reaction? How vigorous will it be? What product will be formed?

6.3 Using Table 6.10, predict some of the properties of the Group II oxide, calcium oxide, and the oxide of the Group VII element selenium.

6.4 Predict some of the properties of the halogen, astatine, which is below iodine in Group VII. You might need to look back at some of the properties of halogens. Predict the following properties.
- Is it a metal or a non-metal?
- Is it a solid, liquid or gas?
- What colour is it?
- How will it react with sodium? Describe the product.
- How will it react with hydrogen? Describe the product.
- How will it react with iron? Describe the product.
- How does its reactivity compare with other Group VII elements?

6.5 Strontium is in period 4 of Group II, the same group as magnesium and in the same block of the Periodic Table as the alkali metals.
- Predict what would happen if you heated some strontium in a flame.
- Predict what would happen if you put a piece of strontium in water.
- Strontium reacts readily with chlorine. Predict the formula and colour of strontium chloride. Predict whether you would expect it to be soluble in water and give reasons for your prediction.

6.6 Using Table 6.1, plot a graph showing how the boiling and melting points of the elements of Group I vary with proton number (x-axis). Use the graph to predict the melting and boiling points of the element francium (proton number 87).

6.7 Rubidium is the fourth element in Group I. Predict the following properties of rubidium and its compounds.
- its appearance
- its hardness
- how it will react with water
- the appearance and solubility of rubidium chloride
- its electrical conductivity

6.8 Sodium is a very good conductor of electricity; scientists are working on ways of using it to make electrical wires. What are the main problems the scientists must try to solve before sodium can be used in this way?

6.9 From the information in Table 6.2 plot a graph showing how the melting point of the halogens changes with proton number (*x*-axis). Use the graph to predict the melting point of the halogen, astatine (proton number 85).

6.10 What, if anything, would you expect to see in the following reactions?
- bromine water is added to a solution of sodium fluoride
- iodine solution is added to a solution of sodium chloride
- fluorine is bubbled through a solution of sodium bromide

Explain your answers.

6.11 Hydrogen combines explosively with fluorine. Give the formula of the product. State whether the product is a solid, liquid or gas. Explain what would be produced if the product were bubbled through water.

6.12 If you were to gently warm a drop of bromine in a test tube which also contained some aluminium foil, describe what would you expect to happen, if anything.

6.13 Explain why the inert gases do not react with other elements.

6.14 Use Table 6.5 to plot a graph showing how the boiling points of the inert gases change as the proton number increases. Explain the general shape of the curve. Use the curve to predict the boiling point of the inert gas radon (proton number 86).

6.15 What is meant by the term 'transition metals'? List their characteristic properties.

6.16 Describe how the reactivity of the transition metals changes (a) across periods and (b) down groups.

6.17 The table below shows some properties of six elements.

Element	Properties	Element	Properties
A	A soft silvery metal which reacts violently with water.	D	A reactive liquid at room temperature.
B	A gas that reacts violently with other elements without heating.	E	A hard solid that conducts electricity, forms coloured compounds and corrodes in moist air.
C	A gas that does not react with anything else and that is heavier than air.	F	A hard solid that conducts electricity and does not corrode easily.

- List the elements that are metals.
- List elements that are probably transition elements.
- State which element is an inert gas and explain where in Group VIII it is likely to be found.
- Describe the product of the reaction between element A and element D.
- Describe the product of the reaction between B and E.
- Name two elements that belong to the same group, state the group and explain your answer.
- When element B reacts, explain what happens to the electrons in its outer shell.

Summary

Now that you have completed this chapter, you should be able to:

- describe the typical properties of Groups I and II elements in the Periodic Table and why their reactivity increases down the groups

- describe the typical properties of transition metals; know that they often form coloured compounds and explain why reactivity decreases across the periods and also decreases down the transition metal groups

- describe the typical properties of the non-metals on the right of the Periodic Table

- describe the typical properties of Group VII elements, the halogens; explain how and why reactivity changes down the group.

- describe and explain the typical properties of Group VIII elements, the inert gases

- describe and explain trends in physical properties such as melting points and density across periods

- describe and explain trends from metallic to non-metallic character across periods

- describe and explain trends in the chemical properties of oxides across periods.

Chapter 7

Acids and alkalis

An early neutralisation reaction

Around 40 BCE, so legend has it, Cleopatra, the Queen of Egypt, won a wager with the Roman general Mark Anthony, who she seemed to spend quite a lot of time with. They had just enjoyed a good dinner together and her wager was that she could provide a feast for them that would cost a fortune. To prove it she dissolved a priceless pearl in vinegar and then drank the resulting solution.

We do not know of Mark Anthony's response. Nor do we know how much wine she had consumed at the meal before she began dissolving her best jewellery and we can only guess what she felt like after drinking calcium ethanoate solution! This is an early example of a reaction of an acid.

The word 'acid' originally meant a sour taste. Foods like vinegar, lemon juice and sour milk have an 'acid taste'. These days the word means the class of substances that cause such a sour taste. There are very many compounds that cause this, but some of them would be very unpleasant indeed to taste! This chapter looks at the class of compounds we call acids and at their reactions.

▲ Figure 7.1
Queen Cleopatra

▶ Figure 7.2
Alkalis were also used in ancient times. The mortar used between the stones of the pyramids contained lime, an alkali made from limestone.

7.1 What are acids and what do they do?

The easiest way to recognise an acid is to use an **indicator**. An indicator is a substance that changes colour when an acid is added to it. **Litmus** is a chemical that is extracted from lichen. It is a purple dye and it is an indicator that has been known for over 400 years. In acid solutions it turns red. Many coloured extracts from plants will change colour when an acid is added to them; the red colour from red cabbage is a particularly good one.

Acids all have a sharp taste. Vinegar and lemon juice are both acids. Many things that we eat that have a sharp taste contain acids. Of course, some acids are poisonous so it is not a good idea to taste acids.

Acids react in other ways also; here are two reactions of acids:

> **Activity 7.1**
> Some reactions of acids

> **Activity 7.2**
> Measuring the pH of some common solutions

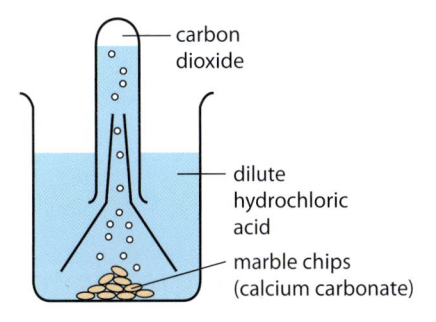

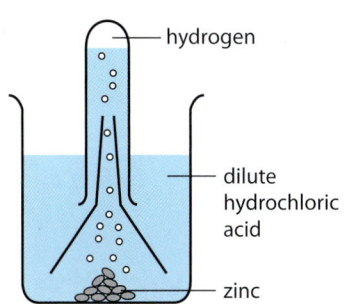

◀ **Figure 7.3**
Reactions of acids to form carbon dioxide and hydrogen.

Some chips of marble are placed in the acid. Carbon dioxide gas is produced. (Marble is a form of calcium carbonate.) The gas can be tested with limewater. The limewater will turn milky.

Some pieces of zinc are placed in the acid. Hydrogen is produced. The hydrogen can be tested by lighting it.

Test for carbon dioxide

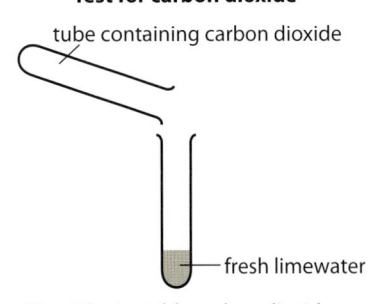

'Pour' the invisible carbon dioxide on to the fresh limewater. Shake the limewater. It will turn milky.

Test for hydrogen

Turn the tube upwards to allow the hydrogen to come out (it is lighter than air) near a flame. An explosion will be heard.

Acids react with carbonates to produce carbon dioxide

The reaction of acid with carbonate is this:

hydrochloric acid + calcium carbonate → calcium chloride + carbon dioxide + water

$2HCl\ (aq) + CaCO_3(s) \rightarrow CaCl_2(aq) + CO_2(g) + H_2O(l)$

Any carbonate will react in this way with any acid. Cleopatra's pearl was made of calcium carbonate, vinegar is an acid (ethanoic acid) and so it would have reacted, giving off carbon dioxide. Instead of forming calcium chloride, it would have formed calcium ethanoate.

There is one interesting exception to this rule, however. If you add marble chips (calcium carbonate) to dilute sulfuric acid, you will see the reaction start but then it will quickly stop again. This is because the product of the reaction, calcium sulfate, is insoluble and coats the marble chips, preventing further reaction with the sulfuric acid.

The test for carbon dioxide

Fresh limewater reacts with carbon dioxide turning milky. Bubble a sample of the gas through limewater (or pour it as shown in the picture above). If the limewater turns milky, the gas is carbon dioxide.

Limewater is a solution of a substance called calcium hydroxide and this reacts with carbon dioxide to form calcium carbonate, which is insoluble and causes the white milky colour.

calcium hydroxide + carbon dioxide → calcium carbonate + water
$Ca(OH)_2 (aq) + CO_2 (g) \rightarrow CaCO_3 (s) + H_2O (l)$

Acids react with the more reactive metals to give hydrogen

A typical reaction is this:

zinc + hydrochloric acid → zinc chloride + hydrogen
$Zn(s) + 2HCl(aq) \rightarrow ZnCl_2(aq) + H_2(g)$

The hydrogen comes from the acid. The metal replaces the hydrogen in the acid. Only those metals that are quite reactive (Chapter 8) will react in this way. Copper, for example, will not react with dilute acids like this.

The zinc chloride that is left in the solution is a substance that is called a salt. If sulfuric acid had been used instead, the salt produced would have been zinc sulfate. Salts are also left behind when acids react with carbonates. The substance in Queen Cleopatra's solution, calcium ethanoate, is another example of a salt.

The test for hydrogen

Hydrogen explodes if it is mixed with a little oxygen (air) and ignited, as shown in Figure 7.3. It is lighter than air and so it can be carried around in an open test tube as long as you keep the test tube upside down. Bring the test tube round so the hydrogen escapes towards a flame and it will 'pop'. You may also see a little water condensation on the glass. The reaction is:

hydrogen + oxygen → water
$2H_2(g) + O_2(g) \rightarrow 2H_2O(l)$

Acids react with metal oxides and hydroxides

We call these metal oxides and hydroxides **bases.** If they are soluble we call them **alkalis.** Acids will react with bases and alkalis. Here are two typical **neutralisation** reactions:

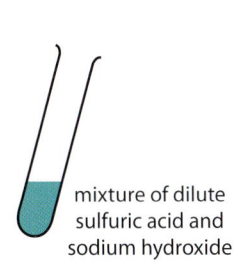

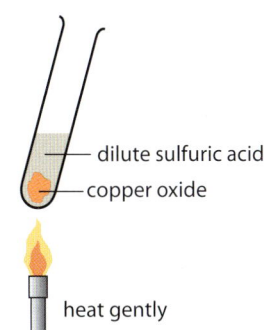

◀ **Figure 7.4**
Reactions of acids with metal oxides and hydroxides.

Mix some dilute sulfuric acid and some sodium hydroxide solution in a test tube. Feel the tube. It will get warm.

The heat produced tells us that a reaction is taking place.

Warm some black copper oxide powder in dilute sulfuric acid. The liquid turns blue and the black powder gradually disappears.

The blue colour is caused by the blue copper sulfate produced. Copper sulfate is soluble. The black oxide gradually disappears as it reacts.

sulfuric acid + copper oxide → copper sulfate + water
$H_2SO_4(aq)$ + $CuO(s)$ → $CuSO_4(aq)$ + $H_2O(l)$

sulfuric acid + sodium hydroxide → sodium sulfate + water
$H_2SO_4(aq)$ + $2NaOH(aq)$ → $Na_2SO_4(aq)$ + $2H_2O(l)$

This reaction is called **neutralisation**. Note that one product of neutralisation is water. The second product is a salt. We can now define what a salt is. A salt is the product of the neutralisation of an acid by a base or alkali.

The neutralisation reaction can be summarised as:
acid + base → salt + water

7.2 A pattern in acids and alkalis – pH

When any substance dissolves in water it forms an **aqueous solution**. Aqueous solutions can be acidic, neutral or alkaline. We can use the indicator, litmus, to find out whether a solution is acidic, neutral or alkaline.

◀ **Figure 7.5**
The three colours of litmus. On the left, acid; on the right, alkaline; in the middle, neutral.

Universal indicator can tell us more about aqueous solutions. Some acidic or alkaline solutions are stronger than others. Universal indicators contain a mixture of dyes and they change to different colours that tell us how strong an acid or an alkali is.

There is a fourteen-point scale which is used to measure the acidity or alkalinity of a solution. It is called the **pH scale**. Strong acids have a low number on the pH scale and strong alkalis a high number (Figure 7.6). A solution that is exactly neutral, that is, it is neither acidic nor alkaline, has a pH of 7. Pure water has a pH of 7.

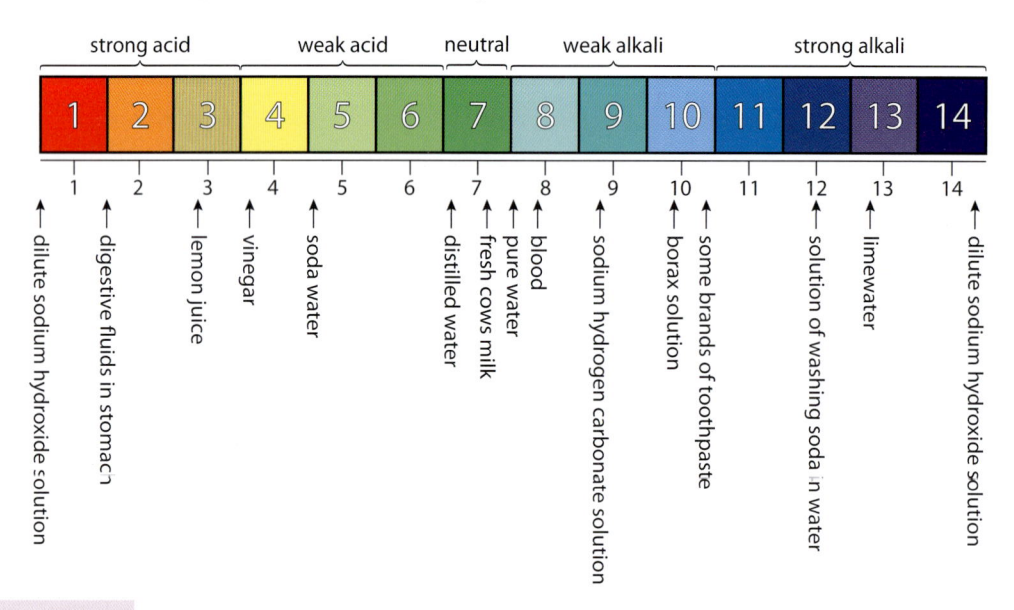

pH	Category	Example
1	strong acid	dilute sodium hydroxide solution
2	strong acid	digestive fluids in stomach
3	strong acid	lemon juice
4	weak acid	vinegar
5	weak acid	soda water
6	weak acid	—
7	neutral	distilled water
8	weak alkali	blood / fresh cows milk / pure water
9	weak alkali	sodium hydrogen carbonate solution
10	weak alkali	borax solution
11	strong alkali	some brands of toothpaste
12	strong alkali	solution of washing soda in water
13	strong alkali	limewater
14	strong alkali	dilute sodium hydroxide solution

▲ **Figure 7.6**
The pH scale showing the different colours of a commonly used universal indicator.

▼ **Figure 7.7**
pH can be measured by a pH meter and by universal indicator paper.

We can measure the pH of any aqueous solution using universal indicator and also measure pH with a pH meter. This is an electronic device with a special electrode that is placed in the liquid. This gives a voltage that depends on the pH of the liquid.

The pH scale classifies acids as strong and weak. Strong acids have a low pH and weak acids have a pH nearer neutral. Similarly there are strong and weak alkaline solutions, the strongest are near pH14 and the weakest just above pH7.

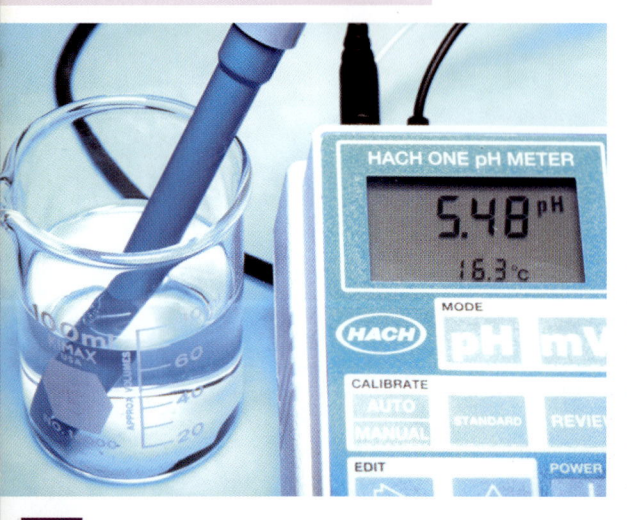

Strong acids

On the pH scale, the acids found at the bottom, with a low pH (less than about 3) are called strong acids and those found nearer 7 are called weak acids. Examples of strong acids are the common ones found in a laboratory such as hydrochloric acid (HCl), sulfuric acid (H_2SO_4) and nitric acid (HNO_3). These kinds of acids are called 'mineral acids' because they are made mainly from minerals that we dig out of the ground.

Weak acids

Weak acids have a pH between about 3 and 6. Examples are the acids we often eat, such as vinegar (ethanoic acid), citric acid (lemon and orange juice) and tartaric acid. These are called 'organic acids' because they are found in living things or they are made from substances that we obtain from living things.

One example of a weak acid is rainwater. Rainwater is acidic because, as it falls, it dissolves some of the gases found in the air, such as carbon dioxide, which make it slightly acidic. Carbon dioxide is slightly soluble and it dissolves to form carbonic acid, which has a pH of about 6. In Chapter 12 you will learn that some gases that are put into the air, mainly by human activities, can cause rainwater to be much more acidic than this and to be harmful to buildings and plants.

The difference between a *strong* acid and a *concentrated* acid.

Acid **concentration** refers to the amount of water present in the acid. A concentrated acid has very little water in it. In a dilute acid, the acid is mixed with a lot of water.

Acid **strength** is a measure of the pH of the acid. This is caused mainly by the structure of the acid molecules, although mixing any acid with a lot of water will raise its pH. So we can have concentrated ethanoic acid which is a weak acid (pH 3) but dilute hydrochloric acid which is a strong acid (pH 1).

Weak alkalis

Weak alkalis have a pH between about 8 and 11. Examples are alkalis we often use in cooking, like baking soda (pH9). Other examples are soap and toothpaste.

Strong alkalis

Strong alkalis have a pH of 12 and above. They must be treated with care, as they are corrosive. They attack substances like wood and skin that are either living or once lived (**organic** substances). Substances that do this we call **caustic**. A good example is sodium hydroxide, often called caustic soda. Caustic soda is often used to clean blocked drains because it reacts easily with the kind of organic household waste that causes blockages.

> **DID YOU KNOW?**
>
> When you run up a lot of stairs quickly you often feel a slight pain in your knees. This is due to the weak acid, lactic acid (this is the acid that makes milk acidic). The lactic acid is produced when the glucose in your muscles reacts to give you energy but cannot get enough oxygen to be converted completely into the usual products, carbon dioxide and water. Instead it is turned into lactic acid. When you stop and rest, the lactic acid is turned back into glucose and the pain goes away.

> **DID YOU KNOW?**
>
> The pH scale is not just a simple scale from 0 to 14 that some chemists have thought up. The pH is actually the negative logarithm of the hydrogen ion concentration in the acid! Don't worry about this; you don't need to know this fact for your exam.

7.3 How we use acids and alkalis

We make use of acids and alkalis almost every day of our lives. We use them in our homes and at work. They are used in agriculture, in building and in almost all industries. The acid, sulfuric acid, and the base, calcium hydroxide (lime), are two of the main substances on which our chemical industry is based

Acids and alkalis in the home

▶ Table 7.1 Acids in the home.

Name	Use
Citric acid	Fruit juice
Ethanoic acid	Vinegar
Lactic acid	Sour milk
Phosphoric acid	Rust remover
Phenolic acids	TCP, Dettol
Sulfuric acid	Car batteries
Carbonic acid	Soda water, fizzy drinks

Water is an extremely good solvent. Whenever something dissolves in water the pH is likely to change. Because of this, the pH of your tap water will probably not be pH 7 (the pH of pure water). If you live in an area where the rocks are made of limestone, your tap water may be slightly alkaline. In other areas, the water may be slightly acidic.

There is a lot of water in our bodies. The pH varies depending on where the water is in the body. Blood is mainly water but has many substances dissolved or suspended in it. It has a pH slightly above 7. The liquid in our stomach is quite strongly acidic, as this helps to break down the food.

Saliva contains an enzyme that helps to break down starch in food into the sugars that your body needs for energy. The enzyme only works well at a pH of about 8, so saliva should be slightly alkaline. The inside of your mouth is a nice warm, wet place for bacteria to live and they have plenty of food from the bits left between your teeth. These bacteria like to live in a slightly acid solution and they make acid as they feed. It is a good idea to clean your teeth regularly to remove the bacteria. Toothpaste is alkaline to help neutralise the acids produced by the bacteria.

Many of the foods we eat, particularly fruit juices, are acidic. Acids have a sharp taste which people like. Acids in food help the food break down during cooking. We also sometimes use alkalis in cooking; baking soda is alkaline. It is used in baking to give off carbon dioxide, which makes dough rise. Adding it to the water when we cook green vegetables helps the vegetables stay green and look good.

Acids are also used in cleaning liquids; toilet cleaners often contain sulfuric or phosphoric acids. Some cleaning liquids may be alkaline; ammonia is an alkaline substance used in many cleaning liquids because it kills germs.

Acids and alkalis in agriculture

Most plants grow best in a soil that is slightly alkaline. Soil is a mixture of minerals formed from the breaking down of rocks by rain and wind, and organic matter formed from the breaking down of plant and animal remains. Fertile soils contain a great variety of organisms. All these are dependent on each other. Many of these organisms only survive well in slightly alkaline conditions.

For the soil organisms to grow well the soil must be 'open' which means that air and water should be able to get into it easily. If the mineral particles in the soil are too small, as in clay, the soil easily becomes waterlogged and this prevents air getting into it.

In order to improve their soils, farmers often spread lime on them to help the soil stay alkaline. This is particularly important in areas where the soil is naturally acid because of the rock from which it is made. Lime is also important where the soil is a heavy clay that easily gets waterlogged. Adding lime also helps to break down heavy clay soils and makes them more open.

Figure 7.8
Lime being spread on the soil.

The 'lime' that is put on the soil can be either one of two chemicals. It is sometimes crushed limestone, calcium carbonate, and sometimes 'slaked lime', calcium hydroxide. The calcium hydroxide is made from limestone (see Chapter 16), which occurs naturally. The limestone acts slowly, being broken down in the soil to calcium hydroxide. The calcium hydroxide acts quickly; it is the hydroxide of the metal calcium and is therefore a base. It is slightly soluble giving an alkaline solution.

7.4 Oxides and pH

Look back at Chapter 6 where you studied trends across the periodic table. Table 7.1 below is taken from Chapter 6 and shows trends in the properties of oxides in Period 3 (sodium to argon).

Element	Group	Formula of oxide	Properties of oxide
Sodium	I	Na_2O	White crystalline solid, soluble in water to give an alkaline solution.
Magnesium	II	MgO	White crystalline solid, slightly soluble in water to give an alkaline solution.
Aluminium	III	Al_2O_3	White crystalline solid, insoluble in water.
Silicon	IV	SiO_2	White solid with giant covalent structure, insoluble in water.
Phosphorus	V	P_2O_5	White solid with covalent structure, which reacts with water to give an acid solution.
Sulfur	VI	SO_2	Gas, soluble in water to give an acid solution.
Chlorine	VII	Cl_2O	Unstable gas, which reacts with water to give an acid solution.
Argon	VIII	–	Does not form an oxide.

▲ Table 7.2
Properties of oxides across Period 3.

Can you see the pattern in Table 7.2? The oxides of the metals on the left of the periodic table dissolve in water to form alkaline solutions. The oxides of the non-metals on the right dissolve in water to form acidic solutions. Many oxides in the middle of the table are insoluble in water and so they do not affect the pH of water.

Acidic oxides and basic oxides

Activity 7.3
The pH of solutions of oxides

The oxides of metals are called **basic oxides**. They will react with acids to form salts. The reaction of copper oxide and sulfuric acid that you have already studied is a typical reaction of metal oxides.

sulfuric acid + copper oxide → copper sulfate + water
$H_2SO_4(aq)$ + $CuO(s)$ → $CuSO_4(aq)$ + $H_2O(l)$

The oxides of non-metals are called **acidic oxides.** They will react with bases and alkalis to form salts. You will learn more about salts and how they are formed in sections 7.5 and 7.6 below.

Neutral oxides

There are some oxides of elements that are neither acidic nor basic. If these oxides dissolve in water they do not affect the pH and they do not react with either acids or bases. These are called neutral oxides. The most common one is water itself. Others that are well-known are carbon monoxide (CO) and two oxides of nitrogen, nitrogen monoxide (NO) and dinitrogen monoxide (N_2O), which was used as one of the first anaesthetics, particularly by dentists.

DID YOU KNOW?

Dinitrogen monoxide is known as 'laughing gas' because sometimes dental patients that come round after being anaesthetised with it burst out in uncontrollable laughter (despite the toothache!).

Amphoteric oxides

Some oxides and hydroxides of elements near the centre of the periodic table are both acidic and basic at the same time. Aluminium hydroxide is one of these. The following flow diagram shows how aluminium hydroxide can be made and how it reacts with both acids and alkalis.

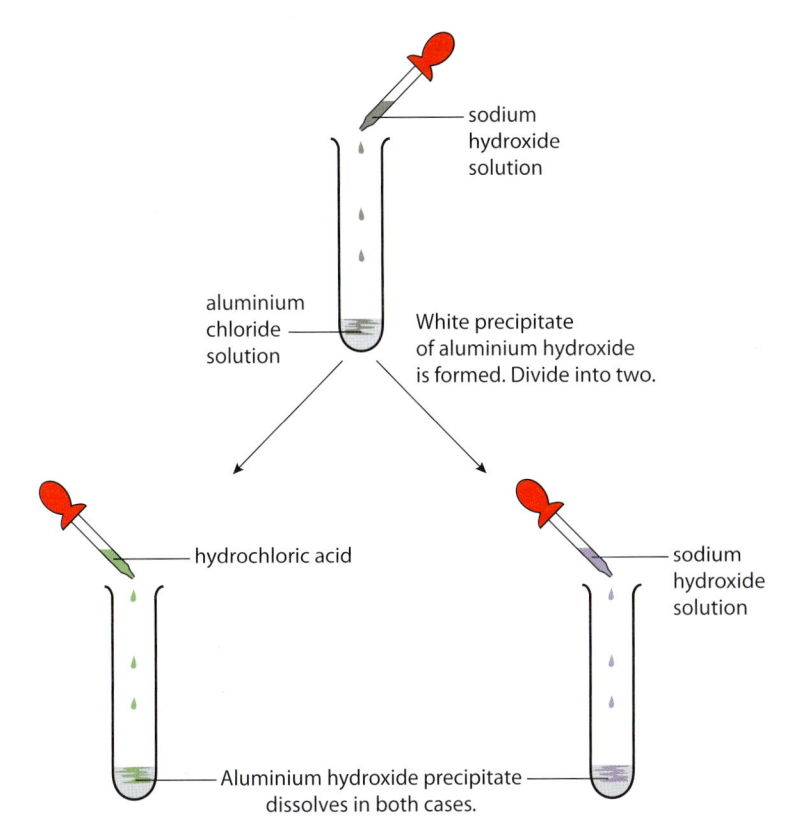

Acids and alkalis

▶ **Figure 7.9**
Flow diagram showing reactions of aluminium hydroxide.

When sodium hydroxide (or any solution containing hydroxide ions) is added to solutions containing the ions of aluminium, the hydroxide of the metal forms as a white precipitate because it is insoluble. This reaction is shown in the equation:

aluminium + sodium → aluminium + sodium
chloride   hydroxide   hydroxide   chloride
$AlCl_3(aq) + 3NaOH(aq) \rightarrow Al(OH)_3(s) + 3NaCl(aq)$

Adding acid to aluminium hydroxide

When acid is added to the precipitate of aluminium hydroxide, a neutralisation reaction occurs, and a salt and water are formed.

acid + alkali → salt + water
hydrochloric acid + aluminium hydroxide → aluminium chloride + water
$3HCl(aq) + Al(OH)_3(s) \rightarrow AlCl_3(aq) + 3H_2O(l)$

Adding alkali to aluminium hydroxide

When alkali is added to the precipitate of aluminium hydroxide, a different neutralisation occurs. This time the aluminium hydroxide is behaving as an acidic oxide.

acid + alkali → salt + water
aluminium hydroxide + sodium hydroxide → sodium aluminate + water
$Al(OH)_3(s) + NaOH(aq) \rightarrow NaAlO_2 + 2H_2O$

Aluminium hydroxide is behaving as both a basic oxide and an acidic oxide. We call oxides like these **amphoteric** oxides (another more recent name is **amphiprotic** oxides). The metals that form amphoteric oxides

Activity 7.4
What is an amphoteric oxide or hydroxide?

are those that are near to the border between metals and non-metals in the periodic table. Lead and zinc are other metals that form amphoteric oxides.

You can now see that the move from metal to non-metal as you go from left to right across the periodic table does not happen suddenly but is gradual. Metals such as aluminium, lead and zinc show some characteristics of non-metals by forming oxides that behave like acidic oxides, and some non-metals on the other side of the line show some metallic properties such as a shiny appearance.

7.5 What happens when acids and bases react together?

The reaction between an acid and a base is called **neutralisation**. The products are a salt and water.

acid + base → salt + water

A salt is an ionic crystalline substance made up of positive ions, which are metal ions that come originally from the base, and negative ions that come originally from the acid. This can be clearly seen in the following examples of neutralisation.

acid	+	base	→	salt	+	water
hydrochloric acid	+	sodium hydroxide	→	sodium chloride	+	water
$HCl(aq)$	+	$NaOH(aq)$	→	$NaCl(aq)$	+	$H_2O(l)$
sulfuric acid	+	copper oxide	→	copper sulfate	+	water
$H_2SO_4(aq)$	+	$CuO(s)$	→	$CuSO_4(aq)$	+	$H_2O(l)$
nitric acid	+	potassium hydroxide	→	potassium nitrate	+	water
$HNO_3(aq)$	+	$KOH(aq)$	→	$KNO_3(aq)$	+	$H_2O(l)$

Figure 7.10 shows two examples of salts. The regular shapes of the crystals can easily be seen.

▶ **Figure 7.10**
Cubic sodium chloride crystals (left) and diamond-shaped blue crystals of copper sulfate (right).

A closer look at neutralisation

In the reactions above, both the acid and the alkali are destroyed. One of the compounds formed in both cases is water. The other compounds formed are salts.

Definition

A salt is an ionic compound formed when an acid reacts with an alkali. It contains a metal ion and a non-metal ion.

All acids contain hydrogen ions. You will remember from Chapter 5 that a hydrogen atom consists of only a proton in the nucleus with just one electron moving round it. A hydrogen ion therefore is just a proton because the electron has left it.

Acids are solutions that contain many protons. This means that the pH scale is a measure of the concentration of protons in a solution. The higher the concentration of protons, then the lower the pH.

Look again at the neutralisation reactions above. Rewrite the equations showing all the ions. The acids contain ions. The copper oxide is ionic. The sodium and potassium hydroxide solution contain ions and the salts formed are all ionic. Only the water is covalent.

$$H^+ + Cl^- + Na^+ + OH^- \rightarrow Na^+ + Cl^- + H_2O$$

$$2H^+ + SO_4^{2-} + Cu^{2+} + O^{2-} \rightarrow Cu^{2+} + SO_4^{2-} + H_2O$$

$$H^+ + NO_3^- + K^+ + OH^- \rightarrow K^+ + NO_3^- + H_2O$$

What has changed in these equations?

The only particles that have changed in these three reactions are the oxide and hydroxide ions and the hydrogen ions. They have joined together to form the covalent compound, water.

$$2H^+ + O^{2-} \rightarrow H_2O$$

$$H^+ + OH^- \rightarrow H_2O$$

Now we can clearly see what is happening during neutralisation. The hydrogen ion (or proton) in the acid is joining oxide or hydroxide ions to form water. This is called a **proton transfer reaction**. The proton is being transferred from the acid to the base to form water.

This can give us a better definition of an acid. The acids in the reactions all contain protons (hydrogen ions), which they *donate* to the alkali to form water. The alkalis in the reactions all *receive* the protons to form water. We can therefore define acids and alkalis like this:

An acid is a proton donor.

An alkali is a proton acceptor.

> **DID YOU KNOW?**
>
> Something for mathematicians. The pH scale numbers have a real meaning. The pH of a solution is the negative logarithm (base 10) of the concentration of hydrogen ions in solution. This means that if a solution has a concentration of 10^{-2} (1/100) moles per litre it will have a pH of 2. Pure water, with a pH of 7, has a concentration of hydrogen ions of 10^{-7} or one 10 millionth of a mole of hydrogen ions per litre. (We measure concentrations in moles per litre, as you will find out in Chapter 17.)

> **Activity 7.5**
> Making salts

7.6 Making salts

Look back at all the reactions of acids; they all produced salts. We can use these reactions to make salts.

acid + base → salt + water
acid + metal → salt + hydrogen
acid + carbonate → salt + carbon dioxide + water

Method 1: Making a soluble salt from an insoluble starting material

We can make salts from bases, metals or carbonates. If the base, metal or carbonate is insoluble, then all we have to do is add enough solid to some acid to use it all up and then filter off the solid that has not been used. We will then have a solution of the salt and water, which we can evaporate. You have studied all these techniques in Chapter 3.

The flow diagram below shows how to make salts using this method.

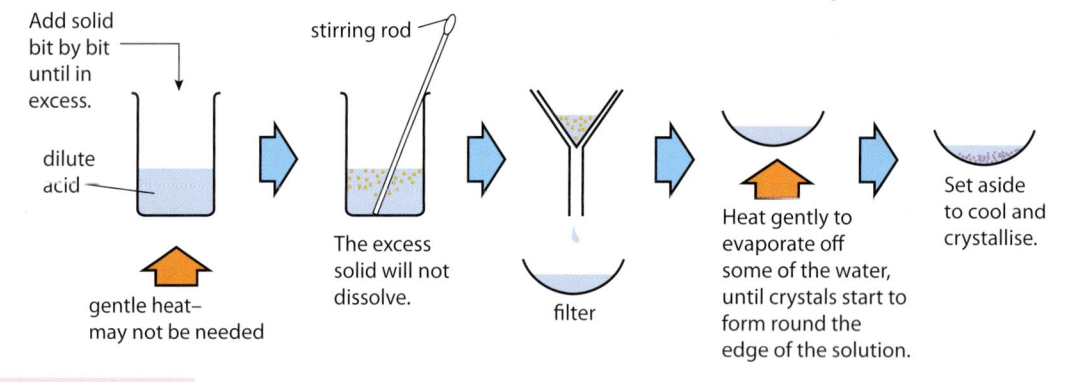

▲ Figure 7.11
Sequence for preparing soluble salts from an insoluble starting material.

In this investigation you have used an insoluble substance to react with the acid. When all the acid was used up, you filtered off the unused insoluble substance. In this way you could be sure that the liquid contained only the salt and water. It was then easy to obtain the pure salt by evaporation and crystallisation.

The last step should always be to leave the salt to crystallise and then filter the crystals off before all the water has evaporated. This ensures that the crystals you get are pure; any impurities are left behind in the water.

Another reason for crystallising the final product is that most salt crystals contain a little water. This is called the 'water of crystallisation' and is part of the crystal structure. The blue copper sulfate crystals, for example, contain water of crystallisation. If you heat these blue crystals, the water is driven off and the crystals break up into a white powder called **anhydrous** copper sulfate (anhydrous means 'without water'). Sodium chloride is one the few salts that does not have any water of crystallisation in its crystals.

The list shows three examples of salts that can be made in this way.

Acid	Insoluble substance to react with the acid	Soluble salt crystallised out
Dilute sulfuric acid	Copper oxide	Copper sulfate
Dilute sulfuric acid	Zinc metal	Zinc sulfate
Dilute hydrochloric acid	Calcium carbonate	Calcium chloride

These three reactions are shown by the equations.

copper oxide + sulfuric acid → copper sulfate + water
$CuO(s) + H_2SO_4(aq) → CuSO_4(aq) + H_2O(l)$

zinc + sulfuric acid → zinc sulfate + hydrogen
$Zn(s) + H_2SO_4(aq) → ZnSO_4(aq) + H_2(g)$

calcium carbonate + hydrochloric acid → calcium chloride + carbon dioxide + water
$CaCO_3(s) + 2HCl(aq) → CaCl_2(aq) + CO_2(g) + H_2O(l)$

Method 2: Making a soluble salt from soluble starting materials

In the next example, an acid is used to neutralise an alkali to give a salt and water. In this case, both of the reactants are soluble. You must therefore add just the right amount of the acid to neutralise the alkali. You cannot filter off any unused alkali after the reaction because the alkali is soluble. In this case you will use an indicator to tell you when you have added just the right amount of acid. At this point, the indicator will change from its alkali colour to its acid colour. We call this point the **end-point**.

Activity 7.6
Making sodium chloride

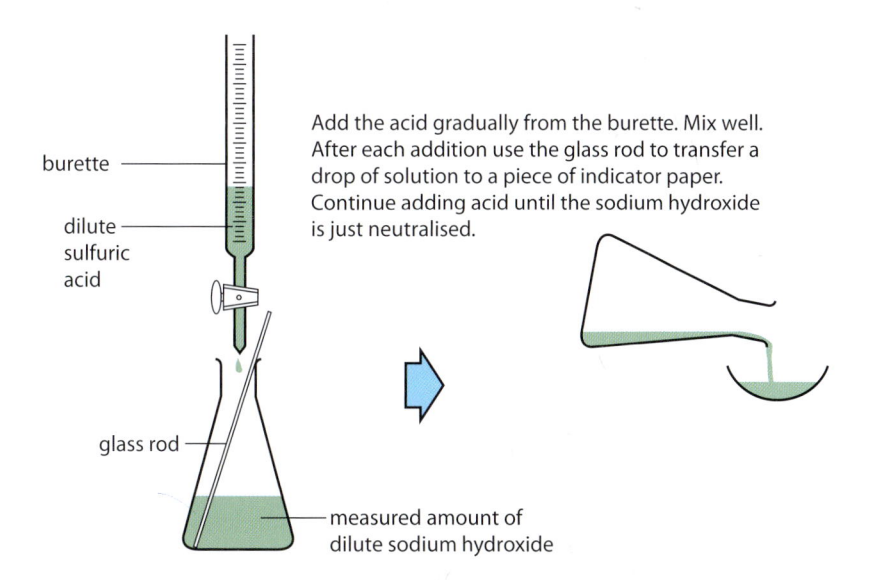

Add the acid gradually from the burette. Mix well. After each addition use the glass rod to transfer a drop of solution to a piece of indicator paper. Continue adding acid until the sodium hydroxide is just neutralised.

burette
dilute sulfuric acid
glass rod
measured amount of dilute sodium hydroxide

Heat gently to boil off some of the water, then set aside to cool and crystallise.

▲ **Figure 7.12**
Preparing a salt using titration.

This process is called a **titration**. It is a process widely used in industrial laboratories, not for making a chemical but for **analysis**. You carry out an analysis of something when you want to find out what it is made of or how much of a particular chemical is present in it.

A piece of equipment used for measuring out the acid in Figure 7.12 is a **burette**. A burette allows you to add the acid very accurately by allowing one drop at a time through the tap. It allows you to measure exactly how much acid is used. You will learn more about this kind of **quantitative** equipment in Chapter 17.

Method 3: Making an insoluble salt

In the two methods of making salts described above, the product has been a solution of the salt in water. The salt is then obtained by evaporation or crystallisation. A different method is needed if the salt you want to make is insoluble. Figure 7.13 shows how you can make lead iodide, a yellow insoluble salt.

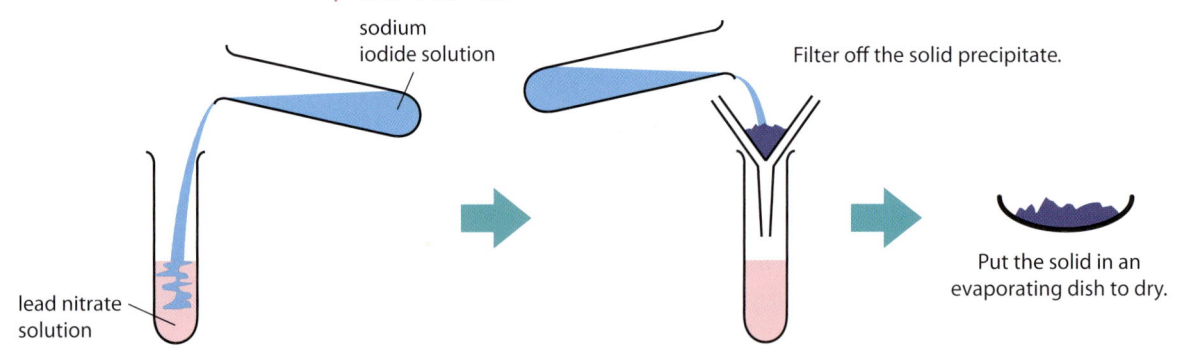

▲ **Figure 7.13**
Making an insoluble salt.

Activity 7.7
Making an insoluble salt, lead iodide

In Figure 7.13, the insoluble lead iodide is made by mixing together solutions of two soluble salts, lead nitrate solution and sodium iodide solution. The insoluble lead iodide is produced immediately as a yellow **precipitate** (insoluble solid).

Any insoluble salt can be prepared in this way. The salt is made of the two ions, the **anion** and the **cation**. To prepare an insoluble salt, all that is needed is a solution of a soluble compound that contains the cation and another of a soluble compound containing the anion. In this case the two solutions were lead nitrate and sodium iodide. Lead ethanoate and potassium iodide would have been just as good.

When the two solutions are mixed, the insoluble salt immediately appears as a precipitate. This is filtered and washed to remove traces of the soluble salt left in the solution.

lead nitrate + sodium iodide → lead iodide + sodium nitrate
$Pb(NO_3)_2(aq)$ + $2NaI(aq)$ → $PbI_2(s)$ + $2NaNO_3(aq)$

Nothing actually happens to the nitrate or the sodium ions in this reaction. In the original solutions, they are present as ions in solution, and at the end they are still there as ions in solution in the filtrate. So we can write a much simpler ionic equation for the reaction by leaving them out.

lead ions + iodide ions → lead iodide precipitate
$Pb^{2+}(aq)$ + $2I^-(aq)$ → $PbI_2(s)$

This is a general equation. It will also apply, for example, if lead ethanoate and potassium iodide were used.

7.7 Identifying ions in salts

You learnt above that analysis is what chemists do when they want to find out what chemicals there are in a substance. **Qualitative analysis** is what chemists do if they want to find out just *what* is present. **Quantitative analysis** is what chemists do when they want to know *how much* of a substance is present. The titration in Figure 7.12 is an example of quantitative analysis. The rest of this section is about qualitative analysis.

Acids and alkalis

Salts contain ions. They contain cations and anions.

The cations in salts are the positive ions and they are almost all metal ions. There is one cation that is not a metal; the ammonium ion. The ammonium ion is a group of atoms (one nitrogen atom and four hydrogens) that are joined together with covalent bonds but the group of atoms has an overall charge of 1^+. This means that the total number of electrons in all the atoms is one less than the total number of protons in the nuclei of the atoms. We can represent the ammonium ion as $(NH_4)^+$.

The anions are the negative ions. Some of these are the ions of non-metal elements such as chloride Cl^- but most of them are made from groups of atoms such as nitrate $(NO_3)^-$, sulfate $(SO_4)^{2-}$, and carbonate $(CO_3)^{2-}$. The atoms within these groups are joined together by covalent bonds.

Chemists often need to know which ions are present in a salt. To do this they carry out tests that identify the ions. The tables below give details of some tests to identify some anions and cations. In each case, the tests should be done using a small amount (about 5 mm depth) of a solution of the salt in a micro test tube. Add the reagent one drop at a time and watch carefully what happens as each drop mixes with the solution.

Activity 7.8
Identifying some unknown chemicals

▼ Table 7.3
Qualitative analysis: cations.

Cation	Test	Result
Aluminium	Add sodium hydroxide solution.	A white precipitate will form that will disappear as more is added.
	Add ammonium hydroxide solution.	A white precipitate will form which does not dissolve when excess ammonium hydroxide is added.
Zinc	Add sodium hydroxide solution.	A white precipitate will form that will disappear as more is added.
	Add ammonium hydroxide solution.	A white precipitate will form that will disappear as more is added.
Calcium	Add sodium hydroxide solution.	A white precipitate will form that will disappear as more is added.
	Add ammonium hydroxide solution.	No precipitate.
Copper	Add sodium hydroxide solution. Add ammonium hydroxide solution.	A blue precipitate will form. A blue precipitate will form. With excess, the precipitate will disappear and a deep blue clear solution will form.
Iron(II)	Add sodium hydroxide solution.	A green precipitate will form, insoluble in excess. This will gradually turn brown on the surface.
Iron(III)	Add sodium hydroxide solution.	A brown precipitate will form, insoluble in excess.
Ammonium	Add four drops of sodium hydroxide solution and warm; hold a piece of moist red litmus paper in the mouth of the tube.	Ammonia gas will be given off which will turn the litmus paper blue.
Sodium		No reaction will be seen when any of these tests are tried.

▶ Table 7.4
Qualitative analysis: anions

Anion	Test	Result
Carbonate	Add dilute acid, test the gas evolved with limewater.	The limewater turns milky.
Sulfate	Add a drop of dilute acid and add barium chloride or nitrate.	A white precipitate will form.
Chloride	Make acid with a drop of nitric acid and add silver nitrate solution.	A white precipitate will form.
Iodide	Make acid with a drop of nitric acid and add lead (II) nitrate solution.	A yellow precipitate will form.
Nitrate	Make alkaline with sodium hydroxide solution, then add aluminium foil and warm.	Ammonia gas is produced.

For the anion table, the order in which you carry out the work is important. For example, you should always test for the sulfate ion before the chloride ion because sulfates can also give a positive result in the chloride test. A carbonate will give a positive result with both the chloride test and the sulfate test so it should always be done first.

When carrying out these tests, always use small quantities. About 5 mm depth of the original solution in a micro test tube is a good guide. When you heat anything, use the smallest flame you can get with your burner and move the tube continuously in and out of the flame. Small quantities will heat up very quickly and boil over suddenly.

The chemistry behind the tests – cations

When you carry out the tests for the cations, the metal hydroxide will be made when you add sodium hydroxide solution. Most metal hydroxides are insoluble and those of transition metals are coloured. The colour of the precipitate therefore tells you which metal is present. Copper forms a blue hydroxide ($Cu(OH)_2$) whereas iron forms two, one green and one brown ($Fe(OH)_2$ and $Fe(OH)_3$).

copper ion + hydroxide ion → copper hydroxide
$Cu^{2+}(aq)$ + $2OH^-(aq)$ → $Cu(OH)_2(s)$ (blue)

iron(II) ion + hydroxide ion → iron(II) hydroxide
$Fe^{2+}(aq)$ + $2OH^-(aq)$ → $Fe(OH)_2(s)$ (green)

iron(III) ion + hydroxide ion → iron(III) hydroxide
$Fe^{3+}(aq)$ + $3OH^-(aq)$ → $Fe(OH)_3(s)$ (brown)

Iron, like many transition metals, can form two different ions with different charges. It can form the iron(II) ion and the iron(III) ion. The iron(II) ion, which is sometimes called the ferrous ion, forms a series of salts that are green in colour. The iron(III) ion is much more common and it forms a series of salts that are brown in colour.

Copper hydroxide has an interesting property in that it will react with excess ammonia to form a clear, deep blue liquid. This liquid contains a coloured ion, which has a complex formula involving the copper and molecules of ammonia.

Aluminium hydroxide and zinc hydroxide are white in colour and they both react with excess alkali. Calcium hydroxide is also white but does not react with alkali.

The ammonium ion is identified by heating it with an alkali such as sodium hydroxide solution. Ammonia gas is evolved which has a very distinctive smell. The gas can easily be identified as it turns moist red litmus paper blue.

ammonium chloride + sodium hydroxide → sodium chloride + water + ammonia

$NH_4Cl(aq) + NaOH(aq) \rightarrow NaCl(aq) + H_2O(l) + NH_3(g)$

This can be seen more easily as an ionic equation:

$NH_4^+(aq) + OH^-(aq) \rightarrow H_2O(l) + NH_3(g)$

DID YOU KNOW?

The common brown colour the you see in so many rocks is caused by the iron(III) ion. It is very widespread and common. Sand is brown because of the iron(III) ion; without it, sand would be colourless and look like sugar.

The chemistry behind the tests – anions

The test for a carbonate is well known. A carbonate will give carbon dioxide when hydrochloric acid is added and this turns limewater milky. This is the first anion test that should be done because the carbonate anion will give a positive result in all the other tests as well.

carbonate ion + hydrochloric acid → chloride ion + carbon dioxide + water

$CO_3^{2-}(aq) + HCl(aq) \rightarrow Cl^-(aq) + CO_2(g) + H_2O(l)$

To identify the other anions, a precipitate of an insoluble salt of the anion is made. The insoluble sulfate is barium sulfate and it is made by adding barium chloride to any sulfate.

sulfate ion + barium chloride → barium sulfate + chloride ion

$SO_4^{2-}(aq) + BaCl_2(aq) \rightarrow BaSO_4(s) + 2Cl^-(aq)$

The insoluble chloride is silver chloride. This is made when silver nitrate solution is added to any chloride. Silver sulfate is also insoluble and so a sulfate will also produce a precipitate. This is why the sulfate test must be done before this one.

chloride ion + silver nitrate → silver chloride + nitrate ion

$Cl^-(aq) + AgNO_3(aq) \rightarrow AgCl(s) + NO_3^-(aq)$

The iodide test is similar. A yellow precipitate of lead iodide is produced when lead nitrate solution is added to an iodide.

iodide ion + lead nitrate → lead iodide + nitrate ion

$2I^-(aq) + Pb(NO_3)_2(aq) \rightarrow PbI_2(s) + 2NO_3^-(aq)$

All nitrates are soluble and so it is not possible to identify a nitrate by making a precipitate of an insoluble one. Instead, the nitrate ion is changed into an ammonium ion by warming it with aluminium powder. The ammonium ion is then identified by warming with alkali as described above.

Tests for gases

In this chapter you have met the tests for a number of gases. These tests are summarised below.

Gas	Test
Carbon dioxide	The gas is bubbled through fresh limewater. The limewater terms milky.
Oxygen	A glowing splint is put into to the gas. It relights.
Hydrogen	The gas is mixed with a little air and brought near a flame. An explosion is heard and sometimes condensation can be seen.
Ammonia	Hold a piece of moist red litmus paper in the gas. It turns blue.
Chlorine	Hold a piece of moist blue litmus paper in the gas. It first turns red and then bleaches.

QUESTIONS

7.1 Write word equations for the following reactions. The action of:
hydrochloric acid on magnesium
nitric acid on sodium carbonate
ethanoic acid on calcium hydroxide.

7.2 'Johnny, finding life a bore
Drank some H_2SO_4
His father, an MD
Gave him $CaCO_3$
Now he's neutralised it's true
But he's full of CO_2.'

The poet did not get his chemistry quite right. Explain why Johnny will not fill up with CO_2.

7.3 Explain the difference between a weak acid and a dilute acid.

7.4 Pure distilled water has a pH of 7. Rainwater often has a pH of between 5 and 6. Explain this.

7.5 Explain why toothpastes are usually alkaline.

7.6 Explain why farmers in some regions spread lime on their soil.

7.7 Classify the following oxides or hydroxides as acidic, amphoteric or basic. The periodic table (Table 4.7) will help you.
Rubidium oxide
Manganese(III) oxide
Selenium dioxide
Lead(II) hydroxide

7.8 Make a table showing the trends in the properties of the oxides across Period 3 of the periodic table (Na to Ar). In your table, consider state, solubility and reaction with acids and alkalis.

Summary

Now that you have completed this chapter, you should be able to:

- describe the characteristic properties of acids in their reaction with litmus, metals, carbonates, and alkalis
- describe the chemical tests for carbon dioxide and hydrogen
- (S) use the pH scale to explain the differences between strong and weak acids and strong and weak alkalis
- describe the important uses of acids and alkalis in the home, in industry and in agriculture
- distinguish between basic, neutral and acidic oxides and described the reaction between acidic oxides and basic oxides to form salts
- (S) show how some oxides of elements near the centre of the periodic table can form acidic and basic oxides at the same time and know that these are called amphoteric oxides.

Chapter 8

Oxidation and reduction

▶ Figure 8.1
Foods rich in antioxidants.

What have all these foods got in common? They all contain things called **antioxidants**. You may have read that antioxidants in food are good for you. But what are they and what do they do? And are they really good for you?

The problem is that our atmosphere contains the gas oxygen, and oxygen is poisonous. Oxygen, as you know, reacts with molecules that contain carbon, and our bodies are made out of molecules that contain carbon. Our bodies struggle all the time to prevent the molecules in our body from being damaged by oxygen. They have complicated methods for repairing this kind of damage. This kind of damage, called **oxidative damage**, is said to contribute to heart disease and cancer and the general aging of the body.

So what do these antioxidants do? They contain chemicals that react with the chemicals in our bodies that can do damage to our cells. Some of the most important antioxidants are the vitamins A, C and E; these are present in most of the foods in the picture.

You can buy pills that contain antioxidants that claim to slow down the effects of aging. Scientists who have studied these matters advise that a balanced diet, containing vegetables rich in these vitamins, is probably more effective than pills, because the vegetables also contain many other substances that help the vitamins in their action.

DID YOU KNOW?

The element selenium is also an antioxidant and is a trace element in many of the foods we eat. Trace elements are elements that are essential to us in very small quantities.

94

8.1 Reducing metal ores

For centuries, chemists have referred to the process of obtaining metals from their ores as **reduction.** This word was used because a large amount of ore is always needed to get a small quantity of metal.

English is a living language, however, and the exact meanings of words are changing all the time. This is particularly true of scientific words. These words often take on extra meanings, as our understanding of nature gets deeper. So we still use the word 'reduction' to mean the extraction of metals from their ores, but the word has other definitions as well, which have been added as our knowledge of chemistry has improved.

In Chapter 11, you will study the reduction of iron ore. In the reaction, the ore, iron oxide, is changed to the metal, iron. In the process, oxygen is removed from the ore. The **reducing agent** (the chemical that is put in the furnace to remove the oxygen) is carbon monoxide. This equation shows what happens:

iron oxide + carbon monoxide → iron + carbon dioxide
  ore   + reducing agent → metal + carbon dioxide
  Fe_2O_3 + $3CO$ →   Fe + $3CO_2$

So we have a chemical meaning for the word 'reduction'. Reduction means the removal of oxygen from a compound.

8.2 Oxidation of metals

In the chapter on the periodic table you studied the formation of oxides. Most metals react with oxygen to form the metal oxide. Some metals, such as magnesium, react readily in a spectacular way by burning. The reaction below shows what happens when iron wool burns in oxygen. The name we give to this kind of reaction is **oxidation.**

iron + oxygen → iron oxide
$4Fe + 3O_2 → 2Fe_2O_3$

So we have a chemical meaning for the word 'oxidation'. Oxidation means the addition of oxygen to a compound.

Oxidation is the reverse of reduction. The reactions we have been discussing are called reduction-oxidation reactions or **redox** reactions for short.

Oxidation and reduction happen together.

Look again at the reduction of iron oxide.

$Fe_2O_3 + 3CO → 2Fe + 3CO_2$

What is happening to the carbon monoxide? It is combining with oxygen. The carbon monoxide is oxidised to carbon dioxide. The two reactions, oxidation and reduction, are always grouped together. Whenever there is a reduction, there is also an oxidation.

8.3 Oxidation state

Some elements, particularly the transition metals, form not one oxide but two or more. Examples are copper and iron. These metals also form two sets of salts like sulfates, nitrates and chlorides. The table shows the two oxides of copper and the two sulfates of iron.

▶ Table 8.1
The oxides of copper and the sulfates of iron.

Modern name	Formula	Colour	Old name	Metal ion
Copper(I) oxide	Cu_2O	Brown	Cuprous oxide	Cu^+
Copper(II) oxide	CuO	Black	Cupric oxide	Cu^{2+}
Iron(II) sulfate	$FeSO_4$	Green	Ferrous sulfate	Fe^{2+}
Iron(III) sulfate	$Fe_2(SO_4)_3$	Orange	Ferric sulfate	Fe^{3+}

The roman number in brackets in the modern name of the oxides refers to the **oxidation state** of the metal. In these simple compounds, the oxidation state is the same as the number of positive charges on the ion formed by the metal when it loses electrons.

One of the typical properties of transition metals is that they form ions with a variable number of charges. It is more accurate to describe them as showing variable oxidation states. For example, the oxidation state of manganese in potassium permanganate is 7. In this compound, the metal manganese is part of the permanganate anion, $(MnO_4)^-$. This does not mean that manganese will form the ion Mn^{7+} with seven charges, but it does have an oxidation state of +7. For this reason, the correct modern name for potassium permanganate is potassium manganate(VII).

Most of the ions containing these transition metals are coloured and the colour depends on the oxidation state of the metal. Iron(III) compounds are all brown and iron(II) compounds are all green.

▲ Figure 8.2
Potassium permanganate, now called potassium manganate(VII). The transition metal, manganese, is part of the anion in this salt and it has an oxidation number of +7. The crystals look almost black but they are dark purple and dissolve to form a purple solution. The purple colour is caused by the manganese in its +7 oxidation state.

8.4 Another definition of oxidation and reduction

Look more closely at the reduction of iron oxide.

$Fe_2O_3 + 3CO \rightarrow 2Fe + 3CO_2$

What has happened to the iron in this reduction reaction? It has changed from iron *ions* in the oxide into iron *atoms* in the pure metal. In order to do this it has gained electrons:

$Fe^{3+} + 3e^- \rightarrow Fe$

Think also about the opposite reaction, the burning of steel wool in oxygen.

$2Fe + 3O_2 \rightarrow 2Fe_2O_3$

In this *oxidation* the iron has changed from atoms into ions. The atoms of iron have lost electrons:

$Fe \rightarrow Fe^{3+} + 3e^-$

This leads us to a better, simpler definition of oxidation and reduction.

Reduction is gain of electrons.

Oxidation is loss of electrons.

Oxidation and reduction

This is a much more useful definition because it is not limited to just reactions involving oxygen. In Chapter 5 you studied the reaction of iron and chlorine. If you lower hot iron wool into a gas jar of chlorine, it will burn and iron(III) chloride will form. If you lower the hot iron into a gas jar of oxygen, it will burn and iron(III) oxide will form.

$2Fe(s) + 3Cl_2(g) \rightarrow 2FeCl_3(s)$

$4Fe(s) + 3O_2(g) \rightarrow 2Fe_2O_3(s)$

The same thing has happened to the iron in both cases. The iron atoms have lost electrons to form iron ions:

$Fe \rightarrow Fe^{3+} + 3e^-$

The iron has been oxidised. In one case the oxidising agent is chlorine, in the other case it is oxygen.

In these reactions the chlorine and the oxygen have both gained the electrons that have been lost by the iron.

$O_2 + 4e^- \rightarrow 2O^{2-}$

$Cl_2 + 2e^- \rightarrow 2Cl^-$

The chlorine and the oxygen have been reduced to chloride and oxide ions.

In Chapter 9 you will find out how metals can displace less reactive metals from solutions of their compounds. For example, if zinc is put in a solution of copper sulfate, copper metal and zinc sulfate are formed.

$Zn + CuSO_4 \rightarrow Cu + ZnSO_4$

In this reaction, the zinc forms zinc ions and the copper ions are changed into copper atoms.

$Zn \rightarrow Zn^{2+} + 2e^-$

$Cu^{2+} \rightarrow Cu + 2e^-$

These equations show that the zinc has been oxidised and the copper ions have been reduced.

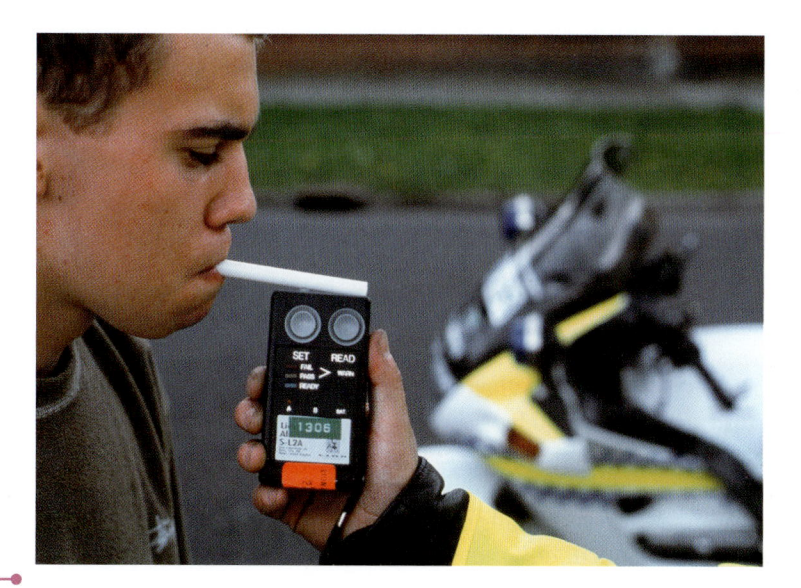

◀ Figure 8.3
Alcohol is a reducing agent. A breathalyser contains an oxidising agent that can be reduced by the alcohol. When it is reduced it changes colour. This colour change is recorded electronically and the breathalyser readout tells the policeman whether there is too much alcohol in the driver's breath.

8.5 Electrolysis

Electrolysis is a process that breaks down liquid chemical compounds into their elements when an electric current is passed through them. This is a process that involves oxidation and reduction. In this section you will study this further.

Which liquids conduct electricity?

Not all liquids conduct electricity. It is easy to test whether a liquid conducts electricity, using a battery, some wires and a bulb. Figure 8.4 below shows which liquids conduct and which do not.

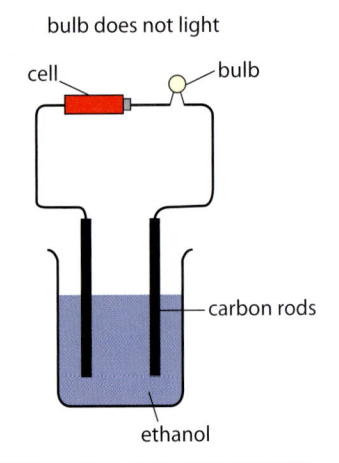

▲ Figure 8.4
Four examples of liquids being tested for conductivity.

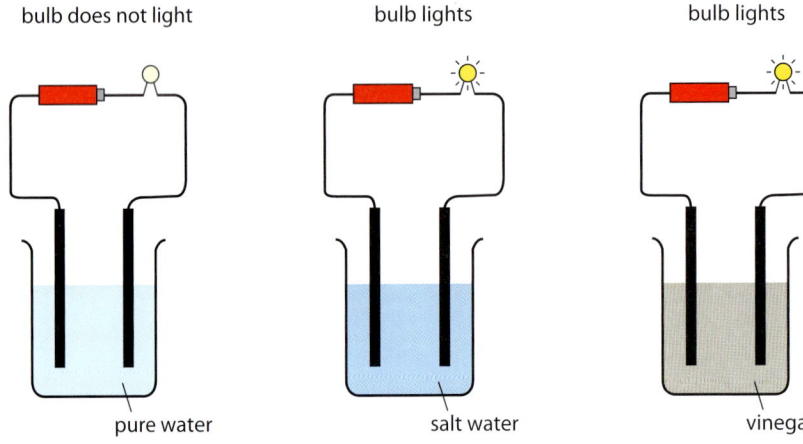

A simple test like this shows that ethanol (alcohol) and pure water do not conduct electricity. But salt water and vinegar, which is mainly water, are good conductors.

Ethanol and pure water are covalent compounds. You learnt this in Chapter 5. Salt solution and vinegar are both mainly water but these solutions both contain ions. It is these ions that make them conduct electricity. The ions carry the electric charge through the liquid.

There is another kind of liquid that will conduct electricity; molten ionic compounds. Salt (sodium chloride) melts at about 800 °C and it is possible to melt it with a strong Bunsen burner flame(but you must use a Pyrex test tube!). It can be tested in the same way as the solutions in Figure 8.4 and the bulb will light up. It will conduct electricity because the ions can move in the molten salt just as they can in salt solution.

▼ Figure 8.5
Electrolysis of molten lead bromide.

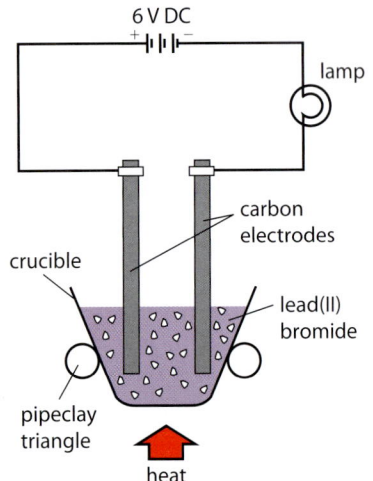

Electrolysis of molten electrolytes

If they have a low enough melting point, it is possible to electrolyse some ionic solids in a school laboratory. Lead bromide melts at 373 °C so it can be easily melted and electrolysed in a porcelain crucible. The equipment is shown in Figure 8.5. When the current is passed, lead is produced at the cathode (−) and bromine is given off at the anode (+). It is not a very pleasant reaction to do as the bromine vapour produced at the anode has an acrid smell and is rather poisonous. The lead is a liquid at this temperature and it falls to the bottom. It can be recovered after the crucible has cooled.

Oxidation and reduction

Electrolysis of water

You have already seen that pure water does not conduct electricity. But if you add an ionic substance to it, it will conduct, so it is possible to study what happens when an electric current passes through water. We usually add a little bit of sulfuric acid to make it conduct electricity. The electrolysis of water can be done in a simple electrolysis cell like the one in Figure 8.6. This cell is made from a short piece of glass tubing about 2.5 cm in diameter. It has a two-hole bung in the bottom and carbon electrodes are inserted through the holes. The tubes are micro test tubes.

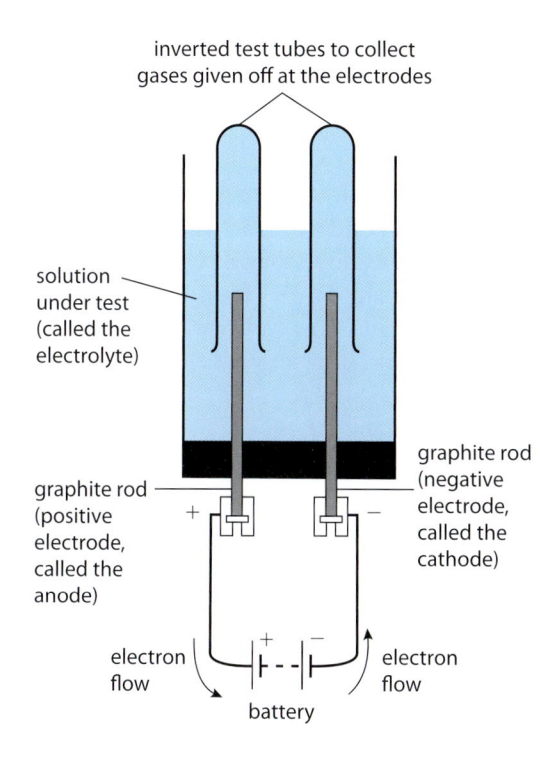

Figure 8.6
Electrolysis cell showing electrolysis of water.

When water is electrolysed there are two products. Hydrogen is produced at the cathode and oxygen is produced at the anode. The volume of hydrogen produced is twice the volume of oxygen produced. This is because a molecule of water contains two atoms of hydrogen and one atom of oxygen.

Note that in both these electrolysis cells, the elements that form ions with a positive charge (the lead and the hydrogen) appear at the cathode. The elements that form ions with a negative charge (oxygen and bromine) appear at the anode.

Electrolysis of some aqueous solutions

When water is electrolysed, two products are hydrogen and oxygen. When solutions of ionic substances in water are electrolysed, the products will depend upon what ions are present in the water. For example, if copper sulfate is electrolysed the product of the cathode is copper. Table 8.2 shows the products of electrolysis of a number of solutions

Activity 8.1
What is the effect of electricity on solutions?

Electrolyte	At the cathode	At the anode
Copper chloride solution	A salmon pink solid collects on the carbon rod. It is copper.	A yellow green gas collects. It bleaches indicator paper. It is chlorine.
Sodium chloride solution	A clear, colourless gas collects. The gas burns with a squeaky pop. This is hydrogen.	**Chlorine** is produced.
Potassium bromide solution	Hydrogen is produced.	A dark red colour forms around the carbon rod. It is due to bromine.
Copper sulfate solution	Copper is produced.	A clear colourless gas collects. It relights a glowing splint. It is oxygen.
Zinc sulfate solution	Hydrogen is produced. Also, there is some grey solid around the rod. It is zinc.	Oxygen is produced.

▲ Table 8.2
The products of electrolysis of a number of solutions.

Electricity, everyone is taught, flows from positive to negative. However, we now know that an electric current is actually a stream of electrons. These are negatively charged and so they actually flow from the negative pole of the battery to the positive one. This is the opposite direction from the direction we are all taught. When you learn about electrolysis it is important to understand this. It means that electrons flow:
- into the solution from the cathode
- away from the solution along the anode.

This electron flow is shown in Figure 8.6.

You will have noticed some gas produced at some of the electrodes. Chlorine gas is easy to identify; it has a well known smell and it bleaches litmus paper. Other gases have to be collected and then tested. This is rather difficult as quite small quantities of the gases are produced. It is difficult to collect and identify oxygen because some of it may react with the carbon of the electrode and so carbon dioxide is also produced.

Table 8.2 shows two important patterns:
- metals or hydrogen are formed at the cathode
- non-metals (except hydrogen) are formed at the anode.

The solutions that are electrolysed all contain an ionic compound and water. Sometimes the product of the electrolysis comes from the water (hydrogen at the cathode and oxygen at the anode) and sometimes it comes from the ionic substance that is dissolved.

Patterns such as these can be seen from the table.

At the cathode:
- The product is the metal when the metal is not very reactive like copper (see Chapter 9).
- The more reactive metals are not produced; instead hydrogen from the water is the product.

At the anode:
- If the solution contains halide ions, these elements are liberated at the anode.
- When the electrolyte is a sulfate, electrolysis liberates oxygen from the water.

8.6 Explaining electrolysis

Figure 8.7
Michael Faraday, 1791–1867 was an English scientist who is best known for his work on electromagnetism and his invention of the electric motor. However, he was a professor of chemistry and was the first to explain electrolysis. In the 1830s he introduced the word 'ion' to mean an electrically charged atom.

Ionic solutions will conduct electricity because the charge is carried by the ions moving through the solution. This is quite easy to demonstrate using a substance that has a coloured ion, such as potassium manganate(VII) (potassium permanganate). Figure 8.8 shows this. A single crystal of potassium manganate(VII) is placed on a moist filter paper that is wrapped round a microscope slide. The terminals of a DC power supply set at about 20 volts are connected either side of the crystal. The coloured anion (MnO_4^-) will stain the paper and the stain can be seen moving towards the positive terminal.

Figure 8.8
Diagram of equipment showing the movement of ions during electrolysis.

Activity 8.2
Studying the movement of ions during electrolysis

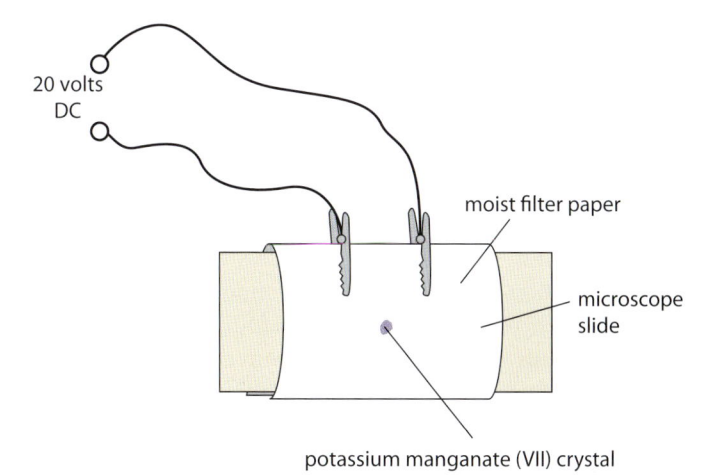

In an electrolysis circuit, the power supply or battery is a source of electrons and also a pump to make them go along the wire. In the electrolyte, the positive ions (cations) are attracted towards the negative electrode (cathode) and the negative ions (anions) are attracted towards the positive electrode (anode). Figure 8.9 shows this.

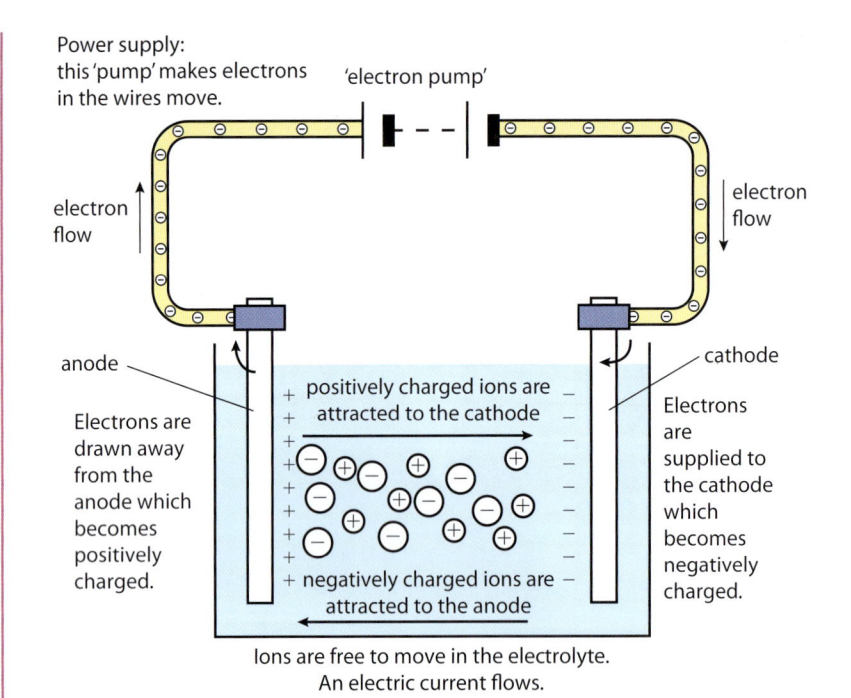

Figure 8.9
Diagram explaining electrolysis.

Power supply: this 'pump' makes electrons in the wires move.

'electron pump'

electron flow

electron flow

anode

Electrons are drawn away from the anode which becomes positively charged.

positively charged ions are attracted to the cathode

negatively charged ions are attracted to the anode

cathode

Electrons are supplied to the cathode which becomes negatively charged.

Ions are free to move in the electrolyte. An electric current flows.

When a cation reaches the cathode, an electron (or two electrons if the cation has two charges) joins the ion and forms a neutral atom. We can begin to see the element made up of these atoms on the electrode. If the cations are copper ions we see a deposit of copper forming on the cathode.

When anions reach the anode, they give up electrons and also form neutral atoms. This element then appears at the anode. In the electrolysis of copper chloride, for example, these reactions happen at the electrodes.

At the cathode:
$Cu^{2+} + 2e^- \rightarrow Cu$

At the anode:
$2Cl^- \rightarrow Cl_2 + 2e^-$

The cathode will become coated in copper and there will be smell of chlorine at the anode.

The products observed at the electrodes will depend on the ions present in the solution. Most of the ionic compounds we have studied in this chapter are called salts. A salt is any ionic compound of a metal, other than its oxide or hydroxide, and they will be studied further in the next chapter. The salt solution will contain ions from the salt and the water, which could be electrolysed as well. In any solution of a salt, therefore, the following products could be produced at the electrodes:

At the cathode:
metal (from the salt)
hydrogen (from the water)

At the anode:
non-metal (from the salt)
oxygen (from the water)

Which of these two products will be formed at the electrodes? This will depend upon two factors:
- the ease with which the ions are discharged
- the concentration of the salt.

What happens at the cathode?

Some ions are discharged more readily than others. You will learn in Chapter 9 that some metals are more easily formed from their ions than others. Metals that are not very reactive, such as copper, are easily made from their ions. Metals that are very reactive, such as sodium, are not easily made from their ions.

A useful general rule is that transition metals can be made from the electrolysis of solutions of their salts, but other metals, such as those in Groups I, II and III cannot. If you electrolyse solutions of salts of these metals, hydrogen is produced at the cathode, not the metal. You will learn more about this when you study the **reactivity series** for metals in the next chapter

If the solution of a transition metal salt is very dilute, however, some hydrogen will be discharged. This is because there are not enough metal ions near the electrodes in the very dilute solution and so some hydrogen will be produced as well.

At the cathode, positive ions are reduced to their atoms by the addition of electrons.

What happens at the anode?

At the anode we find that the usual product is oxygen, except where the salt is a halide (remember that we call salts containing group VII ions, halides). In this case, the halogen is liberated. If the halide solution is very dilute, however, some oxygen will also be produced.

At the anode, negative ions are oxidised to their atoms by the removal of electrons.

Electrolysis of copper sulfate using copper electrodes

There is a different reaction at the anode when we electrolyse copper sulfate solution using copper electrodes. This is shown in Figure 8.10.

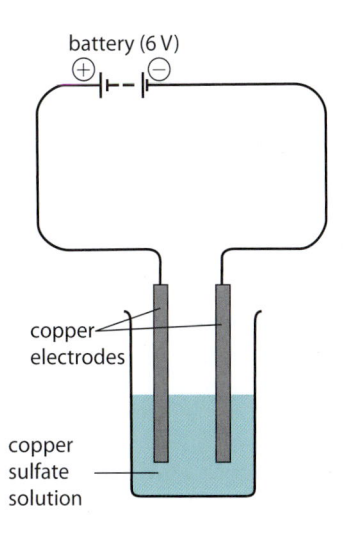

Figure 8.10
Electrolysis of copper sulfate between copper electrodes.

> **Activity 8.3**
> Electrolysis of copper sulfate using copper electrodes

In this electrolysis there are no signs of a gas at either electrode. At the end of the investigation there will be a deposit of copper as expected on the cathode. At the anode, however, a different reaction takes place from the one that happens when carbon electrodes are used. When carbon electrodes are used, oxygen gas, from the water, is liberated. In this case, no anion was discharged at all; instead copper atoms in the electrode give up electrons and they became ions. These ions replace the ones that are discharged at the cathode.

You can see from the equations for this that the action at the anode is the reverse of the action at the cathode.

At the cathode:
$Cu^{2+} + 2e^- \rightarrow Cu$

At the anode:
$Cu \rightarrow Cu^{2+} + 2e^-$

This reaction is a very important one. It is used in industry to purify the crude copper produced by smelting. The crude copper is made into the anode and the cathode is a piece of pure copper. As the electrolysis proceeds, the cathode gets bigger and the anode gets smaller. The impurities fall to the bottom of the cell underneath the anode.

▶ **Figure 8.11**
The commercial purification of copper by electrolysis. The anodes in these rows of cells are made of impure copper and pure copper is deposited on the cathodes.

8.7 Applications of electrolysis

There are two important applications of electrolysis. One is the manufacture of useful elements from their compounds and the other is electroplating.

We make many elements by electrolysis. The manufacture of chlorine is described in Chapter 16 and the use of electrolysis to extract zinc and aluminium will be described in Chapter 11.

Electroplating is widely used to coat one metal with another one. When you electrolyse copper salts you will notice that the cathode became coated in copper. This copper coat is usually rather soft and can be scraped off easily. It is possible, however, to make a very hard-wearing coating if the right conditions are used.

Chromium, nickel, silver and gold are often plated onto less expensive metals. Table 8.3 gives some examples of these. The articles to be plated are placed on the cathode of an electrolysis cell. The electrolyte contains a solution of the ion of the metal to be deposited.

Metal electroplated	Uses
Chromium and nickel	Steel objects are chromium- or nickel-plated to prevent them from corroding. Examples are bicycle wheels, taps, kettles, watches and other household metal items used under conditions where paint would wear off.
Silver	Ornaments or cutlery made out of copper or an alloy of copper and nickel are plated with silver to give an attractive and corrosion-resistant finish. The objects are much cheaper than they would be if they were made out of solid silver.
Gold	Ornamental items are also finished with gold plating. The metal parts of electronic components are often gold plated. This ensures that the surface is free from corrosion and makes good electrical contacts.

◀ Table 8.3
Some uses of electroplating.

QUESTIONS

8.1 Iron ore is reduced in the blast furnace. Explain what is meant by the word 'reduced'.

8.2 Explain what is meant by the word 'oxidation'. Give some examples of oxidation from everyday life.

8.3 In the following reactions, name the substance oxidised and the substance that is reduced.

carbon + carbon dioxide → carbon monoxide

magnesium + copper oxide → magnesium oxide + copper

calcium + water → calcium hydroxide + hydrogen

8.4 Draw a diagram to show how you would electroplate a copper ring with silver. Show which is the anode and which the cathode. Show what electrolyte you would use.

8.5 In the following reactions, write equations showing which particles have gained electrons and which have lost them.

$2AgNO_3 + Pb \rightarrow Pb(NO_3)_2 + 2Ag$

$Zn + CuO \rightarrow ZnO + Cu$

$Mg + I_2 \rightarrow MgI_2$

In each case, state what is the oxidising agent and what is the reducing agent.

8.6 List the products of electrolysis of the following solutions and give reasons for your answer.
Potassium iodide solution
Nickel sulfate solution
Magnesium chloride solution

8.7 Sodium is manufactured commercially by electrolysis of molten sodium chloride. Explain why it is not possible to use a solution of sodium chloride for this.

Summary

Now that you have completed this chapter, you should be able to:

- explain oxidation and reduction as gain or loss of oxygen
- explain oxidation and reduction in terms of loss and gain of electrons and recognise that oxidation and reduction are reactions which happened together
- know that many elements, particularly transition metals, form ions with variable oxidation states
- describe how, during electrolysis, ionic compounds (in solution or molten) are converted into their elements
- explain the changes at the anode and the cathode during electrolysis
- show how water can be electrolysed to form hydrogen and oxygen if a little acid is added to it to make it conduct
- know why the products of the electrolysis of a solution that contains a number of different ions will depend on the reactivity of the elements present as ions in the solution
- list the applications of electrolysis.

Chapter 9

Metals

Your car backs hard into a lamppost. You can imagine what the back of the car will look like. A big dint and the back door will not shut properly. No problem, just throw a bucket of boiling water over it and it will return to its original shape.

Is it possible? Not now, but in the future, perhaps, if the cars are made of 'memory metal'. Figure 9.1 shows how memory metal is used now. The ballerina has a broken toe. The wire in the picture is made of memory metal and was shaped to fit carefully around the broken bone. Then it was cooled and bent around the toe to hold it together. When it is cold it can be bent and stays bent. But when it is warmed up to body temperature it springs back to its original shape needed to hold the bones together tightly while they heal.

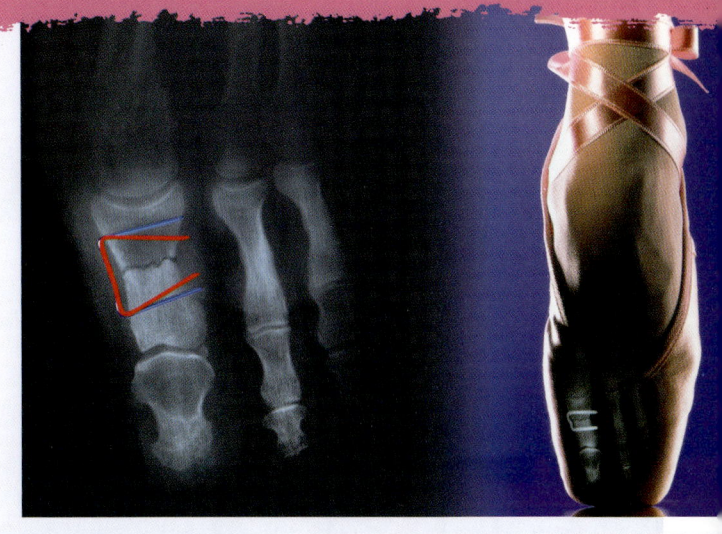

▲ **Figure 9.1**
Using memory metal.

Why don't we make cars of memory metal? At the moment it costs about one US dollar for a gram! How does it work? Turn to Section 11.8.

9.1 Why metals are so useful

▶ **Figure 9.2(a)**
This photograph of the Victoria Falls Bridge across the Zambezi between Zambia and Zimbabwe was taken in 1906. The bridge is made of cast iron in sections made in England and then transported to southern Africa. Cast iron has a very strong *compressive strength*. The forces on the bridge compress the cast iron arch.

◀ **Figure 9.2(b)**
This is one of the world's earliest suspension bridges. It crosses the River Avon in Bristol in England. The chains holding the bridge are made of steel and they are stretched by the weight of the bridge. Steel has a high *tensile strength* which means that it is very strong when it is stretched.

107

▶ **Figure 9.2(c)**
These electricity cables are made from aluminium and they have a steel core in the middle. Aluminium is used because it *conducts electricity* well and the cables are light because aluminium has a *low density*. But aluminium has a low tensile strength and the cables would snap if they were made only from aluminium. So the cables have a steel core.

◀ **Figure 9.2(d)**
This is the propeller of the warship HMS Rattler and it can be seen in the Museum of the SS Great Britain in Bristol, England. It is made of bronze, which is a mixture of copper and tin. Bronze is used because it is *hard* and strong and *does not corrode* in the salty seawater. HMS Rattler was one of the first ships to use a propeller. In March 1845 it took part in a tug-of-war with HMS Alecto, a similar ship but a paddle steamer, to see which form of propulsion was better. HMS Rattler won, pulling the Alecto backwards at about 4 km/hr.

These pictures show that metals are extremely useful materials. Some of their properties that make them useful are shown in italics in the captions. We must understand these properties to make the best use of them. We also need to know how to extract the metals from their ores without doing too much damage to the environment. In this chapter, you will study the physical and chemical properties of metals and what use we make of them and in the next chapter you will learn where we get them.

Metals are elements that you can find on the left side of the Periodic Table. The pictures show some uses and important properties of metals. You can think of many more uses of metals. Think about what properties of metals make them useful. We call these the **physical properties** of metals. Table 9.1 shows some important physical properties of metallic elements compared with non-metallic elements.

▶ **Table 9.1**
Some physical properties of metallic and non-metallic elements.

Metals usually have:	Non-metals usually have:
• high melting points • high boiling points • high densities	• low melting points • low boiling points • lower densities than metals
Metals usually are:	**Non-metals usually are:**
• good conductors of electricity • good conductors of heat • easily pulled out into wires (ductile) • easily hammered into different shapes (malleable)	• electrical insulators • poor conductors of heat • not ductile • brittle (if they are solids)

To understand more about the properties of metals we have to know more about the atoms that make up the metals. The **chemical properties** of the metals depend on the arrangement of the electrons in the metal atoms. The physical properties of the metals depend on the way the atoms are arranged in the metal.

Look carefully at the surface of a piece of new galvanised iron. Galvanised iron is made out of sheets of steel that have been dipped in molten zinc. The zinc forms a coat on the steel, which prevents the iron from rusting. When it is new you can see that the zinc is not one smooth coat but is a lot of small patches (called grains). Each patch is a single crystal of zinc spread out on the iron. These can be seen in Figure 9.3. In each crystal, the zinc atoms are arranged in rows and the rows are arranged in layers like the ions in an ionic crystal. However, there are some important differences between ionic crystals and metal crystals, and these explain why ionic crystals and metal crystals have very different properties.

How metal atoms are held together

Metal atoms are held strongly together by bonds that are called **metallic bonds**. The metal atoms are arranged in rows in metal crystals like ions in ionic crystals. You know that the outer electrons of metal atoms can easily move away from the atom because they are far from the nucleus. In the metallic bond these electrons can move freely around between the atoms. This means that the metal is made of rows of positive ions surrounded by a 'sea' of moving electrons. This 'sea' of negative electrons attracts the positive ions strongly together. Figure 9.4 shows the metallic bond.

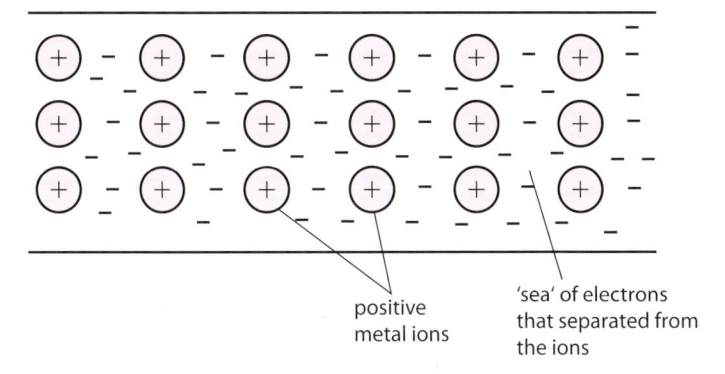

▲ **Figure 9.3**
This photomicrograph shows crystals of zinc.

◀ **Figure 9.4**
Metallic bonding.

The metallic bond explains a number of the properties of metals.

Firstly, because the atoms are held together very strongly, they are close together and a lot of energy is needed to pull them apart. This explains why the melting points and densities of most metals are high. If you look at Table 9.2 you can see that metals with a rather low density also have rather low melting points. Can you explain this?

Secondly, we know that an electric current in a metal is caused by electrons moving through the metal. This can happen because the outer electrons in the metal atoms easily become detached from the atoms to form the 'sea' of electrons. In an electrical wire these electrons move away from the negative terminal in a circuit and towards the positive terminal.

Thirdly, the moving electrons can also help to take heat energy through the metal and so metals are good conductors of heat.

Fourthly, it is the 'sea' of electrons that makes the metallic bond strong but not rigid and so it will deform, not crush, when it is hit.

Melting and boiling points

There are many physical properties of metals that make them useful to us. The high melting and boiling points of metals is one property. Other useful properties that are described below are the high densities of metals, their good electrical conductivity and properties called **malleability** and **ductility**.

If a substance has a high melting point, it means that a lot of energy is needed to pull the particles of the substance apart. The atoms in most metals are held strongly together. This means that a lot of energy is needed to pull them apart and so metals have high melting and boiling points as shown in Table 9.2.

▶ Table 9.2
Density, melting and boiling points of some common metals.

Metal	Density (g/cm³)	Melting point (°C)	Boiling point (°C)
Aluminium	2.7	659	2447
Gold	19.3	1063	2600
Iron	7.9	1540	3000
Magnesium	1.7	650	1110
Tungsten	19.4	3410	5930
Zinc	7.1	420	908

DID YOU KNOW?

Filaments of electric light bulbs are made out of tungsten because it has a particularly high melting point. The filament must be white-hot but it must not melt.

Density

Because the metal atoms are held together very strongly, the atoms are packed close together and so metals have a high density. As you can see from Table 9.2, most metals have a high density compared with typical non-metallic elements and compounds (remember that the density of water, for example, is 1 g/cm³).

Some metals, like aluminium and magnesium, have quite low density. The density of sodium is even lower; it has a density less than 1 g/cm³ so it floats on water. As you discovered in the last chapter, the lower density metals are all on the left hand side of the periodic table, whereas the ones with higher densities are the transition metals.

The metals with the lower densities in Groups I and II are also all rather reactive, which is a pity because we often need to use metals that are light for making such things as electricity cables and aircraft parts. In the section below on **alloys** you will find out how we can design metals that are both light in weight and unreactive.

Metals

> **DID YOU KNOW?**
>
> **Gold – an important metal. Its main use is to be unused!**
> Most of the gold in the world is in little neat piles of bars in bank safes doing nothing very useful.
> What properties of gold make it so useful for storing away in a cupboard? It is rare so it is valuable. It is very unreactive so it does not corrode when you leave it stored away for years. And it is very dense so that it takes up very little space in the cupboard. (Gold has a density of 19.3 g/cm^3; calculate the volume of gold that has the same mass as you.) And, of course, gold has a pretty colour; we all like it so much we do strange things with it like wrap it round our toes or hang it from holes in our ears.
>
> ▶ Figure 9.5
> Gold bars. Each bar weighs around 12.5 kg. Find out on the internet how much each of these is worth.

Electrical conductivity

An electric current in a metal is caused by electrons moving through the metal. This can happen because the outer electrons in the metal atoms easily become detached from the atoms. This means that electrons can move along a wire in a circuit. They move from negative to positive in the circuit because they are negatively charged.

Substance	Conductivity (mho)
Aluminium	3.7×10^7
Copper	5.9×10^7
Nichrome (nickel and chromium)	9.0×10^5
Silver	6.3×10^7
Iron (steel)	1.1×10^7
Silicon	4.3×10^{-4}
Glass	10^{-10} to 10^{-14}

Websites
You can find out everything about gold at the website of the World Gold Council. Go to www.heinemann.co.uk/hotlinks, insert the express code 6799P and click on 9.1.

◀ Table 9.3
Electrical conductivities of various substances.

Table 9.3 shows that some metals are much better conductors than others. Electrical conductivity is measured in a unit called a *mho*. You don't have to know what a mho is to see that some metals are better conductors than others. The good conductors are useful for making electrical wires and components. The filament of an electric fire is made from the metal mixture, nichrome, which has a rather poor conductivity. This means that it has a fairly high resistance and so it gets hot as the current passes through it. Can you think of two reasons why we do not make electric cables out of iron?

> **DID YOU KNOW?**
>
> The elements such as silicon and germanium in the centre of the Periodic Table are known as semi-conductors. As the table shows, they do not conduct as well as metals but they are much better conductors than non-metals. Silicon can be made into a much better conductor by adding tiny amounts of other elements (this process is called 'doping'). It is interesting that doped silicon only conducts electricity well in one direction; it becomes an electrical one way street. Doped silicon is used to make electronic 'chips'.

← force

The layers of atoms can slip past each other.

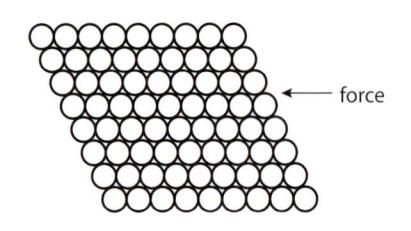

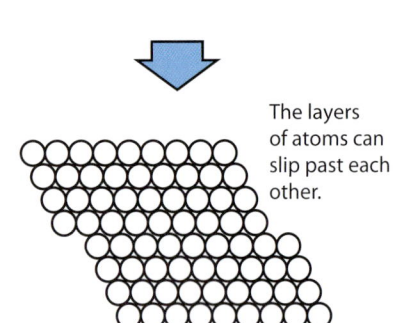

▲ **Figure 9.6**
Metal particles before and after hammering.

▶ **Figure 9.7**
This mask of the Egyptian King Tutankhamun was made 3300 years ago. Why does it look almost new?

Conductivity of heat

Heat is quickly conducted through a solid when the particles are close together. The heat makes the particles vibrate more. The kinetic energy in these vibrating particles is passed on to the next particle easily when the two bump into each other. In a metal this energy can also be transferred by the moving electrons and so metals are the best solid conductors of heat.

Malleability and ductility

The bonds holding the ions together in a crystal of sodium chloride are strong but they are also rigid. The bonds between metal atoms are also strong but not rigid. Because of this, if you hit a crystal of sodium chloride with a hammer it will crush but if you hit a metal with a hammer it will not crush, it will deform. Figure 9.6 shows what happens. The layers of atoms do not move apart, they slide over each other. After they have moved, the close-packed structure is still there. This property is called malleability. Metals are malleable; they can be easily pressed into different shapes without breaking.

Metals can also be stretched into wires when they are warm and soft. The particles in the metal crystals move over each other when this happens in the same way as when metals are pressed into shapes. This property is called ductility; metals are ductile.

It is much easier to hammer a metal into a different shape when it is hot than when it is cold. When the metal is hot, the particles have more energy and are vibrating faster and further away from each other. It is easier for the layers to move over each other when this is happening.

9.2 A pattern of metals – the reactivity series

The reaction of metals with water and oxygen

The mask in Figure 9.7 was made to cover the head of the young King Tutankhamun when he died in Egypt around 3300 years ago, and yet it looks almost new. This is because it is made of gold, and gold does not react with air or water or dilute acids. However, very few metals are unreactive like this. Table 9.4 below shows what happens to some common metals when you heat them in air or put them in water.

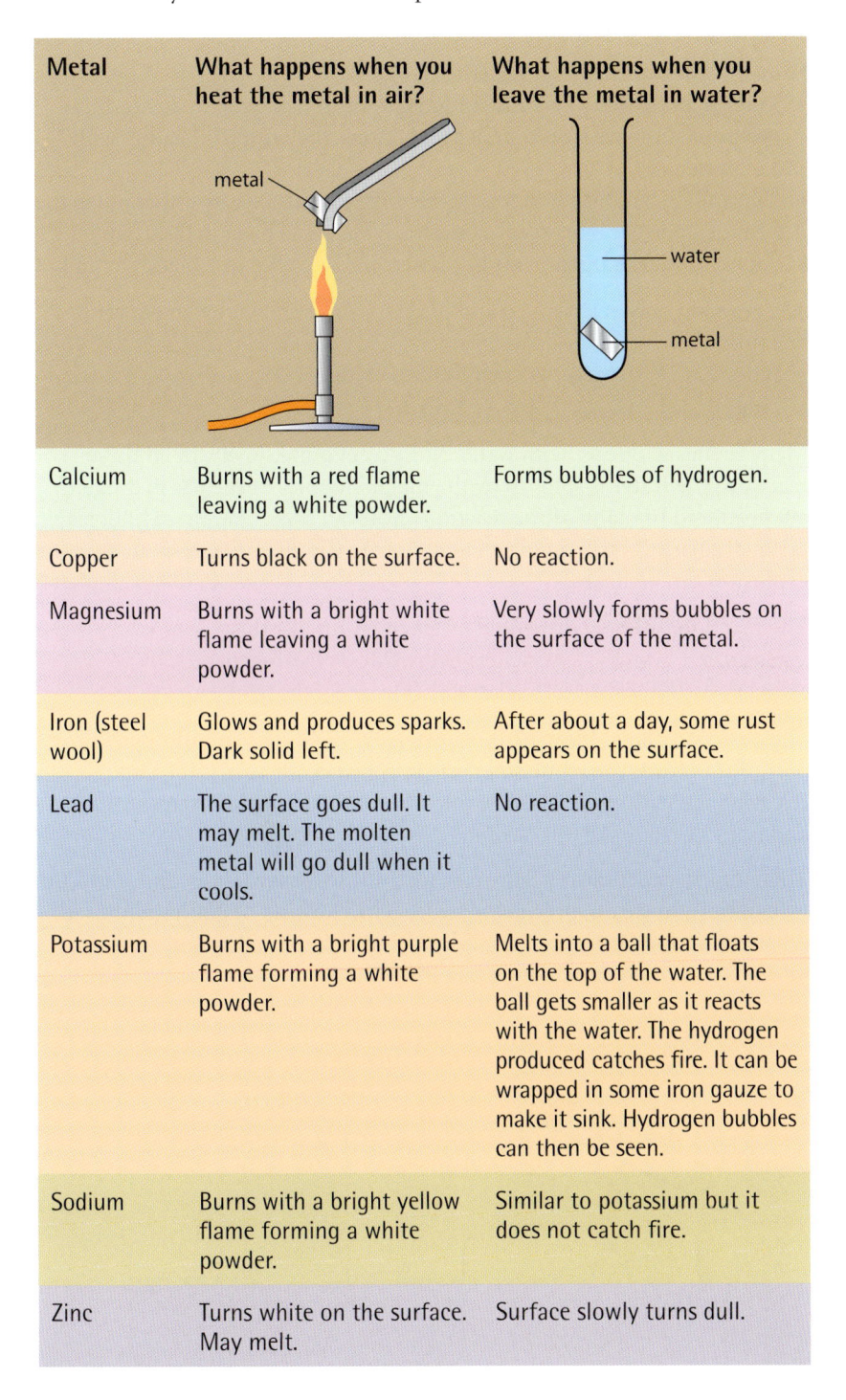

> **Activity 9.1**
> How do metals react with air and oxygen?

> **Activity 9.2**
> How do metals react with water?

◀ Table 9.4
Some chemical reactions of metals.

Metal	What happens when you heat the metal in air?	What happens when you leave the metal in water?
Calcium	Burns with a red flame leaving a white powder.	Forms bubbles of hydrogen.
Copper	Turns black on the surface.	No reaction.
Magnesium	Burns with a bright white flame leaving a white powder.	Very slowly forms bubbles on the surface of the metal.
Iron (steel wool)	Glows and produces sparks. Dark solid left.	After about a day, some rust appears on the surface.
Lead	The surface goes dull. It may melt. The molten metal will go dull when it cools.	No reaction.
Potassium	Burns with a bright purple flame forming a white powder.	Melts into a ball that floats on the top of the water. The ball gets smaller as it reacts with the water. The hydrogen produced catches fire. It can be wrapped in some iron gauze to make it sink. Hydrogen bubbles can then be seen.
Sodium	Burns with a bright yellow flame forming a white powder.	Similar to potassium but it does not catch fire.
Zinc	Turns white on the surface. May melt.	Surface slowly turns dull.

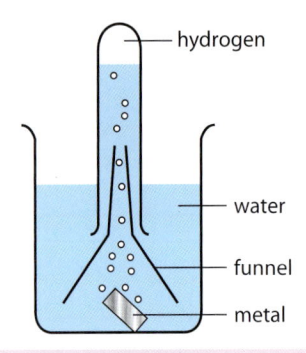

▲ Figure 9.8
Equipment like this can be used to collect any gas produced if the metal reacts with water.

None of the metals in Table 9.4 stay bright like Tutankhamun's mask. Unlike the mask, most metals will tarnish when they are left in air. The surface of the metal gradually becomes dull. This is because the metal slowly reacts with the oxygen in the air and the product is called a metal oxide. Metal oxides are powders and the dull surface is made of tiny particles of these powders. Zinc oxide is a white powder and so the surface of zinc turns from shiny to a greyish white. Copper oxide is black and so copper turns dark when it tarnishes.

Metals react much faster with the air when they are heated. Some, like magnesium and iron wool, burn in air when you put them in the flame.

Some metals react with air faster than others.
- Sodium, potassium, calcium and magnesium will burn in air. Sodium and potassium are stored under oil because they react so readily with the oxygen in the air.
- Aluminium, zinc and iron react easily with air, particularly if they are in the form of a powder or a 'wool'. These three metals all burn in pure oxygen.
- Copper does not burn in air but it becomes covered in a black coating.

The reaction between a metal and oxygen can be shown by an equation like this:

magnesium + oxygen → magnesium oxide
$2Mg(s) + O_2(g) → 2MgO(s)$

Many metals will react with water. Most react quite slowly. In all these reactions the water is split up by the metal. Bubbles of the gas hydrogen are produced in many of the reactions. You can show that these bubbles are hydrogen gas by bringing a flame near to the test tube. A small explosion can be heard.

The reaction can be represented by an equation like this:

calcium + water → calcium hydroxide + hydrogen
$Ca(s) + 2HOH(l) → Ca(OH)_2(s) + H_2(g)$

The equation shows how the metal splits up the water, combining with part of it to form the white solid, calcium hydroxide ($Ca(OH)_2$) and releasing the hydrogen. The formula of water has been written as HOH and not H_2O to make this clearer.

These metals react more vigorously with steam. Magnesium, zinc and iron will all burn in steam, producing hydrogen. The kind of equipment used for this is shown in Figure 9.9. Sodium and potassium explode in steam. Steam is a corrosive and dangerous chemical!

▶ Figure 9.9
When iron wool or magnesium ribbon is heated strongly in steam, in equipment like this, it will burn brightly to form an oxide. Hydrogen is produced and is collected in the gas jar.

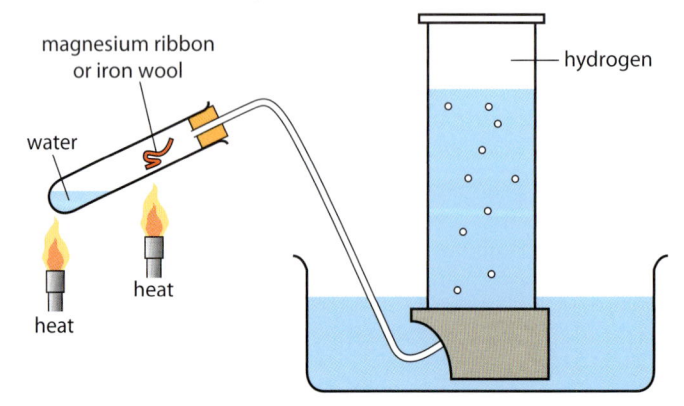

SKILLS QUESTION

9.1 You may have noticed that metals corrode much more if they are near the sea. Steel on ships rusts very quickly and readily. Design an investigation to show if salt water causes metals to rust more than fresh water. Predict what you will expect to happen in your experiment.

The reaction of metals with acids

Dilute acids such as dilute hydrochloric acid contain hydrogen, like water. Acids react more rapidly than water with many metals. For example, magnesium, iron and zinc react very slowly with cold water but they react rapidly with a dilute acid such as dilute hydrochloric acid.

Activity 9.3
How do metals react with dilute acids?

All the metals in Table 9.4, except lead and copper, react with dilute acids. When the metal reacts with the dilute acid, hydrogen is produced. The reaction is **exothermic** which means that heat is produced. The amount of heat that is given off depends on how reactive the metal is. The reaction between metals and acid is very similar to the reaction with water but more vigorous. The reaction of sodium and potassium with acids is dangerous and should not be tried.

The reaction can be represented by an equation like this:
zinc + hydrochloric acid → zinc chloride + hydrogen
$Zn(s)$ + $2HCl(aq)$ → $ZnCl_2(aq)$ + $H_2(g)$

You can see from the equation that the metal replaces the hydrogen in the acid. A new substance is formed, called a **salt**. The salt in this example is zinc chloride.

We can summarise these reactions of common metals with oxygen, water and acids in Table 9.5.

▼ Table 9.5
Metal reactions results table.

Metal	Reaction with oxygen in air	Reaction with cold water	Reaction with steam	Reaction with dilute hydrochloric acid	Symbol
Potassium Sodium	Burns in air on heating to form the metal oxides.	Reacts with cold water to form hydrogen and the metal hydroxide.	Reacts with steam to form hydrogen and the metal oxide.	Violent reaction to give hydrogen.	K Na
Calcium Magnesium				Reacts to form hydrogen and the chloride of the metal.	Ca Mg
Zinc Iron	Does not burn but reacts to form the metal oxide on heating.	Reacts slowly with cold water.			Zn Fe
Lead Copper		Does not react with cold water.	Does not react with steam.	Does not react with dilute acid.	Pb Cu
Silver Gold	No reaction.				Ag Au

potassium
sodium
calcium
magnesium
zinc
iron
lead
copper
silver
gold

most reactive
increasing reactivity
least reactive

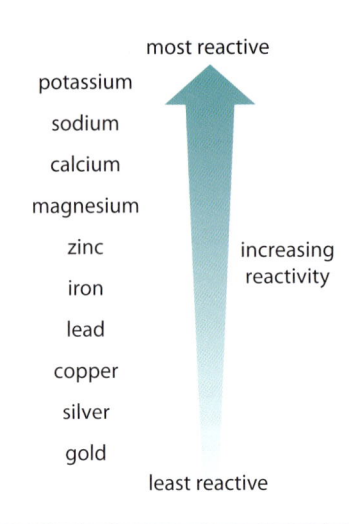

Figure 9.10
The reactivity series.

Table 9.5 shows that for each of these reactions the order of reactivity of the metals is the same. Potassium is the most reactive metal in the table and gold is the least reactive. We call this the **reactivity series** for metals; this series is shown in Figure 9.10.

You can see a pattern in this reactivity series. The most reactive metals are those in Group 1 of the Periodic Table. The next in the series are the Group 2 metals. The transition metals are among the least reactive metals.

Can you also see that in Groups 1 and 2 the reactivity increases down the group? You will remember this from Chapter 6 on the Periodic Table. Where would you place the metal caesium in the reactivity series?

Aluminium has not been included in the series because it is unreactive and yet it is not a transition metal. It does not seem to fit the pattern. We will come back to aluminium later in the chapter.

Something to think about

The metals at the bottom in the table have been known for thousands of years. The ones at the top were not extracted until the nineteenth century. Can you think why this should be so? The answer will be given later in the chapter.

9.3 How readily will a metal form its positive ion?

Look at all the reactions of metals you have studied. In every case when the metal has reacted, it has formed an ionic compound containing the positive ion of the metal. Think of the reaction between zinc and dilute hydrochloric acid.

$$Zn(s) + 2HCl(aq) \rightarrow ZnCl_2(aq) + H_2(g)$$

In this reaction zinc atoms have become zinc ions.

$$Zn \rightarrow Zn^{2+} + 2e^-$$

What has happened to the two electrons? The acid, hydrochloric acid, contains hydrogen ions. The equation shows that two hydrogen ions in the acid change into a hydrogen molecule. Hydrogen ions have no electrons but the hydrogen molecule has two. The two electrons given away by the zinc atom when it became a zinc ion will have been taken by hydrogen ions to make a hydrogen molecule.

$$2H^+ + 2e^- \rightarrow H_2$$

Copper is near the bottom of the reactivity series. It is unreactive. This means that, unlike zinc, copper atoms will not readily give up their electrons to form copper ions. The reactivity series is therefore an order of how readily metals will give up electrons to form ions. This is shown in Figure 9.11.

potassium
sodium
calcium
magnesium
zinc
iron
lead
copper

increasing tendency to form ions

Figure 9.11
Reactivity series showing metal's tendency to form positive ions.

Metals

Metals in competition

What happens when a clean strip of copper is put in a solution containing iron ions? And what happens when some clean iron (such as a nail) is put in a solution containing copper ions? This is shown below:

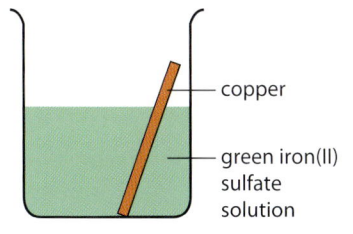

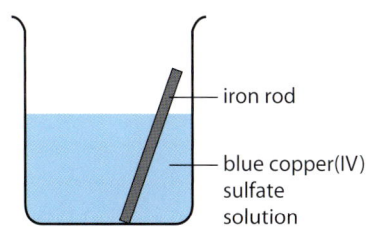

- copper
- green iron(II) sulfate solution

- iron rod
- blue copper(IV) sulfate solution

The copper does not change. The iron sulfate solution does not change.

The iron nail becomes coated in copper which is a reddish-brown colour. The blue copper sulfate solution gradually turns a pale green.

> **Activity 9.4**
> Will metals react with solutions of ions of other metals?

> **Activity 9.5**
> Will metals react with the oxides of other metals?

Iron is higher than copper in the reactivity series. It displaces copper from copper sulfate. Iron atoms in the nail form iron ions by losing two electrons. The copper ions in the solution gain the electrons to become copper. This happens because iron more readily gives up its electrons than copper. Iron and copper compete to form ions and the iron, being more reactive, wins.

The equations show what happens:

$$Cu^{2+} + 2e^- \rightarrow Cu$$
$$Fe \rightarrow Fe^{2+} + 2e^-$$

or, combining them:

$$Cu^{2+} + Fe \rightarrow Cu + Fe^{2+}$$

On the other hand, when you put copper into the solution of iron ions, nothing happens.

$$Cu + Fe^{2+} \rightarrow \text{no reaction}$$

We say that iron will *displace* copper ions from solution but copper will not *displace* iron ions.

We can see metals in competition when we heat one metal in powder form with the oxide of another metal.

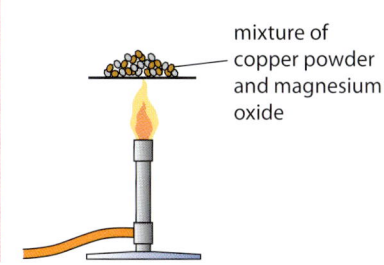

- mixture of copper powder and magnesium oxide

Nothing happens when a mixture of zinc oxide and copper powder is heated.

> **SKILLS QUESTION**
>
> **9.2** Predict what would happen if you put some strips of the following metals in a solution of zinc sulfate?
> copper
> iron
> magnesium
> Plan an investigation to test your prediction and explain the results.

117

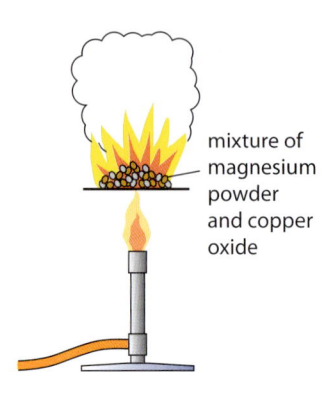

When a mixture of copper oxide and zinc powder is heated there is a bright flash and much white smoke is seen.

mixture of magnesium powder and copper oxide

A mixture of powdered zinc and copper oxide will react quite vigorously. The reaction will leave behind some lumps of copper that was molten during the reaction. The white smoke produced is zinc oxide. Zinc is more reactive than copper and will *displace* copper from copper oxide.

Can you see the pattern? It is the same as before. When the metal used in this reaction is higher in the reactivity series than the metal in the oxide, there will be a reaction, but when it is lower, nothing happens. A reactive metal will displace a less reactive metal from its oxide. This can be shown using equations like this:

zinc + copper oxide → zinc oxide + copper
Zn + CuO → ZnO + Cu

But

Cu + ZnO → no reaction

The ionic equation showing what happens to the metals is:

$Zn + Cu^{2+} → Zn^{2+} + Cu$

The zinc is more reactive than the copper, which means that it gives up its electrons more readily than copper. It will give the electrons to a copper ion, which forms a copper atom.

DID YOU KNOW?

A form of this oxide displacement reaction, using aluminium powder and iron oxide, was once used for welding tramlines in the days before portable oxy-acetylene torches. The lump of molten iron produced welded the lines. The mixture was called the 'thermit' mixture.

9.4 How stable are metal compounds?

Some metal compounds are very stable but others are easily decomposed by heat. We call this kind of reaction **thermal decomposition**.

The thermal decomposition of metal carbonates

Heating calcium carbonate (limestone) to make lime may be one of the earliest chemical reactions deliberately carried out by humans to make a product. Lime was made and used in building by ancient civilisations as long as 7000 years ago in many different parts of the world. In fact, many archaeologists blame the lime industry for destroying ancient forests in places as far apart as Mexico, where the Mayan people made lime, and Egypt, where it was also made at the time the pyramids were built.

Heating calcium carbonate to about 800 °C to 1000 °C causes it to decompose into calcium oxide and carbon dioxide. Calcium oxide is commonly known as quicklime. The equation for this reaction is:

calcium carbonate → calcium oxide + carbon dioxide
$CaCO_3(s)$ → $CaO(s)$ + $CO_2(g)$

All carbonates decompose when they are heated except for carbonates of metals like sodium and potassium at the top of the reactivity series.

The thermal decomposition of nitrates

All nitrates decompose when they are heated but they do not all decompose in the same way.

Most nitrates break down, like carbonates, into the metal oxides. Two gases are given off, nitrogen dioxide and oxygen. This is shown by the equation for the decomposition of copper nitrate when it is heated:

copper nitrate → copper oxide + nitrogen dioxide + oxygen
$2Cu(NO_3)_2(s)$ → $2CuO(s)$ + $4NO_2(g)$ + $O_2(g)$

Copper nitrate is blue; the copper oxide that remains behind is black. Nitrogen dioxide is a brown poisonous gas. It can readily be seen when the nitrates are heated.

The nitrates of the most reactive metals such as sodium and potassium decompose in a different way; they do not give off the nitrogen dioxide, only oxygen is produced:

sodium nitrate → sodium nitrite + oxygen
$NaNO_3(s)$ → $NaNO_2(s)$ + $O_2(g)$

Sodium nitrate and sodium nitrite are both white and oxygen is a colourless gas that cannot be seen. It is difficult to see that a reaction is taking place. We can detect oxygen in the heated test tube using a glowing splint. Light the splint. Blow it out so that it is glowing. Put it in the gas. If the spill relights, the gas is oxygen. This is shown in Figure 9.12.

Activity 9.6
Heating metal compounds

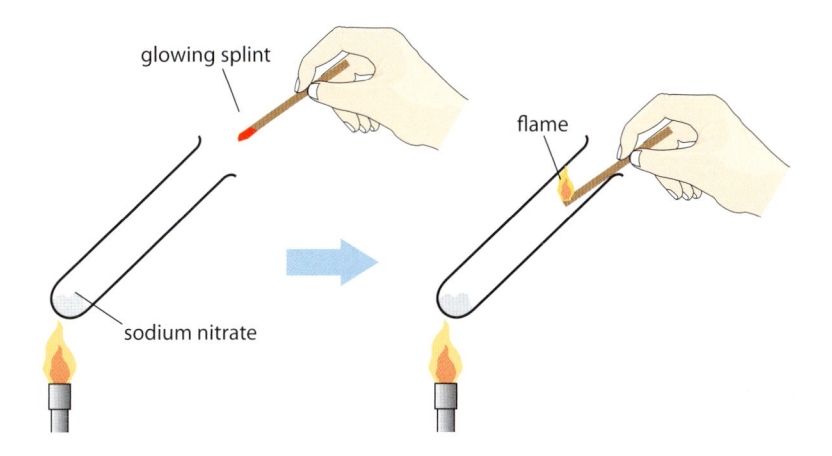

◀ **Figure 9.12**
Heating sodium nitrate and testing for oxygen.

The thermal decomposition of hydroxides

Most metal hydroxides decompose when they are heated. They decompose to give off water and leave the oxide.

zinc hydroxide → zinc oxide + water
$Zn(OH)_2(s)$ → $ZnO(s)$ + $H_2O(g)$

All hydroxides decompose like this, except the hydroxides of sodium and potassium at the top of the reactivity series.

In all these examples of decomposition, the further down the reactivity series the metal is, the more easily it decomposes when heated. Table 9.6 below summarises these reactions.

▶ Table 9.6 The decomposition of some metal compounds.

	Group I metals	Group II metals	Transition metals
Nitrates	Decompose to nitrite and oxygen.	Decompose to oxide, nitrogen dioxide and oxygen.	Decompose easily to oxide, nitrogen dioxide and oxygen.
Hydroxides	No effect on heating.	Decompose to oxide and water.	Decompose easily to oxide and water.
Carbonates	No effect on heating.	Decompose when heated to around 1000 °C to the oxide and carbon dioxide.	Decompose quite easily on heating to the oxide and carbon dioxide.

9.5 The names of some chemical compounds

Some of the substances you will meet in this book have more than one name. One name is the correct name that has been decided internationally and the other is an older name that we still like to use because it is familiar and easier to remember. For example, we are familiar with the name **acetic acid** (vinegar) but the correct name for what you put on your fish and chips is dilute **ethanoic acid**.

The correct name for nitrogen dioxide is nitrogen(IV) oxide. The correct name for nitrate salts such as copper nitrate is copper(IV) nitrate. The correct name for nitrites like potassium nitr**i**te (with an 'i') is potassium nitr**a**te(III) (with an 'a'). Remember that the roman number is known as the **oxidation number** - which you studied in Chapter 8.

The common names are still widely used but you should also know the correct names so that if you see a compound called, for example, potassium manganate(VII) you will know that it is really just potassium permanganate.

9.6 Corrosion and its prevention

Figure 9.13
This Chevrolet Cabriolet was made in 1941. Nobody knows how long it has been in this remote part of Damaraland in Namibia, or how it got there. But why has it corroded? And why, after such a long time, has it not corroded very much?

Metals left around in air often become dull. Steel very often rusts. These processes are examples of corrosion. Corrosion of metals is an extremely expensive problem all over the world. Much thought, time, effort, and money is spent each year trying to prevent it.

SKILLS QUESTION

9.3 What makes iron and steel rust? Design an investigation to find out what makes steel rust. Think about how to make your investigation fair. List all the variables you can think of and decide what will be your independent variable, what you will measure and what variables you will control. You will have to do several experiments using different independent variables.

To start your thinking, here is a list of possible variables:
- the size and shape of the steel object used (small steel nails are cheap and have the same shape)
- how clean the surface of the object is (nails are often coated with a little oil)
- the temperature of the object
- whether the object is in contact with water, water vapour or seawater
- whether the object is in contact with air (remember that water contains dissolved air).

What do you think causes rusting of steel? Make predictions about the results of your investigations based on your ideas. Carry out the investigations to test your predictions.

What happens when metals corrode?

When metals corrode they react with oxygen to form the metal oxide.

Corrosion of metals is often worse when the metal is wet and particularly when the water is salty. This is because corrosion is an ionic process. Ionic reactions take place more readily in water than in air because the ions can move around in the water. The ions in salt water can help the corrosion process go faster. We say that corrosion is an **electrolytic** process. You studied electrolysis in Chapter 8.

Rusting is the name given to the corrosion of iron. Rusting needs both oxygen (from the air) and water to take place. It takes place fast in salty water. The 1941 Chevrolet in Figure 9.13 has been there for many years. Although it has rusted, there is still quite a lot of steel still there because Damaraland is on the edge of the Namib Desert and the rainfall is low. Most of the time it is very dry.

Preventing corrosion

There are two ways of preventing corrosion. The first is to prevent water and air getting to the metal by covering it with something such as paint or oil. The second method is to attach the metal to another that is more reactive. In this case the more reactive metal corrodes first. This is called 'sacrificial' protection, because the second metal is **sacrificed** (used up first) to protect the first one. An example of sacrificial protection is galvanised iron, which is iron coated with zinc. The zinc corrodes before the iron does.

Table 9.7 shows examples of the prevention of corrosion by different methods.

▶ **Activity 9.7**
What causes corrosion?

▶ **Table 9.7**
Ways of preventing corrosion.

Metal object	Method of preventing corrosion	Advantages of using this method
Car bodies	Paint	Easily applied, looks attractive.
Bicycle chain	Oil	Protects moving parts – other coatings will wear off.
Iron roofing	Galvanising. The sheet is coated with a layer of zinc which corrodes away first.	Long-lasting, easy to apply.
Food can	Tin plating. Steel is coated with a layer of tin.	Tin does not corrode easily and is not poisonous.
Silver plated cutlery	Silver electroplating (see Chapter 8).	The coating is very attractive, even and hardwearing.

SKILLS QUESTION

9.4 How effective are the ways of preventing corrosion in Table 9.7? Design an investigation to find out. Choose your independent variable and what you will measure. Control all other variables. You may have to do several investigations.

QUESTIONS

9.5 Explain the words 'ductile' and 'malleable'.

9.6 You are given a sample of an element you have never heard of before. Describe three tests you could do to find out if it is a metal or a non-metal.

9.7 Explain why metals are good conductors of electricity and have high densities and high melting points.

9.8 Mercury is an unusual metal because it is a liquid at room temperature. Explain why it is particularly useful
   a) in thermometers
   b) for making electrical switches for high voltages, where sparking could easily occur.

9.9 Explain how metals can conduct electricity.

9.10 Metals that conduct electricity well usually also conduct heat well. Explain why this is so.

9.11 Explain what is meant by the *reactivity series of metals*.

9.12 Titanium is a metal that reacts quite rapidly with acids but hardly at all with water or steam. Explain where you would place titanium on the reactivity series.

9.13 a) Look at the reactivity series. Then look at the Periodic Table. Can you see any connection between the two?
   b) Barium is low down in Group II. Place it on the reactivity series. Give reasons for the place you have given it.
   c) Describe two experiments you could do with barium to find out whether you have put it in the correct place. State your predictions for the results of the experiments.

9.14 If some zinc is placed in a solution of manganese sulfate there is a reaction and manganese metal is produced. If manganese is placed in a solution of iron(II) sulfate, iron is produced. State where you would place manganese on the reactivity series. Explain your answer.

9.15 Describe what you would expect to see if you put some copper in silver nitrate solution. Describe what would happen to the colour of the solution. Explain your answers.

9.16 Nickel is just above copper in the reactivity series, whereas scandium is just below magnesium. Describe what you would expect to see if you heated the nitrates and the hydroxides of scandium and nickel.

9.17 Predict what you would see if you did the following investigations. Explain your predictions and write ionic equations for the reactions.
   a) Place strips of zinc in solutions of aluminium nitrate, copper nitrate, silver nitrate, sodium nitrate.
   b) Zirconium, element 40, is a transition metal on the left of the Periodic Table. Explain where you think it may be found on the reactivity series. Predict what might happen if you placed some pieces of zirconium in i) copper sulfate solution and ii) magnesium sulfate solution. Write ionic equations for these, given that zirconium forms the ion Zr^{2+}.

9.18 Describe how the following steel articles are treated to prevent them from rusting. In each case describe why this method is the best one for the article.
   a) a bicycle chain
   b) a car body
   c) a steel kettle
   d) a corrugated iron roof
   e) a food can

9.19 Galvanising is one way to stop iron rusting. This is known as 'cathodic protection'. Explain how it works.

9.20 Explain why cars near coasts rust much more than when they are kept inland.

Summary

Now that you have completed this chapter, you should be able to:

- list the physical properties of metals and know where they are found in the Periodic Table
- describe how metal atoms are held together by metallic bonds and show how this type of bonding can explain the typical properties of metals
- know that metals vary greatly in their reactivity and can be arranged in a reactivity series, with the most reactive metals at the top and the least reactive ones at the bottom
- explain, in terms of the reactivity series, how different metals react with air, water and acids
- explain the reactivity series in terms of the ease with which metal atoms form ions
- show how the thermal stability of metal nitrates and hydroxides depend on the position of the metal in the reactivity series
- list the different applications of metals
- explain how and why metals corrode and list different ways of preventing corrosion.

Chapter 10

Chemistry and energy

The engine designed by Brunel that took the SS Great Britain across the Atlantic got its energy from a chemical reaction. It burnt around 800 tonnes of coal in the two-week crossing and the heat made steam to drive the steam engine. The steam engine drove a steel crankshaft shaft 70 cm in diameter and this turned the 4 tonne propeller. The engine turned at a maximum of 20 revolutions per minute. Only about 12% of the energy in the coal was used to turn the propeller; the rest was lost as heat which went up the funnel.

▲ Figure 10.1
(a) Artist's impression of the SS Great Britain at sea. (b) This is part of the four-cylinder steam engine designed to power the SS Great Britain, the first iron-hull steam-powered ship designed by the engineer Isambard Kingdom Brunel. It was launched in 1843. The engine weighed 300 tonnes. Its energy came from burning coal.

▲ Figure 10.2
Some of these cells are so small they can be used to power hearing aids that are small enough to fit inside the ear. Their energy comes from a chemical reaction in which the metal cobalt reacts with oxygen.

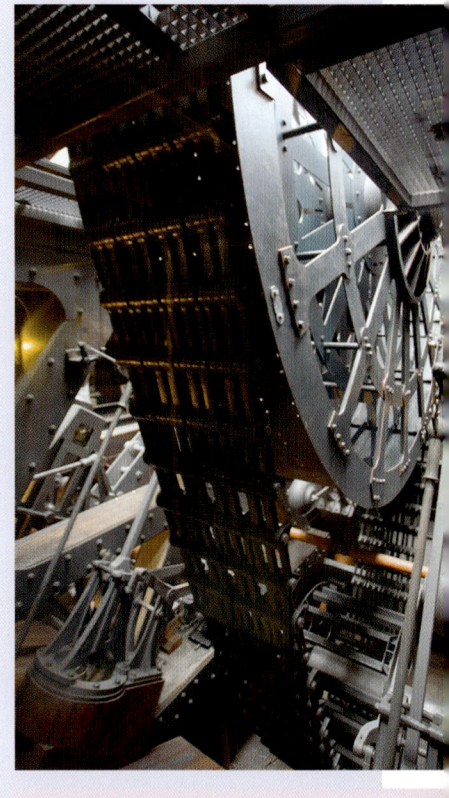

125

Hearing aid batteries will power a hearing aid for about a week and weigh about one gram. They get their energy from a chemical reaction between cobalt (or zinc) and oxygen.

The Brunel engine produced one joule of energy for every half kilogram of its weight (and that does not include its coal!). The hearing aid battery produces one joule of energy for every milligram of its weight.

10.1 Conservation of energy

Driving a car, riding a bicycle, keeping warm, cooking food, listening to a radio: all these activities need energy from chemical reactions to keep them going. So do you. Without energy from the food you eat, you could not use your muscles and your heart could not beat.

Coal is a fuel that is mainly carbon and it burns easily to form carbon dioxide. The energy in coal was used to take people across the Atlantic Ocean in the SS Great Britain in two weeks. Now we use energy from oil to get us across the Atlantic in just a few hours. Electricity is a particularly useful form of energy that we can obtain directly from chemical reactions, such as the reactions that happen inside a battery.

Activity 10.1
Studying some energy changes

You will have learnt from physics that we cannot create energy and we do not use energy up. All we can do is to change it from one form to another. This is known as the *Law of Conservation of Energy*. This chapter is about chemical energy and how we can make use of it by converting it into other forms of energy.

10.2 Energy changes during chemical reactions

All chemical reactions involve energy changes. The diagrams show three chemical reactions that involve energy changes of different kinds.

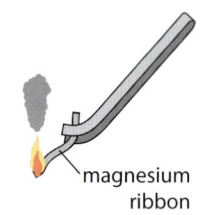

Magnesium burns to produce heat and light energy.

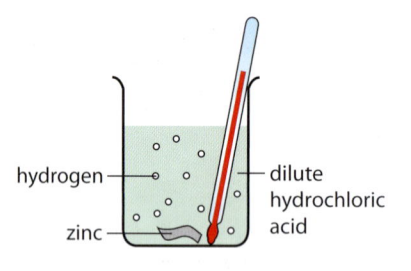

Zinc reacts with dilute hydrochloric acid. The temperature goes up.

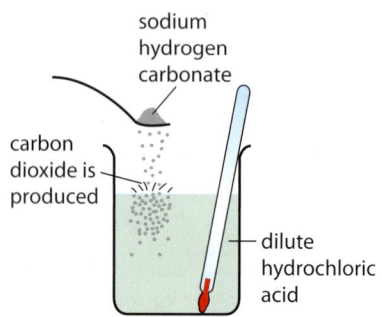

Sodium hydrogen carbonate reacts with dilute hydrochloric acid. The temperature goes down.

In the first reaction, energy is produced in the form of heat and light when magnesium burns. In the second reaction, heat energy is produced as the zinc reacts and the temperature of the solution goes up. In the third reaction, the solution cools down because heat energy is taken in during the reaction.

We call a reaction that gives off energy an **exothermic** reaction. We call a reaction that takes in energy an **endothermic** reaction.

A change in energy, either an endothermic change or an exothermic one, is the sign that a chemical reaction has taken place. Whenever a chemical reaction happens there is an energy change. Most chemical reactions are exothermic. Reactions that involve the breakdown of a compound to produce gases are quite often endothermic; this is because a lot of energy is given to the gas molecules to make them move apart from each other.

Where does the energy in a chemical reaction come from?

Energy is stored in the electrons that make up the bonds between atoms. We call this *chemical energy*. When a chemical reaction happens, these electrons move to make more stable bonds that have less energy stored in them. This stored energy is rather like the stored energy – called *potential energy* – of an object on a table. The object can fall to the floor. When it falls, it loses some of its potential energy, which is changed into energy of movement (kinetic energy). Electrons in an atom can move to a position of lower potential energy during a chemical reaction. When they do, the chemical potential energy that is lost appears as other forms of energy such as heat.

We can show this in a graphical form for a reaction. Think about the reaction where magnesium is burnt in air to form magnesium oxide:

magnesium + oxygen → magnesium oxide
$2Mg(s) + O_2(g) → 2MgO(s)$

◀ **Figure 10.3**
Energy changes in the reaction of magnesium with oxygen.

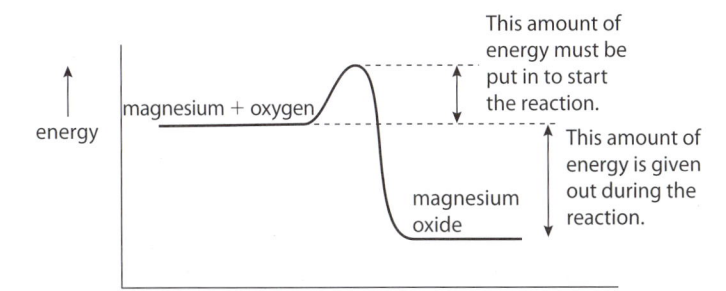

The amount of energy stored in the magnesium and oxygen before the reaction is shown by the line on the left. This is higher than the line on the right, which shows the energy stored in the magnesium oxide. The difference between the two lines shows the energy given out when the magnesium burns.

Magnesium does not burn by itself; a small amount of energy from a flame has to be given to it to start it off. This amount is shown by the hump between the two lines and this is called the **activation energy**.

Energy changes when bonds break and form

Think more about this reaction between magnesium and oxygen:

$2Mg(s) + O_2(g) \rightarrow 2MgO(s)$

What must happen to the bonds in the magnesium and the oxygen when the reaction takes place?

1. The metallic bonds holding the two magnesium atoms to other magnesium atoms must break.
2. The covalent bond between the two oxygen atoms in the molecule must break.
3. The two ions, the magnesium ion and the oxide ion, must form.
4. The ions must come together in the form of a crystal lattice.

The first two of these processes involve the **breaking** of bonds. When bonds are broken and atoms are pulled apart, energy is needed. So in processes 1 and 2, energy is taken in.

Processes 3 and 4 involve the **formation** of an ionic bond in a crystal. When ionic bonds are formed and atoms form ions which come together, energy is given out. In this reaction, the amount of energy given out in processes 3 and 4 is greater than the amount needed to make the first two steps happen. This means that over all four steps, energy is given out.

▼ **Figure 10.4**
Marshmallow chemistry. There are two chemical reactions going on here. The firewood burning is exothermic. The cooking of marshmallows is also exothermic. When the marshmallows are eaten, another exothermic reaction will happen inside the bodies.

Energy in food

We get our energy from the food we eat. In our body, chemical reactions break this food down and the energy is released. Food is made out of molecules that contain carbon. The logs in the fire also contain carbon. Carbon changes to carbon dioxide when the wood burns. This reaction is exothermic. The energy in the food is not released all at once like the energy in the firewood; if it were, we would all explode into flames after a meal! The energy is given out in a number of small steps in amounts small enough for the muscles to use. The carbon in the food, like the carbon in the logs, changes to carbon dioxide, which we then breathe out.

Some foods contain much more useful energy in the chemical bonds than others. This is shown in Table 10.1. The unit of energy is the joule (J) but this is rather small, so we usually measure food energy in kilojoules (kJ).

Chemistry and energy

High-energy foods	kJ/100g	Low-energy foods	kJ/100g
Most fats	>3000	Most raw vegetables	<100
Sweet biscuits	2000	Most fresh fruit	<200
Hard cheeses	1500	Boiled rice	500
Most pasta	1500	Eggs	650
Roast meat	>1000	Most bread	<1000

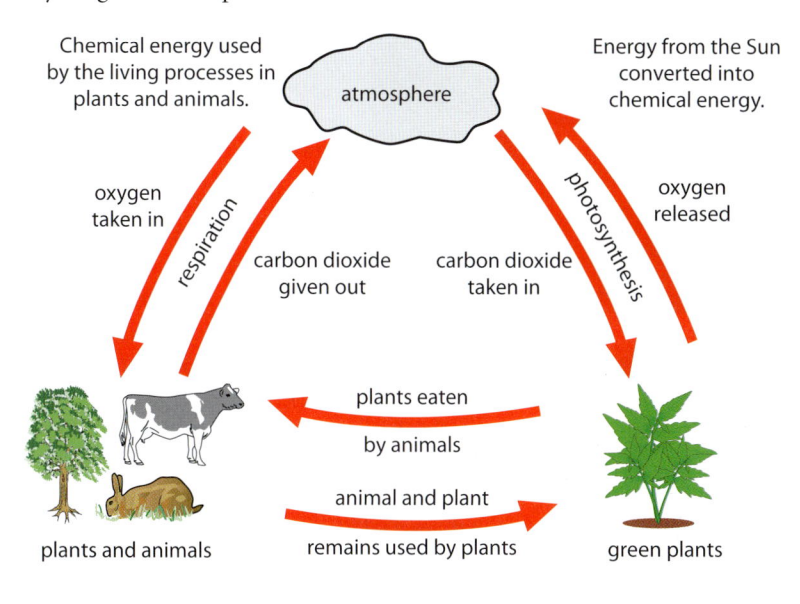

◀ Table 10.1
Energy in food.

The energy used by our muscles comes from glucose. The glucose is produced when the food we eat is digested. It is taken to the muscles by the blood and there it reacts with oxygen. The products are carbon dioxide and water, and the reaction produces a lot of energy. This reaction that happens in our muscles is called **respiration**.

glucose + oxygen → carbon dioxide + water + *energy*

Where did the energy in food come from?

The energy in food came from plants. The energy in plants originally came from the Sun. The green plants, which we eat to obtain glucose, made the glucose originally from carbon dioxide in the air and water from the ground. This reaction is endothermic, taking in light energy from the Sun. It is a very important reaction and is called **photosynthesis**. This reaction is the reverse of the respiration reaction in our muscles. Compare this equation for photosynthesis with the one above for respiration.

carbon dioxide + water + *energy* → glucose + oxygen

The two reactions, respiration and photosynthesis, together form a **cycle** in nature. Green plants take up carbon dioxide and turn it into other molecules that contain carbon; all living things get their energy from respiration. In respiration, these carbon molecules are turned back into carbon dioxide. The carbon cycle is shown in Figure 10.5 and you will study it again in Chapter 12.

DID YOU KNOW?

The process of breaking down food starts with the cooking. This means that energy is given out during cooking; cooking is exothermic. This may surprise you because you usually put energy into cooking. However, if you start cooking a stew in a pot and then you take it off the stove and put it into a well-insulated box, it will continue to cook with no extra heat. In the past, a box like this was used quite often. It was called a 'haybox' because the insulating material was hay.

◀ Figure 10.5
The carbon cycle.

129

10.3 Fuels

The SS Great Britain in the 1840s used 800 tonnes of fuel to cross the Atlantic, carrying about 250 people (plus several cows and sheep and many chickens to keep the passengers fed) in two weeks. An airliner 170 years later can do the same journey carrying 400 people in about 6 hours using about 80 tonnes of fuel (and does not need to carry cows and chickens!). What are these fuels, where do they come from, and what happens to them when they are used?

All our common fuels contain the element carbon. We can classify them into two groups, **renewable** fuels and **non-renewable** fuels.

The renewable fuels come from living things – after we have used them we can replace them by growing more. The non-renewable fuels were made over 150 million years ago, when living things died and their remains decayed in the absence of air.

Fuels from the Carboniferous age

Around 200–300 million years ago, in what is now called the **Carboniferous age**, the world was a very different place from what we see today. There were no humans – we have only existed for a few million years. The plants then were unlike the kinds we see around today; they were more like giant ferns. Much of the land was swampy, the climate was hot and the air was damp. The ferns were huge, much bigger than most of the trees we have today.

▼ Figure 10.6
Carboniferous period environment.

When this vegetation died it fell into the swampy water where there was very little oxygen. The lack of oxygen prevented the vegetation from decomposing completely. Instead it was gradually compressed at the bottom of the swamps. Later, more soils were deposited on top of the vegetation and under the great pressures of the layers above, it gradually turned into coal.

At the same time, in the warm seas, small shellfish lived and died and their remains fell to the sea bottom. The same thing happened to their remains, but instead of forming coal, they changed into oil and gas. Oil and gas can often escape though rocks, as many rocks are porous (which means that they have small holes in them that liquids and gases can get through). One rock that is not porous, however, is rock salt and this was formed when ancient seas dried up. If the rock salt formed on top of the oil and gas deposits, it trapped them and we can now use them.

Chemistry and energy

We call these fuels **fossil fuels** because, like fossils, they are the remains of once-living things. It is important to realise that our climate today is very different from, the carboniferous age and so the plants and animals are very different. Fossil fuels are not being made today from living things and so these fuels are non-renewable. Once we have used them, they are gone for ever.

The fuels we use

Figure 10.7
World energy use 1972–2005 (from 'Key World Energy Statistics, International Energy Agency, 2007).
*MTOE: million tonnes oil equivalent i.e. amount of energy obtained from one million tonnes of oil.

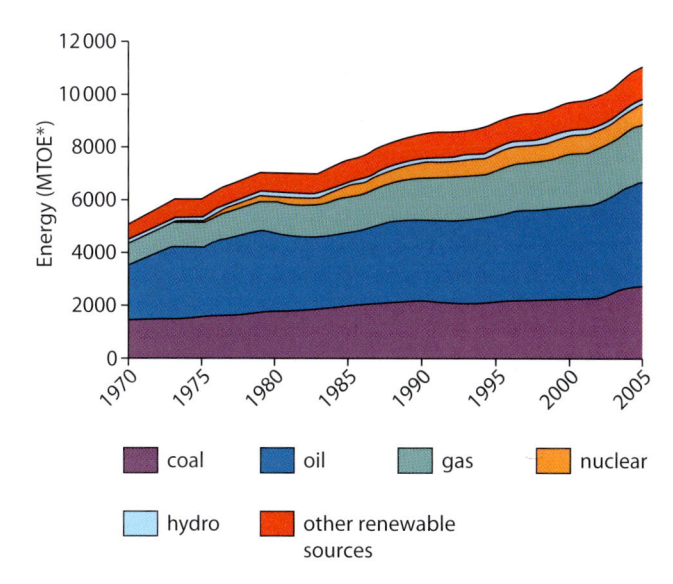

Figure 10.7 shows how our use of different fuels has increased over the last 40 years. It shows that fossil fuels account for most of the energy we use. Almost all the energy that is called 'renewable' comes from burning wood and also from burning rubbish. Hardly any of our energy comes from sources like solar power and wind power. So one chemical reaction, the burning of chemicals that containing carbon, gives us almost all of our energy.

There are a number of different chemicals that are used as fuels and some of these are shown in Table 10.2. All except hydrogen contain carbon. Coal and coke are impure forms of carbon. Ethanol contains carbon, hydrogen and oxygen. All the other fuels are **hydrocarbons**, which means they are molecules made from the two elements hydrogen and carbon

State	Renewable fuels	Non-renewable fuels
Solid fuel	Wood	Coal Coke (made from coal)
Liquid fuel	Ethanol	Petrol Diesel oil Kerosene (paraffin) – used by aircraft
Gas fuel	Hydrogen	Natural gas (methane) 'Bottled' gas (butane and propane)

Table 10.2 Fuels

Carbon burns to produce carbon dioxide. Hydrocarbons burn to produce carbon dioxide and water vapour. A typical reaction is the burning of the hydrocarbon propane, a gas that is used for cars in many countries. The reaction is very exothermic. You will learn in Chapter 12 that we are now burning so much fuel that we are polluting the atmosphere with too much carbon dioxide and this is affecting our climate.

propane + oxygen → carbon dioxide + water + energy
$C_3H_8(g) + 5O_2(g) → 3CO_2(g) + 4H_2O(g)$

It is easy to show that carbon dioxide and water are produced when hydrocarbons burn, by collecting the gas that is produced by the flame and testing it. This is shown in the flow diagram below. Remember that the test for carbon dioxide is that it will turn fresh limewater a milky colour. The water that is produced by these reactions will appear as condensation. How do you know it is water?

There are two tests for water. Remember that blue copper sulfate contains water and that when it is heated this water is driven off and the copper sulfate turns white. We can use this white (**anhydrous**) copper sulfate to test for water; when we add a drop of water to it, it will turn to blue **hydrated** copper sulfate.

An alternative is to use blue cobalt chloride paper. If you touch water with it, it turns pink. You can turn it blue again by warming it. The paper has cobalt chloride in it and this changes colour like copper sulfate; *anhydrous* cobalt chloride is blue and *hydrated* cobalt chloride is pink.

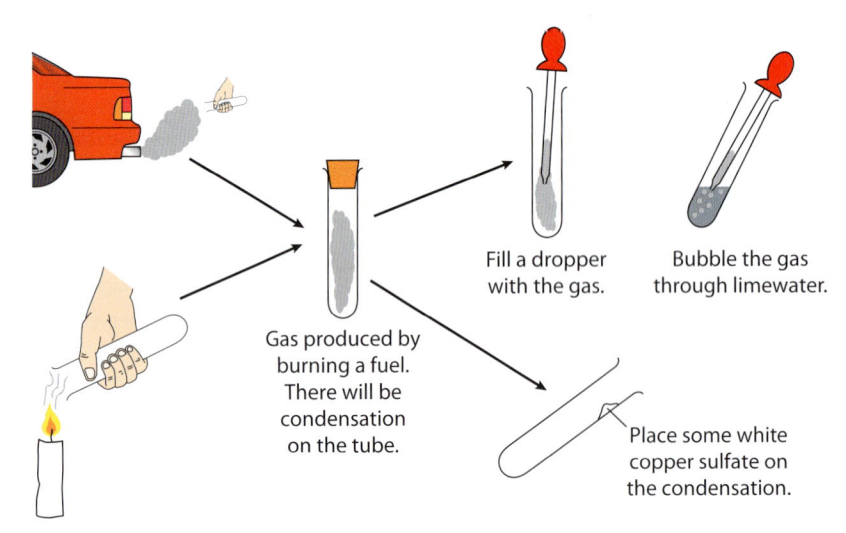

> **Activity 10.2**
> What are the products when fuels burn?

▶ **Figure 10.8**
Identifying the products of burning. Flow chart showing collection of gas from a car exhaust and a burning candle and testing for carbon dioxide with limewater and for water with white copper sulfate.

Coal

Coal is mainly carbon but it also contains a lot of compounds of carbon. Many of these compounds are useful chemicals and so they are often removed from the coal by heating it in the absence of air. When this happens, the chemicals distil off. The solid that is left behind is coke. Coke, unlike coal, burns without much smoke and it burns at a higher temperature than coal. This means that coke is more useful to industry and causes less pollution than coal.

Although coal is quite cheap to extract and is very plentiful in many parts of the world, it is expensive to use. Coal cannot be transported by pumping it along pipes. Instead it has to be transported by train and lorry, which is very expensive. It is also much more difficult to control in a furnace than oil and gas, which can be easily switched on and off using taps. It is therefore used mainly in very large-scale furnaces, such as large power stations and blast furnaces. These large furnaces are made to run continuously because it is very difficult and wasteful to relight coal furnaces often.

Coal can quite easily be turned into a gas fuel and in some parts of the world, such as South Africa, coal is also made into diesel fuel. As the world gradually uses up its supplies of oil, these processes will become more important.

Crude oil

Crude oil – its correct name is **petroleum**, which means 'liquid stone' – is a mixture of hydrocarbons. Hydrocarbons are compounds made from the two elements, hydrogen and carbon.

Crude oil is **refined** to give us many very useful substances. This process will be described in Chapter 13. The fuels we get from oil are particularly useful for transport as they can easily be carried around and, being liquid, are easily carried through pipes and burnt in different types of engines.

Natural gas

When we talk of natural gas we mean methane gas. Methane was formed in the same way as oil was between 150 million and 300 million years ago. It is the simplest hydrocarbon, having only one atom of carbon in its molecule, CH_4. It is present in gas fields in a number of places in the world. In many countries it is pumped directly to industry and to houses through a long network of pipes in the same way as water is delivered to homes.

Incomplete burning of hydrocarbons

Very often, when fuels burn, not enough oxygen can get to the flame to burn the hydrocarbon completely. When this happens, carbon monoxide (CO) is one of the products and sometimes unburned carbon (C) is produced. You will probably have seen unburned carbon coming from diesel vehicles, particularly if they are old. The unburned carbon appears as a black smoke.

Carbon monoxide is a dangerous gas because it has no colour or smell, and it is poisonous. Whenever you see a yellow flame when fuels are burnt you can be sure that some carbon monoxide is being produced, because when fuels burn completely, the flame is blue. Sometimes when people light a heater inside at night the carbon monoxide cannot escape and it can kill people. Heaters that burn fuels should only be used where there is good ventilation.

10.4 Sustainable fuel supplies

Our supplies of coal, oil and gas will eventually be used up. This is predicted to happen for oil within the next few decades. It is important that we use more and more sources of energy that are renewable.

DID YOU KNOW?

Scientists are working on ways to convert coal into gas underground so that it will not have to be mined. This will allow us to use small seams of coal or seams that are dangerous to mine because of weaknesses in the surrounding rocks.

DID YOU KNOW?

You can find a process similar to the production of oil happening on a very small scale today. Poke around with a stick in the muddy bottom of a pond or marsh. You may see bubbles coming up out of the mud. These bubbles are the hydrocarbon gas, methane, which is sometimes called 'marsh gas'.

Something that is **sustainable** is something that can be kept going indefinitely. If we use renewable energy resources it means that our supply of fuel is sustainable.

Renewable energy sources often come indirectly from the Sun. We can generate electricity from hydroelectric schemes, which use the potential energy of water. The water was given this energy by the Sun. We can also use plant matter such as wood as a source of energy. The energy in the plants originally came from the Sun and was converted into chemical energy in the plant during the process of photosynthesis.

Wood is a renewable source of energy. In most parts of the world it is the main source of energy in the home. It is only renewable, however, if new trees are allowed to grow, or planted, to replace the ones used. In many places this is not happening. In these places the people will gradually run short of the energy they need to live.

Ethanol (alcohol) is another renewable energy source. It is commonly available throughout the world as methylated spirits. It can be made from plant matter by fermentation. This is a process that uses the micro-organism, yeast, to convert sugars into ethanol. Sugars are available naturally in many plants and can be made from cellulose, the material that all plants are made of. You will study this further in Chapter 14.

▶ Figure 10.9
This is a new ethanol plant in North America. It converts maize grain into ethanol by fermentation. The ethanol is then used as a fuel instead of petrol.

Ethanol has the formula C_2H_5OH. When it burns, carbon dioxide and water vapour are produced.

ethanol + oxygen → carbon dioxide + water + *energy*
$C_2H_5OH(l) + 3O_2(g) \rightarrow 2CO_2(g) + 3H_2O(g)$

Hydrogen is a possible fuel of the future. It can be made from water using electricity (Section 8.5). When it burns, the only product is water vapour and so it does not cause pollution.

hydrogen + oxygen → water + *energy*
$2H_2(g) + O_2(g) \rightarrow H_2O(g)$

Chemistry and energy

Hydrogen can be used by car engines without a major modification in the design. Hydrogen is the lightest gas and was once widely used to keep large airships aloft before the days of passenger aircraft. The main problem with hydrogen is that it can be dangerously explosive as the picture shows. Scientists are working on ways of storing and using it safely.

▶ **Figure 10.10**
The airship Hindenburg showed how explosive hydrogen is. It was filled with hydrogen, which burned very quickly after the varnish on the skin of the airship caught fire from a static electricity spark when it earthed itself on its mooring mast.

Case study: Drax power station
Making electricity; how can we use more renewable sources and make less pollution?

Drax power station is one of the largest in the world. It has six generator units each supplying 660 MW of electricity making a total output of around 4000 MW. This is almost enough electricity for the whole of London. It was built in the 1970s in a little village called Drax above a newly discovered coal seam near the town of Selby in the north of England. The coal was mined and brought up into the power station, which used 36 000 tonnes a day.

Towards the end of the twentieth century, the coal supply was used up and coal had to be imported. Gradually it became clear that the power station was a huge source of pollution. The coal contained sulfur which caused acid rain (see Chapter 12) and the power station produced 20 million tonnes of carbon dioxide every year, which was more than was produced each year by over 100 non-industrialised countries.

Visit the website of Drax power station and find out how they have reduced sulfur dioxide pollution, how they are reducing the amount of carbon dioxide it produces and how they are changing from coal to burn renewable fuels and waste.

◀ **Figure 10.11**
Drax power station is one of the largest in the world. The chimney is 260 metres high and is the second highest concrete structure in Britain. The clouds above it are always there and are caused by the evaporation of water in the cooling towers.

Websites

Find Drax Power Station on Google Earth. You can easily recognise its twelve cooling towers. Look at the large flat building to the west. This is a large greenhouse where tomatoes are grown all year round. It was originally built there to use waste heat from the power station. Sadly this ran into problems and an oil heater was installed when oil was cheap. Now that oil is expensive, they may once again use the waste heat.

Websites

Go to www.heinemann.co.uk/hotlinks, insert the express code 6799P and click on Activity 10.1.

135

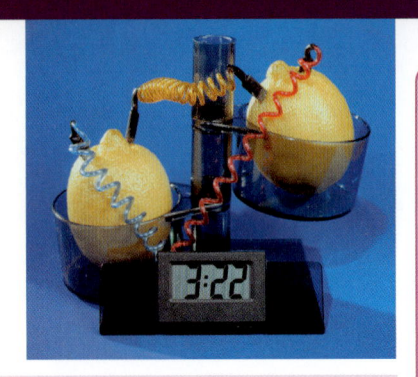

▲ **Figure 10.12**
This electric clock seems to be powered by two lemons. How does it work?

10.5 Cells and batteries

The clock in the picture seems to get its energy from two lemons. There are two pieces of metal sticking into each; one is copper and the other is magnesium. The energy comes from a chemical reaction involving these two metals; the metals form part of an electric cell. The lemon provides an ionic solution that allows electrons to move between the two metals. The lemon could be replaced by a beaker of salt solution.

The diagrams below show three different cells. Each is connected to a voltmeter.

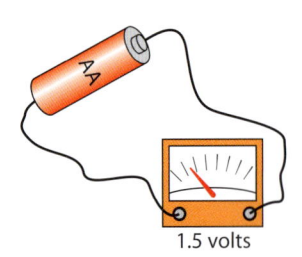

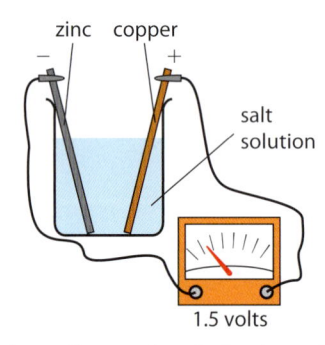

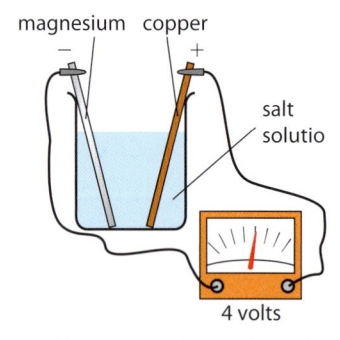

1.5 volts | 1.5 volts | 4 volts

This cell is a commercial AA cell. It is full of a gel that conducts electricity.

It has a zinc cathode (−) and a carbon anode (+). The voltage is 1.5 volts.

This cell is made of a beaker of salt solution with two different metals dipping into it.

It has a zinc cathode (−) and a copper anode (+). The voltage is 1.2 volts.

This cell is made of a beaker of salt solution with two different metals dipping into it.

It has a magnesium cathode (−) and a copper anode (+). The voltage is 4 volts.

Activity 10.3
Electricty from chemicals

The salt solution and the gel are called the **electrolyte**. An electrolyte is any solution that will conduct electricity; it is a solution that contains ions.

You can see that the voltage depends on the metals used to make the cells. If the metals are far apart in the reactivity series, like magnesium and copper, the voltage is large. If they are closer together, like zinc and copper, the voltage is smaller.

You can also see that the less reactive metal is always the positive pole of the cell.

When the cell is connected and electricity flows along the wire, the most reactive metal, which is always the negative pole, is eaten away while the current flows through the voltmeter. Metals react by losing one or two electrons and some (those high on the reactivity series) lose them more easily than others.

If the two metals are placed in a solution containing ions and connected together with a wire, a circuit is formed. When the metals react and form ions, the electrons the atoms lose can flow back around the circuit. This will mean that one metal is pushing electrons one way and the second is pushing them the other way. The more reactive one pushes harder (we say it has a greater potential) and so the current is set up, flowing from the more reactive metal to the less reactive one. This is shown in Figure 10.13 with the metals copper and zinc.

Chemistry and energy

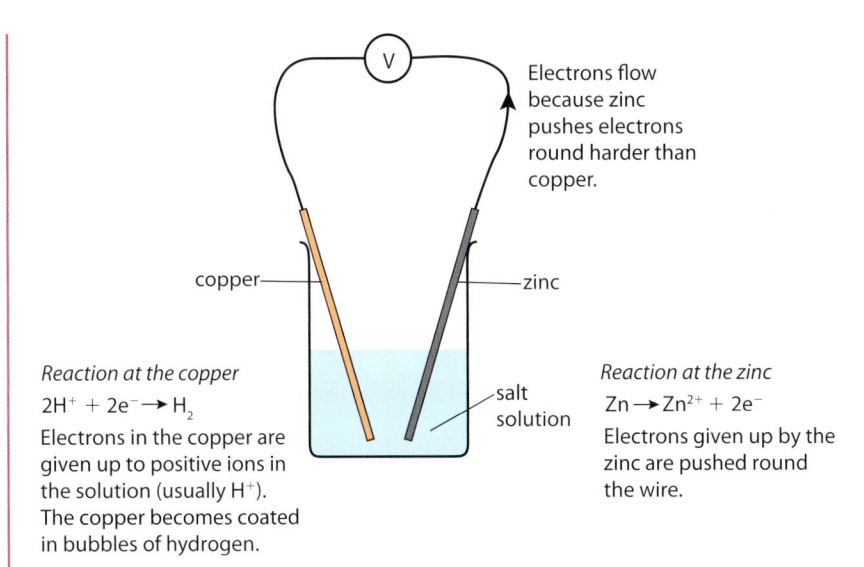

◀ **Figure 10.13**
Why the copper – zinc cell works.

Electrons flow because zinc pushes electrons round harder than copper.

copper — zinc

salt solution

Reaction at the copper
$2H^+ + 2e^- \rightarrow H_2$
Electrons in the copper are given up to positive ions in the solution (usually H^+). The copper becomes coated in bubbles of hydrogen.

Reaction at the zinc
$Zn \rightarrow Zn^{2+} + 2e^-$
Electrons given up by the zinc are pushed round the wire.

SKILLS QUESTION

10.1 If two metals in the same reactivity series are connected in a cell, the highest in the series will always be the cathode. Design an investigation to show whether this is true. Decide what your independent variable will be and what you will measure.

Commercial cells

The picture shows many different commercial cells of different sizes. The smallest at the front is not as small as pencil tip-sized batteries used in muscle implants. The largest at the back is small compared with some commercial cells such as ones used on ships.

Cells are a convenient, portable source of electrical energy. All of them work in the same way as the ones in the chart above. The two poles are always made out of different conducting materials (usually metals), which dip into a solution containing ions. In 'dry' cells, the solution is a paste or a gel so that it does not spill out. The voltage of a cell depends on the difference in the reactivity between the materials of the two poles.

Some cells are **rechargeable**. This means that the chemical reactions that happen when the cell gives electricity can be made to go backwards when an electric current is passed through the cell. The current is passed through the cell in the opposite direction from the current that it produces when it is used.

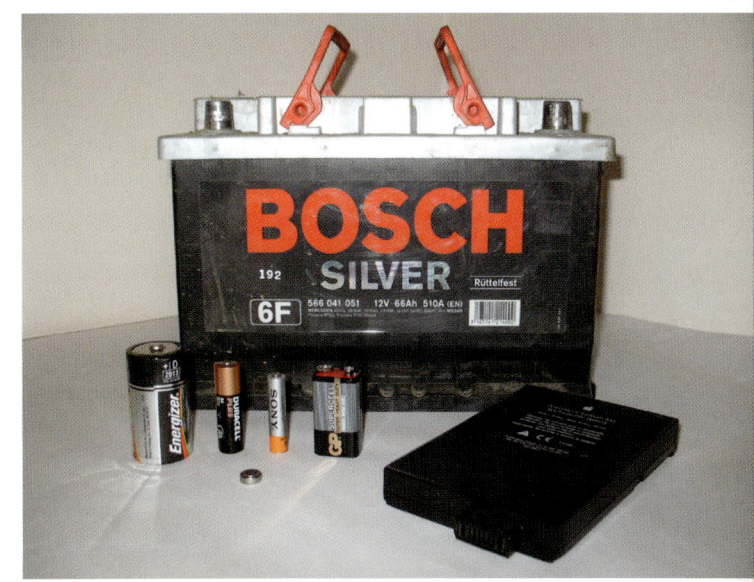

▲ **Figure 10.14**
Some commercial batteries showing a range of sizes.

137

▶ **Figure 10.15**
The first working battery: Volta's pile.

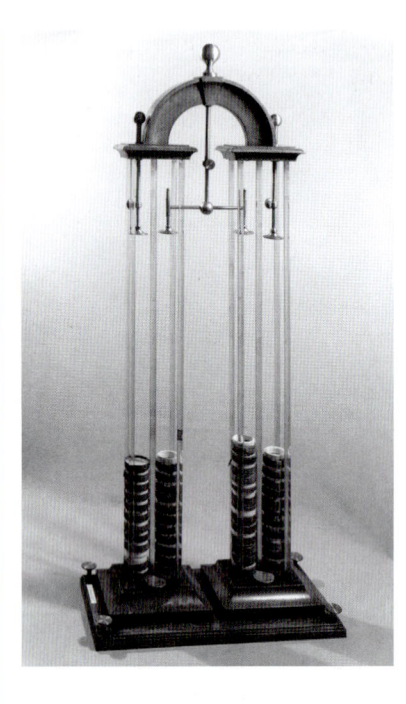

A short history of batteries

The first battery

The first working battery was made by Count Alessandro Volta, an Italian, in 1800. He used a pile of alternating discs of zinc and silver. In between the sheets he put cloth soaked in salt water. Because it was a pile of discs it came to be called a **voltaic pile**. The picture shows a reconstruction of a voltaic pile in the Tempio Voltiano, a museum in Como in Italy, the town where Volta was born.

DID YOU KNOW?

Leclanché made his discovery in 1866 and by 1868 had set up a factory that had produced 20 000 of his cells. These were used everywhere to power the latest invention – the telegraph.

The big battery problem – the voltage drop

If you make your own voltaic pile, or your own lemon clock, you will find one big problem. It works fine for a while but then the voltage starts dropping. If you stop using it and leave it for a bit and then try it again it will work (but only for a while).

The solution: Leclanché's cell of 1866

Leclanché spent some years trying to solve the voltage drop problem in his spare time. He realised that the problem was caused by small bubbles of hydrogen that formed on the cathode of the battery. He solved it by coating the cathode with a black chemical called manganese dioxide mixed with a bit of crushed carbon. This stopped the hydrogen forming.

DID YOU KNOW?

Did Volta really make the first battery? Figure 10.16 shows a clay pot in the Baghdad museum, which some archaeologists think may have been a battery that was in use 200 years BCE. Next to the vase was found a sheet of copper soldered into a cylinder and an iron rod, both having pitch on one end. Was the iron rod sealed inside the cylinder and the two put into the clay pot filled with an electrolyte? We will probably never know. The archaeologists looked for wires but did not find any.

But there may be more evidence. If it was a battery, the most probable use for it would be electroplating; coating copper objects with gold (see Section 8.7). Some objects that look as though they were electroplated have been found near Baghdad and they date from as far back as 2000 BCE. Did the ancient peoples of the Middle East, who invented writing and books and so much else, also invent the battery?

▲ **Figure 10.16**
Baghdad battery

Chemistry and energy

The common torch cell that you can buy today is a Leclanché cell. If you cut it open you can see the little bag of manganese dioxide powder around the carbon cathode. The electrolyte is a whitish paste containing the salt ammonium chloride. Take a little, mix it with sodium hydroxide and warm; you will smell ammonia (see Section 7.7).

Rechargeable cells

A rechargeable cell is one where the chemical reactions can be made to go backwards when a voltage is applied backwards through the cell. The first rechargeable cell was also invented by a Frenchman. His name was Gaston Planté and he developed the first practical lead acid battery in 1859. This kind of battery is still used in cars today.

> **Activity 10.4**
> Making a rechargeable lead-acid cell

Modern batteries

Have you ever tried to lift a battery out of the car? If you have, you will know the biggest problem car batteries have – they are very heavy. They are heavy because they use lead electrodes; the cathode is made of lead and the anode is made of lead metal that is coated in lead dioxide. The lead acid battery is still widely used because it lasts a long time and it is not easily damaged. But scientists are working on newer batteries that are lighter.

Light batteries must be made from light elements. The lightest elements are the smallest elements; they are the ones that occur in the first two rows of the periodic table. Modern batteries often contain the element lithium, because lithium is the metal that has the lowest density. Many of these light batteries also contain the elements sulfur or fluorine, so the chemical reactions in them are the reaction between lithium and non-metals like sulfur or fluorine.

Fuel cells – twenty-first century batteries

Although the first fuel cell was made in 1843 (by a Welshman called William Grove, who was a lawyer by profession and a brilliant amateur scientist) they only became important when satellites were first developed and needed quite large amounts of electrical energy. There is a big difference between fuel cells and batteries. Batteries contain all the chemicals they need inside them, but fuel cells are continuously supplied with the chemicals, a bit like an engine being continuously supplied with fuel.

The most common fuel cells use two chemicals, hydrogen at the anode and oxygen (from air) at the cathode. The hydrogen splits up into a proton and an electron at the anode and the electron flows round the circuit to reach the cathode. Meanwhile the proton goes through a membrane to get to the cathode, where it joins up with the oxygen and electrons coming around the circuit, to form water. Although a single cell has only a small output, many cells are used together in commercial fuel cells and they can produce many kilowatts of power.

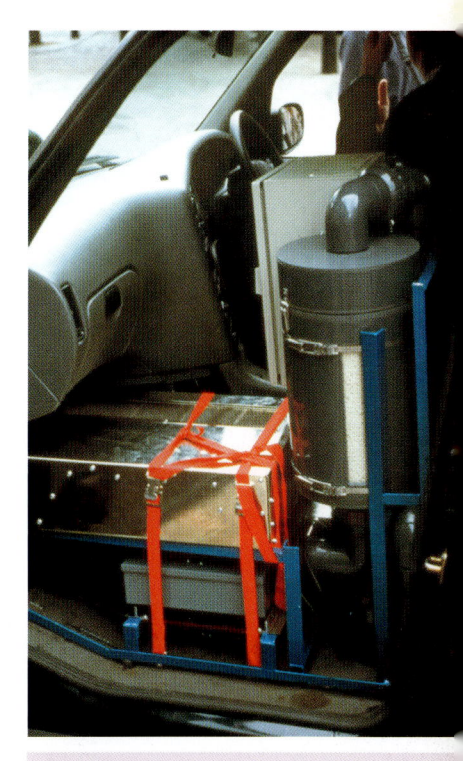

▲ **Figure 10.17**
Fuel cells are beginning to replace batteries for many tasks such as powering pollution-free buses in towns. They run on hydrogen and the only waste is water. They can have power outputs of many kilowatts; this one is a 1.2 kW cell.

QUESTIONS

10.2 We get our energy from glucose. In our muscles it reacts with oxygen and is converted into water and carbon dioxide. Explain where the energy comes from.

10.3 Explain, giving examples, what is meant by 'endothermic' and 'exothermic' reactions.

10.4 This decomposition reaction of calcium carbonate is endothermic:
calcium carbonate → calcium oxide + carbon dioxide
Explain what you must do to calcium carbonate to make it decompose. Draw an energy diagram (similar to Figure 10.3) for the reaction.

10.5 Explain why the reactions that take place during cooking food are usually exothermic.

10.6 Reactions that produce gases are often endothermic. Explain why this is so.

10.7 A Bunsen burner burns methane or propane as a fuel. List the products of the burning. The burner gives a different flame according to whether the air hole is open or closed. State which flame gives the most complete combustion. Describe the evidence for incomplete burning in the other flame.

10.8 Explain why coal is used mainly in large power stations, whereas oil is burnt in small ones that are used to increase the supply of electricity at peak times.

10.9 Hydrogen is a fuel that can easily be made from water and causes hardly any pollution when it is burnt. Give two reasons why it is not widely used.

10.10 Study the graph of world energy consumption in Section 10.3. Our supplies of oil will begin to run out in the next few decades, gas a little after that, but there are known coal reserves to last another century at present rates of production. Predict how you think the graph will change in the next 30 years. Give reasons for your predictions.

10.11 Describe how you would use a tomato to light a 1.5 amp bulb. What else will you need besides a tomato and a bulb? Explain how your idea will work.

10.12 A cell has two electrodes dipping into salt water. The electrodes are made out of iron and copper. State which metal is the positive pole of the cell and give a reason for your answer. Explain how you would make the cell produce a higher voltage.

Summary

Now that you have completed this chapter, you should be able to:

- know that all chemical reactions involve energy changes
- distinguish between endothermic and exothermic reactions and give examples of each
- draw energy change diagrams representing endothermic and exothermic reactions and explain what is meant by activation energy
- (S) explain energy changes in terms of the breaking and formation of chemical bonds
- know that our bodies get energy from the food we eat and explain where the energy and food originally came from
- explain how we can get useful energy from fuels and know the difference between renewable and non-renewable fuels
- explain the origins of fossil fuels and list and describe the main ones
- know the products of burning of fossil fuels
- understand why it is important that we should use less fossil fuel and more renewable fuels
- describe ways in which we are making our fuel supplies more sustainable
- (S) describe how electrical energy is made from chemical energy in cells and batteries.

Chapter 11

Extracting and using metals

▲ Figure 11.1
A zinc processing plant, Rosh Pinah, Namibia. This is a modern plant for making zinc. Note there is no chimney; the modern process used here does not pollute the air (see page 151).

▲ Figure 11.2
The last Bessemer converter to be used in England. A blast of air was blown up through the molten pig iron in the converter to change it into steel.

◀ Figure 11.3
This old lead smelter in the Yorkshire Dales in the north of England closed down in 1888. This area was once covered in trees but they were all cut down to make charcoal for this industry.

Extracting and using metals

◀ Figure 11.4
Rössing uranium mine, Namibia

Most metals are extracted from ores that are found in the ground. A few metals such as silver and gold, and also some copper, are found in nature as elements. They do not have to be extracted from ores. Humans have been extracting metals from ores using chemical reactions called **smelting** for almost 6000 years. The earliest smelting was probably done in what is modern Iraq when the earliest examples of the alloy, bronze, was made. Bronze is a mixture of copper and tin.

Metals have brought great benefits but extracting them has brought many problems. The old lead smelter in Figure 11.3 is in the middle of what seems to be beautiful countryside. But two hundred years ago, this area was so polluted by sulfur dioxide that few plants grew. The whole area was once thick woodland until the trees were chopped down to be made into charcoal for the smelting. Mining metals now involves digging bigger and bigger pits because all the richest ores have been used up; we need to dig up much more ore to get just a small amount of metal. The uranium ore being dug out of the pit in Figure 11.4 is less than 1% uranium.

11.1 Mining and concentrating the ore

Rocks are usually mixtures of many different compounds. The compounds that make up rocks are called **minerals**. These minerals are compounds that contain metals and many of these minerals are useful sources of the metals. They often have special names: **haematite** is an important mineral containing iron; **galena** contains lead ore; and **bauxite** is a common mineral that contains aluminium. The rocks that contain these useful minerals are called **ores**.

There are usually four steps in the process of obtaining metals from their ores:
- mining or quarrying the ore
- concentrating the mineral in the ore
- reducing the ore to crude metal or a compound of it
- refining the metal.

DID YOU KNOW?

Many rich countries are now building nuclear power stations and they need a lot of uranium but they do not have any of their own. One uranium pit in Namibia will eventually cover an area of 40 km² and be 20m deep. The uranium ore is only 0.01% which means that 1kg of uranium, enough to fill a coffee mug, will make at least 10 tonnes of waste. The uranium that is produced will be used to make electricity for the people of France, not Namibia where the environment will be destroyed. What do you think of this?

Websites

You can find a lot of information about different minerals and gemstones (including pictures) on the internet. Go to www.heinemann.co.uk/hotlinks, insert the express code 6799P and click on 11.1.

143

> **DID YOU KNOW?**
>
> Most of the gold that has ever been mined has been found in a part of South Africa near Johannesburg. If all the gold that has been mined there were made into one golden ball it would be 16m in diameter! Can you work out how much this ball is worth?

Mining the ore

Some metals occur uncombined in nature. Gold is one of these; the uncombined gold is sometimes washed down rivers and is found in riverbeds. It can be extracted by an old process called 'panning'. The crushed material from the riverbed is washed in running water. The impurities are washed away and the very dense pieces of gold are left behind.

Most metals are combined with other elements in minerals. Because most rocks only contain a small amount of the metal, quarries are often very large, like the one in Figure 11.4. The process of extracting the metal leaves a lot of waste and this is often poisonous to plants. The waste may also contain soluble compounds that may leak into the ground and pollute water supplies. This means that extracting metals can do much damage to the environment.

Concentrating the ore

The ore is one particular mineral found in a rock that is usually made of many minerals. Most of the rock is therefore not wanted; sometimes more than 99%. The first purification step is often a process called **froth flotation**. In this process the crushed rock is mixed into a mixture of oils and water. The mixture is carefully designed so that the particles of the mineral that contains the metal stay floating in the oil but the impurities, such as sand, sink to the bottom. The mineral particles are held in the liquid by electrostatic forces.

A modern way of concentrating some ores is to use a process called **solvent extraction**. This uses two liquids that do not mix. The metal in the ore reacts with a special organic acid or alkali to form salts that mix with one of the liquids while everything else stays in the other. The concentrated ore is then separated from the liquid with the ore in it and it is converted into a salt of a common acid such as sulfuric acid. The organic acid or alkali can be recovered and reused. The metal can be extracted from its sulfate using electrolysis (see Chapter 8). This process produces very little waste and pollution, as all the chemicals used are recycled.

The zinc extraction plant at Rosh Pinah in Namibia shown in Figure 11.1 is one of the most modern in the world. All the chemicals used, including water, are recycled in the plant and no gases are made that can cause air pollution.

11.2 Reducing the ore to the metal

There are three important ways of reducing the ore to the metal.
   1. Heating the ore
   2. Heating the ore with carbon
   3. Electrolysis of the molten ore or of a solution

Heating the ore is only possible with certain metals. Mercury is an example. The common ore of mercury is mercury sulfide (called cinnabar). When it is heated in air the sulfur combines with the oxygen leaving mercury behind.

Some copper ores can be treated in the same way. This is possible when the ore contains copper sulfide. Heating the ore produces copper and sulfur dioxide.

The equation shows what happens:

copper sulfide + oxygen → copper + sulfur dioxide
$CuS(s) + O_2(g) → Cu(s) + SO_2(g)$

Heating the ore with carbon is the most common method of extracting metals from their ores. The ores are the oxides of the metals. The form of carbon used in earlier times was charcoal. There are remains of furnaces all over the world that used charcoal; one is the lead-smelting furnace shown in Figure 11.3 above. These furnaces were used to make lead, tin or iron.

A major problem with using charcoal to smelt metal ores is that so many trees had to be cut down to make it. In 1709 this problem was solved when coke, a form of carbon made from coal, was first used instead of charcoal to smelt iron. This process was invented by a man called Abraham Darby in Coalbrookdale, England. The iron bridge at Ironbridge, shown in Figure 6.4, is the first major structure to be built using Coalbrookdale iron. It was built in 1779.

More modern furnaces use graphite electrodes that are heated by sparking high voltage electricity between them. Graphite is the pure form of carbon that we know in pencil 'leads'.

In all these processes the ore is heated with the carbon in the furnace. The heat comes from the carbon that burns. One of the products of the burning of carbon is carbon monoxide and it is this carbon monoxide that reacts with the ore and changes it to the metal. The carbon monoxide combines with the oxygen in the metal ore and the molten metal is left behind.

The equation shows the reaction with iron oxide to form liquid molten iron.

iron oxide + carbon monoxide → carbon dioxide + iron
$Fe_2O_3(s) + 3CO(g) → 3CO_2(g) + 2Fe(l)$

This process is called the **reduction** of the ore to the metal and carbon monoxide is called the **reducing agent**.

Using limestone to remove impurities during smelting with carbon

From earliest times limestone has been added to the reduction furnace. It helps to remove impurities from the ore. In the furnace limestone forms calcium oxide, which is basic and will react with any acidic impurities in the ore. A common acidic impurity is sand, silicon dioxide. This reacts with the calcium oxide to form calcium silicate, called **slag**, which is molten and floats on top of the metal. The slag and the metal can be run off from time to time through two taps at the bottom of the furnace.

limestone (calcium carbonate) → calcium oxide + carbon dioxide
$CaCO_3(s) → CaO(s) + CO_2(g)$

calcium oxide + silicon dioxide (sand) → calcium silicate
$CaO(s) + SiO_2(s) → CaSiO_3(l)$

▲ Figure 11.5
This is Abraham Darby's furnace at Coalbrookdale, now a World Heritage site. Darby (1678–1717) lived only 39 years but was responsible for the invention that started the industrial revolution, a blast furnace that could smelt iron using coke instead of charcoal.

▲ Figure 11.6
One of the reasons why Abraham Darby wanted a better and cheaper way of making cast iron was that, together with one of his young employees, John Thomas, he had developed a way of making the now well-known three legged cast iron pot. Until then, these had been made of brass (by the Dutch mainly and so they were called 'Dutch ovens') and they were very expensive. The industrial revolution started in the kitchen!

Smelting sulfide ores

Not all ores are in the form of oxides. Some are sulfides (such as galena, lead sulfide) and others are carbonates. These ores are usually heated in air first to convert them to the oxides. The oxides are then reduced with carbon. You can see from the equation below that the process of heating a sulfide ore in air produces sulfur dioxide. This is an unpleasant choking gas that damages plants and buildings as well as being poisonous to animals. The furnaces in which the sulfide ore is heated often have high chimneys, so that the sulfur dioxide can be carried a long way in the air before it finally returns to the ground.

These equations show how some ores are converted into the metal oxides by heating in air.

lead sulfide + oxygen → lead oxide + sulfur dioxide
$$2PbS(s) + 3O_2(g) \rightarrow 2PbO(s) + 2SO_2(g)$$

zinc carbonate → zinc oxide + carbon dioxide
$$ZnCO_3(s) \rightarrow ZnO(s) + CO_2(g)$$

▶ **Figure 11.7**
This is the flue (chimney) of an old lead smelter in England used over 200 years ago to make lead from the lead sulfide ore. The flue leaves the back of the furnace and runs along the ground for several kilometres to the top of the nearby hill. The long flue ensured that the sulfur dioxide from the smelter was taken well away and also allowed lead vapour escaping from the furnace to condense in the soot. The flue was swept regularly by small boys climbing inside it and the soot was put back in the smelter.

Electrolysis of the molten ore is the process used to smelt ores that cannot be reduced by carbon. Only metals in the bottom half of the reactivity series can be extracted by carbon. Metals such as sodium, magnesium and aluminium are extracted instead by electrolysis of a molten compound. Sodium, for example, is obtained by electrolysing molten sodium chloride.

As you will have learnt in Chapter 8, if an electric current is passed through a solution that will conduct electricity (which we call an electrolyte), ions in the electrolyte are converted into atoms and so these elements appear at the electrodes.

Aluminium is made by electrolysing molten aluminium oxide and so the two products of the electrolysis are aluminium and oxygen. Aluminium appears at the cathode (negative electrode) and oxygen is collected at the anode.

11.3 Extraction of metals and the reactivity series

Look back at the reactivity series for metals. Can you see a pattern in the method used for extraction metals? Those metals that are least reactive form compounds that are easily broken down. This means that these metals are easily extracted. Those metals high in the reactivity series form strong bonds in their compounds. A lot of energy is needed to break these bonds. These metals are not extracted easily. This pattern is summarised in Figure 11.8.

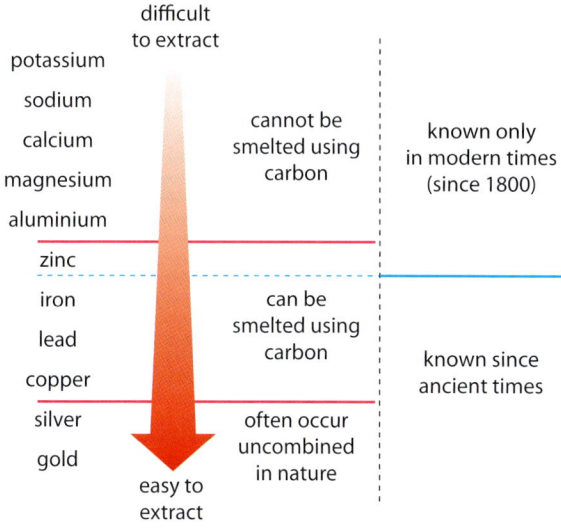

◀ **Figure 11.8**
The reactivity series related to methods used to extract metals.

Electrolysis is now used in modern smelters even for metals low on the reactivity series that could be extracted using carbon. One reason for this is that it is a clean process that does not cause much pollution. Another reason is that electrolysis always gives a pure metal that does not have to be further purified.

11.4 Making iron and steel

Pure iron is very rare. It is rare for two reasons: firstly, pure iron is very difficult to make and secondly, it is not much use to us because it is very soft; a one-centimetre diameter bar can easily be bent by hand. When we talk about iron we usually mean steel. Steel is iron with a small percentage of carbon in it.

Steel is very common and one of the most useful materials we have. It is common partly because there is a lot of iron in the earth's crust (about 5% of the crust is iron) and partly because the iron from which it is made is quite easy to extract. In 2006, the amount of steel made in a year went over a billion tonnes for the first time.

Extracting crude iron from iron ore

The iron is extracted using carbon, in the form of coke, heated either by electricity (the electric arc furnace) or by burning the coke (the blast furnace).

▶ Figure 11.9
Electric arc furnace.

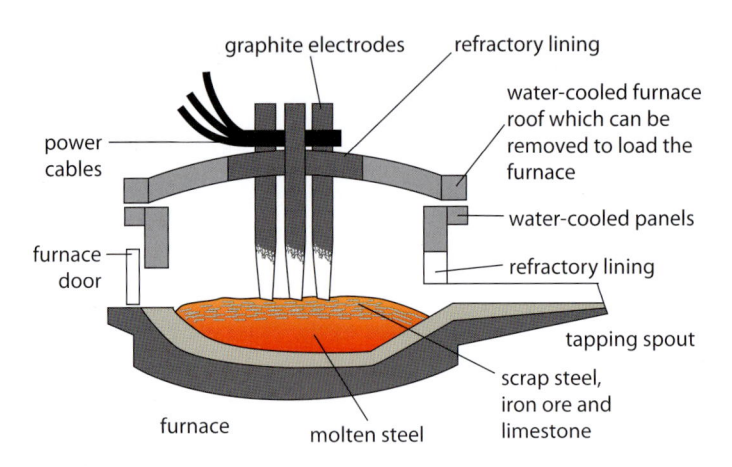

DID YOU KNOW?

A modern electric arc furnace takes a charge of about 100–120 tonnes of ore and scrap steel. It uses 70–90 megawatts at full power, which is about the same as needed by a small town.

In the electric arc furnace, the heat comes from electrical sparks (arcs) jumping between large carbon electrodes lowered into the furnace. Scrap steel in the furnace helps the arcing process as it conducts electricity. The carbon from the electrolytes burns away to form carbon monoxide, which then reduces the iron ore.

carbon + oxygen → carbon monoxide
$$2C(s) + O_2(g) \rightarrow 2CO(g)$$

carbon monoxide + iron oxide → iron + carbon dioxide
$$3CO(g) + Fe_2O_3(s) \rightarrow 2Fe(l) + 3CO_2(g)$$

In the blast furnace the reactions are the same but the heat is generated by burning coke (using a blast of air forced in near the bottom). Limestone is added to the contents of the furnace (called the 'charge') to react with impurities. Look back to Section 11.2 for more about this reaction.

These two furnaces are shown in Figure 11.9 and Figure 11.10.

Because carbon is used in the extraction process, the metal that comes out of the blast furnace contains about 4% of dissolved carbon. It is called 'pig iron' or 'cast iron'. It is very hard but rather brittle. To make a more useful material, steel, the amount of carbon must be reduced to between 0.5–2%. The electric arc furnace is used to make steel directly in one process, as the amount of the carbon electrodes that is allowed to enter the molten iron can be carefully controlled.

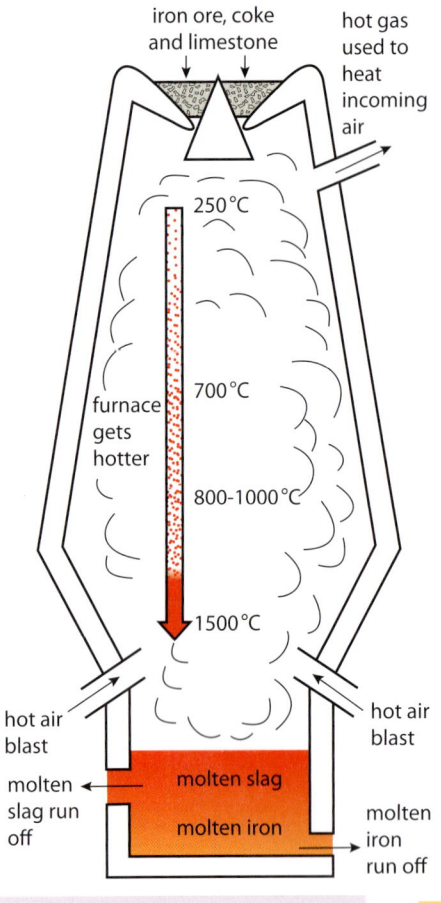

▲ Figure 11.10
Blast furnace.

DID YOU KNOW?

Why it is called 'pig iron'?
In the nineteenth century the molten iron was run out of furnaces in troughs made by pressing a mould into sand. The iron ran from the furnace down a long trough into a lot of smaller ones at right angles to it. The small ones looked like piglets being fed by the longer one that was called the 'sow'. Each 'pig' was about 100 kg and was snapped off the sow when it went solid. The sand was then raked and new troughs made. It was extremely dangerous manual work done outside, night and day, in all kinds of weather. The process was automated in the 1920s.

Websites

You can see photographs of iron production in the nineteenth century on the internet. Go to www.heinemann.co.uk/hotlinks, insert the express code 6799P and click on 11.2.

Extracting and using metals

Converting pig iron from the blast furnace into steel

To make steel, the carbon in the pig iron is partly burnt away using oxygen. For the last 150 years this has been done by blowing air or oxygen through the molten pig iron in a large bucket-shaped furnace that usually holds about 250 tonnes. One of these is shown in Figure 11.2. The oxygen reacts with the carbon in the pig iron and burns off at the top of the furnace in a very spectacular way.

The older versions of these furnaces (like the one in the picture) were called Bessemer converters and they use an air blast blown through the bottom. More modern ones are called basic oxygen furnaces (Figure 11.11) in which an oxygen pipe (called a lance) is put into the molten pig iron and exactly the right amount of oxygen is blown through.

While the metal is in this furnace, any other additives can be put in it to make 'special' steels for different uses. The molten metal is then poured out of the furnace, which can be tipped and cast into blocks called ingots.

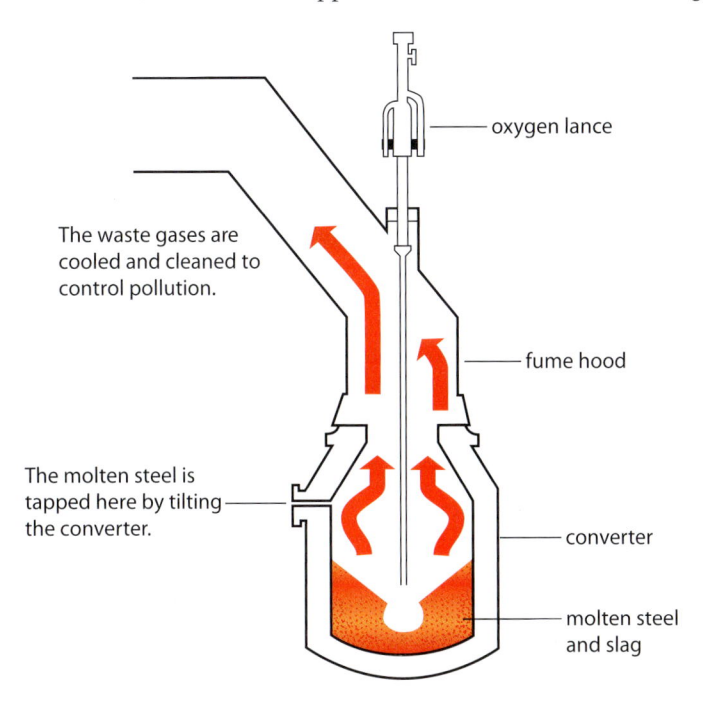

◀ **Figure 11.11** Basic oxygen furnace.

11.5 Making aluminium

Aluminium is high in the reactivity series and is too reactive to be extracted with carbon. Instead, electrolysis must be used. The main aluminium ore is **bauxite**, which is a form of aluminium oxide. Aluminium oxide, however, has a very high melting point (2015 °C) and so it is not possible to melt it easily to carry out the electrolysis.

This is why aluminium was a very rare metal until the 1880s, when it was discovered that the oxide would dissolve in another aluminium compound called **cryolite** (sodium aluminium fluoride) at a much lower temperature (about 950 °C). This mixture is electrolysed in a cell with carbon electrodes.

149

Figure 11.12
Electrolysis cell for producing aluminium.

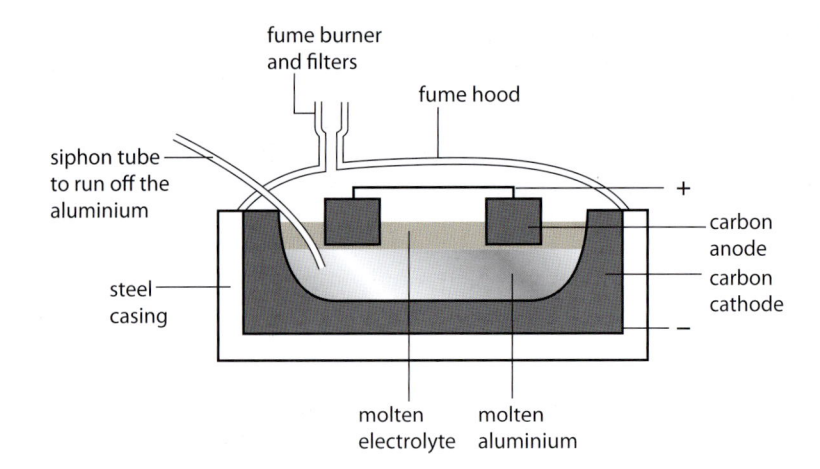

DID YOU KNOW?

Two unknown young scientists (both in their twenties), the Frenchman Paul Héroult and the American Charles Hall, invented this process for making aluminium. They did not know each other and both filed patents for the process in 1886. The process became known as the Hall-Héroult process. In 1890 the world production by this process was less than 50 tonnes. By 2005 this had risen to about 30 million tonnes.

The liquid aluminium collects at the bottom of the cell and from time to time is run off. The heat produced by the resistance of the electrolyte keeps the cell hot and the aluminium is run off each day.

The ionic reactions are these.

At the cathode:
$Al^{3+} + 3e^- \rightarrow Al$

At the anode:
$2O^{2-} \rightarrow O_2 + 4e^-$

The carbon anodes gradually burn away because the carbon reacts with the oxygen produced on them. They are replaced every 24 hours.

Because the electrolyte contains fluoride ions, the waste gases contain fluorine. This could cause damage to the surrounding countryside and so fluorine is usually removed from the flue gases before they leave the chimney.

11.6 Making zinc

The most common ore of zinc is called zinc blende and it is zinc sulfide (ZnS). In the older processes for making zinc, the sulfide ore is first converted to the oxide by roasting in air. This produces a lot of sulfur dioxide as an unpleasant by-product.

zinc sulfide + oxygen → zinc oxide + sulfur dioxide
$2ZnS(s) + 3O_2(g) \rightarrow 2ZnO(s) + 2SO_2(g)$

The zinc oxide is then heated with coke. The coke forms carbon monoxide in the furnace and this is the reducing agent that converts zinc oxide to zinc. Because zinc boils at only 913 °C it does not sink to the bottom of the furnace like iron but escapes with the waste gases as zinc vapour. The gases are cooled rapidly and the zinc condenses.

carbon + oxygen → carbon monoxide
$2C(s) + O_2(g) \rightarrow 2CO(g)$

zinc oxide + carbon monoxide → zinc + carbon dioxide
$ZnO(s) + CO(g) \rightarrow Zn(g) + CO_2(g)$

Zinc is often extracted together with lead because the ores occur together, but the molten metals do not mix. The zinc floats on top of the lead and can be run off.

Modern zinc extraction plants do not use coke as the reducing agent. As explained in Section 11.1, the zinc oxide is allowed to react with an organic acid and this is separated using a technique of solvent extraction. The separated zinc salt is then mixed with sulfuric acid to make zinc sulfate. The zinc is then extracted using electrolysis. This is a much cleaner process than using carbon; it does not pollute the air and all the chemicals used in the process are recovered and used again.

If you look at the photograph of the Rosh Pinah zinc plant in Namibia (Figure 11.1) you can see that there are no chimneys and so no polluting smoke is made.

11.7 Uses of metals

Metals are extremely useful substances because of the important properties listed in Table 9.1. Different metals have different properties and so they have different uses.

Uses of steels

There are many different kinds of steel. The hardness of steel depends on how much carbon remains dissolved in it. To make steel for a particular purpose, it is important to know exactly how much carbon there is in it. This is why exactly the right amount of oxygen is blown through the basic oxygen furnace, so that not all the carbon is burnt off. Table 11.1 shows some steels and their uses.

Kind of steel	Percentage of carbon	Typical uses
Cast iron	4+	Engine blocks, drain covers
Carbon steels		
Low carbon	Less than 0.3	Car bodies, rivets
Medium carbon	0.3 to 0.8	Railway lines, springs
High carbon	0.8 to 1.5	Knives, razor blades

Uses of aluminium

If you look back at the reactivity series, you will see that aluminium is quite high up. Aluminium *should* be a reactive metal, and yet it is not. It seems to be almost as unreactive as copper. This is because aluminium metal is always covered with a very thin layer of aluminium oxide. This layer of oxide is stuck firmly to the metal; it is insoluble and unreactive and prevents further attack on the aluminium. This can be shown quite easily. If you remove the oxide coating, by scratching the aluminium, and put it straight into acid, it reacts quickly where it has been scratched. If

DID YOU KNOW?

It is said that the French Emperor Napoleon III had, in the 1860s, a very rare dinner set. It became well known because it was made of a metal many times more expensive than silver. It was made out of aluminium! Aluminium was first named by the English chemist Sir Humphrey Davy in 1808, who also discovered sodium and potassium, but never managed to make any. It was finally made in 1827 by the German chemist, Friedrich Wöhler, but it was not made in large amounts until the modern process was patented in 1886 by Héroult and Hall. This was several years after the death of Napoleon III.

◀ Table 11.1
Some steels and their uses.

▶ **Figure 11.13**
This Airbus 380 is higher than a three-storey house but even when it is full with 525 passengers and 300 tonnes of fuel it only weighs as much as 16 large lorries. This is because it is made mainly from aluminium alloys.

it were not for this property of aluminium oxide, anything made of aluminium would crumble into a hot heap of aluminium oxide in just a few minutes.

This property of aluminium oxide is extremely useful. It allows us to use aluminium to make articles where lightness, corrosion resistance and good heat conductivity are important. The list of these articles is very long. It includes aircraft, car engines, pans, kitchen foil, window frames, some coins and some statues. In 1900 the amount of aluminium made was about 1000 tonnes. A century later this had risen to 32 million tonnes.

Websites
You can fine much interesting information about aluminium at the website of the International Aluminium Association. Go to www.heinemann.co.uk/hotlinks, insert the express code 6799P and click on 11.3.

Uses of copper

Copper is an important element in the electrical industry, because it conducts electricity so well, does not corrode and is not too expensive. It is widely used to make electrical wire and all kinds of electrical equipment. It is also used to make domestic water pipes because it is not easily corroded and is not as poisonous as lead. Because it is not corroded easily and is a good conductor of heat, it is used to make high quality cooking pans. The pans are always lined with tin or plated with nickel, as copper can be toxic over long periods of time.

Uses of zinc

Zinc has many uses. It is used as the case of the cell (the negative terminal) in ordinary torch cells. A most important use of zinc is to coat steel to stop it rusting. This is a process called **galvanising;** clean sheets of iron are dipped into vats of molten zinc. The zinc stops the iron from rusting because it is more reactive than iron; it reacts with air and water before the iron does. Only when all the zinc has corroded away does the iron underneath begin to rust badly.

Zinc is used to make a number of alloys, particularly bronze and brass. Brass is a mixture of zinc and copper (see Table 11.2), which is liked because it looks like gold but is very much cheaper. These alloys are useful because they are hard and do not easily corrode; brass screws are often used instead of steel screws because of this.

▲ **Figure 11.14**
The statue of Eros in Piccadilly in the centre of London. It is not the Greek God Eros, it is the Christian Angel of Charity, and when it was made in 1893 it was the first major statue to be made of aluminium.

DID YOU KNOW?
In the nineteenth century, tin-lined copper pans were common but the tin gradually wore away. So people often used to take their pans to the local tinsmith to have them re-lined. Being a tinsmith was a common occupation in the days before plastic.

Extracting and using metals

11.8 Alloys

An alloy is a mixture of two or more metals. Alloys are useful because they often have properties that are different from the metals they are made out of. In particular, they are often stronger than the metals they are made out of. This allows us to take two rather weak, but light, metals, aluminium and magnesium, and make them into a strong alloy, called duralumin, which can be used to make aircraft. Table 11.2 shows some useful alloys

Alloy	Main components	Some uses	Useful properties of the alloy
Duralumin	Aluminium, copper, magnesium	Aeroplanes	Light and strong,
Brass	Copper, zinc	Door knobs, ornaments	Corrosion resistant and hard, readily pressed into shapes.
Bronze	Copper, tin	Ship's propeller, church bells, statues	Corrosion resistant and hard, readily pressed into shapes.
Cupro-nickel	Copper, nickel	'Silver' coins	Corrosion resistant, looks like silver.
Titanium alloy	Titanium, iron, carbon	Aeroplanes	Light and strong, low expansion when heated.
Solder	Lead, zinc	Joining wires	Very low melting point.

◀ Table 11.2
Some alloys and their uses.

It is quite easy to see how metals can be made stronger when they are mixed with a small amount of another metal that has atoms of a different size. Figure 11.15 shows an alloy. Notice that the atom of the second metal is slightly larger than the atoms of the main metal. When a force is applied to the alloy at the point shown, the layers cannot move very far because the atom of the second metal stops them.

Copper is a very useful metal because it is resistant to corrosion. Unfortunately it is rather soft and cannot be used for anything that requires strength. There are two alloys of copper, however, which have the resistance to corrosion of copper but also have strength. One is bronze, which is 97% copper and 3% tin and zinc. One important use for it is casting ship's propellers, which have to be very strong and resistant to corrosion by the seawater.

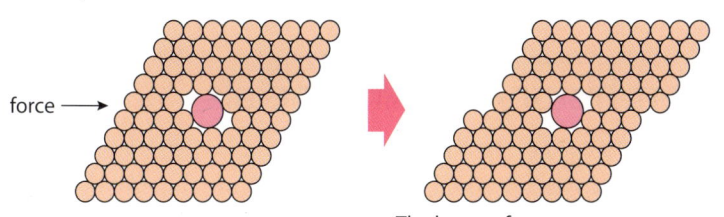

force →

The layers of atoms cannot slip any further than this.

◀ Figure 11.15
An atom in an alloy preventing slipping of layers.

Another way that alloying makes the metal stronger is by making the individual metal crystals smaller. The atoms of the second metal prevent the metal forming large crystals as it cools because they stop the regular build up of layers. The crystals are therefore smaller. Deforming can only happen inside a crystal. It cannot happen across the boundaries (called grain boundaries) between two crystals. This means that it is much more difficult for an alloy to deform than a pure metal and so it is stronger than the pure metal.

Steel is the most widely used alloy. It is called an alloy even though the element mixed with the iron is not another metal but is the non-metal carbon. You have already seen in Table 11.1 how the percentage of carbon in the steel alters its properties. The steels in Table 11.3 contain only carbon and they are called 'carbon steels'. But we can mix steels with other metals to form 'alloy steels'. This allows us to make a great variety of steels with properties exactly suited to our needs. Table 11.3 below shows some alloy steels.

▼ Table 11.3
Some alloy steels and their uses.

Name	Typical composition	Some uses
Chromium steel	Up to 5% chromium	Ball bearings
Cobalt steel	Up to 10% cobalt	Magnets
Molybdenum steel	Up to 4% molybdenum	Gun barrels
Stainless steel	Usually 18% chromium, 8% nickel	Sinks, cutlery, vessels to make corrosive chemicals and foodstuffs
Tungsten steel	Up to 18% tungsten	Armour plate
Vanadium steel	Up to 2% vanadium	Spanners, tools

DID YOU KNOW?

You do not have to add other metals to steel to make it harder. You can do it just by heating it. If you heat it up to red heat and then suddenly cool it by putting it in water, the surface becomes very hard. This is because at red heat the 'grains' (iron crystals) are small. When the steel is cooled suddenly, the grains do not have a chance to get bigger and a metal with small grains is hard, because slippage of atoms cannot take place across the grain boundaries. This kind of hardening of steel is called 'case hardening'. Blacksmiths case harden horses' shoes before they nail them on, and tools like chisels are case hardened.

Memory metal – an alloy with special properties

At the beginning of Chapter 9 you met 'memory metal'. How does it work? Memory metal is an alloy that can form two different crystalline structures. One of these is stable at a higher temperature than the other and this is a very rigid strong structure. The alloy can be made into a shape at the high temperature. When it cools and is made to bend, it changes to the lower temperature structure that can be bent. But if it is then heated up, the atoms return to the arrangement they had in the first rigid structure.

The wire mending the ballerina's bone can be made into the correct shape at the high temperature. The bone can then be set using the metal when it is cold and can be bent. Then her body warms it up to the high temperature and returns it to the correct shape.

A short history of using metals

Au, Cu, Ag, Pb, Sn, Fe, Hg. These seven metals have Latin names and the symbols are short for the Latin names. They are the seven metals known to the ancient world because they were extracted quite easily with charcoal. Do you know their names?

Extracting and using metals

Our early civilisations could not have developed without these metals. Civilisations need tools to make things. They also need weapons to defend against any threatening armies. The axe in Figure 11.16 was probably a weapon of war rather than a tool for peaceful use. Bronze is a hard alloy of tin and copper and could be forged to give a very sharp edge. Without bronze, the first civilisation (the Sumerians, in what is now Iraq) could never have developed as it did 5000 years ago.

Iron is more difficult to smelt than copper and tin; it needs a much higher temperature and early iron was five times more expensive than gold! But there was another source of iron – iron from space. Many meteorites are a mixture of iron and nickel and these have been used to make iron tools. It was only a little over 3000 years ago that iron swords and iron-tipped spears and other tools were first made. Iron tools also revolutionised agriculture. Can you imagine growing crops without a spade?

The next big advances in metallurgy did not happen until some 2500 years later. They started with the discovery of how to use coke, made from coal, as a reducing agent. This was discovered around 1700 by Abraham Darby who lived at Coalbrookdale on the River Severn in England. This was the discovery that started the Industrial Revolution. Iron and steel suddenly became cheap and readily available for making ever more complex machines.

The processes of extracting metals damages the environment. Figure 11.18 shows the other side of our advances in metallurgy; air and water pollution. Figure 11.4 shows another problem; large quarries that destroy our landscapes. These are two examples of a serious problem, caused by our need for metals.

Modern methods of extracting metals produce less waste than older methods – but all methods require energy, usually electrical energy. As you will learn in Chapter 12, making electricity produces a lot of carbon dioxide, which is causing our atmosphere and seas to warm up.

▲ Figure 11.16
Bronze Age axe head.

▲ Figure 11.17
Many early iron tools were made from iron from outer space like this meteorite found in southern Namibia. We know when Iron Age tools were made out of meteorites and not smelted iron because they are about 10% nickel.

◀ Figure 11.18
This print shows the air pollution in Sheffield, England in the nineteenth century when Sheffield was the centre of the world's steel industry.

Websites

For more on the Coalbrookdale Ironworks go to www.heinemann.co.uk/hotlinks, insert the express code 6799P and click on 11.4.

We need cheap metals. How can we make sure we have a supply of cheap metals without doing serious damage to our environment? One way is to re-use scrap metal. We call this 'recycling'. It is often cheaper to recycle metals than to make them new but this may depend on how metal objects are made. Drink cans used to be made of two metals, aluminium and steel. Now they are all made either of steel only or of aluminium only and this makes them cheaper to recycle. Many modern electronic devices are being made so that they can be recycled more easily. Do you recycle metal objects like batteries and drink cans?

▲ Figure 11.19
In 2007, two out of three drinks cans in the world were recycled. This sounds good but it means that 30 000 000 000 cans are still thrown away each year!

QUESTIONS

11.1 List the materials that are added to the blast furnace to make iron. Explain why the product of the blast furnace contains 4% carbon.

11.2 Describe how the product of the blast furnace is turned into steel. List the advantages of the electric arc furnace over the older blast furnace for making steel.

11.3 Name the reducing agent in the blast furnace and write an equation showing the reduction reaction.

11.4 Explain the purpose of the limestone added to the charge in the blast furnace and the electric arc furnace.

11.5 List the main uses of aluminium.

11.6 Describe how the properties of steel depend on how much carbon is dissolved in it. State one use for a high-carbon steel (1.5% carbon) and one for a low-carbon steel (0.3% carbon).

11.7 Pure iron (called wrought iron) is easily bent by hammering it when cold. Mild steel contains about 0.5% carbon and is much stronger, but can be bent in a press and is used to make car bodies. Cast iron contains about 4% carbon and cannot be bent, but breaks if hit hard. Explain how these different properties can arise.

11.8 Aluminium is a very soft metal that can be easily bent by hand. Explain why large aircraft can be made mainly of aluminium.

11.9 Find out what the different coins in your country are made of. Explain why they are made of these alloys. Give a reason why 'silver' and 'gold' coins are no longer made of silver and gold.

11.10 State what metals the following household objects are made from. Give reasons why they are made from the metal.
(a) door hinges
(b) cooking pans
(c) car bodies
(d) house electrical wiring
(e) water taps.

Extracting and using metals

11.11 State what method is most likely to be used for the extraction of the following metals.
(a) potassium
(b) nickel.
Explain your answer.

11.12 Explain why copper smelters often have very tall chimneys and are often found in places where there are not many people.

11.13 Discuss the advantages and disadvantages of using electrolysis rather than heating with coke to extract zinc.

11.14 Zinc is not run off at the bottom of the furnace in which it is made. Describe how it is removed and explain why it is removed in this way.

11.15 Aluminium is high in the reactivity series and yet it is used to make items such as cooking pans, which are often used with substances such as dilute acids and salt, which cause corrosion of metals. Explain why aluminium can be used in this way.

Summary

Now that you have completed this chapter, you should be able to:

- understand that metal smelting is a very important process but that it can have a very negative impact on the environment
- describe how the crude metal ore is first concentrated by processes such as flotation or solvent extraction
- describe the three important ways of reducing metal ores to the metal
- understand the purpose of using limestone during this smelting process
- understand why the method of extracting metals is often related to the position of the metal in the reactivity series
- describe the two common processes of extracting iron from iron ore using the blast furnace and the electric arc furnace and also the process for converting pig iron into steel
- describe the process of making aluminium from bauxite using electrolysis of the molten ore
- describe and explain the uses we make of aluminium, copper and zinc
- understand the importance of alloys and explain why the properties of an alloy can often be very different from the properties of the metals from which it is made
- account for the apparent unreactivity of aluminium.

Chapter 12

Chemistry and the environment

▲ **Figure 12.1**
Our planet is the only place we know about in the whole of the Universe, where water can exist most of the time as a liquid, without most of it slowly evaporating. This is vital for the survival of life. This photograph was taken from the moon by astronauts on the Apollo 8 mission in 1968. In 2010 another planet was discovered orbiting near another star where the liquid water might exist. Scientists call these 'Goldilocks Planets'. If you know the Goldilocks fairytale you might be able to work out why.

▲ **Figure 12.2**
Mars does not have much air. The white patches at the poles are not ice but solid carbon dioxide, so the temperature there must be around −100 °C. In 2008 water ice was found in the Martian soil so it may be possible for some kind of life to exist on Mars.

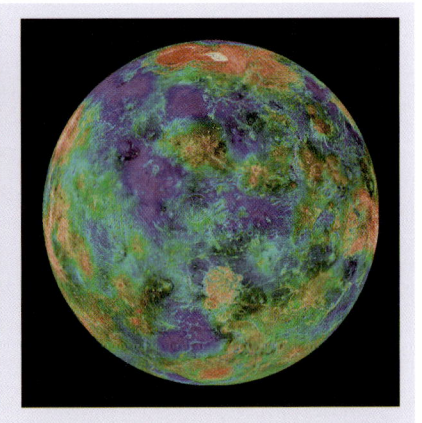

▲ **Figure 12.3**
This is a false colour image of Venus. Venus is too near the Sun to allow life. All the water on the planet is in the form of vapour in the atmosphere and the clouds are mainly sulfuric acid droplets. The temperature on the surface is nearly 500 °C.

Are we alone? Are we the only place in the Universe with life? The answer is that we just do not know. What we do know is that any planet that supports life, at least our kind of life, must be very special. Look at our neighbours in the pictures. Mars is a little too far away from the Sun to be warm enough and a little too small to keep hold of its small water molecules; they have diffused into space long ago, but water ice has been discovered underground. The water molecules were moving fast enough to overcome gravity.

Look at our closest neighbour, Venus. It is too near the Sun and everything that boils below about 500 °C has evaporated into its thick atmosphere. Spacecraft that have landed there have survived about 20 minutes before melting.

We are just the right distance from the Sun. Or rather, we were a few million years ago. But the Sun is naturally getting hotter as it grows older and now we are a bit too close. When the planet was cooler, a few

Chemistry and the environment

hundred million years ago, it was covered by much richer vegetation, both in the sea and on land, than it is now (see Figure 10.6). Today our planet is rather too hot and dry for healthy life and it is struggling. Our green plants in the sea and on land are not using as much carbon dioxide as we would like them to. This chapter tells you more about this problem and what we can try and do to help our green-blue planet remain a pleasant place for all its millions of species. Including us.

12.1 Our atmosphere

The atmosphere forms a very thin layer around the surface of the planet. (If our planet were a golf ball, the air would be the thickness of the layer of white paint on it.) Without it, most life could not exist. Pure dry air is a mixture of nine gases but is mainly **nitrogen** and **oxygen**. Oxygen is a very important gas for us; to get the energy we need to survive, a wide variety of substances must react with oxygen. We burn fuels in oxygen to keep us warm, to power our vehicles and to generate most of our electricity. It is the reaction between oxygen and sugars in our body that provides us with the energy that keeps us alive.

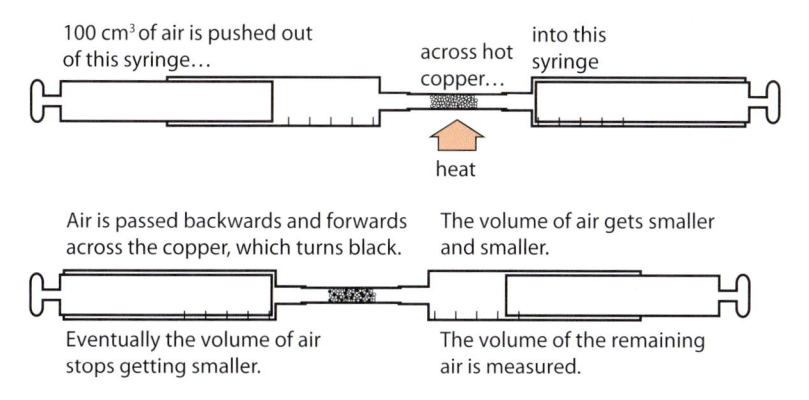

Activity 12.1
The composition of the air

◀ **Figure 12.4**
Apparatus to measure the oxygen content of the air.

We can use gas syringes to measure the percentage of oxygen in the air. Gas syringes are accurately made glass syringes with tightly fitting airtight plungers. They are usually calibrated and can hold 100 cm³ of gas. 100 cm³ of air is passed slowly backwards and forwards across granules of copper that is heated strongly in a silica tube. (A silica tube is used because a glass one would melt.)

In the experiment, the oxygen combines with the hot copper as it is passed slowly over it. Eventually all the oxygen has combined with the copper. The remaining air is allowed to cool to the original temperature and the new volume is read. Subtracting this from the original 100 cm³ gives the volume of oxygen. Because the original volume of air was 100 cm³, this number is also the percentage of oxygen in air. It will be 21% if all the oxygen has been used.

Table 12.1 shows the main constituents of dry air. It shows that a little less than four-fifths of the air is nitrogen and a little over one-fifth is oxygen. The remaining seven gases account for only around 1%. One substance that is not included in the table is water vapour. The amount of this in the atmosphere is variable and depends on the weather.

DID YOU KNOW?

Oxygen is a poisonous gas. We could not survive for long if we had to breathe pure oxygen. Air is safe because the oxygen is 'diluted' with nitrogen and the dilution is just right for life. If the amount of oxygen were more than about 25%, things would be constantly catching fire. If it were less than about 15%, we could not breathe.

▶ **Table 12.1**
The composition of dry air by volume.

Gas	Percentage by volume of dry air
Nitrogen	73.03
Oxygen	20.99
Argon	0.93
Carbon dioxide	0.03
Neon	0.001 5
Hydrogen	0.001 0
Helium	0.000 5
Krypton	0.000 1
Xenon	0.000 008

DID YOU KNOW?

You breathe in and out approximately 15 000 litres of air each day. When you are doing vigorous exercise, you need up to 40 litres every minute.

Oxygen and nitrogen

▶ **Table 12.2**
The properties of the two main gases, nitrogen and oxygen.

Oxygen	Nitrogen
Boiling point −183 °C.	Boiling point −196 °C.
Molecular formula O_2.	Molecular formula N_2.
Colourless gas.	Colourless gas.
Has no smell.	Has no smell.
Slightly soluble in water.	Less soluble than oxygen.
Solution is neutral.	Solution is neutral.
Does not burn.	Does not burn.
Necessary for other substances to burn.	Does not help other substances burn.
Relights a glowing splint.	

Oxygen and nitrogen are physically very similar but chemically very different. Oxygen is very reactive. When elements burn in air they are combining with oxygen. Substances that burn in air will burn very brightly in pure oxygen. A glowing wooden splint will burst into flame if it is put into pure oxygen. This is the chemical test for oxygen.

Nitrogen, however, is very unreactive. It will not allow substances to burn in it and if a glowing splint is put into it, it will be extinguished.

The oxygen cycle

The proportion of oxygen in the air stays constant, even though it is continually being used up when substances burn and when living things respire. This is because another process, **photosynthesis**, produces oxygen. The chemical reaction that happens when living things respire converts carbohydrates to carbon dioxide and water. The chemical reaction that happens during photosynthesis is the opposite; carbon dioxide and water are converted into carbohydrates. Because of these processes, oxygen is continuously recycled. This is shown in Figure 12.5.

The equations for the two reactions show that oxygen is used up during respiration and produced during photosynthesis. The balance between these reactions has kept the amount of oxygen in the atmosphere almost the same for many hundreds of millions of years.

Chemistry and the environment

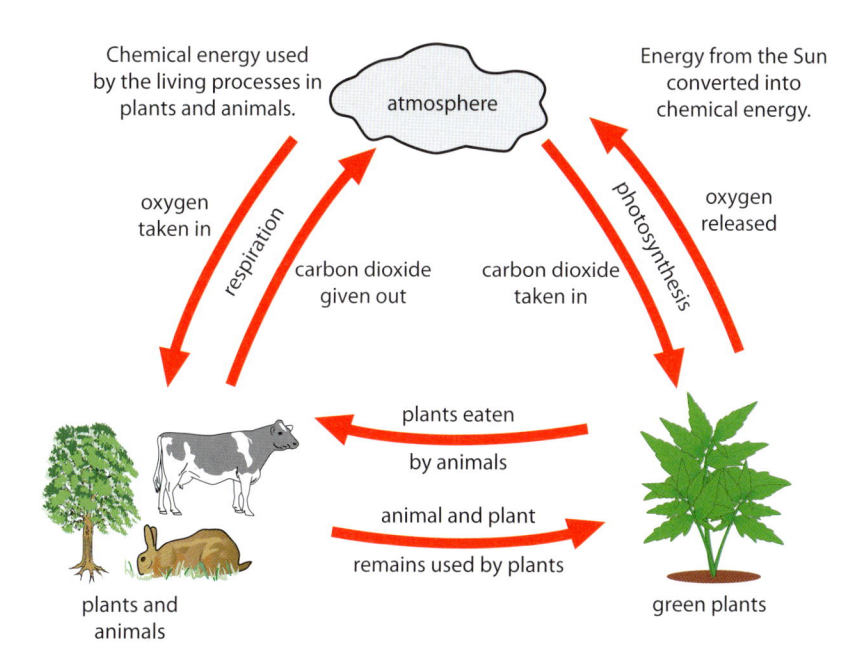

Figure 12.5
Oxygen and carbon cycles showing respiration and photosynthesis.

Respiration:
glucose + oxygen → carbon dioxide + water
$C_6H_{12}O_6$ (aq) + $6O_2$(g) → $6CO_2$(g) + $6H_2O$(g)

Photosynthesis:
carbon dioxide + water → glucose + oxygen
$6CO_2$(g) + $6H_2O$(g) → $C_6H_{12}O_6$ (aq) + $6O_2$(g)

Carbon dioxide

Carbon dioxide makes up only about 0.03% of the atmosphere. This means that when we take a deep breath, we only breathe in about a tenth of a cubic centimetre of it with each breath. However, it is a very important gas in the atmosphere. It is given off when materials that contain carbon combine with oxygen in processes such as burning and respiration. It is absorbed from the air during photosynthesis. Carbon, like oxygen, is continuously recycled in these processes. The same processes recycle both elements (Figure 12.5).

The proportion of carbon dioxide in the atmosphere in 1890 was about 20% less than it is today. This proportion has increased because we are burning an increasingly large amount of fossil fuels and also because the green plants, particularly ocean plants, are not removing as much from the air as they used to. This increase is worrying scientists and this is studied further below.

The properties of carbon dioxide are summarised in Table 12.3

Carbon dioxide

Sublimes at −78 °C (solid turns to gas).
Molecular formula CO_2.
Colourless gas.
Has no smell.
Slightly soluble in water.
Solution is a weakly acidic.
Does not burn.
Extinguishes burning materials.
Turns limewater milky.

▲ Table 12.3
The properties of carbon dioxide.

The inert gases

The inert gases, you will recall, are the elements in Group VIII of the periodic table. All of them are found the atmosphere. Argon makes up about 1% of the atmosphere. This means that an average classroom will contain 3–4 cubic metres of it. It is quite a common gas! The other inert gases are more rare, as Table 12.4 shows.

▶ **Table 12.4**
Some properties of inert gases.

Gas	% in dry air	Boiling point (°C)
Helium	0.0005	−269
Neon	0.002	−246
Argon	1	−186
Krypton	0.0001	−152
Xenon	0.00001	−107

The discovery of the inert gases is an interesting story. As long ago as 1785, only ten years after the discovery of oxygen in the air, a British scientist called Henry Cavendish was working on the problem of the composition of air. He carried out some difficult experiments in which he absorbed all the oxygen and nitrogen from the air. Every time he did the experiment he was surprised to find that a little bit of the air was left over; 'Not more than $\frac{1}{120}$th part of the whole' he wrote at the time. Nobody could explain it then and the work was forgotten for a hundred years.

In 1895, the physicist Lord Rayleigh made some nitrogen from dry air by removing oxygen and carbon dioxide from it. He noticed that this nitrogen was slightly denser than nitrogen prepared chemically. He then isolated argon from it and found that argon had a density that was 50% more than nitrogen. It was only then that scientists realised how important the work of Cavendish was a century earlier.

Rayleigh named the gas 'argon' and in 1904 he was awarded the Nobel physics prize for his work. His colleague, the Scottish chemist William Ramsay, won the chemistry prize in the same year for discovering the other gases and putting them in their places in the Periodic Table.

How scientists work

Scientists look for evidence. They do this by designing investigations and making observations. Based on the observations, they then design more investigations to give more evidence.

Then they think up theories that explain the evidence. Sometimes they find evidence that cannot be explained by the theory. What do they do then? They must either adapt the theory to fit the new evidence. Or they must develop a completely new theory.

An important theory about air and burning was the Phlogiston theory. This was a powerful theory; it stated that substances that burn contain something called 'phlogiston'. When they burn, the phlogiston is given off into the air. This explains why things gradually disappear when they burn.

Things burn very brightly in oxygen. Oxygen, it was said, was a special form of air that had no phlogiston in it and so it made things burn better as the phlogiston was sucked out of the burning object more rapidly. Oxygen was called 'dephlogisticated air'.

Things did not burn in nitrogen because, it was said, nitrogen was saturated with phlogiston and could not absorb more. It was called 'phlogisticated air'.

The phlogiston theory was replaced by our modern theory of burning, mainly due to the French chemist Lavoisier (who was guillotined in the French Revolution because he was an aristocrat). He showed that substances actually increased in weight when they burnt, not decreased. The phlogiston theory could not explain this evidence.

Chemistry and the environment

Here are some paragraphs from one of the most famous chemistry research papers. It was published by Henry Cavendish in a scientific journal called *Philosophical Transactions of the Royal Society*, Volume 75, page 372, in 1785. It describes some of the earliest accurate work on the composition of the air. The original paragraphs are on the left and an explanation is on the right. This is the paper where he reported the existence of what was later called argon.

Figure 12.6
Henry Cavendish, 1731–1810, a member of the English aristocratic family that includes the Dukes of Devonshire. He discovered hydrogen and worked on the composition of air. The Cavendish Laboratory, the physics laboratory at the University of Cambridge, was named after him. The Cavendish has produced 29 Nobel prizewinners.

Websites

There is an excellent online collection of the original research papers that describe many of the discoveries mentioned in this book. Go to www.heinemann.co.uk/hotlinks, insert the express code 6799P and click on 12.1.

From the original paper

… As far as the experiments hitherto published extend, we scarcely know more of the nature of the phlogisticated part of our atmosphere, than that it is not diminished by limewater, caustic alkalis, or nitrous air; that it is unfit to support fire, or maintain life in animals; and that its specific gravity is not much less than that of common air; so that, though the nitrous acid, by being united to phlogiston, is converted into air possessed of these properties, and consequently, though it was reasonable to suppose that part at least of the phlogisticated air of the atmosphere consists of this acid united to phlogiston, yet it might fairly be doubted whether the whole is of this kind, or whether there are not in reality many different substances confounded together by us under the name of phlogisticated air…

…I then, in order to decompound as much as I could of the phlogisticated air which remained in the tube, added some dephlogisticated air to it, and continued the spark till no further diminution took place. Having by these means condensed as much as I could of the phlogisticated air, I let up some solution of liver of sulphur to absorb the dephlogisticated air; after which only a small bubble of air remained unabsorbed, which certainly was not more than $\frac{1}{120}$ of the bulk of the phlogisticated air let up into the tube; so that if there is any part of the phlogisticated air of our atmosphere which differs from the rest, and cannot be reduced to nitrous acid, we may safely conclude, that it is not more than $\frac{1}{120}$ part of the whole.

Some notes explaining the work

In this first quotation Cavendish describes the properties of the part of the air he has discovered, which he called phlogisticated air (and which we call nitrogen). He says it does not react with limewater or alkali (as carbon dioxide does). It does not react with 'nitrous air'. This is the gas nitrogen monoxide, which reacts with oxygen to form brown nitrogen dioxide, which is soluble in water. It does not support burning or life (this was tested with a mouse which died). Yet it is otherwise the same as air ('common air').

He refers to 'nitrous acid, by being united to phlogiston'. This is pure nitrogen, which he knew how to make, probably from ammonium nitrite. The key question he asks is whether his 'phlogisticated air' is indeed pure nitrogen or a mixture of different gases ('confounded together').

This is the famous quotation from the end of the same paragraph as above. He created a static electricity spark, which he discharged through the air. This caused nitrogen to combine with oxygen to form nitrogen dioxide, which then dissolved in water. This used up ('condensed') the nitrogen ('phlogisticated air'). He then absorbed any remaining oxygen with 'liver of sulphur' a substance that is mainly potassium sulfide and reacts readily with oxygen.

But there was always a 'small bubble' left behind that did not react. It is clear that he did not believe that this was experimental error as he always found it every time he did the experiment. He had discovered the inert gas argon, which is $\frac{1}{120}$th of air, but he did not know it.

163

12.2 Pollution of the atmosphere

Some of the planets and moons in our solar system have atmospheres; others do not. The ones that have no atmosphere are all either very cold, if they are far from the Sun, or very hot, if they are near the Sun. Mercury is the nearest planet to the Sun and it has no atmosphere. The temperature of the side facing the Sun is very hot, about 425 °C, and the temperature of the side facing away from the Sun is very cold, about −180 °C. Venus, the next planet from the Sun, has a thick atmosphere and it has a temperature all over its surface of about 500 °C, hotter than Mercury. It is the atmosphere on Venus that keeps it warm, even on the night side. The atmosphere is like a blanket that traps the heat of the Sun.

Our atmosphere contains just the right amount of gases to keep the temperature of the surface of the Earth at an average of about 25 °C. This is very important because life on Earth depends on the existence of liquid water, and water is only a liquid between 0 °C and 100 °C. Life could not have evolved if the temperature was either too high or too low for water to exist as a liquid.

If life is to continue on Earth, it is important that the temperature of the surface does not change much. This temperature is kept at a temperature suitable for life by our atmosphere. It is very important, therefore, that we should look after our atmosphere. Unfortunately we often use it as a huge dustbin for any gas or smoke that we want to get rid of.

> **DID YOU KNOW?**
>
> The body temperature of all warm-blooded animals is about the same, 37 °C. This is because the important molecules called enzymes, which catalyse the chemical reactions in the body, work best at this temperature. This means that there can only be similar life on planets that have a similar constant temperature to the Earth.

▶ **Figure 12.7**
Large industrial works often use the atmosphere to get rid of unwanted sulfur dioxide and other gases through high chimneys.

We cause pollution of the atmosphere whenever we put into it any waste gases that are not normally there. We also put into the air many gases (such as carbon dioxide or sulfur dioxide) that are there naturally. If we cause the concentration of these gases to increase much above their natural concentrations, then we cause pollution. Table 12.5 and Figures 12.8 and 12.9 show some of the ways we pollute the air and the problems the pollution can cause.

Chemistry and the environment

Pollutant	Source	Effect
Carbon monoxide	Incomplete burning of fuels.	Poisonous. It combines with haemoglobin in the blood and so prevents the blood carrying oxygen around the body.
Carbon dioxide	Combustion of fuels.	Too much carbon dioxide in the air causes the temperature of the surface of the Earth to rise. This is called the greenhouse effect and it is described later in this chapter.
Sulfur dioxide	Burning of fuels that contained sulfur as an impurity and the smelting of sulfide ores.	Dissolves in rain, making the rain acidic. This causes damage to limestone and concrete buildings. It also makes some soils very acidic killing the vegetation. This is a particular problem in some eastern parts of Europe where large areas of evergreen forests are dying. Sulfur dioxide also prevents the proper growth of plants by stopping photosynthesis.
Oxides of nitrogen	Formed in car engines when oxygen and nitrogen in the air combine at the high pressures and temperatures of the engine.	Causes acidic rain with effects similar to those described above.
Chlorofluorocarbons (CFCs)	From aerosol sprays and refrigerators.	Destroys the layer of gas called the ozone layer in the upper atmosphere. This is described later in this chapter.

▲ Table 12.5
Some common air pollutants.

▲ Figure 12.8
Acid rain damage to limestone carvings.

▲ Figure 12.9
The acid rain that has killed these trees came from factories many miles away and upwind.

DID YOU KNOW?

When there are a lot of pollutant gases from motor vehicles, the Sun can cause them to react with each other and make a lot of very unpleasant substances that are poisonous and can irritate the eyes and throat. This effect is particularly bad when the warm air near the surface of the Earth is trapped under a layer of cold air. The pollutants cannot then escape into the upper atmosphere and spread out. This effect is called 'temperature inversion' and occurs in cities near coasts where cool winds blow in off the sea and rise to go over hills behind the city. There are a number of cities where this can happen and air pollution is often particularly bad there. Examples include Los Angeles, Tokyo and Rio de Janeiro.

One form of air pollution that used to be serious but has now been stopped is pollution by particles containing the metal lead. This was taken in when we breathed and taken by the blood to the brain where it caused damage. Some years ago, the petrol companies phased out the use of lead in petrol (it was added to make the petrol burn more smoothly) and such pollution has largely disappeared. This is a good example of how we can stop air pollution if we want to.

165

Figure 12.10
People who work outside in our cities often wear masks to protect their lungs against the effects of the chemicals that are produced from pollutants in the air.

Pollution caused by our cities

Scientists have only recently begun to understand all the different chemical reactions that go on in the different layers of the atmosphere. These reactions all help to keep the gases in the atmosphere at the correct concentration. We are learning now how some of the pollutants can interfere with these reactions and cause changes in the natural balance of the gases.

Summer is usually the worst time for air pollution in our cities. This is because the chemical reactions that take place in the air between the pollutants often need sunlight. These reactions are called **photochemical** reactions. The starting materials for these reactions are the gases that are produced by car exhausts. These react together in the sunlight and the air in some of our cities becomes a gaseous soup of many unpleasant compounds that can make breathing quite difficult. Some of these compounds are known to cause cancers.

This is why many towns and cities are creating pedestrian areas, where vehicles are not allowed. Many towns are also encouraging people to travel by vehicles that do not cause air pollution, such as electric buses and trains. The air in these towns is now of a much better quality.

Another way of reducing air pollution in our cities is to ensure that all the vehicles are fitted with catalytic converters. These are devices which are placed in the exhaust pipe of the vehicles and which contain very small quantities of metals such as platinum. Figure 12.11 shows how a catalytic converter works; when the hot exhaust passes through these converters, many of the nasty chemicals in the exhaust are oxidised. Unburnt petrol is converted to carbon dioxide. Carbon monoxide is converted to carbon dioxide. The converter also changes oxides of nitrogen back to nitrogen. These oxides of nitrogen (often called 'NO_x') are produced in the high temperature and pressure of the engine from the oxygen and nitrogen in the air that the engine uses.

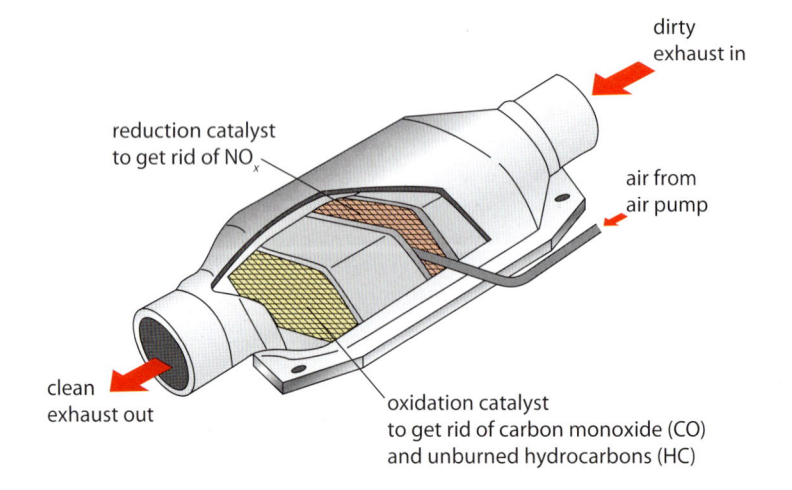

Figure 12.11
Section of a catalytic converter.

dirty exhaust in

reduction catalyst to get rid of NO_x

air from air pump

clean exhaust out

oxidation catalyst to get rid of carbon monoxide (CO) and unburned hydrocarbons (HC)

Chemistry and the environment

Two more ways in which pollutants can interfere with the balance of gases are by causing the atmosphere to heat up, and by destroying the ozone layer.

The greenhouse effect

Everything gives off heat. Radiant heat is a form of electromagnetic radiation, like light. Substances that are very hot give off heat radiation that has a higher frequency than substances that are cool. This is well known; a very hot fire is yellowish white and a cooler one is red. Red light is radiation with a lower frequency than yellow light. The Sun is very hot; its surface is about 6000 °C. Much of the radiation it gives off has a high frequency. This radiation comes through the atmosphere and warms the Earth.

The Earth is only around 25 °C and so it emits heat radiation of a lower frequency than the Sun. This heat radiation can be absorbed by certain molecules in the atmosphere. Compounds that can absorb this energy are water vapour, methane and carbon dioxide. This is why a cloudy night in winter is usually warmer than a clear night; the water in the clouds stops the heat escaping.

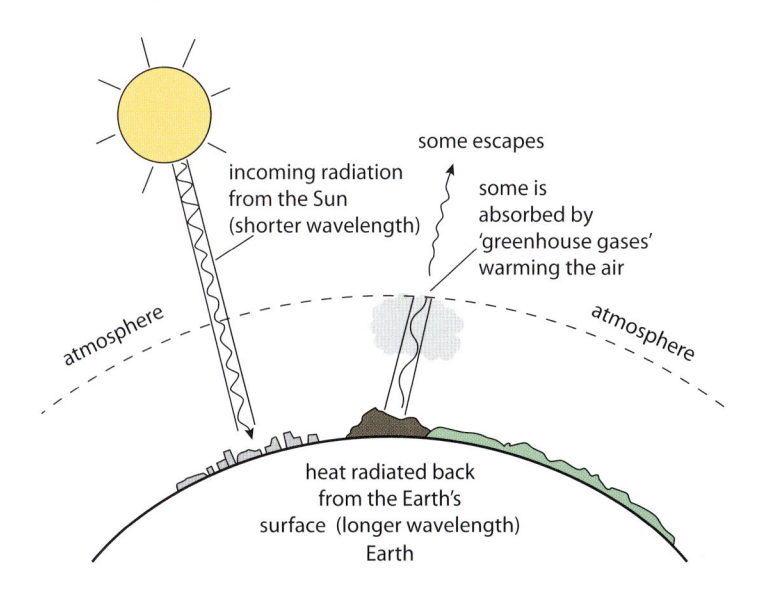

◀ Figure 12.12
The greenhouse effect.

It is the presence of gases such as methane, water vapour and carbon dioxide in the air that keeps our planet warm. This is called the 'greenhouse effect' and these gases are sometimes called 'greenhouse gases'. If the concentration of these gases increases, then there is a possibility that the planet might heat up too much. We do not yet know much about what might happen if the planet were to heat up, but we can guess that it will cause the water in the oceans to expand. The sea level will rise and could flood low lying cities. Some of the Pacific Island countries could even disappear. It is also becoming clear that this effect will cause climate change, often bringing us more extreme weather such as heavier storms.

The United Nations organisation has recently held a number of important meetings at which nations have tried to plan for a gradual

DID YOU KNOW?

If all the sea heats up by just 0.1 °C, the amount of energy it will absorb is more than all the electricity we have ever generated. It is not surprising that this will cause some changes in our climate.

reduction in the amounts of greenhouse gases they put into the atmosphere. So far there has been very little agreement on what action to take.

The ozone layer

Ozone is a form of oxygen. Instead of two atoms in the molecule, ozone has three. It is formed in the upper atmosphere when high frequency radiation (called cosmic radiation) from the Sun causes oxygen molecules to form ozone. Ozone is a very important gas to us, as it forms a shield in the upper atmosphere that prevents cosmic radiation and ultraviolet radiation, which are harmful to living things, from reaching us.

Some chemicals used in refrigerators and aerosol spray cans can damage the ozone layer. These compounds are called chlorofluorocarbons or CFCs. They are very unreactive substances and therefore they stay in the atmosphere a long time. Gradually they diffuse up to the upper levels of the atmosphere. Here they break down when cosmic radiation hits them to produce chlorine atoms. It is these chlorine atoms that react with ozone. One chlorine atom can destroy many molecules of ozone because it acts as a **catalyst** and is not used up itself. In recent years, the ozone layer has been getting thinner because of this. This has been most noticeable over the South Pole where the CFCs diffuse during the quiet winter months when there is not much wind. In the spring when radiation from the Sun first hits the atmosphere over the South Pole, chlorine atoms are formed and the ozone is destroyed.

The ozone 'hole' in the southern spring allows harmful radiation to reach the Earth's surface and this has caused damage to the eyes of farm animals in the south of South America. It is predicted that there will be an increase in skin cancer amongst people who sunbathe in spring in countries like Australia and South Africa. This skin cancer is caused by an increase in the amount of harmful radiation getting through the atmosphere.

Most of the nations have now agreed to reduce the amount of CFCs they produce but many scientists studying the ozone 'holes' which appear now above both poles in spring believe that more must be done. One point that particularly worries the scientists is that the CFCs stay in the atmosphere so long that even if all use were stopped now, it would be over ten years before the ozone layer stopped getting thinner.

12.3 Water

The water we use in our homes comes from rivers, lakes and boreholes and even in some cases, the sea. Before it can be used for drinking it must be purified, as water is the most common carrier of disease. Water is a very good solvent and so the water we drink always contains dissolved substances. Water without any dissolved material in it tastes very dull and bland.

> **DID YOU KNOW?**
>
> Ozone is quite a well-known gas. Photocopiers and any other source of static electricity can cause it to form from oxygen. You may have noticed a strange bitter smell near photocopiers; this is ozone. It is a poisonous gas and is formed on hot days in badly polluted cities.

> **DID YOU KNOW?**
>
> One of the substances that is dissolved in the water we drink is oxygen gas. In fact the concentration of oxygen dissolved in water saturated with oxygen, is about one and a half times greater than the concentration of oxygen in air. This dissolved oxygen is very important as it helps chemical and biological reactions that naturally clean up dirty water.

Chemistry and the environment

The water cycle

Because water is such a good solvent, most of the water on the planet is salty. Rain has dissolved the salt out of the rocks on the Earth's surface and washed it down into the sea. However, the water that we drink does not come directly from the sea. It first evaporates from the sea and then condenses as rain. This process is called the water cycle.

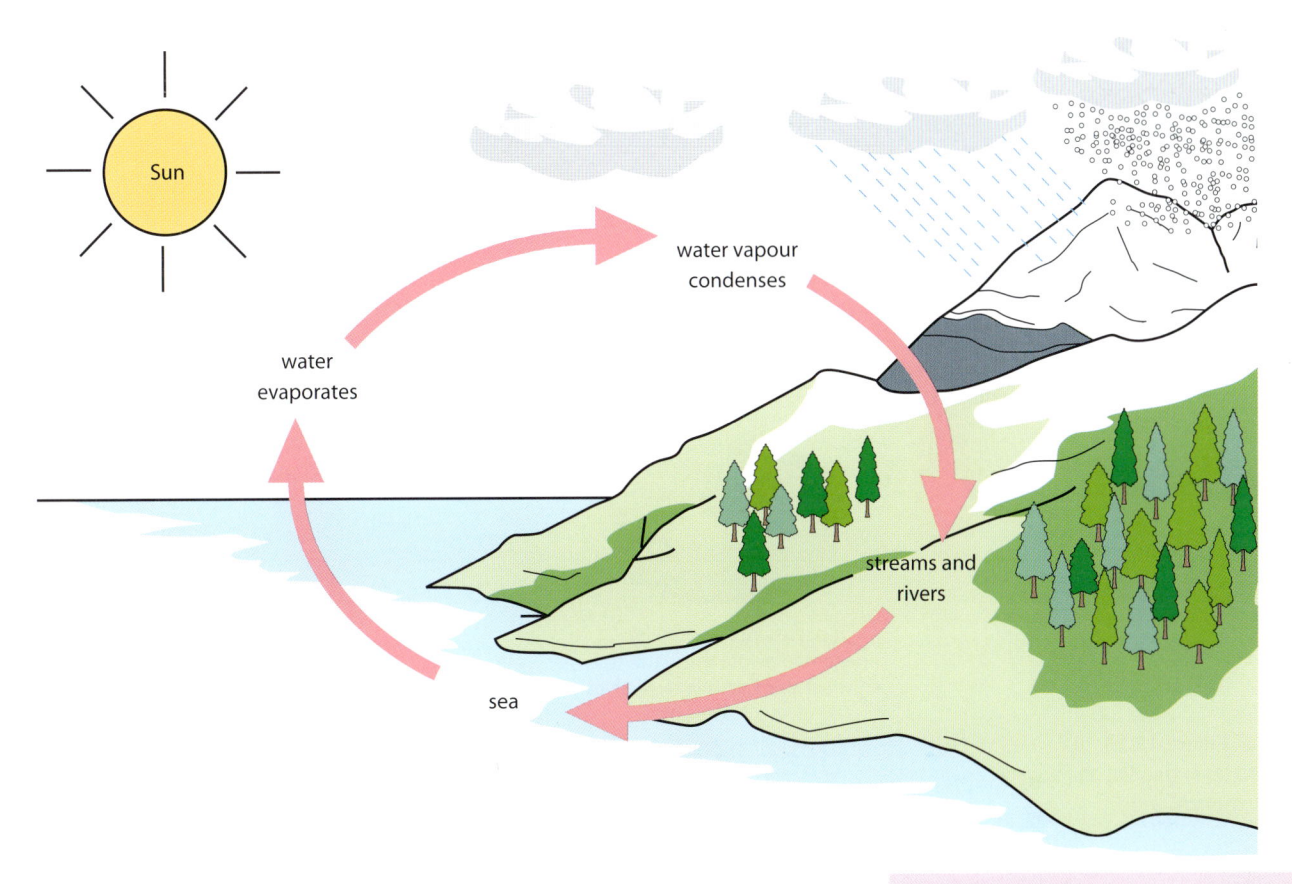

▲ Figure 12.13
The water cycle.

Using water

The water in the lakes and the rivers that we drink is fresh water. It may, however, contain suspended solids. These are particles of solids which are insoluble but which the river water is carrying along as it flows. These are removed from the water by filtering it though a bed of sand. Bacteria in the water will pass though the sand filter and therefore these have to be killed before the water is suitable for drinking. To do this, some chlorine gas is bubbled though the water. You can often smell the chlorine in drinking water.

Sewage is 98–99% water and it is sensible to recover the pure water from it. To do this it is first filtered to remove large solids. It is then held in tanks to allow more solids to settle out. The liquid is then passed through gravel beds, which contain bacteria that decompose the organic substances in the water. This water is good enough to be put into a purification plant to make drinking water. It is often said that the water drunk in a city such as London has been drunk ten times before on its way down the river!

Water is pumped out of the river.

It is filtered to remove solids.

It is chlorinated to remove bacteria.

It is pumped to the storage tank.

It goes to the houses.

It leaves the houses as sewage.

The sewage is filtered.

It passes into a sprinkler system to aerate the water to allow aerobic bacteria to clean it.

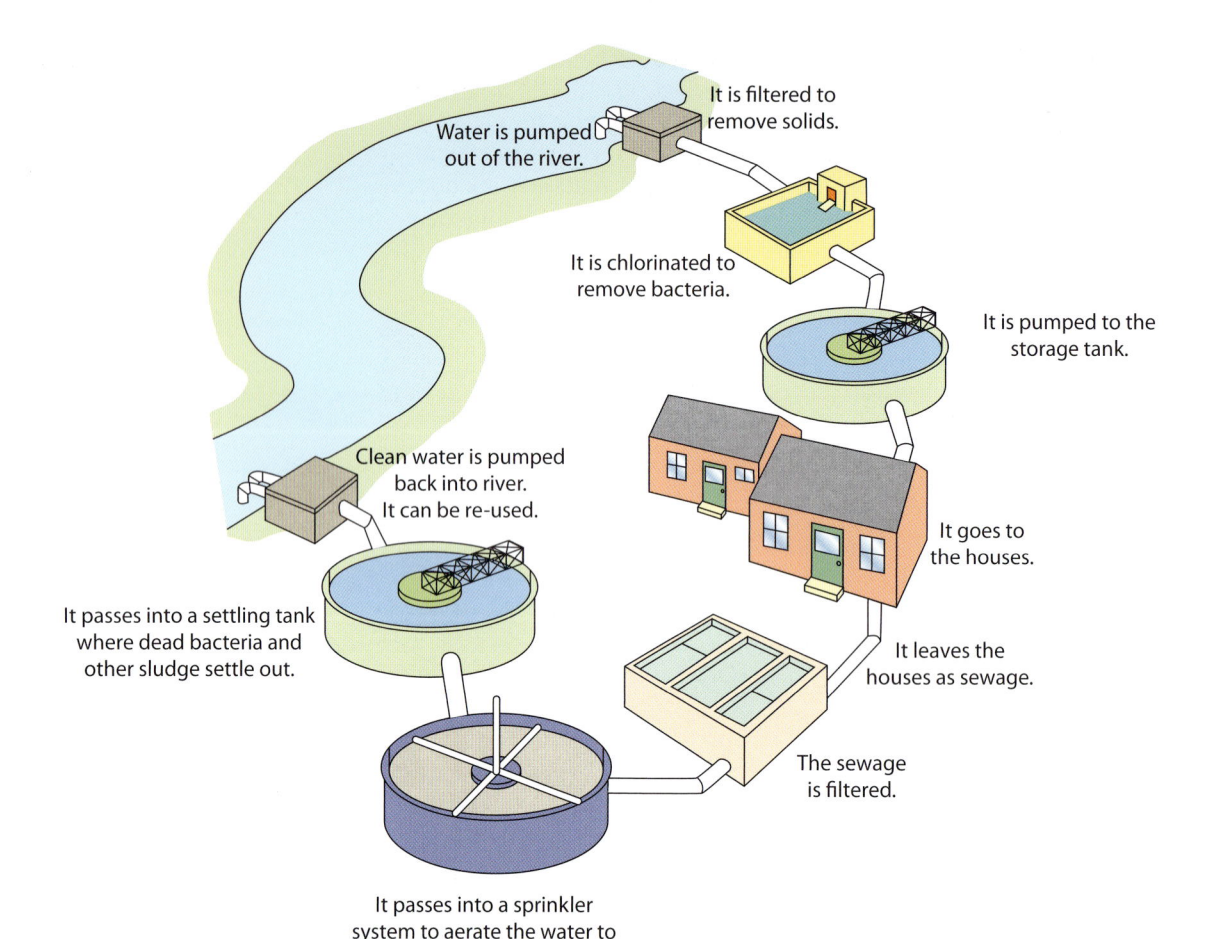

It passes into a settling tank where dead bacteria and other sludge settle out.

Clean water is pumped back into river. It can be re-used.

▲ Figure 12.14 Water extraction and sewage treatment.

Uses of water

We often think that the main use of water is in our homes, but in many parts of the world this is not the case. Water is used industrially for cleaning and cooling. Slaughterhouses, for example, use a lot of water to ensure that the meat they produce is clean. A particularly important use for water is in cooling. Many power stations cool the steam that has been used to drive turbines with water. In fact some power stations use so much water for cooling that when we are asked to save water in times of drought, we can save a lot by just turning off the lights!

Pollution of water

When we use water we make it dirty. Very often after it has been used, it is returned to rivers and lakes without being properly treated to clean it. This causes water pollution.

A serious form of pollution occurs when the soluble impurities in the water are phosphates or nitrates. These are plant nutrients and cause the growth of a lot of algae (an algal 'bloom') in the water. When these algae eventually die, they rot. When rotting takes place bacteria are involved that need oxygen. If there is too much algae rotting then all the dissolved oxygen in the water is used up. This means that all the other life in the water that needs oxygen dies. This process is called **eutrophication.**

The nitrates and phosphates that cause pollution often come from fertilisers or from dairy farms that wash out their dairies (which contain droppings from the cows) into slurry tanks. The slurry is usually spread on the fields but it quite often gets into streams and rivers. Badly polluted rivers can often be found in open country far away from the polluting industry.

QUESTIONS

12.1 Draw a pie chart showing the composition of air. Include the four most common gases by name but include all the others in a single segment.

12.2 Devise an experiment that you could do to find the percentage of oxygen in the air you breathe out. Describe the measurements you would make and the calculations you would do.

12.3 When we breathe and when we burn things we are continually using up oxygen from the air. Yet the percentage of oxygen in the air stays constant. Explain why this is so.

12.4 Respiration is a chemical reaction. Explain what happens during the reaction. Describe the similarities between this reaction and photosynthesis.

12.5 Look at Table 12.5 of the causes of air pollution. For each gas, write down at least one way that you can think of that will reduce the pollution.

12.6 Design an experiment to show that gases from the burning of fuels are acidic.

12.7 Sometimes farmers have to throw away supplies of milk that are accidentally contaminated or which go sour before they reach the dairy. Some of them throw it away in a river. Explain how this can cause serious water pollution.

12.8 Draw a flow chart to show how sewage can be converted into water that can be safely drunk.

12.9 Explain the how air pollution can cause:
(a) the greenhouse effect
(b) the thinning of the ozone layer.
Suggest ways that this pollution can be reduced.

Summary

Now that you have completed this chapter, you should be able to:

- describe a method for determining the percentage of oxygen in air
- know the names of the main gases that make up the atmosphere and of their approximate proportions
- understand how the oxygen cycle works to regulate the proportion of oxygen and carbon dioxide in the air
- know the main physical and chemical properties of oxygen, nitrogen and carbon dioxide
- name the main gases in the atmosphere and know the common uses we make of them
- know the main sources and consequences of atmospheric pollution and be able to discuss knowledgeably how such pollution can be reduced
- understand the origins of the atmospheric 'greenhouse effect' and why it is important to take action to reduce it
- understand how the ozone layer is created and why it is important to life on Earth.
- explain the water cycle and why it is essential to the survival of life
- understand how drinking water is prepared and how sewage is treated to minimise pollution of our water supplies
- describe the main kinds and causes of water pollution
- **S** describe and explain the presence of oxides of nitrogen in car exhausts and their catalytic removal.

Chapter 13

Fast and slow reactions

Chemical reactions go on around us (and inside us) all the time. They all go at different speeds.

▶ Figure 13.1
Softening onions – a slow reaction that breaks down some of the cellulose of the cell walls. If you try to speed this up, some of the molecules will break down completely into black carbon.

▶ Figure 13.2
This reaction is over in a fraction of a second.

▼ Figure 13.3
This kudu is respiring. In all its body cells, glucose is being converted into water and carbon dioxide. All around it this reaction is going backwards. In the leaves of the plants, carbon dioxide and water are being converted into glucose.

▲ Figure 13.4
This apple is reacting but very slowly. A complex series of reactions are going on inside it that make it produce more of a sugar called fructose as it ripens. Interestingly, you can make these reactions speed up by putting it in a box with other, riper, apples, or with a ripe banana. What do you think makes that happen?

173

▶ **Figure 13.5**
You know that the protein in the egg in the top photograph can be converted into the protein in the photograph below by heating in boiling water for four minutes. Did you know that if the temperature were only 90 °C and not 100 °C this reaction would take many hours.

Some reactions are slow, such as the reactions in cooking and in our stomachs. Other reactions, such as a bush fire, are fast. In this chapter you will study some reactions and find out why some reactions are faster than others. You will also look at some reactions, like photosynthesis and respiration, that can work both ways. These reactions can be made to go one way or the other just by changing the reaction conditions. How fast a chemical reaction proceeds, and in which direction, depend on a number of factors; these will be studied in this chapter.

13.1 Making reactions go faster

For any chemical reaction to take place two things have to happen.
- Firstly the two reacting molecules or ions have to hit each other.
- Secondly, the collision has to result in a reaction with bonds broken and new ones made.

So if we want reactions to speed up, we must think of ways of causing *more* collisions and by causing *harder* collisions. First, however, it is necessary to think up some ways of measuring how fast a reaction is going. Figures 13.6 and 13.7 show two ways. The second is the better one but it needs a balance that will permit quick accurate weighing.

The reaction in both figures is the well-known one between an acid and a carbonate in which carbon dioxide is produced.

calcium carbonate + hydrochloric acid → calcium chloride + water + carbon dioxide
$$CaCO_3(s) + 2HCl(aq) \rightarrow CaCl_2(aq) + H_2O(l) + CO_2(g)$$

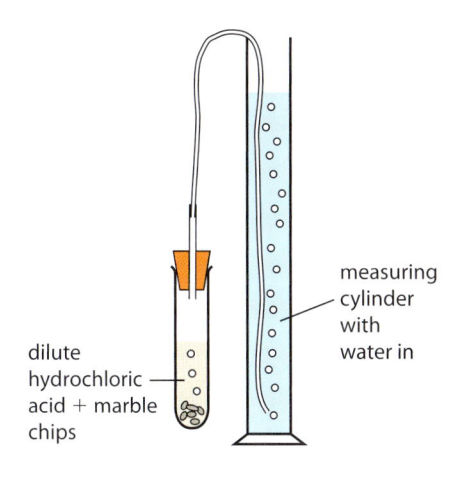

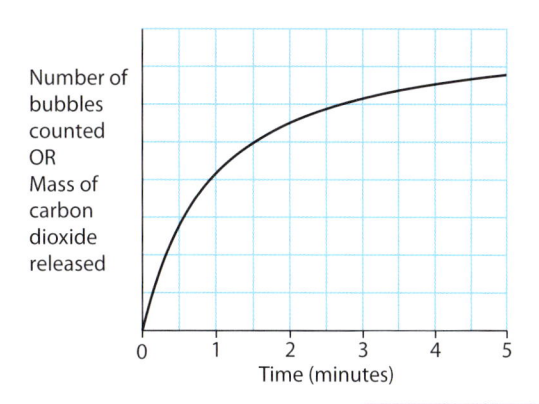

Fast and slow reactions

▲ Figure 13.6
Apparatus for bubble counting.

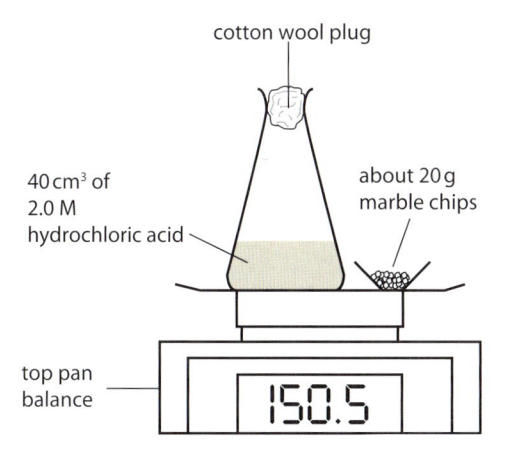

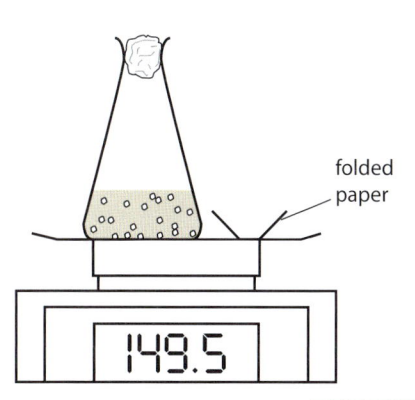

▲ Figure 13.7
Rate measuring apparatus using a top pan balance

We can measure how fast the reaction is going using either of these methods. In the first method, we can count the number of bubbles produced and we can then plot a graph for the number of bubbles produced in the reaction against time.

In the second method, we can record the mass of the reaction vessel each minute. This will decrease as the gas is given off. If we subtract the mass recorded each minute from the original mass, we get the mass of carbon dioxide given off. We can plot the graph of carbon dioxide release against time.

Both graphs will look like the curve in Figure 13.6 and they show that the reaction proceeds fast initially and then slows down and finally stops. It stops because all the acid has been used up. This measures what we call the **rate of reaction**.

⚡ Activity 13.1
Measuring a reaction rate

What happens to the rate if we change the size of the particles of marble or if we change the concentration of the acid?

The graphs below show the effect of particle size and concentration. In both cases the units on the y-axis will depend on what is measured and it will either be number of gas bubbles or the loss of mass.

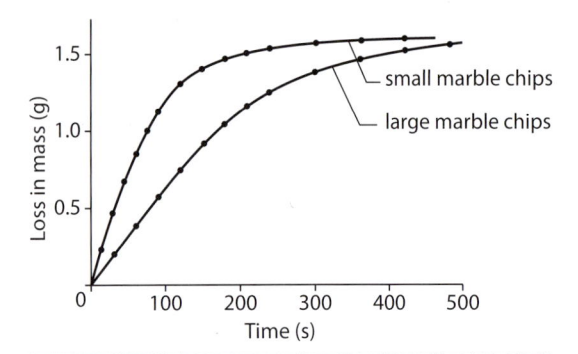

▲ **Figure 13.8**
How the size of the marble chip particles affects the rate of reaction.

▲ **Figure 13.9**
How the concentration of the acid affects the rate of reaction.

You can see the following points from this graph.
- The overall amount of carbon dioxide lost in both experiments is the same. This is because the reaction stopped when all the acid had been used and the amount of acid used in each experiment was the same.
- In both cases the reaction started rapidly and gradually slowed down as the acid was used up.
- The rate of reaction to begin with for the small chips was faster than with the larger chips and the reaction was over sooner.
- The reaction with the small particles is faster because the larger number of small particles will have a greater surface area than a small number of large particles. This will mean more collisions with the acid ions.
- The reaction gets slower as the acid is used up because there are fewer acid ions around and therefore there will be fewer collisions.

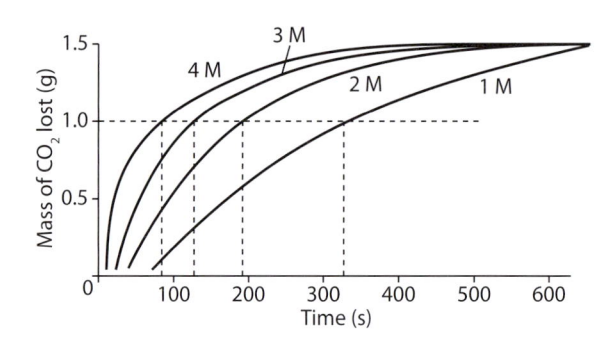

Some important points can be noted from the curves above. (Note that the acid concentration is expressed as the molarity of the acid. The most concentrated acid is 4 M and the least concentrated is 1 M. This idea will be explained in Chapter 17.)
- Again the overall amount of carbon dioxide lost in all experiments is the same because the amount of acid used in each experiment was the same.
- Again the reaction started rapidly and gradually slowed down as the acid was used up.
- The reaction went fastest when the concentration of acid is greatest. This is because when there are more acid ions around there will be more collisions with the calcium carbonate particles and therefore more particles will react.

Looking further at the results in Figure 13.9

The graph in Figure 13.9 can be analysed further. For each concentration, read from the graph the time taken for a particular mass (or number of bubbles) of carbon dioxide to be lost. In Figure 13.9 the mass of 1 g of carbon dioxide has been chosen. Note that this time is shortest for the highest concentration. Make a table of the results from the graph like Table 13.1.

▶ **Table 13.1**
Results from Figure 13.9.

Concentration (molarity)	Time to lose 1 g CO_2 (seconds)	Rate of loss of CO_2 (1/time)
4 M	80	0.0125
3 M	120	0.0083
2 M	190	0.0060
1 M	325	0.0030

The graph of time against concentration of the acid can be plotted. This should give a curve like the first one in Figure 13.10. This is not a

Fast and slow reactions

particularly useful shape to draw any conclusions from. However, we are really interested in finding out how the *rate* of the reaction varies with concentration, not the *time* taken to produce 1g of carbon dioxide.

The rate of reaction is the amount of carbon dioxide produced *per second*. To calculate this, we simply divide the mass of carbon dioxide (1g) by the time taken to produce it. These results are shown in column 3 of Table 13.1. The second graph in Figure 13.10 is a plot of this rate ($\frac{1}{t}$) against concentration.

> **Activity 13.2**
> How does particle size affect reaction rate?

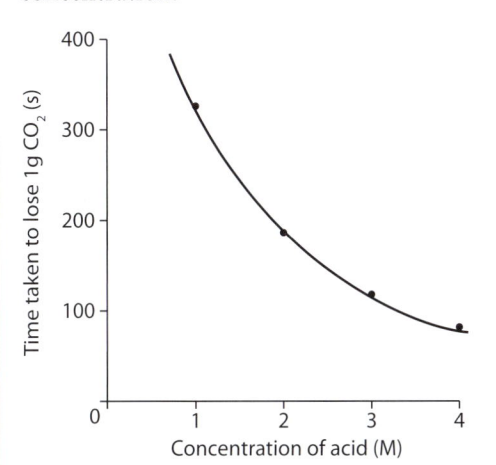

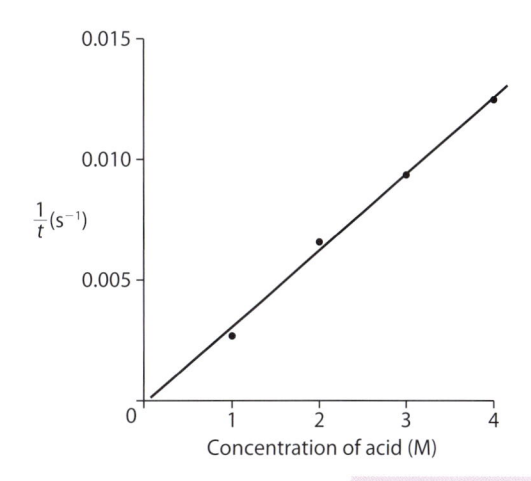

The graph of reaction rate against concentration is a straight line passing through zero. You will know from your mathematics that this means that the rate of the reaction is directly proportional to the concentration of the acid. This means that if the concentration of the acid doubles, the reaction goes twice as fast.

▲ **Figure 13.10**
Rate of reaction graphs for acid/marble experiment.

If you think of what is happening to the particles, you would expect this result. If we double the number of particles per cm³, we will double the number hitting the marble in any given time. This will double the number of collisions that result in a reaction and so double the rate of reaction.

> **Activity 13.3**
> How does concentration affect reaction rate?

What is the effect on the rate of changing the temperature of the reaction?

Can you predict what would happen to the shape of the curve if you repeated the same reaction but at a higher temperature? Figure 13.11 shows this for two different temperatures on the same axes.

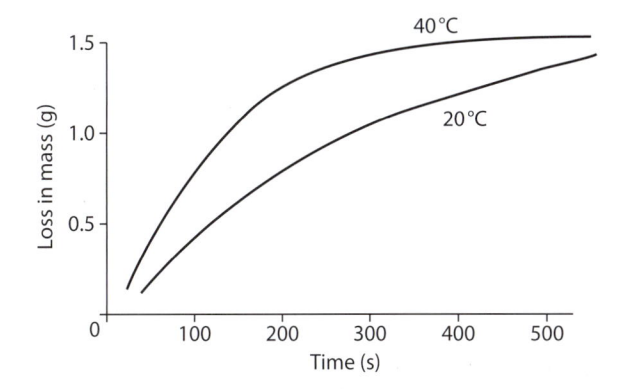

◀ **Figure 13.11**
Graph of rates of reaction at different temperatures.

177

The graph clearly shows that the reaction at the higher temperature is faster than the reaction at the lower temperature. This is a very common observation; we know, for example, that detergent reacts with grease on clothes faster if we use hot water in the wash (and think about the egg boiling in Figure 13.5).

Particle theory can explain the observation that a reaction gets faster if the temperature is increased. If the temperature of the acid is higher, the particles will be moving faster. If they move faster they will hit the particles of marble more frequently and they will also hit the marble harder. There would be therefore be more collisions and the collisions would be more likely to result in a reaction. The rate of the reaction would therefore be expected to increase.

> **Activity 13.4**
> How does temperature affect reaction rate?

How does a catalyst affect the rate of reaction?

There have been many references to catalysts throughout this book. The use of transition metals as catalysts is discussed in Chapter 9. The use of catalysts in the manufacture of ammonia and of sulfuric acid will be covered in the next chapter, and in Chapter 15, the use of catalysts in the manufacture of margarine and of polythene will be mentioned. Not all catalysts are good for us, however; you have also read in Chapter 12 about how chlorine atoms can catalyse the destruction of the protective ozone layer.

> **Activity 13.5**
> What is the effect of a catalyst on reaction rate?

Catalysts are very important because they speed up chemical reactions and allow us to carry them out using much less energy. An important property of catalysts is that they are not themselves used up during the reaction.

Here is a simple example of the use of a catalyst.

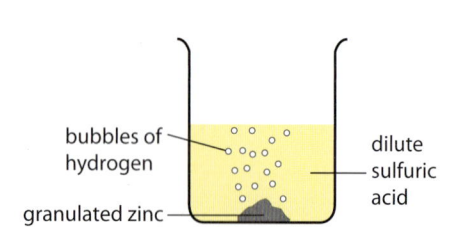

The dilute sulfuric acid in the beaker is reacting with zinc to produce hydrogen gas.

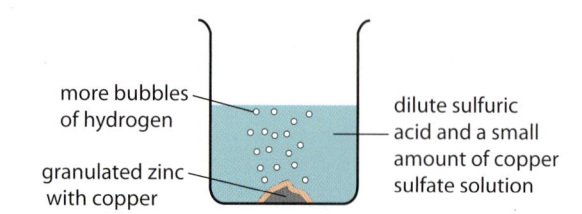

In this beaker the reaction to produce the hydrogen gas is going much faster because the zinc is coated in a small quantity of copper. The copper has been produced by the reaction between the zinc metal and copper ions in the solution.

The copper is acting as a catalyst in this reaction. It is not used up.

Figure 13.12 shows a spectacular demonstration of the effect of a catalyst. Hydrogen is a very flammable gas but normally it needs energy in the form of a flame to ignite a gas jar full of it. However, the metal platinum will catalyse the burning of hydrogen so well that the energy in the air at room temperature is then sufficient to ignite it. Just opening the jar and putting the platinum in the gas will cause it to burst into flame.

Remember from Chapter 12 that platinum in a catalytic converter will cause unburnt fuel and carbon monoxide in a car exhaust pipe to burn to form carbon dioxide.

How does a catalyst work? A catalyst works by helping the reactants get close enough to each other for long enough for a reaction to occur. The hydrogen gas in Figure 13.12 is held close to the oxygen of the air on the surface of the platinum metal.

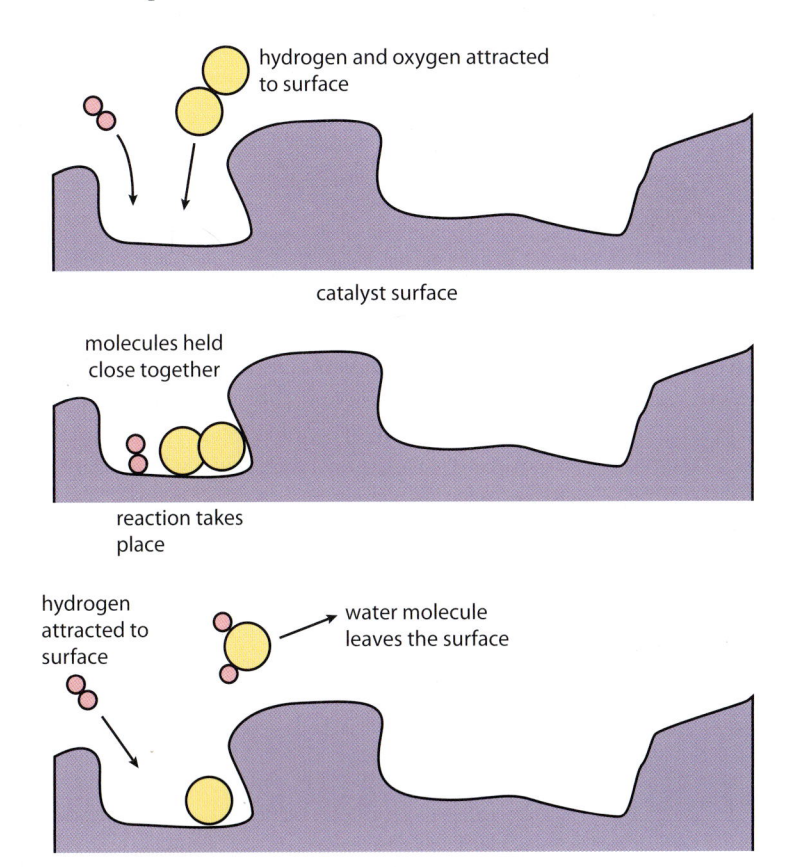

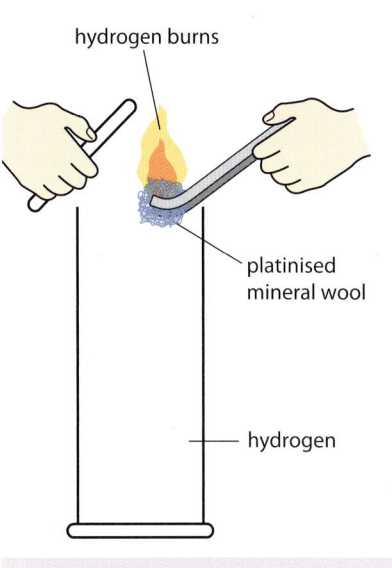

▲ **Figure 13.12**
Platinised mineral wool will make hydrogen burn at room temperature.

◀ **Figure 13.13**
Action of surface action catalyst.

In this case, once the catalyst has started the reaction, so much heat is given out by the reaction that it is able to carry on without the catalyst and all the hydrogen burns.

Enzymes

There is an important group of catalysts that are very common in living things. These are called **enzymes**. Enzymes are large, complicated molecules that catalyse chemical reactions in living things. Each reaction has its own particular enzyme. The enzyme **ptyalin** is present in your saliva and it starts off the process of breaking down your food. Another very useful enzyme is called **pectinase** (most enzyme names end in '–ase'). Pectinase catalyses the reaction that breaks down the molecules that make up plant cell walls. We use it to help us extract fruit juice from fruit; it breaks down the cell walls that hold the juice in the cell. Fungi use it to help them break down the cells of the materials they grow on so that they can get to the nutrients in the cells.

DID YOU KNOW?

Louis Pasteur, the famous French chemist, studied the fermentation of sugar by yeast to make alcohol in the 1870s. He came to the conclusion that the yeast contained some 'vital force' (which means a force associated only with living things) that it used to make the alcohol. It was not until 1897 that a German chemist called Eduard Buchner extracted the substance from yeast that catalysed the fermentation. He called it zymase and he used it to show that fermentation could be done in the laboratory and did not require living things. Zymase was the first enzyme to be extracted and studied. Buchner won the 1907 Nobel Prize for this work.

13.2 Light and chemical reactions

Heat speeds up chemical reactions. Heat is just one form of energy and there are many other forms. One other form is light and so it should not be surprising that light can also affect some chemical reactions. One example is shown in Figure 13.14.

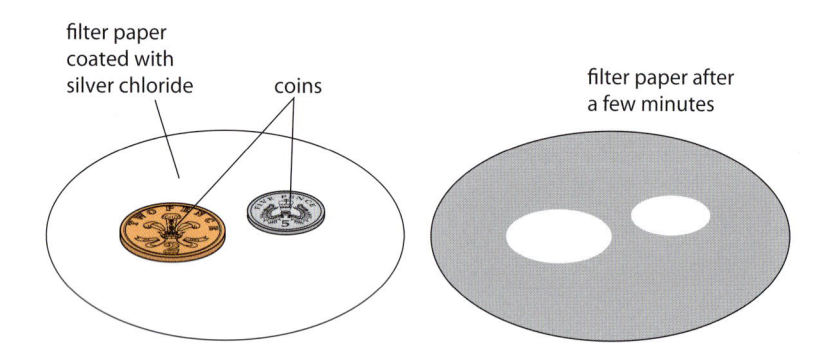

▶ **Figure 13.14**
Light is needed for this reaction to work.

The filter paper on the left is coated with silver chloride. This is made by soaking the paper in silver nitrate solution and allowing it to dry. It is then dipped very quickly into a solution of hydrochloric acid. The hydrochloric acid reacts with the silver nitrate forming silver chloride, which is an insoluble solid and coats the filter paper.

silver nitrate + hydrochloric acid → silver chloride + nitric acid
$AgNO_3(s)$ + $HCl(aq)$ → $AgCl(s)$ + $HNO_3(aq)$

The filter paper is then left in the light for a few minutes with something on top of it (like two coins). After a few minutes the coins are removed and the filter paper looks light grey except for the places where the coins were, which are white circles.

Activity 13.6
Light causing a chemical reaction

This reaction is the basis of black and white photography. The silver chloride slowly decomposes into silver and chlorine. The reaction is very slow in the dark but goes much faster in light.

silver chloride → silver + chlorine
$2AgCl(s)$ → $2Ag(s)$ + $Cl_2(g)$

What you see on the filter paper is a fine coating of silver metal on the parts of it that were exposed to light. This makes the filter paper look greyish in colour.

Another chemical reaction that requires light energy is a very important one. Without this reaction we could not exist. The reaction is photosynthesis, which you met in the last chapter. It takes place in the leaves of green plants but only during the day. The leaves take in carbon dioxide from the air and water from the ground. In the reaction these are converted into glucose.

carbon dioxide + water → glucose + oxygen
$6CO_2(g)$ + $6H_2O(l)$ → $C_6H_{12}O_6(aq)$ + $6O_2(g)$

This reaction only takes place during the day in the presence of sunlight. It requires a catalyst called chlorophyll, which is green in colour and is responsible for the green colour of leaves.

Fast and slow reactions

13.3 Reactions that go both ways

Look at the pictures at the beginning of this chapter. Are these reactions **reversible** or **irreversible**? Can they go backwards? Is it possible to unboil a boiled egg? Most reactions are irreversible but in this book so far you have met some reactions that can go both ways.

Here is one that can go both ways. Chew a piece of bread or some flour for several minutes but don't swallow it. You will notice that it gradually gets sweeter. Bread contains a large molecule called starch. Starch is slowly changed to glucose in your mouth by an enzyme **ptyalin** in your saliva. This process is called the **hydrolysis** of starch; starch and water react together to form a substance called **glucose**, which is one of a class of compounds called **sugars**.

starch + water → glucose

Plants make glucose by photosynthesis in their leaves. They then convert most of it into starch in their leaves. This reaction is the reverse of the one that happens in your mouth when you chew bread.

glucose → starch + water

This reaction is the opposite of hydrolysis and it also has a special name, it is called a **condensation** reaction (it is called a condensation reaction because it produces water).

This reaction can be made to go both ways under different conditions. These conditions are summarised in Table 13.2. There are many reactions like this. They are called **reversible reactions**.

Starch → glucose	Glucose → starch
37 °C	10–40 °C (approx)
Ptyalin catalyst	Several enzymes including chlorophyll
Alkaline solution	Light

◀ Table 13.2 Conditions for starch and glucose reaction.

A simple reversible reaction; heating blue copper sulfate

Activity 13.7
Heating copper sulfate

If you heat some blue copper sulfate crystals gently on a tin lid or gauze, the crystals lose their shape and slowly turn white and powdery. You can also see some steam given off.

blue copper sulfate $\xrightarrow{heat}$ white copper sulfate + water

The white copper sulfate changes back into the blue form when a drop of water is added to it

white copper sulfate + water → blue copper sulfate

Blue copper sulfate crystals contain water. These water molecules are part of the crystalline structure of the blue form of copper sulfate and without them, blue copper sulfate crystals cannot form. We call the blue crystals **hydrated** copper sulfate. When the blue crystals are heated, the water is driven off leaving white copper sulfate. We call this form of copper sulfate **anhydrous** copper sulfate. The word hydrated means 'with water' and anhydrous means 'without water'. The anhydrous form can be converted back to the hydrated form by adding water.

The equation for a reversible reaction is written with a special double arrow sign to indicate that they go both ways.

hydrated copper sulfate $\rightleftharpoons$ anhydrous copper sulfate + water
$$CuSO_4.5H_2O \rightleftharpoons CuSO_4 + 5H_2O$$

There are many other hydrated crystals that change their colour when they lose water. Another example is cobalt chloride – a deep blue when anhydrous and pink when it is hydrated. Both the blue form of cobalt chloride and the white form of copper sulfate can be used as a test for water. Other liquids – like paraffin – will not cause these crystals to change colour.

How changing the reaction conditions affects the products of a reversible reaction

If we warm a blue hydrated copper sulfate crystal it will gradually decompose, giving off water and leaving the white crystals behind. As soon as some water is produced, however, the reverse reaction can happen. The water can react with the white crystals to form the blue ones. We can prevent the reverse reaction happening by driving off the water by evaporating it. If we do this we will convert all the blue crystals to the white ones. But if we do not take all the water vapour away – if we heat it in a sealed container, for example – the reverse reaction will always be happening and we will never get the pure white form.

You can show this just by leaving a crystal of blue copper sulfate around in the air. If you look at it in dry weather you will see a coating of white copper sulfate on the outside of it. In dry weather the water is removed from the reaction and the white form is left. In wet weather there is a lot of water vapour around in the air and this will react with the white coating on the crystal to form the blue copper sulfate again.

So we can control a reversible reaction by altering the reaction conditions. This is a general equation for a reversible reaction in which the materials A and B react to form the products C and D. These products will also react to give back A and B

$$A + B \rightleftharpoons C + D$$

We can make the reaction go to the right by removing either C or D as soon as it is formed. On the other hand, we could make the reaction go to the left by adding C or D or by removing A or B. Many important industrial reactions are reversible and these ideas are used to make sure that the reaction goes the way we want it to.

Another reversible reaction; a reversible thermal decomposition

Another example of a reversible reaction, that can easily be investigated, is the reaction between ammonia and hydrogen chloride. Both these compounds are gases. Ammonia gas is given off all the time from concentrated ammonia solution, and hydrogen chloride is the gas that can be smelled when a concentrated hydrochloric acid bottle is opened. If these two bottles are brought near each other and the stoppers removed, white fumes of ammonium chloride can be seen.

Activity 13.8
Thermal decomposition of amnionium chloride

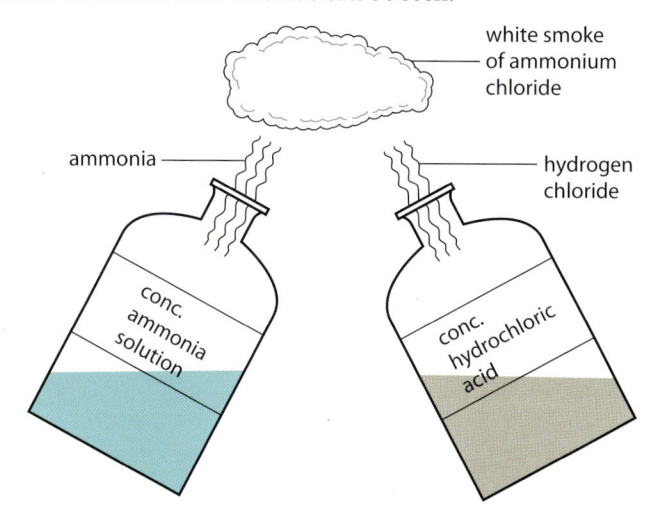

◀ **Figure 13.15**
Formation of ammonium chloride.

The reaction is:

ammonia + hydrogen chloride ⇌ ammonium chloride
$NH_3(g)$ + $HCl(g)$ ⇌ $NH_4Cl(s)$

If ammonium chloride is heated, the reaction is reversed and hydrogen chloride and ammonia are formed. This kind of reaction is called a **thermal decomposition**. The apparatus in Figure 13.16 shows how these can be detected. The ammonium chloride is heated in the tube and forms the two gases, ammonia and hydrogen chloride.

Ammonia gas dissolves in water to form an alkaline solution. Hydrogen chloride, on the other hand, forms hydrochloric acid when it dissolves. The gases formed rise up the tube but the ammonia rises faster because it is much less dense than air and very much less dense than the hydrogen chloride. When the gases first reach the moist litmus papers on the side of the tube, the red one turns blue, indicating the presence of ammonia. A little later the hydrogen chloride turns both of the papers red.

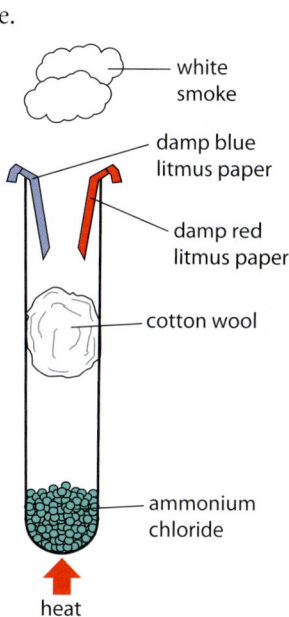

◀ **Figure 13.16**
Thermal decomposition of ammonium chloride.

When the mixture of gases cools above the tube the decomposition reaction reverses and the gases recombine to form white clouds of ammonium chloride.

QUESTIONS

13.1 Explain the following observations.
  a) A car engine does not work very efficiently just after it has started on a cold day.
  b) When you throw some iron filings into a flame they spark immediately but when you put an iron rod into a flame for the same time nothing happens.
  c) A piece of paper that has been rolled into a ball burns more slowly on a fire than one that has not been rolled up.
  d) Magnesium burns more brightly in pure oxygen than in air.
  e) Vegetables cook faster in a pressure cooker than in an open pan.
  f) If you want potatoes to cook faster you slice them up.
  g) Plants grow faster in warm wet climates than in cool dry ones.

13.2 Table 13.3 shows the results for the formation of hydrogen from a sample of magnesium placed in excess dilute acid.

▶ Table 13.3
The production of hydrogen by the reaction between magnesium and acid.

Time (s)	Volume of hydrogen (cm^3)
0	0
10	5
20	15
30	26
40	40
50	55
60	75
70	90
80	100
90	115
100	128
110	133
120	136
130	137
140	137
150	137

  a) Plot a graph showing the production of hydrogen.
  b) State the total amount of hydrogen produced in the reaction.
  c) Explain why the rate of production of hydrogen was greatest at the beginning of the reaction.
  d) Explain why hydrogen eventually stopped being produced.
  e) Draw on the same axes another line showing how the hydrogen would have been produced if the concentration of the acid was halved. Label this curve 'c'.

f) Draw on the same axes another line showing how the hydrogen would have been produced if the temperature of the acid was increased. Label this curve 't'.

g) Sketch the apparatus suitable for carrying out this investigation.

13.3 What is meant by a 'reversible reaction'? Give an example.

13.4 Cobalt chloride forms pink crystals. When the crystals are heated, water is produced and they turn blue. Explain how you could use cobalt chloride as a test for water.

Summary

Now that you have completed this chapter, you should be able to:

- know that different chemical reactions proceed at different rates
- explain, in terms of particle collisions, the effects of temperature and concentration on reaction rates
- explain why reactions proceed faster when any solid reagents used are ground to a fine powder
- plot and interpret reaction rate graphs
- explain, with examples, how the rate of a reaction can be changed using a catalyst and propose a mechanism that explains how catalysts work
- [S] give examples of reactions that require light to make them work
- know that many reactions are reversible and explain how changing reaction conditions can affect the products of a reversible reaction.

Chapter 14

Organic chemistry

Amyl acetate

This is the smell of nail varnish solvent. It has a sweet and pleasant smell. It is one of a class of compounds called **esters**. They all have a pleasantly sweet smell. Many natural smells such as the smell of apples and bananas are caused by esters.

$CH_3COO(CH_2)_4CH_3$

$CH_3-\overset{\overset{O}{\|}}{C}-O-CH_2-CH_2-CH_2-CH_2-CH_3$

Civetone

This is the compound that male cats (particularly the African civet cat shown) leave when they are marking their territory, or attracting a mate, using their scent gland near their anus. It is one of the most revolting smells known. It is used in very expensive perfumes to give the perfume an 'edge'. It sensitises our noses to the perfume.

$C_{17}H_{30}O$

Limonene

This is one of a large class of compounds called **terpenes**. They are also called **essential oils** (from the word 'essence'). They smell rather pleasant and are used in perfumes. This one smells of lemons. Lavender oil and eucalyptus oil, basil and the scent of roses are all due to terpenes.

$C_{10}H_{16}$

3-Methylbutanoic acid

This is an organic acid rather like vinegar but it has a much stronger smell. It is the compound that gives the smell to old socks and vomit. It is also a substance given off by many female animals (including humans) to attract a mate. So many perfumes contain this chemical; look for it on the label!

$C_5H_{10}O_2$

186

Chemists who know about **organic chemistry** can look at the structure of all the compounds shown opposite and be able to predict that: (a) they are liquids, and (b) they probably have quite a strong smell. They will know they are liquids because they all have between 5 and 15 carbon atoms in them and they know that compounds of this size are likely to be liquids. They will know that they have a smell because the particular groups of atoms shown in colour often give a smell to a compound that contains them. They might even be able to predict that amyl acetate and limonene will smell quite nice but that you should avoid smelling the others!

> **DID YOU KNOW?**
>
> The strange 17-member ring structure of civetone was discovered in the 1920s by a Croatian chemist called Leopold Ruzicka working in Utrecht in the Netherlands. He also discovered that the smell of musk, produced when male deer mark their territories, is caused by a molecule called muskone that has almost the same structure. Ruzicka was awarded the Nobel Prize in 1939 but could not receive it until 1945 after the war.

14.1 Carbon, a special element

What can we learn from the four scented molecules?

1. All these compounds, and many millions more, are made out of a carbon skeleton. Each carbon atom in the skeleton has four covalent bonds. These bonds are formed mainly with other carbon atoms and hydrogen, but also with other elements like oxygen and nitrogen.

2. The properties of these compounds depend on particular groups of atoms in their structure. Groups such as the double-bonded carbons and the double-bonded carbon-oxygen give molecules certain properties.

3. These molecules are made by living things and are found in living things or in substances like oil and gas, which were once living. They are called **organic compounds** and their chemistry is called organic chemistry.

This chapter is about organic chemistry, the chemistry of compounds formed by the element carbon.

Carbon is at the top of Group IV in the centre of the Periodic Table. It forms four covalent bonds by sharing its four electrons with other elements. What makes it different from other elements is that it can form long chains of carbon atoms joined strongly together by covalent bonds. These chains can be straight or branched and other elements can join onto them.

Table 14.1 shows some well known compounds. Note that the bonds formed by carbon point away from the atom towards the corner of a tetrahedron (look at the structure of methane in the table). This means that a chain of carbon atoms is not actually straight but crooked. The 'space-filling' model of the atoms gives us a better idea of what the molecule really looks like as it shows the space around the atoms that is taken up by the electrons. The table also shows the compound, water, for comparison.

Name	Molecular formula	Structural formula	Ball and spring model	Space-filling model
Water	H_2O			
Methane	CH_4			
Butane	C_4H_{10}			
Octane	C_8H_{18}			
Polythene	C_nH_{2n}			
Ethanol	C_2H_5OH			

▲ **Table 14.1**
Structure of water, methane, butane, octane (in petrol), polythene, and ethanol (alcohol).

The most convenient and quick way of drawing formulae, that also tells you much about the structure, is to use drawings like the ones at the beginning of this chapter. In these, only the important bonds are fully drawn; the bonds between carbon and hydrogen are not shown.

We can classify all organic compounds into groups of compounds that are similar. You have already met the names of some of the more complex groups such as esters and terpenes. Compounds within a group will have a similar structure and properties. In the rest of this chapter you will study a few of these groups starting with a group called **alkanes**.

14.2 Alkanes

Table 14.2 shows the structure of four hydrocarbons - methane, ethane, propane and butane. All of them are gases. Methane is natural gas that is obtained from gas fields found in many parts of the world. Methane is also produced in the stomachs of animals that feed on grass and it is excreted from time to time as a (dangerously flammable!) waste product. Propane and butane are commonly used throughout the world as a fuel for cooking.

Name	Methane	Ethane	Propane	Butane
Formula	CH_4	C_2H_6	C_3H_8	C_4H_{10}
Structural formula	H–C(H)(H)–H	H–C(H)(H)–C(H)(H)–H	H–C(H)(H)–C(H)(H)–C(H)(H)–H	H–C(H)(H)–C(H)(H)–C(H)(H)–C(H)(H)–H

▲ Table 14.2 Structure of the first four alkanes.

The four compounds in Table 14.2 are the first four of a series of **hydrocarbons** with similar structures that we call the alkanes. Notice that the as you go along the series, the next compound contains one more carbon atom and two more hydrogen atoms than the previous one.

Can you also see that if an alkane contains n carbon atoms, it will have $2n+2$ hydrogen atoms? We can write the general formula for the alkanes as $C_nH_{(2n+2)}$.

There are many alkanes. As the number of carbon atoms gets larger and the molecule gets bigger, the boiling points of the alkanes rise. This means that the smallest, such as the ones in Table 14.2, are gases but larger ones, such as octane shown in Table 14.1 are liquids. Petrol is a mixture of hydrocarbons, one of which is octane. Candle wax is also a mixture of alkanes that are solids. The main alkane in candle wax is called eicosane and contains 20 carbon atoms ($C_{20}H_{42}$).

The most important property of the alkanes is that they burn easily to form carbon dioxide and water. You may recall this reaction from Chapter 10. The carbon dioxide is produced by the carbon in the alkane and the water comes from the hydrogen. We can write equations showing this. The first shows the burning of methane and second equation is a general one for all alkanes.

methane + oxygen → carbon dioxide + water
$CH_4 + 2O_2 \rightarrow CO_2 + 2H_2O$

alkane + oxygen → carbon dioxide + water

Activity 14.1 Burning alkanes

The alkanes are a series of compounds with a similar structure and similar properties. They have similar properties because they have similar structures. We call a series of compounds like this a **homologous series**.

The reaction of alkanes with halogens

The only reaction of alkanes of importance other than burning is the reaction with halogens (Group VII elements). In this reaction, one or more of the hydrogens is replaced by a halogen. This reaction requires light energy to make it happen. Any of the hydrogens can be replaced. The reaction can continue until all the hydrogens have been replaced by the halogen and so a mixture of products is often obtained.

$$CH_4 + Cl_2 \rightarrow CH_3Cl + HCl$$

Other products can be CH_2Cl_2, $CHCl_3$ (which is the anaesthetic called chloroform), and CCl_4.

This is an important reaction commercially as these 'halocarbons' are useful as solvents, anaesthetics and refrigerants. Tetrachloroethane (CCl_4) is useful for putting out fires. Fire extinguishers in vehicles often contain this because it is useful for electrical fires, being a non-conductor.

Branched chain hydrocarbons

In all the hydrocarbons you have studied so far the carbon atoms have been arranged in a single chain. Many alkanes, however, are branched chain compounds. Consider the alkane, C_5H_{12}. How many structures can you draw for this, if you also draw all the possible branched structures? The answer is three and they are shown in Table 14.3.

Structural formula	(pentane structure)	(2-methylbutane structure)	(2,2-dimethylpropane structure)
Name	Pentane	2-methylbutane	2,2-dimethylpropane
Boiling point (°C)	37	29	9

▲ Table 14.3 Three isomers of pentane (C_5H_{12}).

These molecules, which have the same molecular formula but different structures, are called **structural isomers.** Structural isomerism is very common in organic chemistry. The three isomers in the table all have different names and different properties. You may be able to see a pattern in the names, the basic name is that of the longest straight carbon chain in the molecule and each of these carbons is numbered. You can see that the third isomer, 2,2-dimethylpropane has the lowest boiling point. This is because it has the most compact structure of the three, rather like a ball, and needs least energy to make the molecule escape from the liquid.

Organic chemistry

14.3 Alkenes

Another homologous series of compounds is the **alkenes**. Table 14.4 shows the structure of some members of this series.

Name	Molecular formula	Structural formula	Ball and spring model	Space-filling model
Ethene	C_2H_4			
Propene	C_3H_6			
Butene	C_4H_8			

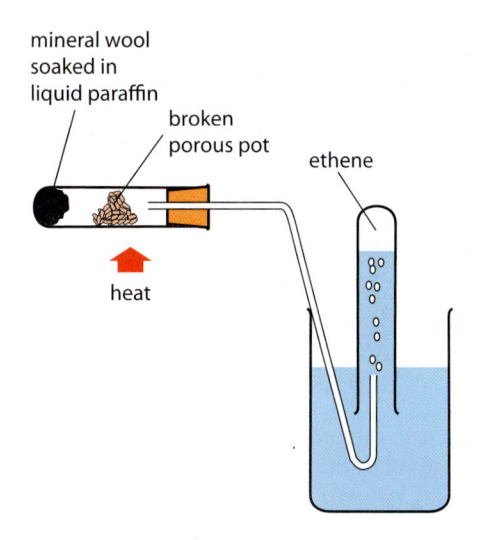

▲ Table 14.4 Structure of ethene, propene, and butene.

You can see that these three, ethene, propene, and butene are very similar to the alkanes, ethane, propane and butane. The only difference is that the alkenes contain a **double bond**. This is a bond that is made by sharing not two, but four electrons. This difference between the structure of alkenes and alkanes means that there is an important difference between the properties of the two series of compounds.

Alkenes are not as readily available as alkanes and so they are usually made from alkanes. Figure 14.1 shows how the simple alkene, ethene (ethylene) can be made from liquid alkanes simply by heating them. It is heated by passing it over some heated pottery chips and the alkane breaks down into ethene. Ethene is a colourless gas that has a sweetish smell.

Activity 14.2 Making ethene

◀ Figure 14.1 Making an alkene from an alkane.

The gas collected is ethene. This process for making ethene is called **cracking**. It is the way ethene and other small hydrocarbon molecules are made industrially from larger alkane molecules.

Properties of alkenes

> Activity 14.3
> Properties of ethene

The reactions of ethene shown below are typical of all alkenes. The double bond makes alkenes much more reactive than alkanes. Table 14.5 shows some of these reactions

Reaction	Set fire to the ethene.	Add some drops of bromine water (bromine dissolved in water) to the ethene and shake.	Add some drops of potassium manganate(VII) solution and shake.
Observation	It burns with a yellowish flame and the gas produced turns limewater milky. Condensation is also seen if a cold beaker is held above the flame.	The brown bromine water turns colourless.	The solution turns colourless (if a little acid is added).
Explanation	Ethene burns to form carbon dioxide and water.	The bromine has reacted with the ethene.	The potassium manganate(VII) is an oxidising agent. It has oxidised the ethene.

▲ Table 14.5 Some reactions of ethane.

Alkenes react with both bromine and potassium manganate(VII), decolourising them because of the presence of the double bond. Alkanes do not do this because they have no double bonds and are therefore unreactive. We can use these two simple reactions to test for the presence of a double bond in some organic substances. An interesting experiment is to use these two reactions to compare lard and cooking oil.

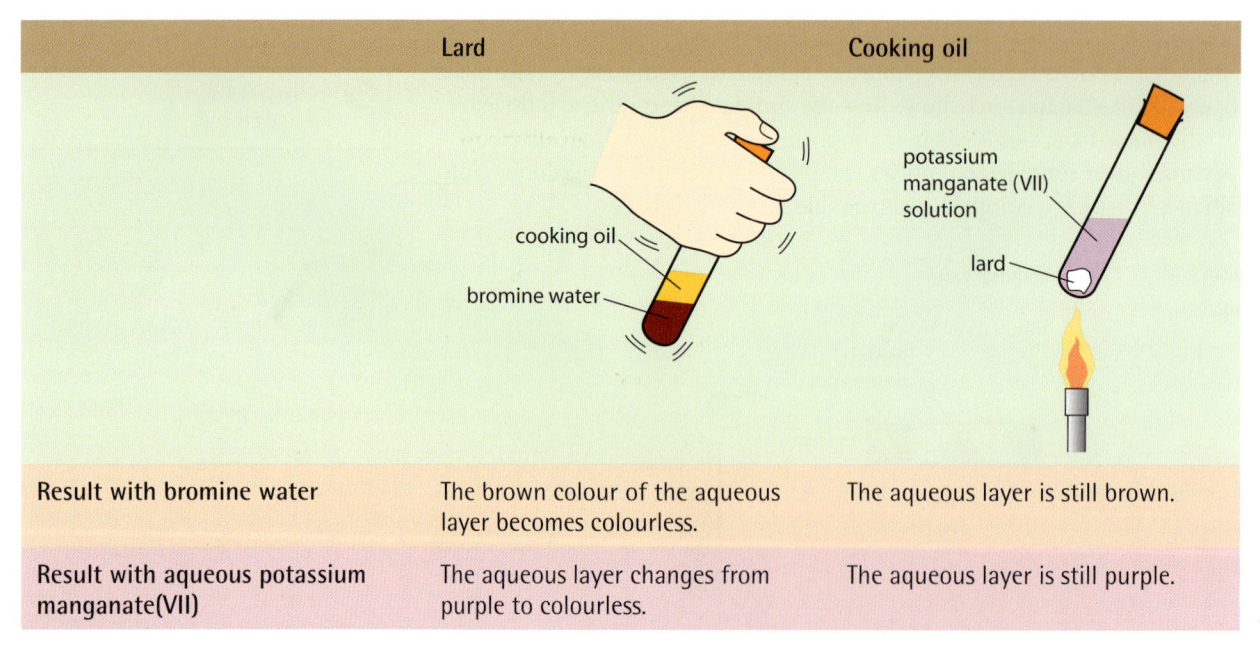

	Lard	Cooking oil
Result with bromine water	The brown colour of the aqueous layer becomes colourless.	The aqueous layer is still brown.
Result with aqueous potassium manganate(VII)	The aqueous layer changes from purple to colourless.	The aqueous layer is still purple.

> Activity 14.4
> Testing for double bonds

Cooking oil and margarine both contain carbon-carbon double bonds whereas lard does not. The double bonds will cause the decolourisation of the potassium manganate(VII) and the bromine water.

Organic chemistry

We have a special name for compounds such as the margarine and the cooking oil that contain double bonds. We say they have in them **unsaturated** hydrocarbon chains. Compounds, such as the lard, that do not have double bonds in them are called **saturated**. You may have read about unsaturated and saturated **fatty acids** in your food. There is evidence that unsaturated compounds such as cooking oil are better for you than saturated ones.

Addition of bromine to double bonds

The reason why potassium manganate(VII) and bromine water are decolourised when they are added to alkenes is that they react with the double bond. The bromine breaks the double bond, forming two extra single bonds to bromine atoms. This is shown in Figure 14.2.

This kind of reaction, in which a reagent like bromine adds on to double bond, is called an **addition reaction** to a double bond. It is a very important reaction because it allows a great many useful substances to be made from ethenes. In the next chapter you will study useful substances called polymers. One polymer, a very well known substance called polyethene or polythene, is made when molecules of ethene are made to *add* onto each other.

Addition of hydrogen to a double bond

One important addition reaction of alkenes is the addition of hydrogen. This is shown in Figure 14.3. If you compare the structure of alkenes and alkanes that have the same number of carbon atoms, the difference is in the number of hydrogen atoms. It is possible to change an alkene to an alkane by adding hydrogen. This is an important process in the food industry. Vegetable oils such as sunflower oil are easily obtained from plants. These can be used unchanged for cooking. However, if the double bonds in them are made to combine with hydrogen, these oils become solids. These solids are margarines.

The hydrogen is passed through the heated oil, which contains a catalyst of powdered nickel. At the end of the reaction the nickel is filtered off and can be used again. Some margarines are soft and some are hard. The soft ones still have some double bonds in them but the hard ones do not.

> **DID YOU KNOW?**
>
> This is the origin of the use of the words 'saturated' and 'unsaturated' applied to fats and oils. We say that the hard margarines, which have no double bonds left, are 'saturated' with hydrogen whereas the soft ones are 'unsaturated'.

◀ Figure 14.2
Bromine adding to a double bond.

◀ Figure 14.3
Addition of hydrogen to a double bond.

193

Addition of water to a double bond

Another important addition reaction of alkenes is the reaction with steam. Like the reaction with hydrogen, a catalyst is used to speed this reaction up. It is important because, as Figure 14.4 shows, the product has the atoms OH attached to one of the carbons that was part of the double bond. This group of atoms is called the **hydroxyl group** and organic compounds that contain this group are called **alcohols**.

▶ Figure 14.4
Addition of steam to a double bond.

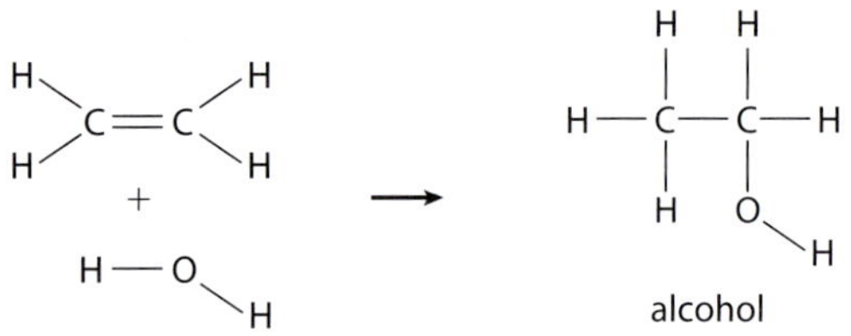

This process is used in industry as one way of making the common alcohol called ethanol. It is described in the next section.

14.4 Alcohols

Ethanol is the scientific name for the liquid commonly known as alcohol. It is the substance produced by the fermentation of sugar in fruits. It is the chemical in wines and beers that causes drunkenness. Ethanol, as shown in Figure 14.5, has the same structure as ethane but it also contains the -OH group. In organic chemistry we use the word 'alcohol' to refer to any compound that contains this -OH group.

▶ Figure 14.5
Structures of ethane and ethanol.

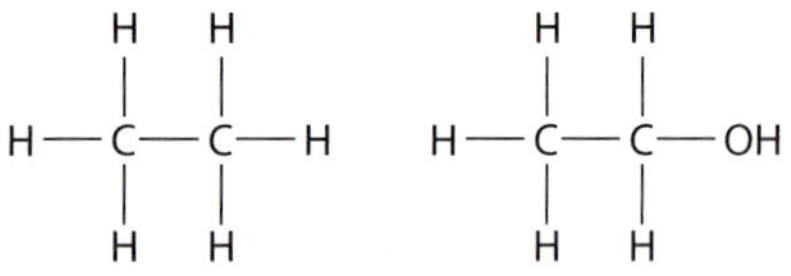

Ethanol is one example of a homologous series of compounds called the alcohols. Figure 14.6 shows three typical alcohols in this series.

▶ Table 14.6
Structure of methanol, ethanol, and 1-propanol.

Name	Nolecular formula	Structural formula	Ball and spring model	Space-filling model
Methanol	CH_3OH	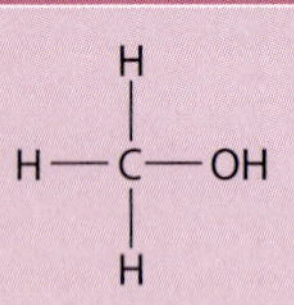	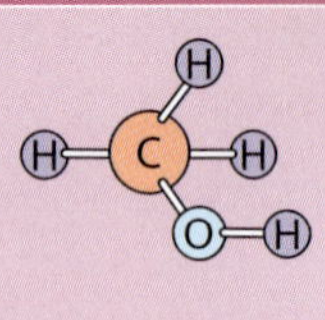	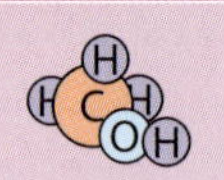
Ethanol	C_2H_5OH	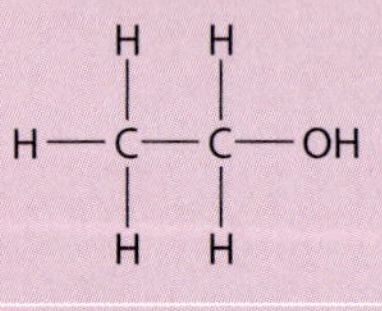	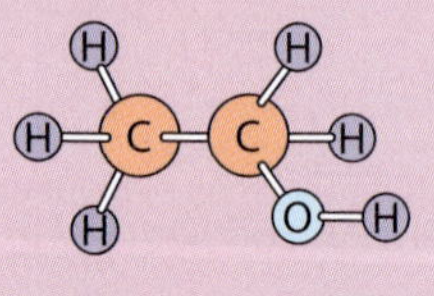	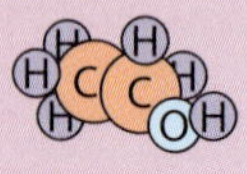
Propanol	C_3H_7OH	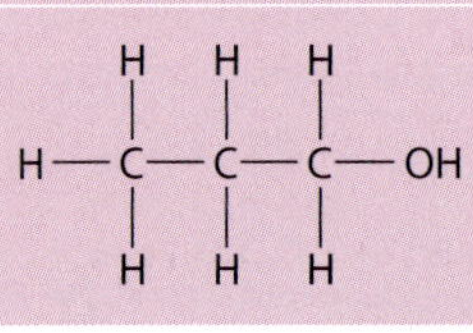	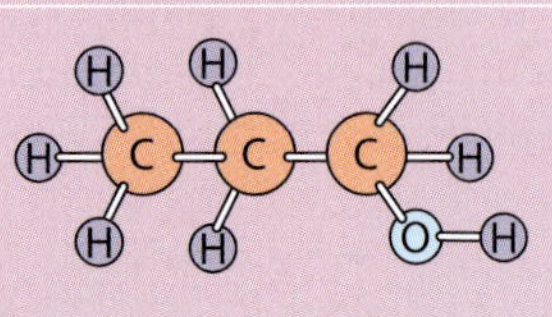	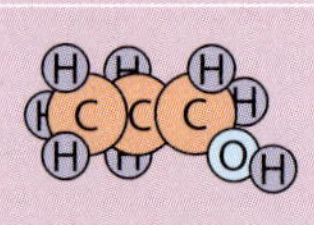

194

Organic chemistry

Methylated spirit, fuel, and solvent

Methylated spirit is a well-known fuel and solvent. It is mainly ethanol but also contains some methanol, which is poisonous, causing blindness and death if it is drunk in sufficient quantity. The methylated spirit that is used industrially is colourless, but when it is sold to the public as a fuel, a purple dye is added to it so that people always know what it is and do not accidentally drink it.

When ethanol burns, it produces carbon dioxide and water.

ethanol + oxygen → carbon dioxide + water
$C_2H_5OH + 3O_2 \rightarrow 2CO_2 + 3H_2O$

Methylated spirits is also widely used in industry as a solvent for paints, soaps and dyes.

Making ethanol

Ethanol is made in two ways. One way uses oil as the raw material. Ethene is made from the oil by cracking. The ethene is then heated to 300 °C under pressure with steam and phosphoric acid. The phosphoric acid is a catalyst in the reaction. Most of the ethanol used in industry is made this way but because this method starts from oil, this ethanol is non-renewable, and more modern methods start with plant material.

Ethanol in wines and beers is made from sugars by a process called **fermentation**. This is a natural process carried out by organisms called yeasts. They convert sugar into alcohol and carbon dioxide. In the process they are able to obtain, and make use of, some of the energy in the sugars. The process can be represented by the equation:

sugar → ethanol + carbon dioxide
$C_6H_{12}O_6 \rightarrow 2C_2H_5OH + 2CO_2(g)$

Figure 14.6 shows how this reaction can be done and how carbon dioxide can be detected.

> **Activity 14.5**
> Making ethanol by fermentation

◀ **Figure 14.6**
Apparatus for the fermentation of sugar.

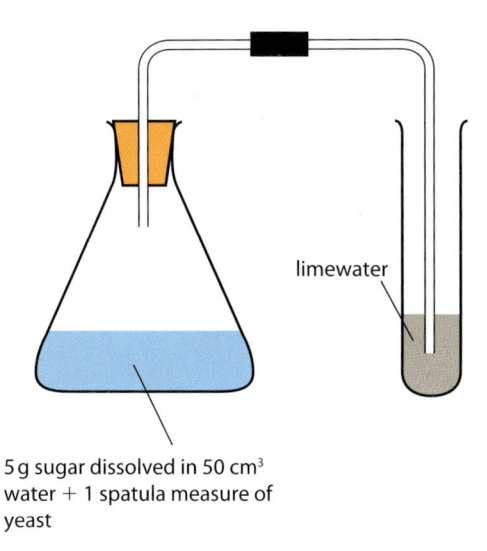

The limewater in the initial fermentation step will turn milky, showing that the process of fermentation produces carbon dioxide.

The reaction will continue for several days and then gradually stop. It will stop either because the sugar has been used up or because the yeast has been poisoned by the alcohol it has produced. The solution is then filtered to get rid of much of the yeast and the alcohol is extracted by fractional distillation (see Chapter 3). The mixture is distilled (Figure 14.7) and the liquid that comes over at around 78 °C (the boiling point of ethanol) is collected.

▶ **Figure 14.7**
Distillation of alcohol.

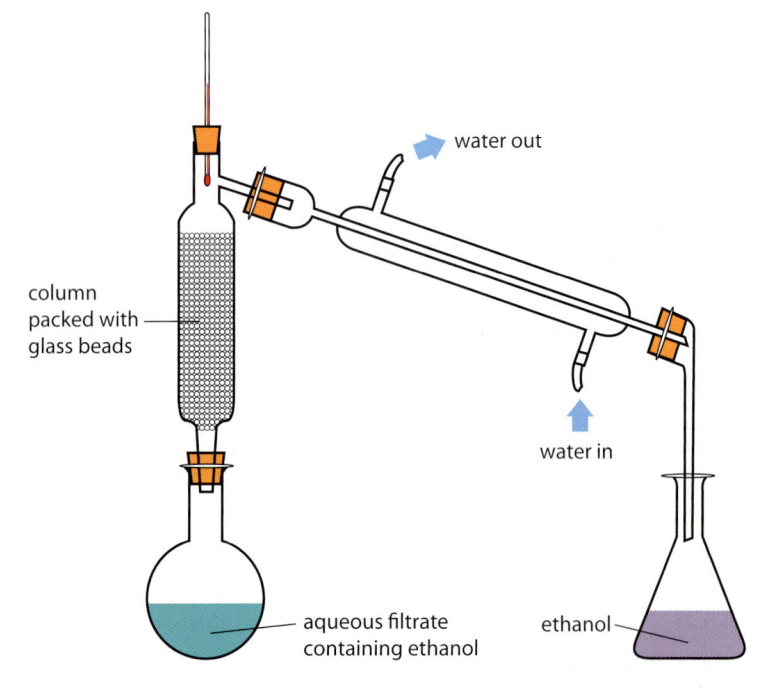

▶ **Figure 14.8**
Scotch whisky is made from barley. The grain is allowed to germinate. During germination the starch in the grain is turned into a sugar called maltose. This is fermented using yeast and finally the mixture is distilled using copper flasks like these. It is said that the taste of the whisky depends in part on the shape and size of these stills.

A wide variety of plant material can be fermented in this way to produce ethanol. The plant material is renewable and so this process is a way of making a useful fuel that is renewable. It is possible to adapt car engines to run on ethanol. Some countries, such as Brazil and the USA, which do not have enough oil reserves of their own, make ethanol which they add to petrol sold at the pumps.

14.5 Organic acids

When an alcoholic drink, like wine, is left open to the air it turns rather unpleasant and acidic. This is a natural process caused by a bacterium. The alcohol is oxidised by the oxygen in the air and the product is an acid. The acid produced when ethanol is oxidised is called ethanoic acid. Its old name is acetic acid and its common name is vinegar.

ethanol + oxygen → ethanoic acid

The oxidation of ethanol, which bacteria are able to carry out, uses air as the oxidising agent. This is an important industrial reaction; vinegar is made in this way. The reaction can also be done in the laboratory using a suitable oxidising agent such as potassium manganate(VII) or potassium dichromate. Both these reagents are well known inorganic substances that can give up oxygen to other compounds. In the process they are themselves reduced. The reaction is easy to follow because there is a colour change; potassium manganate(VII) changes from purple to light pink and potassium dichromate changes from orange to green.

The ethanol is heated for some time with the oxidising agent. The mixture is then distilled and the fraction distilling at around 118 °C, the boiling point of ethanoic acid, is collected. It is a liquid at room temperature and has a very strong vinegary smell.

Table 14.7 shows a number of carboxylic acids. They all have rather pungent smells. You will notice that butanoic acid has a structure that is very similar to the molecule that causes the smell in vomit at the beginning of the chapter. All these carboxylic acids have the –COOH group of atoms.

Name of acid	methanoic	ethanoic	propanoic	butanoic
Formula	HCOOH	CH_3COOH	C_2H_5COOH	C_3H_7COOH
Structure of molecule	H–C(=O)OH	H–C(H)(H)–C(=O)OH	H–C(H)(H)–C(H)(H)–C(=O)OH	H–C(H)(H)–C(H)(H)–C(H)(H)–C(=O)OH
Number of carbon atoms	1	2	3	4
Boiling point	101 °C	118 °C	141 °C	165 °C

▲ Table 14.7 The structures and properties of some carboxylic acids.

Carboxylic acids are very common in our daily lives. We use many in cooking. Table 14.8 shows some that are well known.

Acid name	Where we find it or use it
Formic acid (methanoic acid)	The 'sting' in an ant bite (it actually bites you and quickly turns round and squirts the acid into the bite from a gland in its tail).
Acetic acid (ethanoic acid)	Vinegar
Citric acid	Orange and lemon juice.
Tartaric acid	Used in cooking.
Malic acid	The sharp taste in apples.
Lactic acid	In milk. It is also made in your muscles when they are tired and cannot get enough oxygen. It causes muscle cramp. If you run upstairs fast it is the substance that causes pain in your knees.
Aspirin (acetyl salicylic acid)	Originally found in the bark of the willow tree. Now it is made artificially and used as a medicine.
Stearic acid	Soaps

▲ Table 14.8
Some carboxylic acids.

Carboxylic acids react in two characteristic ways. They react with alkalis like all acids and they also react with alcohols. You will recall from Chapter 7 that alkalis are solutions that contain the hydroxide ion, OH^-. Alcohols are organic compounds that contain the covalently bonded –OH group. These two reactions are compared below.

Ethanoic acid as a typical acid

Ethanoic acid will react as a typical acid. Below are four reactions of acids: the reaction with indicator paper; the reaction with a reactive metal like magnesium; the reaction with a carbonate; and the reaction with an alkali.

Activity 14.6
Reactions of ethanoic acid

The action of indicator paper

Ethanoic acid turns blue litmus paper red and has a pH of around 3 (shown by universal indicator). It is a weak acid. The equation shows how it **dissociates** into an ethanoate ion and a hydrogen ion in solution. This is a reversible reaction so not all the acid has dissociated and this is why it is a weak acid.

$$\text{ethanoic acid} \rightleftharpoons \text{ethanoate ion} + \text{hydrogen ion}$$
$$CH_3COOH(aq) \rightleftharpoons CH_3COO^-(aq) + H^+(aq)$$

The reaction with a reactive metal such as magnesium

If a piece of magnesium is placed in some dilute ethanoic acid, the gas hydrogen is given off and the product is magnesium ethanoate. Magnesium ethanoate is a colourless, ionic crystalline solid like any other salt made in this way.

Organic chemistry

ethanoic acid + magnesium → magnesium ethanoate + hydrogen
2CH$_3$COOH(aq) + Mg(s) → (CH$_3$COO)$_2$Mg(aq) + H$_2$(g)

$$2H_3C-C\genfrac{}{}{0pt}{}{\diagup O}{\diagdown O-H} + Mg \rightarrow \left(H_3C-C\genfrac{}{}{0pt}{}{\diagup O}{\diagdown O}\right)_2 Mg + H_2$$

The reaction with a carbonate such as sodium hydrogen carbonate (baking soda)

If some sodium hydrogen carbonate is added to ethanoic acid, the gas carbon dioxide is produced and the product is sodium ethanoate (sodium acetate) which is a colourless crystalline ionic salt.

ethanoic acid + sodium hydrogen carbonate → sodium ethanoate + carbon dioxide + water
CH$_3$COOH(aq) + NaHCO$_3$(s) → CH$_3$COONa(aq) + CO$_2$(g) + H$_2$O(l)

$$H_3C-C\genfrac{}{}{0pt}{}{\diagup O}{\diagdown O-H} + NaHCO_3 \rightarrow H_3C-C\genfrac{}{}{0pt}{}{\diagup O}{\diagdown O^- Na^+} + CO_2 + H_2O$$

The reaction with an alkali such as sodium hydroxide solution

If some sodium hydroxide solution is mixed with ethanoic acid, no reaction will be seen but the solution will get warm. This tells us that a reaction is taking place. It is the neutralisation reaction and the product which can be crystallised is sodium ethanoate, a typical colourless ionic crystalline salt.

ethanoic acid + sodium hydroxide → sodium ethanoate + water
CH$_3$COOH(aq) + NaOH(aq) → CH$_3$COONa(aq) + H$_2$O(l)

$$H_3C-C\genfrac{}{}{0pt}{}{\diagup O}{\diagdown OH} + NaOH \rightarrow H_3C-C\genfrac{}{}{0pt}{}{\diagup O}{\diagdown O^- Na^+} + H_2O$$

The molecule of ethanoic acid contains four hydrogen atoms. When it reacts as an acid, only one of these hydrogen atoms takes part in the reaction. You will recall from Chapter 7 that when an acid reacts, it donates a hydrogen ion (a proton) to the base or the carbonate. Only one of the four hydrogen atoms in ethanoic acid is donated. You can see from the structure of the acid in the equations above that one of the hydrogens is joined to an oxygen, whereas the others are joined to a carbon atom. It is the one joined to the oxygen that ionises.

The reaction of ethanoic acid with alcohols

A very useful reaction of carboxylic acids is their reaction with alcohol. If you add equal quantities the ethanoic acid and ethanol in a test tube and heat it gently with a few drops of concentrated sulfuric acid (a catalyst), after a few minutes you will be able to detect a rather pleasant sweet smell. When ethanoic acid reacts with an alcohol an ester is formed. In this case the ester is called ethyl ethanoate.

ethanoic acid + ethanol ⇌ ethtyl ethanoate + water

$$H_3C-C\overset{O}{\underset{O-H}{}} + H-O-\underset{H}{\overset{H}{C}}-CH_3 \underset{}{\overset{conc. H_2SO_4}{\rightleftharpoons}} H_3C-C\overset{O}{\underset{O-CH_2-CH_3}{}} + HOH$$

Esters are very common in nature. The taste and smell of fruits is often caused by an ester. Fats and vegetable oils, though not sweet smelling, are also esters. The solvent for removing nail varnish is an ester with a particularly sweet smell. The amyl acetate referred to at the beginning of this chapter is an ester.

We can compare the reaction of ethanoic acid with an alkali and with an alcohol.

ethanoic acid + sodium hydroxide → sodium ethanoate + water
$CH_3COOH(aq)$ + $NaOH(aq)$ → $CH_3COONa(aq)$ + $HOH(l)$

The general reactions can be written like this:

ethanoic acid + alkali → salt + water
ethanoic acid + alcohol ⇌ ester + water

This kind of reaction, in which the only by-product is water is called a condensation reaction.

These two reactions look very similar. In fact they are very different. The first one forming a salt is an ionic reaction. The second one forming an ester is a covalent reaction and it is reversible.

Activity 14.7
Reaction of ethanoic acid as a carboxylic acid

QUESTIONS

14.1 Explain what the names of the alkanes have in common. What is the general formula of the alkanes? Draw the structure of the straight chain alkane with 7 carbon atoms.

14.2 Table 14.9 shows the melting points of the first 10 alkanes. Plot a graph of the melting point against the number of carbon atoms in the molecule and use it to predict the melting point of $C_{12}H_{26}$. Why do you think the melting points get higher as the molecule gets longer?

▶ **Table 14.9**
Some data on straight-chain alkanes.

Number of carbon atoms	Formula	Name	State at room temperature	Boiling point (°C)
1	CH_4	Methane	Gas	−161
2	C_2H_6	Ethane	Gas	−89
3	C_3H_8	Propane	Gas	−42
4	C_4H_{10}	Butane	Gas	0
5	C_5H_{12}	Pentane	Liquid	37
6	C_6H_{14}	Hexane	Liquid	70
7	C_7H_{16}	Heptane	Liquid	99
8	C_8H_{18}	Octane	Liquid	127
9	C_9H_{20}	Nonane	Liquid	152
10	$C_{10}H_{22}$	Decane	Liquid	174

14.3 You are given two flammable liquid hydrocarbons. One of them is an alkene and another is an alkane. Describe how would you find out which was which.

14.4 Propene has a formula C_3H_6. Draw its structure. Describe how it reacts with:
(a) bromine
(b) steam.
Draw the formula for the product of the reaction with bromine.

14.5 Explain, giving examples, what is meant by 'addition reaction' and 'substitution reaction'.

14.6 Explain how margarine is made from vegetable oils. A margarine is advertised as 'high in polyunsaturates'. Explain what you think the makers mean by this.

14.7 Describe two ways of making ethanol, one starting from plant matter and the other from crude oil. Explain which of these methods is sustainable.

14.8 List the main uses of ethanol. Ethanol is the main constituent of methylated spirit. Describe what other compounds are present in methylated spirit. Explain why a purple dye is added to methylated spirits.

14.9 Draw all the possible structural isomers of C_6H_{14}.

14.10 State how many possible products are there when chlorine reacts with ethane. Draw the structures of them all.

14.11 There are four hydrogen atoms in a molecule of ethanoic acid. Explain why only one of them takes part when ethanoic acid reacts as an acid.

14.12 Carboxylic acids react with alkalis and with alcohols. Show one similarity and one difference between these two reactions.

Summary

Now that you have completed this chapter, you should be able to:

- recognise that the element carbon is a special one in that it can form a very large number of different covalent molecules
- know that the properties of carbon are related to its position in the Periodic Table
- draw structural formulae of common hydrocarbons containing single and double bonds
- understand how the physical and chemical properties of alkanes and alkenes are related to their structure
- describe reactions of alkenes in terms of addition reactions
- describe the reactions of alkenes with oxygen [burning in air], halogens and potassium manganate(VII) solution
- draw the structural formulae of common alcohols such as methanol, ethanol and glycerol
- describe how ethanol can be made commercially and list its uses
- draw the structural formulae of common carboxylic acids such as ethanoic acid and list their main properties and uses
- describe esters as the product of a condensation reaction between a carboxylic acid and an alcohol.

Chapter 15

Macromolecules

Graphenes, buckyballs, nanotubes, '100 times stronger than steel', 'the hardest substance known', electrical superconductors, nanofabrics one atom thick, single molecule computer chips. All these phrases refer to a new family of materials based on the graphite form of carbon. The development of these is happening so fast that anything written here may be long out of date by the time you read it.

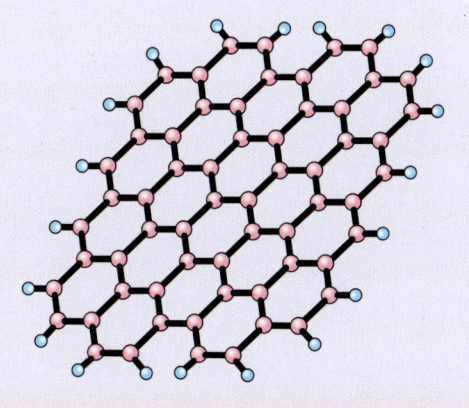

▲ **Figure 15.1**
The basis of many new materials is this chicken-wire structure made out of carbon atoms. It is called graphene and was first discovered in 2004. Carbon normally forms four bonds but these only have three. This means that there is an unused electron on each carbon. These electrons can move, so the sheet can conduct electricity well.

▲ **Figure 15.2**
This structure is made out of 60 carbon atoms. It was originally called a Buckminster Fullerene after the famous American architect Buckminster Fuller, who made buildings looking like this. This became shortened officially to fullerene and, less officially, to 'buckyball'. If a buckyball is compressed to about 70% of its original size, it becomes harder than diamond.

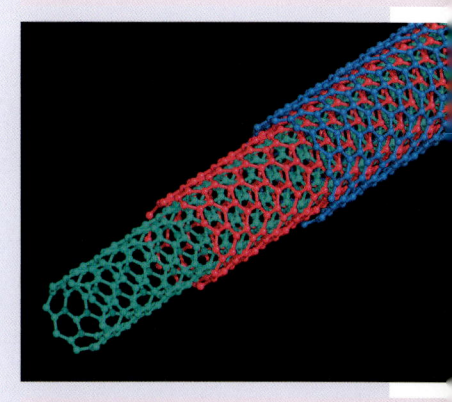

These unusual substances can be given even more unusual properties by modifying them slightly. A 'crystal lattice' containing buckyballs and alkali metal atoms can be made to become superconducting; this means it has no electrical resistance. **Graphene** strips a few carbon rings wide can be made to conduct like transistors, so a whole chip could possibly be made from a single graphene molecule. Single graphene sheets can be made to bind tightly to some vapour molecules, enabling them to be used as 'sniffers' in places like airport baggage security checks. We are only now beginning to discover how useful these graphene-based molecules might be.

The bonds that carbon atoms form with each other are very strong. Some of the compounds that carbon forms are quite small but most of the others, such as graphene, are large molecules; some of them are so large it is not possible to draw their structure on this page. We call them **macromolecules**.

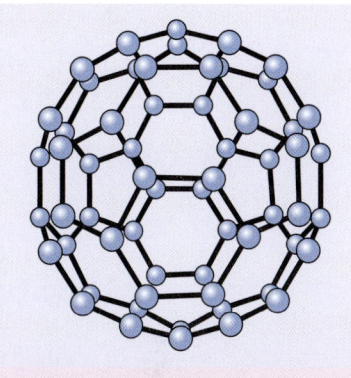

▲ **Figure 15.3**
If you roll up a graphene layer you get a nanotube. If you roll up several, you get a series of nanotubes, one inside another. Nanotubes are the strongest fibres known. A single perfect nanotube is about 10 to 100 times stronger than steel per unit weight.

15.1 Big molecules

The picture shows some large molecules that are part of our everyday lives; we eat them, we wear them, we build with them, we use them to keep us clean. We make some of them, but others are made naturally by plants and animals.

▼ Figure 15.4
Everyday macromolecules.

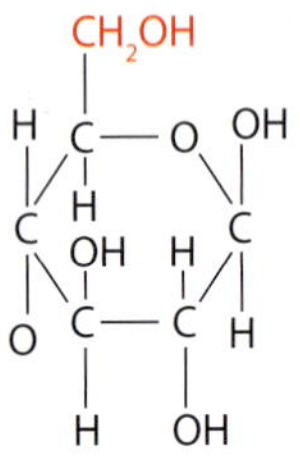

a glucose molecule

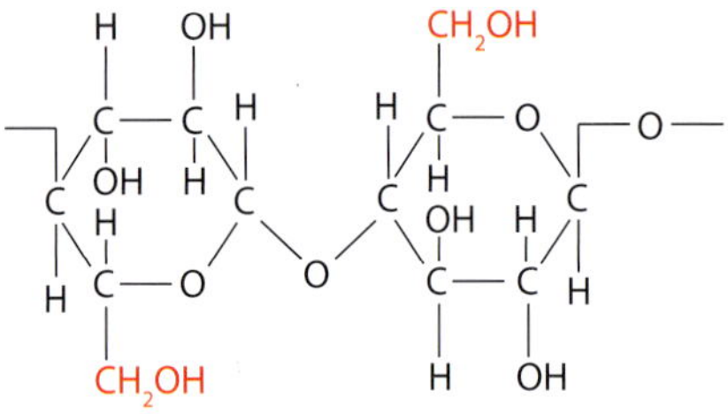

a cellulose molecule

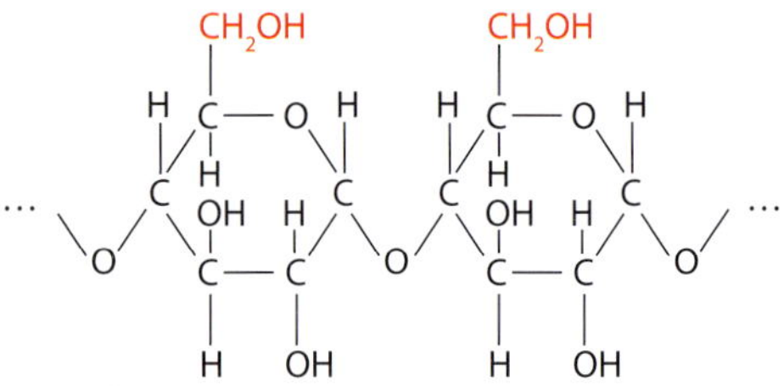

part of a starch molecule

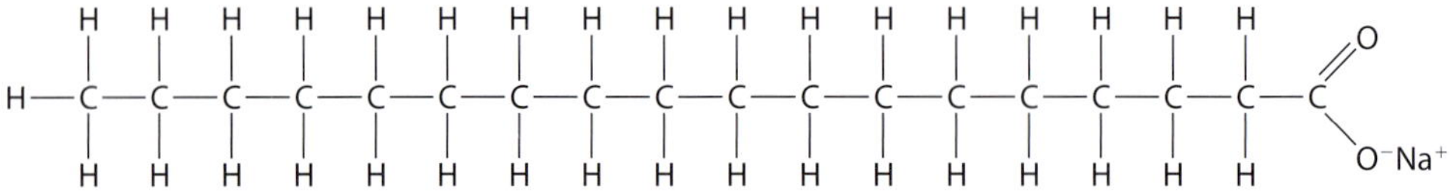

a soap molecule

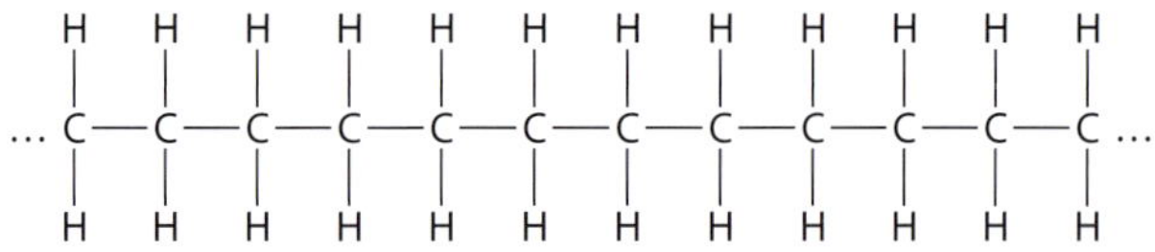

part of a polyethene (polythene) molecule

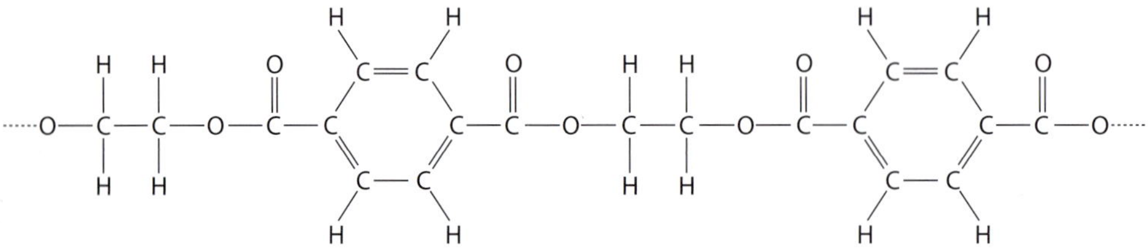

part of a terylene molecule

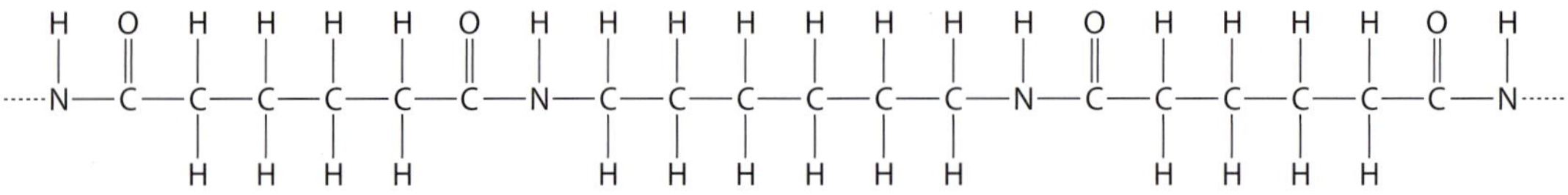

part of a nylon molecule

These molecules all look rather complicated and big. However, if we look carefully at them we find that there are patterns in their structure that make them quite simple to understand. These patterns also allow us to explain some of the interesting and useful properties of these molecules.

Macromolecules

15.2 Synthetic polymers

Three of the molecules in Figure 15.4 (polythene, terylene and nylon) are **synthetic polymers**. Synthetic means that they are made by people and do not occur naturally. Polymer means 'many parts' in ancient Greek. They are called polymers because the molecules are made up of many small parts joined end to end like links in a chain. Each individual small part is called a **monomer**, which means 'one part'.

Addition polymers

Polythene is a very common material. Its correct name is polyethene because the monomer from which it is made is ethene. In the early days of the manufacture of polythene, there were many explosions in the plant. This was because very high pressures (2000 times atmospheric pressure) were needed to make the ethene molecules **polymerise** (combine with each other). Modern polythene plants make use of catalysts, which allow the reaction to happen at much lower and safer pressures.

▲ **Figure 15.5**
The polymer, polythene, is made from molecules of ethene.

▲ **Figure 15.6**
Karl Ziegler (1898–1973) was a German chemist who discovered a process for making polythene from ethylene at atmospheric pressure. He was awarded the Nobel Prize for this discovery in 1967. The discovery was made by accident when a chemical he was using with ethene was accidentally contaminated by some nickel.

The polymerisation of ethene is an addition reaction. In the last chapter, you studied how substances reacted with ethene by adding on to the double bond. In this polymerisation, the molecules of ethene add on to each other.

Polythene is the simplest of many polymers made from alkenes but there are many others which we use every day. Table 15.1 shows a number of other common polymers that are made from alkenes or from compounds made from alkenes.

▼ **Table 15.1**
Addition polymers made from alkenes.

Monomer		Polymer		
Name	Structure	Name	Structure	Use
Propene (propylene)	CH₃, H / C=C / H, H	Polypropylene	(chain with CH₃ and H on alternating carbons)	Water pipes
Chloroethene (vinyl chloride)	Cl, H / C=C / H, H	Polyvinyl chloride (PVC)	(chain with Cl and H on alternating carbons)	Electrical insulation
Tetrafluoroethene (tetrafluoroethylene)	F, F / C=C / F, F	Polytetrafluoroethylene 'Ptfe' 'teflon'	(chain with F on all carbons)	Non-stick pans

205

Condensation polymers

Another synthetic polymer in Figure 15.4 is terylene. This is very different from the addition polymers based on alkenes. One difference is that there are two monomer building blocks and not one. Many polymers have this kind of structure. The two building blocks occur alternately in the polymer. Figure 15.7 shows how these form.

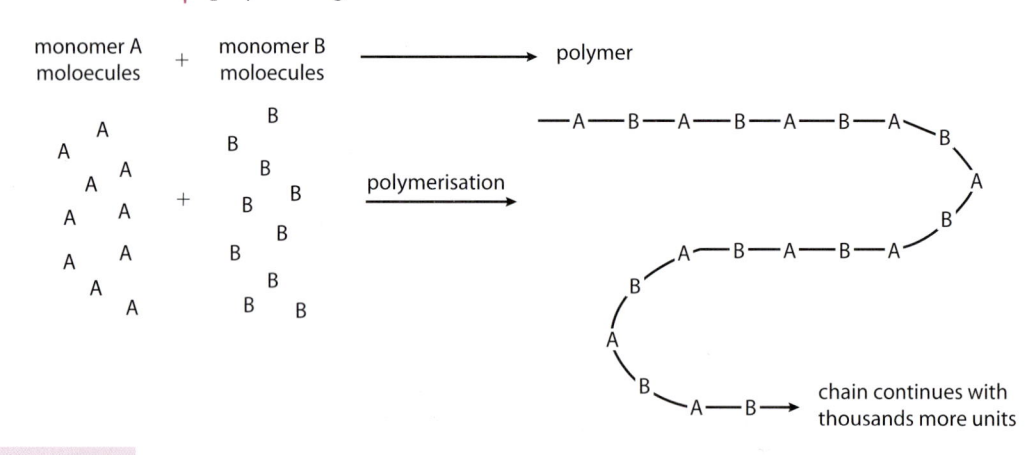

▲ **Figure 15.7**
Formation of a polymer from two different monomers.

In the last chapter you studied the formation of esters from acids and alcohols. If an organic acid has two carboxylic acid groups, one at each end of the molecule, it can react with two molecules of an alcohol to form a di-ester. If the alcohol also has two hydroxyl groups on it then it is possible to obtain a **polyester** from the reaction. A polyester is a long chain compound containing alternately the alcohol part and then the acid part of the ester. Figure 15.8 shows this. We call acids such as these **dicarboxylic acids** and the alcohols are called **diols**.

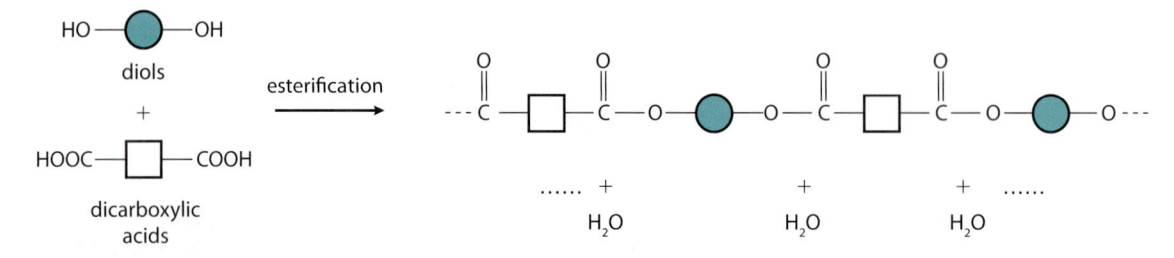

▲ **Figure 15.8**
How a polyester (such as terylene) is formed from a diol and a dicarboxylic acid.

You can see that during this reaction, water is produced. One molecule of water is produced every time a polymer bond is formed between the monomers. As you read in the last chapter, this kind of reaction is called a condensation reaction. Polymers like these are called **condensation polymers.**

Terylene is an example of a polyester made like this. The monomers used to make terylene are the diol, ethane diol (which is also used as antifreeze in car radiators) and a dicarboxylic acid called terephthalic acid.

Another well known condensation polymer is nylon. Nylon is not a polyester but a polyamide. Instead of an alcohol, which contains the -OH group, a substance called an amine, which contains instead the -NH$_2$ group, is used. Otherwise the reaction is the same. The structure of the polymer that is formed is almost the same as a polyester but with an oxygen replaced by a nitrogen atom.

Macromolecules

Figure 15.9 Formation of polyamide (such as nylon).

Both terylene and nylon are used to make fibres which are then woven into fabrics. They are harder-wearing than natural fibres, such as cotton and wool, and dry more quickly after washing. However, they are often less comfortable and not as warm.

15.3 Natural polymers

Some of the macromolecules shown in Figure 15.4 occur naturally. These natural polymers are condensation polymers and many have the polyester or polyamide structures like terylene and nylon.

Polymers in food – proteins

You will learn in biology that the main constituents of food are proteins, fats, and carbohydrates.

Proteins are natural polymers with a polyamide structure. Unlike nylon, which is made only out of two monomers, proteins are made out of up to twenty different monomers (called amino acids). These monomers are arranged in different orders in different proteins and it is the difference in this order that determines the different properties of the protein. Figure 15.10 shows the way amino acids are joined together in a protein; the different shapes represent different amino acids. Compare this with the structure of nylon above.

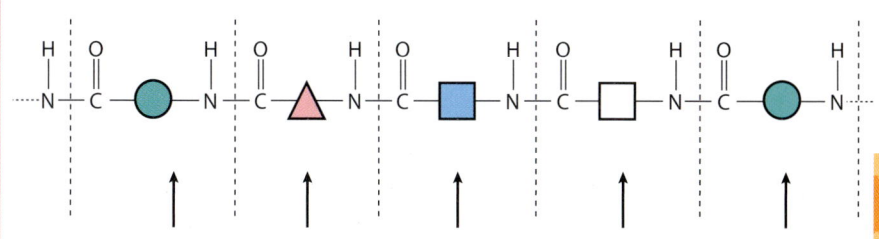

Figure 15.10 Structure of a protein.

each amino acid has a carboxylic acid group on one end and an amine group on the other

Your hair, your red blood cells and the white of an egg are all proteins. The only difference between them is the length of the protein chain and the arrangement of the twenty building blocks, the amino acids. Proteins are large complex compounds. Some proteins, called enzymes, are very important as they control all the chemical processes that keep our bodies going.

Proteins can be broken down into the amino acids from which they are made. This is a process called **hydrolysis**. Hydrolysis is the reverse of

DID YOU KNOW?

The first synthetic plastic was developed by a Belgian chemist, Leo Baekeland (1863–1944) who went to live in the USA. Baekeland was the first to develop plastic commercially, in 1906, and he called it Bakelite. It still has some uses, particularly as a hard electric insulator. Baekeland also invented the first commercial photographic paper.

DID YOU KNOW?

The protein insulin helps controls the level of sugar in the blood. Its structure was discovered by Dorothy Hodgkin (see Chapter 1). Even though it is one of the simplest proteins, it has the formula $C_{254}H_{377}N_{65}O_{75}S_6$! When you have studied Chapter 17 you can come back and calculate its molecular mass.

condensation. Condensation is the process in which two compounds join together, with water as the only by-product. Hydrolysis is the process in which a substance is broken down by heating it with water. The water is usually made either acidic or alkaline which makes the reaction proceed faster.

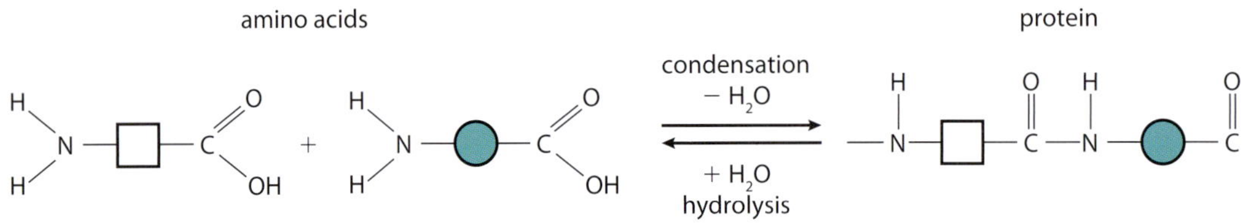

▲ Figure 15.11 Condensation and hydrolysis in proteins.

It is often useful to know which of the twenty amino acids are present in a protein. To do this, the protein is first hydrolysed by boiling it in an acidic solution and then the mixture of amino acids is separated by chromatography. The amino acids are not coloured, so it is impossible to see them on the chromatography paper. To make them visible, the paper is sprayed with a substance that forms coloured compounds when it reacts with amino acids. We call a substance that is used in this way a **locating agent**. The chemical that is used as a locating agent for proteins is called ninhydrin.

Another way of hydrolysing protein is to use an **enzyme**. Enzymes are themselves proteins and they are complex molecules that catalyse reactions in living cells. There are many different enzymes and each one only catalyses one reaction. An enzyme (pepsin) in the digestive tract catalyses the hydrolysis of proteins. It does this at normal body temperature; the protein does not have to be boiled in the stomach!

Polymers in food – carbohydrates

Carbohydrates are substances that are made by plants. The name tells us that they contain the elements carbon (carbo-), hydrogen (-hydr-) and oxygen (-ate). Examples of carbohydrates are sugars, starch, and cellulose. All these three substances have a very similar structure. This is not surprising, as plants make a sugar called glucose during photosynthesis and then they use the glucose to make the starch and the cellulose. Starch and cellulose are both condensation polymers of glucose.

The structure of glucose is shown in Figure 15.4 on page 204. You can see that it has a hexagonal ring structure with many hydroxyl groups attached to the ring. Starch and cellulose are polymers that are both made of glucose. The structures of starch and cellulose are also shown in Figure 15.4 and you can see that they are both made of many glucose rings joined together. The only difference is that in cellulose, every second sugar ring is upside down.

It is interesting to compare the physical properties of starch with those of cellulose. White flour is almost pure starch. It is soluble, and anything made of starch (like bread) has no tensile strength at all. Cellulose, on the other hand, is the material that gives all plant matter its strength. Wood is mainly cellulose and is an extremely strong substance.

The difference in the structures of the two is that the cellulose chain can be straight, because every second monomer is upside down. This allows space for the -CH2-OH group that sticks out from the ring (shown in red in Figure 15.4 and as a red rectangle in Figure 15.12 below). When these are all on the same side, as in starch, the chain has to bend round and curl up.

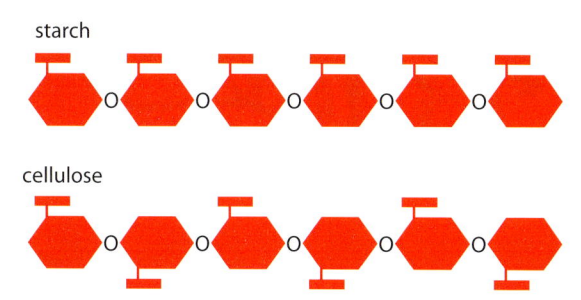

Figure 15.12
Comparative structures of starch and cellulose.

Activity 15.1
Hydrolysis of starch

Like proteins, starch can be hydrolysed with the help of enzymes. The enzyme ptyalin is present in saliva. This breaks down starch into glucose. There is a good chemical test for starch; it forms a black substance when a drop of iodine solution is added to it. If a small amount of starch solution is mixed with some saliva, you can test for starch in the mixture every minute by taking out a drop and mixing it with a drop of iodine solution. After a few minutes the starch test will show that the amount of starch in the solution is decreasing. Eventually all the starch will have been hydrolysed and the iodine test will be negative.

It is interesting that we have evolved an enzyme in our mouths that can easily and quickly break down starch but nowhere in our digestive system is there an enzyme that can digest cellulose. Yet cellulose has a very similar structure and would break down, like starch, into glucose.

15.4 Fats and oils

Unlike proteins and starch, fats are not polymers. They are esters. The alcohol that the esters are made from is called **glycerol**, which is better known by its common name, **glycerine**. It is a small molecule, only three carbon atoms long, and it has three hydroxyl groups, one on each carbon. The acid part of the ester varies according to fat or oil. These acids usually have 14 to 18 carbon atoms and a carboxylic acid group on one end. Three acid molecules are combined with the glycerol molecule in the fat or oil. Figure 15.13 shows a typical fat made from an acid called stearic acid, which has 18 carbon atoms.

DID YOU KNOW?

Some animals, such as cattle, horses, antelope and elephants, have evolved ways of breaking down cellulose in their stomachs. Unfortunately, it is so complicated and inefficient that, in order to get enough glucose from the cellulose, they have to eat almost all the time. It is a fermentation process, which generates a lot of the flammable gas, methane, which has to be released from time to time into the air. If the animals do not keep moving all the time, this methane builds up inside them and cannot escape. This is why, if an elephant is stunned with a dart, it must be brought to consciousness after no more than about 20 minutes, or the build up of methane in its stomach will be so great that it could burst like a balloon.

Figure 15.13
A fat is an ester – here we can see the typical structure of three carboxylic acids attached to a glycerol molecule.

3 carboxylic acids 18 carbons long (stearic acid)

an alcohol with 3 –OH groups (glycerol)

The jagged line represents a hydrocarbon chain, 18 carbons long.

▶ **Figure 15.14**
The label on this margarine pack advertises the fact that the acids in the margarine are unsaturated.

Recipe for making soap from beef fat

Melt some fat the size of your fist in a pan on a fire.

(Optional) Remove from the fire and add a cup of methylated spirit and mix it with the fat.

Make some alkali by shaking up some old wood ash with water and filter it and boil it down to concentrate it.

Add a cup of the strong wood ash liquid to the fat and warm the mixture very gently on the fire. The mixture will become stiff like honey.

Heat up about half a cup of strong salt solution in a pan until it boils and then pour the mixture into it.

Boil gently to evaporate the liquid to about half its volume and then leave it to cool. The solid product formed is soap and you can test it by shaking a bit with water in a mug to see if you can get a lather.

▼ **Figure 15.15**
Saponification of a fat.

In Chapter 14, you studied the difference between saturated and unsaturated hydrocarbons. The acids in fats are saturated; they have no double bonds in them and the esters made from them are solids, like lard. The acids in oils, such as sunflower oil or palm oil, are unsaturated; they have one or more double bonds in them. These esters are all liquids like olive oil. You will recall from Chapter 14 that margarine is made from vegetable oils by the addition of hydrogen to some, but not all, of the double bonds. The margarine is solid but is still 'unsaturated'. Unsaturated fatty acids are healthier for you than saturated ones and so margarine cartons often advertise that the margarine they contain is unsaturated.

Soaps

In Chapter 14, you studied how esters are made from an alcohol and an acid by a condensation reaction. The reverse of condensation is hydrolysis and esters can easily be hydrolysed. The hydrolysis of fats and oils has been an important reaction for many hundreds of years. If a fat or an oil is heated with an alkali it is hydrolysed to glycerol and the acid. The alkali will react with the acid, forming a salt. These salts are **soaps**. The manufacture of soaps by hydrolysis of oils and fats is such an important reaction it has been given a special name, 'saponification'. Look at the traditional recipe for soap that has been used, probably for thousands of years, throughout the world.

The hydrolysis reaction requires alkali to make it happen. In the traditional recipe this was obtained from wood ash, which contains potassium hydroxide.

The reaction can be written as an equation.

Macromolecules

How does soap work?

The structure of a soap molecule gives us an idea of how it works. Soaps make grease soluble. The soap molecule has an ionic 'head' and a covalent 'tail'. The covalent bit is the long chain of carbons and hydrogens. The ionic bit is the carboxylic acid group. The covalent part of the soap molecule is attracted towards the grease particle in a fabric or on your hands. Water readily dissolves the ionic compounds and so the ionic end causes the soap molecule to be soluble. A grease particle that is surrounded by soap molecules becomes soluble. This is shown in Figure 15.16.

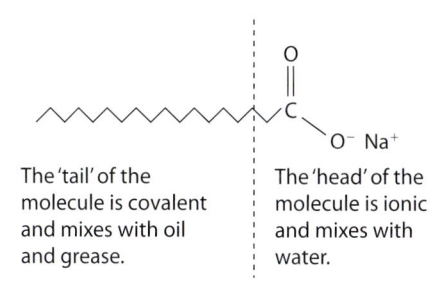

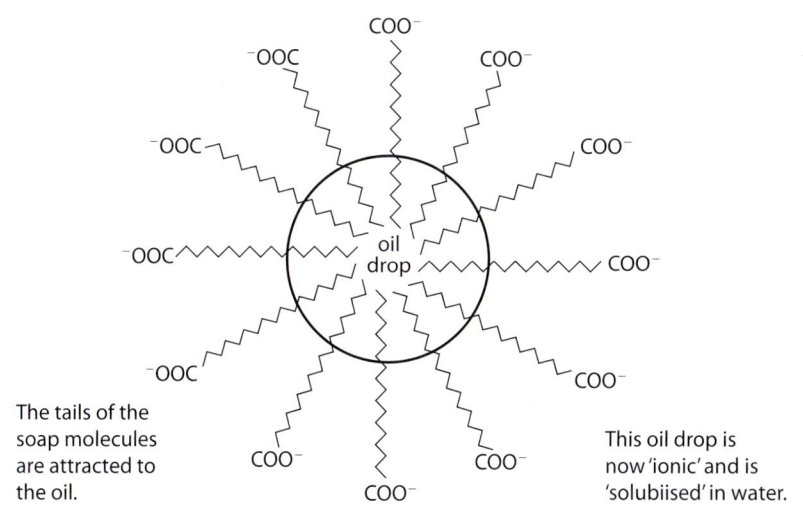

Activity 15.2
Saponification of fats and oils

The 'tail' of the molecule is covalent and mixes with oil and grease.

The 'head' of the molecule is ionic and mixes with water.

The tails of the soap molecules are attracted to the oil.

This oil drop is now 'ionic' and is 'solubiised' in water.

◀ **Figure 15.16**
How soap molecules can solubilise oil and grease.

The process of making soap from fats and oils requires a lot of alkali. It was the demand for soap for cleaning that originally led to the **alkali industry** being set up, and the invention of the chemical processes it uses, almost 200 years ago. Now, of course, there are many other useful materials being produced by the industry, as you will read in the next chapter.

QUESTIONS

15.1 Explain, with examples, the difference between addition polymers and condensation polymers.

15.2 List six synthetic polymers in a table. Also show in the table the structure of the monomers, the structure of the polymer, and at least one of its uses.

15.3 Name three naturally occurring polymers. Name also the building blocks from which the polymers are made.

15.4 Describe one similarity and one difference between starch and cellulose.

15.5 Describe how it is possible to find out which amino acids are present in a protein.

15.6 The two chemical processes, hydrolysis and condensation, are similar in one way. Explain this similarity.

15.7 Show, with the aid of a diagram, the similarity in the structures of proteins and nylon.

15.8 Describe, giving reasons for your answers, which classes of organic compounds (a) fats and (b) soaps fall into.

15.9 Describe how soap is made from fats and oils. Name the two raw materials that are needed for this process and describe where they both come from.

15.10 Explain with the aid of diagrams how soap can solubilise a grease spot.

Summary

Now that you have completed this chapter, you should be able to:

- understand that carbon can join with other elements to form a very large number of large complex molecules – which we call macromolecules – and that many of these are vital for life

- know that polymers are long chain molecules made up of many small molecules, called monomers, joined end to end

- know that some polymers are natural and others are synthetic

- describe the structure of well known synthetic polymers such as polythene, PVC, teflon, nylon, and terylene

- explain the difference between condensation polymers and addition polymers

- describe, in outline, the structure of common natural polymers such as proteins, carbohydrates, fats and oils

- describe the importance of these polymers in our lives

- describe how soap can be made by the hydrolysis of fats and oils and explain how soap molecules can solubilise oil.

Chapter 16

Industrial chemistry

These days we take fertilisers like nitrates for granted. They are made everywhere and are cheap. But just a little over a century ago we did not know how to make them, so we had to go and look for them. What we found was bird droppings. Not just a shovel-full here and there, but thousands of years of droppings that had formed layers several metres deep. It is called **guano**.

Sadly, there is no record of the conversations that must have taken place between the many traders who spotted piles of guano, and the local inhabitants, when they explained why they had come a long way across dangerous oceans in their sailing ships to negotiate permission to help themselves to this pile of bird droppings!

An important source of guano was the small Pacific island of Nauru. There, millions of years of droppings had been compacted with coral, a form of calcium carbonate, to form calcium phosphate rock. This, at one time, made the inhabitants of the island among the richest people in the world. Now the whole island is devastated by mining: the deposits are all mined out, the country is bankrupt and the people have nothing to support them.

The world hunt for bird droppings ended abruptly in 1913 when a brilliant German chemical engineer thought up a way of making fertiliser out of air. Read on.

▲ Figure 16.1
Flying fertiliser factories. Fish go in at one end and a perfectly balanced nitrate and phosphate fertiliser emerges at the other.

▲ Figure 16.2
Halifax Island is a desert island off the Namibian coast. It never rains there, so millions of years of bird droppings were not washed away. This derelict house was, in the 1870s, occupied by the man in charge of shovelling the deposits into visiting ships. It is now occupied by a lone jackass penguin (can you see it?) whose ancestors' made the deposits.

16.1 Making use of the gases of the air

Air is a very important raw material in the chemical industry. Hot air is blown into many furnaces – such as the blast furnace – as a convenient source of oxygen. Air is also used as a cooling fluid for many processes. The cooling towers in large power stations are familiar sights all over the world. Air is also separated into the gases that it is made from. All of them have their uses as shown in Table 16.1.

▼ Table 16.1
Uses of gases of the air.

Gas	Use
Oxygen	Breathing apparatus in hospitals to help patients with breathing difficulties. Mountaineers and divers use oxygen mixed with other gases to breathe in places where air is not available. For welding and cutting steel. The hydrocarbon gas acetylene is burnt with oxygen to give a flame hot enough to melt steel. Making steel from cast iron (see Chapter 9).
Argon	Filling filament light bulbs.
Nitrogen	For making ammonia which is then used mainly to make fertilisers.
Carbon dioxide	Added to drinks to make them fizzy. Much of the carbon dioxide used for this purpose is a by-product of the fermentation process used to make beer. The carbon dioxide is dissolved under pressure. When the can is opened the pressure falls and the gas can escape from the liquid causing the fizz. For refrigeration. Lumps of solid carbon dioxide (called dry ice) are placed inside some refrigerators to keep the contents cold. In fire extinguishers. The gas is heavy and this smothers the fire, preventing oxygen getting to it.

Separating the gases in the air

The gases that make up the air are separated by fractional distillation. The air is first cooled until it liquefies. This process makes use of the common observation that when a gas is compressed, it gets hot, and when a compressed gas expands, it cools. (Let a tyre down and feel the gas that comes out!) Air is compressed and it gets warm. The compressed gas is then cooled by cold nitrogen and then allowed to expand. As it expands, it cools sufficiently for some to liquefy. The air that has turned to liquid is tapped off and the rest goes back into the compressor. Figure 16.3 shows this.

▼ Figure 16.3
Flow chart showing liquefaction of air.

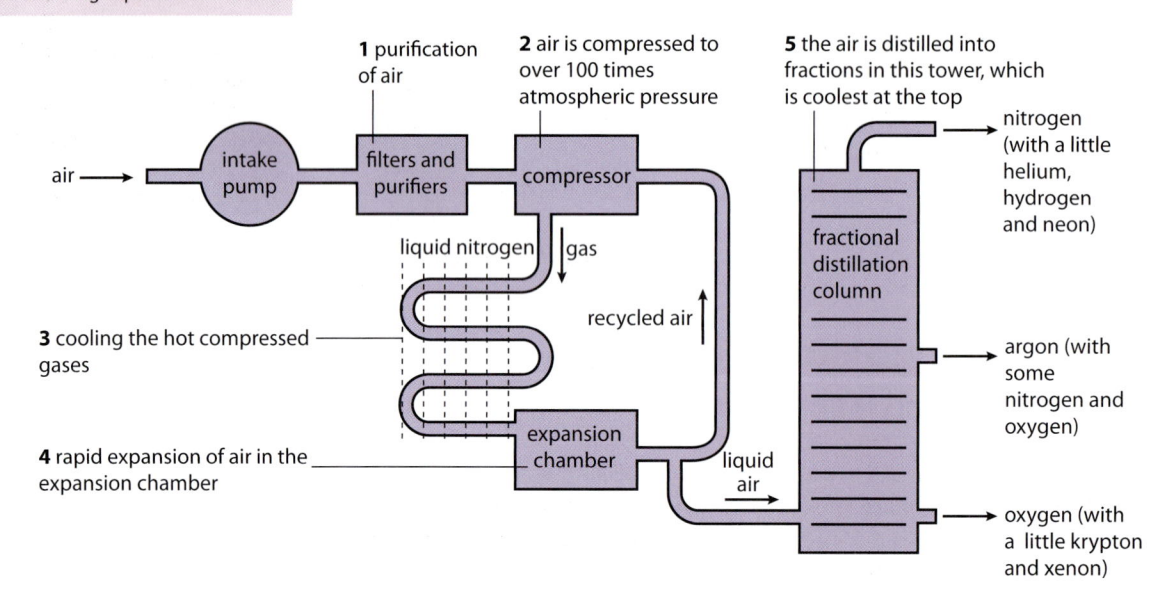

1 purification of air
2 air is compressed to over 100 times atmospheric pressure
3 cooling the hot compressed gases
4 rapid expansion of air in the expansion chamber
5 the air is distilled into fractions in this tower, which is coolest at the top

air → intake pump → filters and purifiers → compressor

liquid nitrogen | gas
recycled air
expansion chamber → liquid air → fractional distillation column

→ nitrogen (with a little helium, hydrogen and neon)
→ argon (with some nitrogen and oxygen)
→ oxygen (with a little krypton and xenon)

Industrial chemistry

The liquid air is then separated into pure gases by fractional distillation. The top of the column is the coldest part and nitrogen distils off here. Oxygen has the highest boiling point of the three main gases of the air and so is tapped off near the bottom of the column.

Using nitrogen to make fertilisers

All plants need nitrogen to grow. They need the nitrogen in the form of nitrates or ammonia, which are ionic and soluble, and so can be taken up easily by the plant. Most plants cannot make use of the huge supply of nitrogen gas all around them in the air, because nitrogen is very unreactive and the plants have not evolved a way of absorbing it and converting it into nitrates.

There are two natural ways in which nitrogen in the air is converted to nitrates that can be used by plants. We call this process 'fixing' nitrogen. When lightning discharges through the air, it causes nitrogen to combine with oxygen to form nitrogen dioxide, which reacts with water to form the nitrate ion. The second natural way is carried out by tiny bacteria found on the roots of some plants, such as acacia trees and peas and beans. These 'nitrogen-fixing' bacteria can convert nitrogen gas into nitrates, which can then be used by the plant they are living on.

The expanding populations of industrial countries towards the end of last century needed feeding. The food crops needed nitrate fertiliser and at that time the only source of nitrates, guano, was running out. These fertilisers had to be brought to Europe by boat. The Germans realised that if they were ever to be at war with a country that could cut off their supply of fertiliser coming in by sea, they would not be able to feed their people.

It became very important for Germany to invent a process for making nitrate fertiliser from nitrogen in the air like the bacteria on the roots of peas were able to do. A chemical engineer, Fritz Haber, invented the process in 1908. By 1913, a giant industrial plant had been built in Ludwigshaven in Germany to manufacture nitrates using the Haber process. (Only a few months later, war in Europe cut off Germany's supply of nitrates from across the seas.)

▲ Figure 16.4
Air is distilled in the tower in this picture.

◀ Figure 16.5
This is an acacia tree ('thorn tree'). The soils of the plains of southern and eastern Africa are not very rich in nitrates because nitrates are very soluble and are easily washed out in the heavy rains that fall there from time to time. Much of the nitrogen in the soil there is 'fixed' by bacteria on the roots of these acacia trees, which are very common there. The tree also provides rich food for animals, shade and firewood from its dead branches.

215

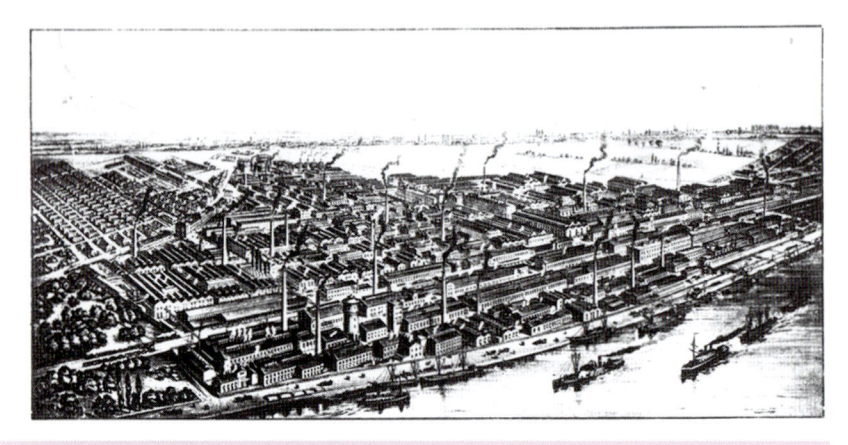

Figure 16.6
The huge BASF plant at Ludwigshaven opened in 1913 to make nitrate fertilisers from nitrogen. The plant used the process Fritz Haber invented only five years earlier. His original apparatus is shown on the left.

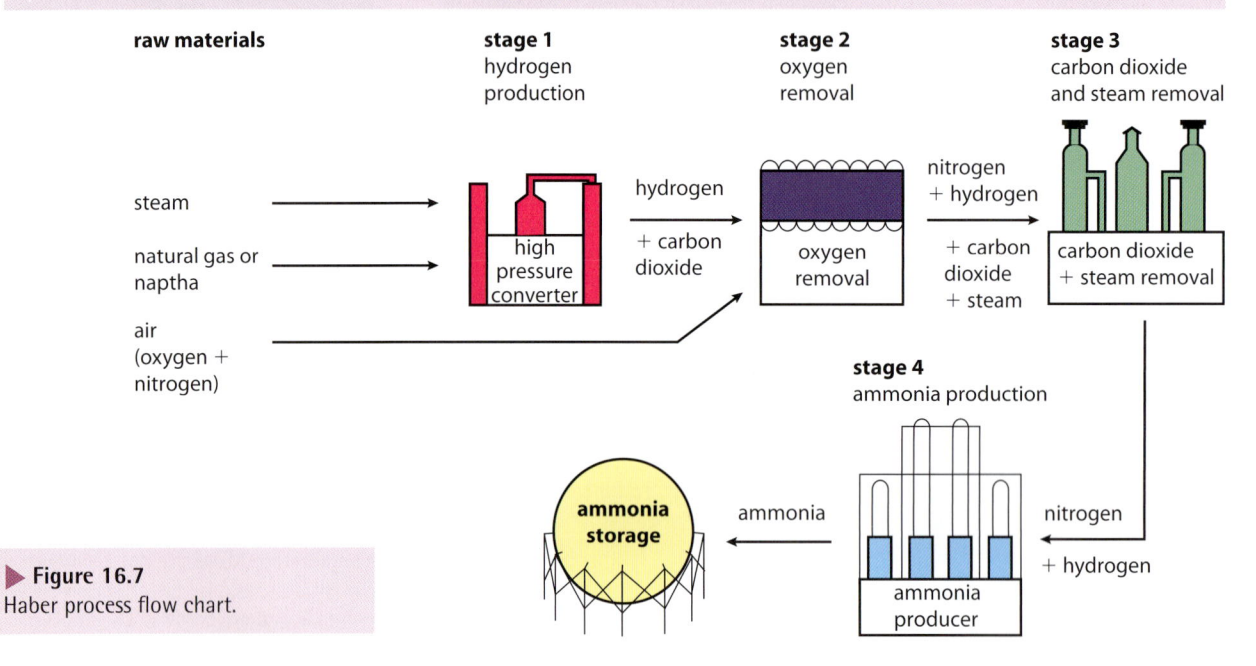

Figure 16.7
Haber process flow chart.

The flow chart shows the process invented by Haber. The first stage is the manufacture of hydrogen from methane or naphtha (a similar gas to methane obtained from coal). In this stage, the methane reacts with steam, giving a mixture of hydrogen and carbon dioxide.

At the second stage, air is added to provide the nitrogen. Unfortunately, air also contains oxygen, which is not needed and has to be removed. To do this, some of the hydrogen is burnt, combining with the oxygen to form water (steam). The mixture now contains nitrogen, hydrogen, steam, and carbon dioxide.

In the third stage, the mixture is bubbled through alkali, such as potassium hydroxide solution. This removes the water and the carbon dioxide, leaving just nitrogen and hydrogen.

In the fourth stage, the two gases are made to combine by passing them over a catalyst made of iron at a pressure of about 200 atmospheres (200 times the pressure of the atmosphere) and a temperature of 450 °C. The hot gases are cooled to liquefy the ammonia and the unchanged hydrogen and nitrogen are recycled. You will see that this last reaction is reversible. Haber's great discovery was to find the right conditions to make the reaction go as far as possible to the right. The very high pressure is important in this; at a lower pressure the amount of ammonia produced would have been very small.

Reactions of the Haber process:

Stage 1
$CH_4(g) + 2H_2O(g) \rightarrow CO_2(g) + 4H_2(g)$

Stage 2
$2H_2(g) + O_2(g) \rightarrow 2H_2O(g)$

Stage 3
$CO_2(g) + 2KOH(aq) \rightarrow K_2CO_3(aq) + H_2O(l)$

Stage 4
$N_2(g) + 3H_2(g) \rightleftharpoons 2NH_3(g)$

The Haber process converts nitrogen from the air into ammonia. To make ammonia into useful fertilisers it is converted either into ammonium salts or into nitrates.

To convert ammonia gas into ammonium salts it is bubbled through an acid. It will react, for example, with sulfuric acid to form ammonium sulfate (the fertiliser 'sulfate of ammonia').

$2NH_3(g) + H_2SO_4(aq) \rightarrow (NH_4)_2SO_4(aq)$

To convert ammonia into nitrates it must first be converted into nitric acid. To do this, air is mixed with the ammonia and the mixture is passed through a platinum gauze heated to red heat. The ammonia is oxidised to nitrogen dioxide and this is dissolved in water to form nitric acid. The nitric acid is then neutralised with alkali to make nitrates.

16.2 Sulfur and the sulfuric acid industry

Apart from industry based on oil, the chemical industry based on acids and alkalis is the most important economically. These are the industries that produce the chemicals on which all the other chemical industries are based. There are three important ones to be considered, the manufacture of sulfuric acid, the industry based on lime and the alkali industry.

The manufacture of sulfuric acid is one of the biggest of the world's chemical industries. 165 million tonnes of the acid was made in 2001. Sulfuric acid is a chemical from which many other useful materials are made. It is a heavy, extremely corrosive liquid which causes burns almost immediately if a spot comes into contact with the skin.

The reason why it is so dangerous to living tissue is not because it is an acid but because it is a **dehydrating agent**. This means that it will remove water from anything that contains it. If it comes into contact with the skin it removes water from it just like a fire does. The result is a burn just like a burn caused by fire. The acid should be handled with very great care and

> **DID YOU KNOW?**
>
> On fertiliser bags you can often see some letters with numbers, like N:P:K and 2:3:2. Have you ever thought what they mean? The letters refer to the three elements nitrogen, phosphorus and potassium, which are essential for the good growth of plants. The numbers refer to the ratio of these elements in the fertilisers.

eye protection should always be worn. Any splashes of the acid should be washed off immediately with a large quantity of water.

Sulfuric acid is made from sulfur dioxide gas. Most of the sulfur dioxide gas is produced by burning sulfur, which is obtained from large deposits found in a number of places in the world. Some sulfur, however, is obtained from natural gas where it is present as an impurity in the form of the gas hydrogen sulfide (H_2S). The sulfur is burned in air to form sulfur dioxide.

sulfur + oxygen → sulfur dioxide
$S(s)$ + $O_2(g)$ → $SO_2(g)$

The sulfur dioxide is then converted into sulfur trioxide by mixing it with oxygen and passing it over a catalyst at about 450 °C. The catalyst is the oxide of the transition metal vanadium, vanadium pentoxide. This process is called the **contact process**.

$$\text{sulfur dioxide} + \text{oxygen} \xrightleftharpoons{V_2O_5 \text{ catalyst}} \text{sulfur trioxide}$$
$$2SO_2(g) + O_2(g) \rightleftharpoons 2SO_3(g)$$

The sulfur trioxide produced in this way must be added to water to make sulfuric acid. However, this process produces much heat and it is easier to dissolve it first in concentrated sulfuric acid. The product of this is a substance called **oleum**, a kind of super-concentrated sulfuric acid. This oleum is then transported to where it is to be used, before the water is added. This saves money in transport costs. The whole process is summarised in the flow chart Figure 16.8.

sulfur trioxide + water → sulfuric acid
$SO_3(g)$ + $H_2O(l)$ → $H_2SO_4(l)$

▼ **Figure 16.8**
Flow diagram of contact process.

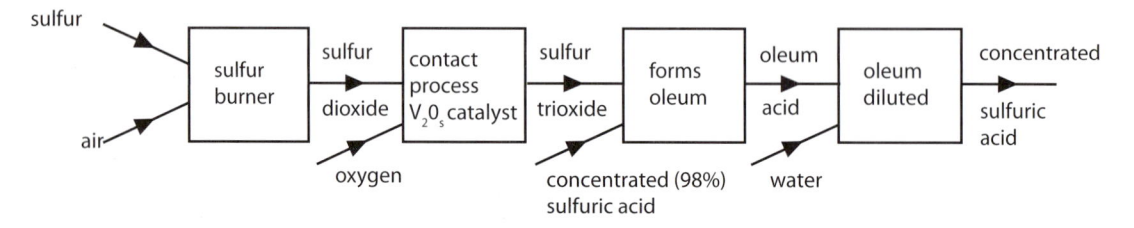

◀ **Figure 16.9**
Sulfuric acid plant.

Industrial chemistry

The uses of sulfuric acid

Sulfuric acid is the basic acid of the chemical industry. It is used, in one way or another, in the manufacture of nearly everything else. The pie chart shows some of the main uses of sulfuric acid.

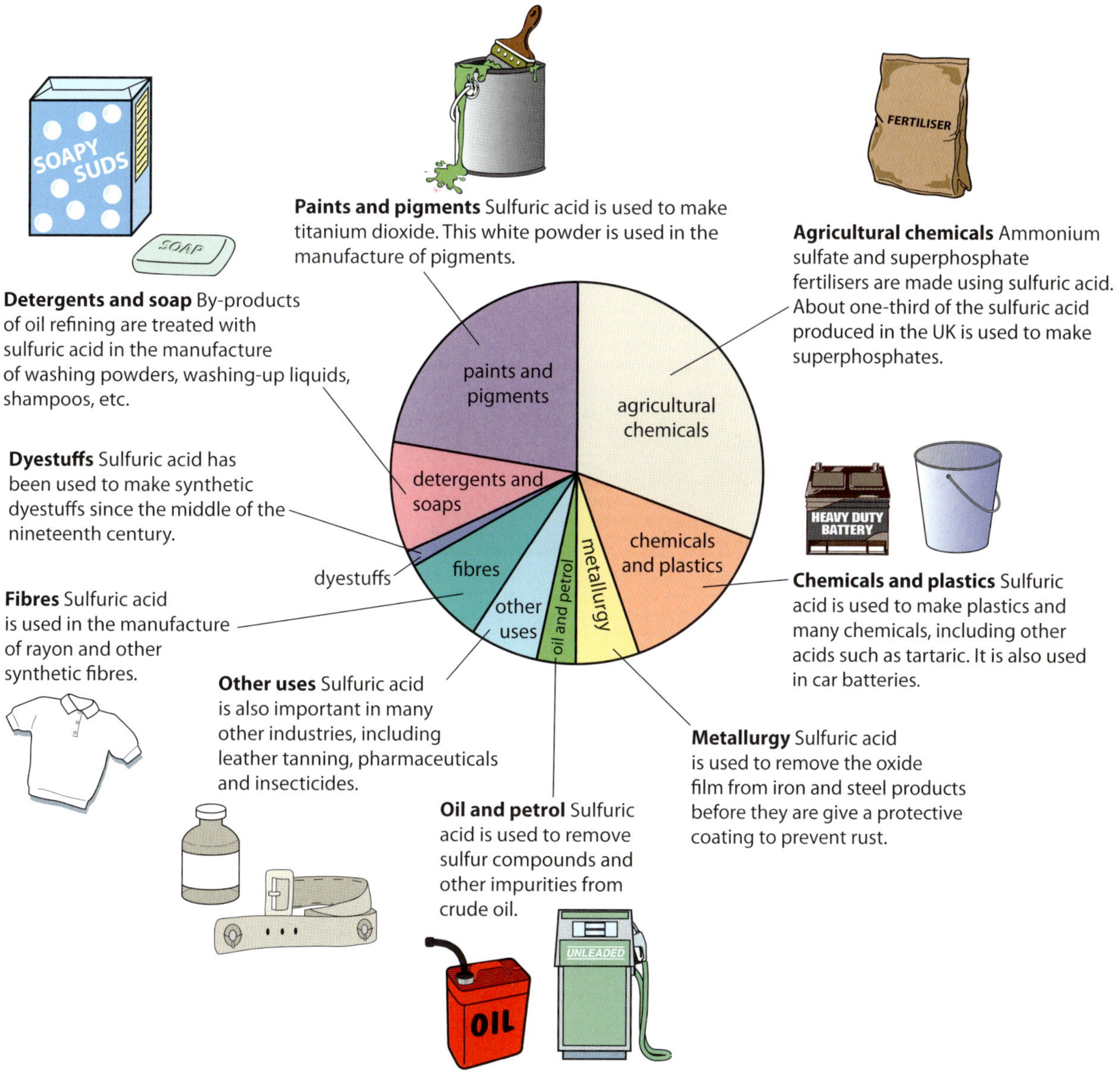

▼ Figure 16.10
Uses of sulfuric acid.

Paints and pigments Sulfuric acid is used to make titanium dioxide. This white powder is used in the manufacture of pigments.

Agricultural chemicals Ammonium sulfate and superphosphate fertilisers are made using sulfuric acid. About one-third of the sulfuric acid produced in the UK is used to make superphosphates.

Detergents and soap By-products of oil refining are treated with sulfuric acid in the manufacture of washing powders, washing-up liquids, shampoos, etc.

Dyestuffs Sulfuric acid has been used to make synthetic dyestuffs since the middle of the nineteenth century.

Fibres Sulfuric acid is used in the manufacture of rayon and other synthetic fibres.

Chemicals and plastics Sulfuric acid is used to make plastics and many chemicals, including other acids such as tartaric. It is also used in car batteries.

Other uses Sulfuric acid is also important in many other industries, including leather tanning, pharmaceuticals and insecticides.

Metallurgy Sulfuric acid is used to remove the oxide film from iron and steel products before they are give a protective coating to prevent rust.

Oil and petrol Sulfuric acid is used to remove sulfur compounds and other impurities from crude oil.

Other uses of sulfur dioxide

An important use for sulfur dioxide is as a bleach. If you hold a piece of moist blue litmus paper in sulfur dioxide gas, it first turns the paper red, because a solution of the gas is acidic. Then it bleaches the paper because the gas is also a bleach. It is used as a bleach in the paper industry to bleach the wood pulp that paper is made from.

Sulfur dioxide is also widely used as a preservative in foods because it kills bacteria, but is not poisonous to humans in small quantities. Sulfur dioxide (or sulfites) are often listed as one of the contents of food sold in tins and jars.

219

16.3 Industries based on lime

Limestone rock (calcium carbonate) occurs widely throughout the world. It was formed many millions of years ago when shellfish and other sea creatures died and their remains fell to the bottom of the sea. These shells are made from calcium carbonate. Over millions of years these shells became compressed into layers of limestone. Rock that is made in layers like this is called **sedimentary rock**.

Marble and chalk are also forms of calcium carbonate. Marble is produced when limestone is subjected to high temperatures and pressures in the Earth's crust, which causes it to melt and then solidify again. We call this kind of rock **metamorphic rock**.

Limestone is widely quarried. Its main use is as a building material; because it is sedimentary and has a layer structure, it is easily cut into regular shaped stones that make particularly good buildings.

▲ Figure 16.11
Limestone is quarried all over the world for building stone and also for the chemical industry.

Making cement and concrete

The main use for limestone is making cement. It is heated with clay in a furnace at about 1400 °C and the product is a mixture of calcium and aluminium silicates. These are in a powder form when they come out of the furnace. When water is added to the mixture the two silicates form long crystals, which lock around each other as they grow. If sand is added to the cement, the particles of sand are also locked into the crystals and the whole mass is very strong. This is called **concrete**.

When concrete sets, it does not dry out, the water in it becomes part of the silicate crystals that are formed. We call water that is part of crystals, **water of crystallisation**. The slower the crystals are allowed to form, the bigger and stronger they are. This is why it is a good idea to keep the concrete moist for a week as it sets, particularly in warm climates. Concrete will even set under water!

Other uses of limestone

An important use of limestone is as a **flux** in furnaces for extracting metals. This use was described more fully in Chapter 11.

Quicklime and **slaked lime** (calcium oxide and calcium hydroxide) are made from limestone. This is a very large chemical industry. To make quicklime, the limestone is heated to over 1000 °C in a furnace. At this temperature it decomposes, losing carbon dioxide. What is left is calcium oxide, which is given the name quicklime.

calcium carbonate → calcium oxide + carbon dioxide

$CaCO_3(s) \rightarrow CaO(s) + CO_2(g)$

> **DID YOU KNOW?**
>
> The world production of cement has increased from 103 million tonnes in 1950 to 2300 million tonnes in 2005. This is a 20-fold growth and is a measure of the rapid increase in the amount of building that has happened in the last half century.

Industrial chemistry

The quicklime is then 'slaked' with water to form slaked lime, calcium hydroxide. In this process, water is added and much heat is released.

calcium oxide + water → calcium hydroxide
$CaO(s)$ + $H_2O(l)$ → $Ca(OH)_2(s)$

Calcium oxide does not have many uses because it reacts with water so easily that it reacts, on standing, with the moisture of the air. This means that it is difficult to store, as it must be kept in sealed bags or bottles. Once these have been opened, the quicklime soon reacts to give slaked lime. It has the unpleasant property that it reacts rapidly with living or dead animal matter. It must therefore always be handled with great care. Because of this property, it is used to destroy diseased animal carcasses, such as cattle that have been slaughtered because they had foot and mouth disease.

Three important uses for slaked lime are: (a) as a fertiliser; (b) for making sodium hydroxide from salt in the alkali industry (see Section 16.4) and (c) for neutralising acidic industrial waste products.

One common industrial waste product is sulfur dioxide. This is produced when coal that contains sulfur is burnt or when sulfide ores are smelted (see Chapter 11). The sulfur dioxide goes into the atmosphere and in some parts of the world has become a serious pollutant. To remove it, the chimney gases are passed over calcium hydroxide (a base) that neutralises the acidic oxide, sulfur dioxide. Big coal-fired power stations, such as Drax power station described in the case study (Section 10.4), remove sulfur dioxide from their flue gases in this way. The product formed is calcium sulfate, which is used to make plaster and plasterboard for houses.

The many uses for limestone are summarised in Figure 16.12

DID YOU KNOW?

The Romans knew how to make concrete. They used clay that had been heated in a natural furnace; the ash that covered the city of Pompeii when the volcano Vesuvius erupted. They mixed it with lime and sand, and the mixture set hard. The Romans realised that any heated clay would be suitable. This is one reason why so many Roman buildings have survived.

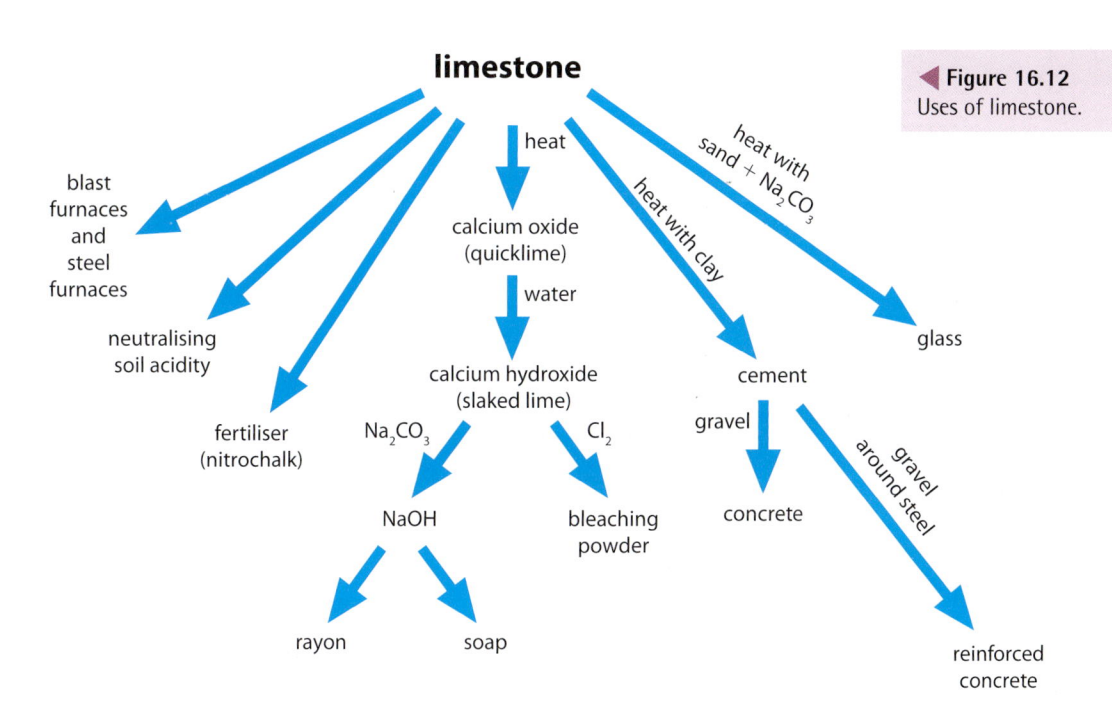

◀ Figure 16.12
Uses of limestone.

16.4 The alkali industry

This is the oldest chemical industry. The first chemical to be produced industrially was soap. This was needed in large quantities to wash the cloth made by the wool and cotton textile industries that developed first during the eighteenth century in northern England. If you look back at the way soap was traditionally made (Section 15.4) you will see that it requires a fat, alkali, salt and, of course, a source of energy such as coal.

Methods were invented for making the alkali needed for soap from salt, sodium chloride. It also requires a source of energy, usually coal, and a supply of calcium hydroxide. The industry has therefore become established where these three are plentiful. Salt is found in large quantities where ancient oceans have dried up and the rock salt formed is mined or quarried. These are all found in the north west of England and that is where the industry grew up.

▲ Figure 16.13
An underground salt mine.

The sodium chloride is converted into sodium carbonate or sodium hydroxide, both of which are alkalis. These alkalis are then used to make other materials, which we use in large quantities, such as soap and detergents. There are two processes that are used to make alkali from salt. One is a process that uses electrolysis and the other is a process invented well over a century ago, called the Solvay process. Figure 16.14 shows the products and starting materials for these processes.

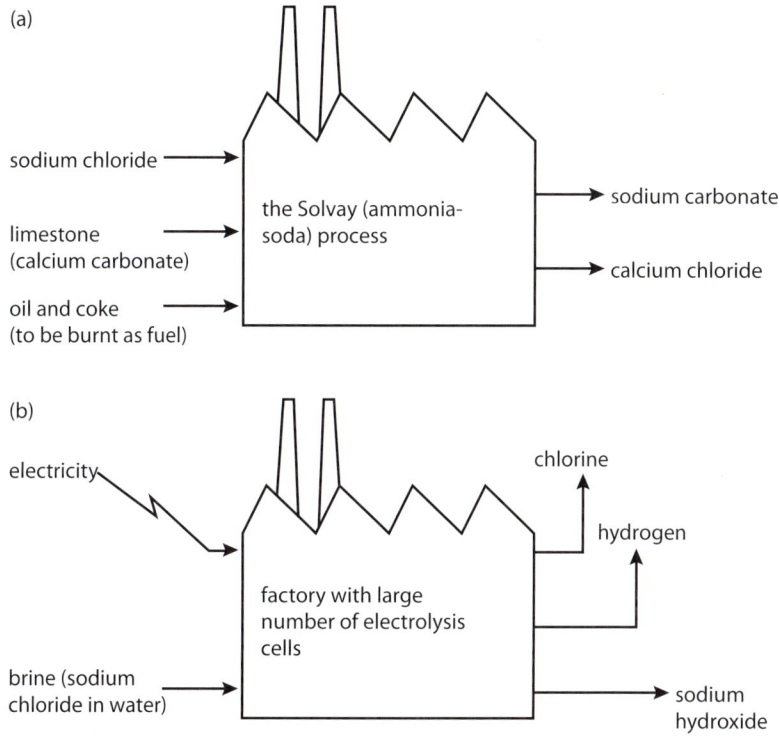

Industrial chemistry

(a)

sodium chloride →
limestone (calcium carbonate) →
oil and coke (to be burnt as fuel) →

the Solvay (ammonia-soda) process

→ sodium carbonate
→ calcium chloride

(b)

electricity ↘
brine (sodium chloride in water) →

factory with large number of electrolysis cells

↑ chlorine
↑ hydrogen
→ sodium hydroxide

◀ **Figure 16.14**
Inputs and outputs of the alkali industry: (a) the Solvay process and (b) electrolysis of brine.

Sodium chloride is also the main source of the element chlorine and so the alkali industry produces this as well. Chlorine is used in several other industries. The main industry that uses chlorine is the plastics industry, because one of the most useful plastics is polyvinyl chloride (or PVC), which is a strong but flexible plastic with many uses from clothing to electrical insulation. The world currently produces about 50 million tonnes of chlorine each year and this is rising by about 2% per year.

The cheapest alkali is produced by the Solvay process, but unfortunately, this process does not also make chlorine from the salt. In recent years the demand for chlorine for making chemicals such as PVC has risen. This means that more alkali is now being made by the more expensive process, electrolysis.

In the electrolysis process, an electric current is passed through a solution of sodium chloride. In the solution there are four ions, the positive ions, hydrogen (H^+) and sodium (Na^+), and the negative ions, chloride (Cl^-) and hydroxide (OH^-). The sodium and chloride ions come from the salt and the others from the water. The electricity causes two of the ions to form elements, hydrogen and chlorine (see Chapter 8). These two gases escape from the solution and are collected. The ions left behind in the solution are sodium and hydroxide. Solid sodium hydroxide can be obtained from this solution.

Figure 16.15 summarises the main uses for the products of the alkali industry. Almost all the major industrial chemistry processes use products from the alkali industry. It is not surprising therefore, that the world centres of the chemical industry have grown up in areas where there is a good supply of salt, limestone and coal.

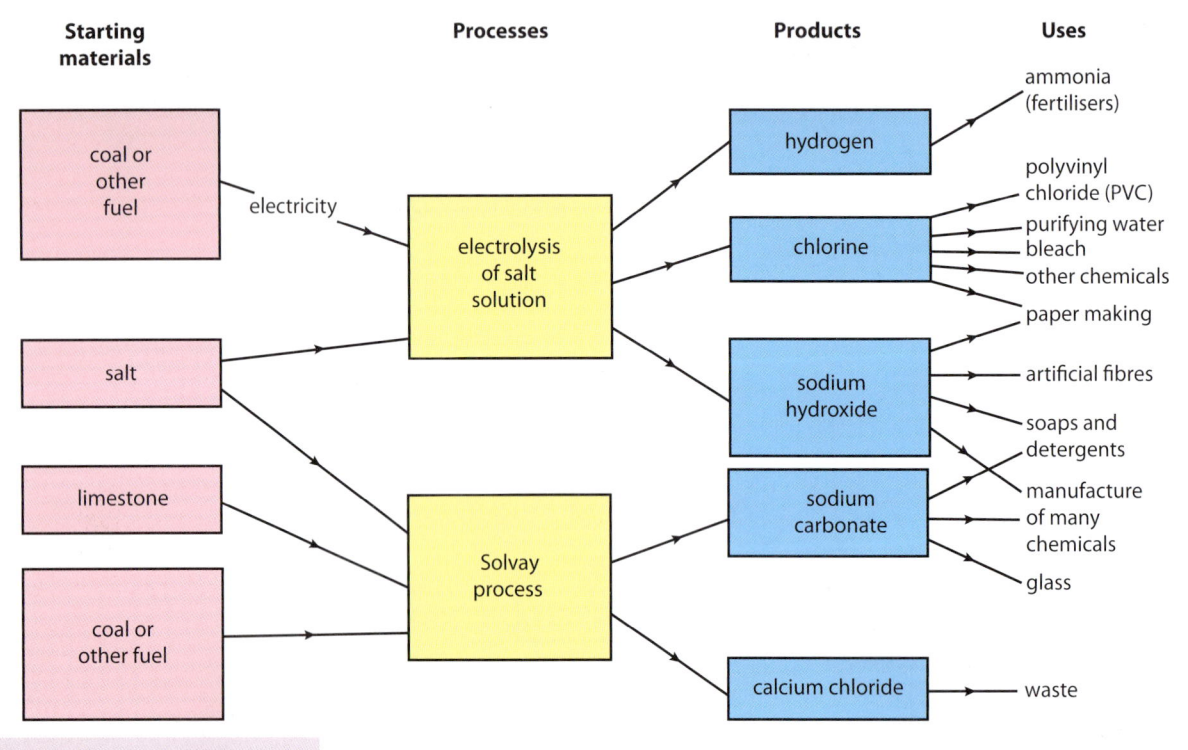

Starting materials	Processes	Products	Uses
coal or other fuel	→ electricity → electrolysis of salt solution	hydrogen	→ ammonia (fertilisers)
salt		chlorine	→ polyvinyl chloride (PVC), purifying water, bleach, other chemicals, paper making
limestone	Solvay process	sodium hydroxide	→ artificial fibres, soaps and detergents
coal or other fuel		sodium carbonate	→ manufacture of many chemicals, glass
		calcium chloride	→ waste

▲ **Figure 16.15**
Schematic diagram of the alkali industry.

▼ **Figure 16.16**
To make paper, wood pulp is purified by soaking in concentrated sodium hydroxide solution. The bleach used to make the paper white is made from chlorine.

Industrial chemistry

16.5 The petroleum industry

Fossil fuels

As you discovered in Chapter 10, coal, oil, and gas were formed millions of years ago from living things, and are now trapped under layers of rock. This is why we call them fossil fuels. They are very important to us. Coal is mainly carbon but also contains many other useful chemicals. Oil is a mixture of many hydrocarbons, and natural gas is mainly methane, CH_4. We make use of them all the time as fuels and as raw materials from which we make many useful chemicals and materials, such as plastics, that are now part of our everyday lives.

Fuels are either renewable or non-renewable. Wood is an example of a renewable fuel because we can grow more to replace what we use. Fossil fuels, however, are non-renewable. This means that once we have used them they are gone; remember the graph in Section 10.3 showing the increase in the use of fuels in recent years.

We know the approximate amount of these fuels still left in the ground (what we call the **reserves** of fuel). It is quite easy to make a rough calculation of how long these fuels are likely to last us if we keep on using them as we are at present. These calculations show that we will run short of oil and gas in a generation or so and as this happens the price will start going up. Many believe that this has now started to happen. It is difficult to imagine life without fossil fuels; we should use them carefully and not waste them. Also we must learn to develop alternative sources of the basic chemicals we use to make the things we now make from petroleum.

What can we make from fossil fuels?

We make many useful materials from fossil fuels. Figure 16.17 shows some of these. To make these materials we must first extract useful pure chemicals from the fuel. This is done by heating it and distilling it.

We can even distil coal. When coal is heated (in the absence of air so that it does not burn), we get a liquid from it that contains a number of useful chemicals, from which some of the items in Figure 16.17 can be made. Detergents and aspirin are two examples of materials that we can make from chemicals in coal.

Crude oil can be distilled using the simple equipment shown in Figure 16.18. A small volume of crude oil is put in the test tube together with some mineral wool to help it boil smoothly. It is heated gently with a small flame and the lowest boiling liquids are distilled first. Liquids with a higher boiling point are distilled over later, as the temperature of the crude oil rises. These liquids – we call them fractions – with different boiling ranges are collected in separate tubes.

DID YOU KNOW?

The word petroleum is made of two Greek words, 'petra', meaning a rock and 'oleum' meaning a liquid. Petroleum, often called crude oil, is 'liquid rock'.

▲ Figure 16.17
Common things we make from fossil fuels.

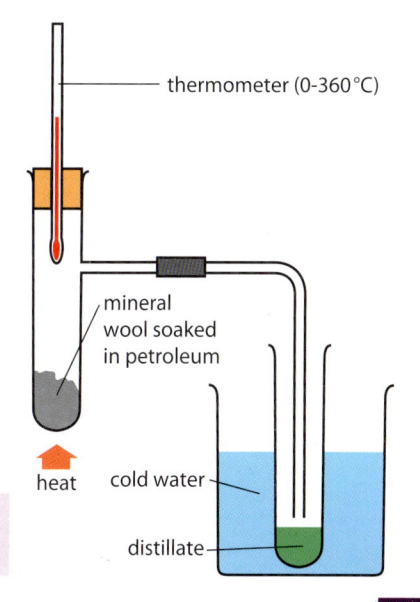

▶ Figure 16.18
Petroleum distillation apparatus.

225

▼ Table 16.2
Petroleum fractions obtained in the small-scale fraction distillation of crude oil.

The lowest boiling point fractions burn easily with a clear flame. The higher boiling point fractions need a wick to burn well and they have a smoky flame. Table 16.2 summarises this. It shows the commercial name and properties of four fractions from crude oil.

Boiling range	20–70 °C	70–120 °C	120–170 °C	170–240 °C
Name of fraction	Petrol	Naphtha	Paraffin	Diesel oil
Colour	Pale yellow	Yellow	Dark yellow	Brown
Viscosity	Runny	Fairly runny	Fairly viscous	Viscous
How does it burn?	Easily, with clear yellow flame.	Quite easily with yellow flame, some smoke.	Harder to burn, quite smoky flame.	Hard to burn, smoky flame.
Number of carbon atoms in the molecules	5–10	8–12	9–16	15–30

Activity 16.1
Distilling petroleum

Each fraction is a mixture of hydrocarbons, which are compounds of hydrogen and carbon. The higher the melting point of a hydrocarbon, the greater the number of carbon atoms each molecule contains.

The uses of the different fractions from petroleum depend on the properties of the fraction. The 'light' fractions that vaporise and burn easily are useful for fuel in cars. The 'heavier' fractions are more viscous and are useful as lubricating oils. (A liquid that is viscous is one that does not flow easily, like treacle). Candle wax is made from the lubricating oil fraction and is a mixture of hydrocarbons with about 20 atoms in the molecule. Table 16.3 summarises the uses made of the different fractions from the distillation of petroleum.

▼ Table 16.3
Uses of petroleum fractions.

Fraction	Approximate boiling range (°C)	Uses
Fuel gas	−160–20	Fuels for gas ovens, LPG, chemicals.
Petrol (gasoline)	20–70	Fuel for vehicles, chemicals.
Naphtha	70–120	Chemicals.
Paraffin (kerosene)	120–240	Fuel for central heating and jet engines, chemicals.
Diesel oils and lubricating oils	240–350	Fuel for diesel engines, trains and central heating, chemicals lubricants.
Bitumen	Above 350	Roofing, waterproofing, asphalt on roads.

DID YOU KNOW?

The diesel fuel sold in winter is usually a different mixture of hydrocarbons from the mixture sold in summer. This is because diesel sets rather like vaseline at a little below 0 °C and will not work as a fuel. More of the lighter fractions are added in winter to prevent this.

Industrially, the distillation of crude oil takes place on a very large scale and is a continuous process. The crude oil is continuously fed into the heated vessel at the bottom and the oil is vaporised. The fractionating column varies in temperature from about 360 °C at the bottom near the heater to 100 °C at the top. The different fractions are tapped off up the column as shown in Figure 16.20.

▶ Figure 16.19
An oil refinery showing the tall fractional distillation columns.

Industrial chemistry

◀ **Figure 16.20**
Fractionating column showing the products obtained from the fractionation of crude oil.

Fractionating column labels:
- fuel gas, 20 °C → bottled LPG
- petrol (gasoline), 70 °C → petrol for vehicles
- naptha, 120 °C → chemicals
- kerosene (paraffin oil), 170 °C → jet fuel, paraffin for lighting, and heating
- diesel oils, 270 °C → diesel fuels
- fuel oil → fuel for ships, factories, and central heating
- lubricating oil → lubricating oils, waxes, polishes
- 350 °C bitumen → bitumen for roads and roofing

crude oil → heater → fractionating column

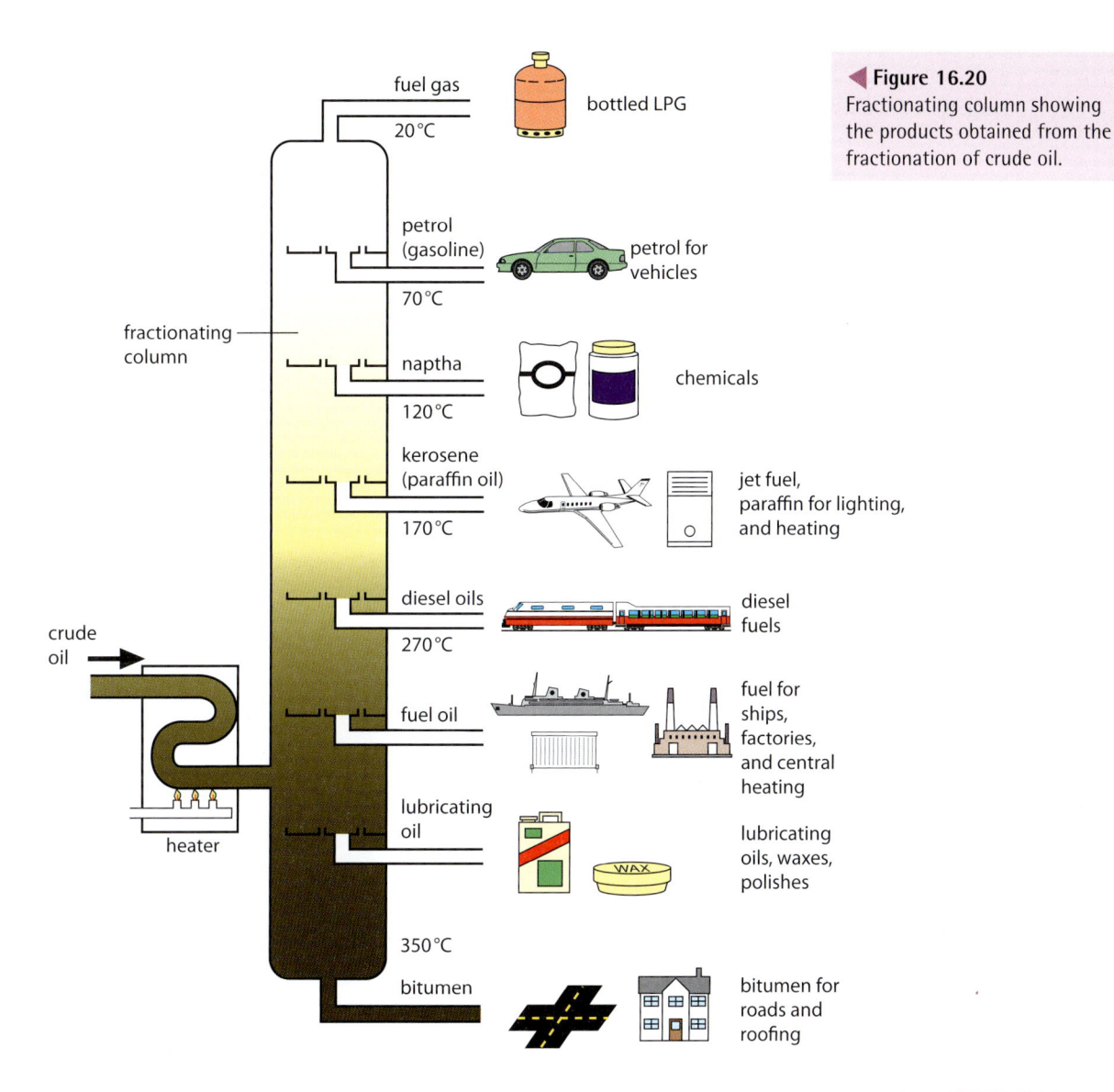

QUESTIONS

16.1 Plants need nitrogen, in the form of nitrates, to grow. They cannot make use of the nitrogen in the air because they cannot convert the nitrogen into the nitrates. There are two natural ways in which this can happen. Describe them.

16.2 Haber invented a process to make nitrate fertiliser from the nitrogen in the air.
  a) List the other materials needed for this process.
  b) Describe the conditions used in the main reaction between nitrogen and hydrogen.
  c) Describe how the ammonia made by the Haber process is converted into useful fertiliser.

16.3 Describe the process we use to obtain oxygen and nitrogen from the air.

DID YOU KNOW?

Arabic scientists were carrying out the fractional distillation of crude oil over a thousand years ago. Roads in Baghdad were first tarred in the eighth century and kerosine street lamps were being used there in the tenth century.

227

16.4 Draw schematic diagrams showing starting materials, processes, and products for the manufacture of the following substances:
sulfuric acid
sodium hydroxide
calcium hydroxide
cement

16.5 Explain why many of the major centres of the chemical industry in the world have arisen where there is a plentiful supply of salt and limestone.

16.6 Describe what concrete is made of. Explain how it is possible for it to set hard under water.

16.7 Explain why sulfuric acid causes very nasty blisters if it comes into contact with skin.

16.8 List the most important uses for the following chemicals:
sulfuric acid
chlorine
sodium carbonate
calcium carbonate (limestone)
calcium hydroxide (slaked lime)
sodium hydroxide

16.9 Explain why crude oil is so important to us. Suggest what could be done to ensure that it is used more economically.

16.10 Describe how crude oil separates into different fractions. List the boiling range and main uses of each fraction.

16.11 Explain why coal, oil, and gas are sometimes called fossil fuels.

16.12 'When oil is burned, the energy that is released originally came from the Sun.' Explain this statement.

Summary

Now that you have completed this chapter, you should be able to:

- know how fractional distillation is used to separate air into its component gases
- list the main uses of the common gases in the air
- describe how nitrogenous fertilisers can be made from nitrogen using the Haber process and the conversion of ammonia into nitric acid
- describe how sulfuric acid is made commercially from sulfur and list the common uses of sulfuric acid
- describe how the limestone is used as the basis of many industries including the manufacture of cement, glass, the smelting of metals and in the alkali industry
- describe the manufacture of alkali from salt by electrolysis and by the Solvay process, and describe the main uses of alkali
- understand how fractional distillation of crude oil is used to provide us with a wide variety of different fuels and with the raw materials for making organic chemicals such as plastics, drugs etc.

Chapter 17

How much?

When we study any chemical reaction, we are interested usually in two things. Firstly we like to know *what* is produced by the reaction. Secondly we like to know *how much* of the product is made. Most of this book has been about *what*. This chapter, however, is about *how much*.

17.1 Relative atomic and molecular masses

If you go back to Chapter 4, you will remember that atoms of different elements have different masses. The lightest element is hydrogen, and one hydrogen atom has a mass of one. We call this the **relative atomic mass** (or A_r) of hydrogen. All other atoms are heavier; carbon for example, has a relative atomic mass of 12, and oxygen has a relative atomic mass of 16.

Molecules are made up of atoms of several elements. For example, methane (CH_4) is made of one atom of carbon and four atoms of hydrogen. A molecule of water (H_2O) is made of two atoms of hydrogen and one of oxygen. We can calculate the **relative molecular mass** (or M_r) of a molecule such as methane, by adding up the atomic masses of all its atoms. So the relative molecular mass of methane (CH_4) will be $12 + (4 \times 1)$ which is 16. The relative molecular mass of water (H_2O) is $16 + (2 \times 1) = 18$.

Ionic compounds do not form molecules. Instead they form crystals containing large numbers of ions. So we cannot talk about the relative molecular mass of ionic compounds. But all ionic compounds have a formula; the formula for magnesium oxide for example is MgO. So we can talk about the **relative formula mass** (also M_r) of an ionic compound. The relative atomic mass of magnesium is 24 and that of oxygen is 16, so the relative formula mass of magnesium oxide is $24 + 16$, which is 40.

We can use these ideas to give us information about reacting masses.

WORKED EXAMPLES

1. In the beaker there is 360 g of water. How much of this mass is made up of the oxygen atoms and how much is hydrogen atoms?

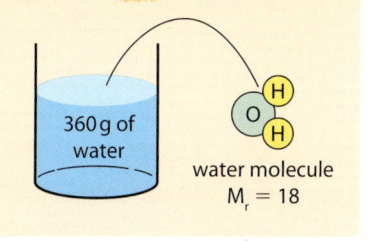

   360 g of water

   water molecule $M_r = 18$

M_r of water = 18
A_r of oxygen = 16
Therefore the proportion of 360 g water that is oxygen = $\frac{16}{18} \times 360$
= 320 g

We can conclude that the water in the beaker is made up of 320 g of the element oxygen and 40 g of the element hydrogen. If we were to split up this water by electrolysis (Section 8.5), this is the mass of the two elements that we would get.

2   How much magnesium oxide would you have if you burnt 12 tonnes of magnesium?
A_r of magnesium is 24
M_r of magnesium oxide (MgO) is 40
So 24 tonnes of magnesium would be needed to make 40 tonnes of magnesium oxide.
Therefore 12 tonnes of magnesium would make 20 tonnes of magnesium oxide.

The meaning of an equation

When hydrogen and oxygen are mixed and ignited, there is an explosion as they react and water is formed. The equation for the reaction is:

$2H_2(g) + O_2(g) \rightarrow 2H_2O(l)$

What information can we get from this equation?
- It tells us that hydrogen and oxygen combine to form water.
- It tells us that each molecule of hydrogen consists of two hydrogen atoms.
- It tells us that each molecule of oxygen consists of two oxygen atoms.
- It tells us that a molecule of water is made up of two atoms of hydrogen joined to an atom of oxygen.
- It tells us that two molecules of hydrogen react with one molecule of oxygen to form two molecules of water.

It also tells us something about the masses of hydrogen and oxygen that react together. It tells us that 2 relative molecular masses of hydrogen react with 1 relative molecular mass of oxygen to give 2 relative molecular masses of water.

But the relative molecular mass of:

hydrogen (H_2) is 2 (2 × 1),

oxygen (O_2) is 32 (2 × 16),

water (H_2O) is 18.

So we can say that 4 amu (atomic mass unit) of hydrogen ($2H_2$) reacts with 32 amu of oxygen (O_2) to give 36 amu of water.

Put another way, this means that 4 g of hydrogen reacts with 32 g of oxygen to give 36 g of water.

17.2 The mole
Counting atoms

The relative atomic mass of hydrogen is 1 and that of oxygen is 16. This means that an atom of oxygen is sixteen times as heavy as an atom of hydrogen. This means that 1 g of hydrogen contains the same number of atoms as 16 g of oxygen. But how many atoms is this?

An Italian called Count Amadeo Avogadro, professor of physics at Turin University, first worked this out as long ago as 1811. The number became known as the Avogadro constant and is around 600 000 000 000 000 000 000 000 (or 6×10^{23}). This number is known as a **mole** (just as 12 is known as a dozen and 144 is known as a gross) and it is a very useful number for chemists.

Why is this a useful number? Knowing this number enables us to count atoms and molecules by weighing them, just as bank clerks often count cash by weighing it.
- 1 mole of hydrogen atoms has a mass of 1 g
- 1 mole of carbon atoms has a mass of 12 g
- 1 mole of oxygen atoms has a mass of 16 g

To obtain a sample of an element that contains 1 mole of atoms all we have to do is to weigh out its relative atomic mass in grams.

The relative molecular mass of water (H_2O) is 16 + 1 + 1 which is 18. This means that 18g of water contains a mole of water molecules.

Go back to the reaction between hydrogen and oxygen in Section 17.1 above and use this idea of moles to tell us something about it.

$2H_2(g) + O_2(g) \rightarrow 2H_2O(l)$

This equation now tells us even more about the reaction. For instance:

If ...

two molecules of hydrogen react with one molecule of oxygen to form two molecules of water

then ...

two dozen (or gross) molecules of hydrogen react with one dozen (or gross) molecules of oxygen to form two dozen (or gross) molecules of water.

And so ...

two moles of hydrogen molecules react with one mole of oxygen molecules to form two moles of water molecules.

How do we convert this number of moles into grams?

The relative atom mass of hydrogen is 1, therefore the relative molecular mass of the hydrogen molecule (H_2) is $2 \times 1 = 2$

Similarly the relative molecular mass of oxygen (O_2) is $2 \times 16 = 32$

The reactive molecular mass of water (H_2O) is 1 + 1 + 16 = 18

> **KEY TERMS**
> The relative atomic mass, in grams, of any element contains 1 mole of atoms.

> **KEY TERMS**
> The relative molecular mass, in grams, of any compound contains 1 mole of molecules.

And so:

The mass of 2 moles of hydrogen molecules is 2 × 2 = 4 g

The mass of 1 mole of oxygen molecules is 32 g

The mass of 2 moles of water molecules is 2 × 18 = 36 g

So the equation also tells us the very useful fact that:

4 g of hydrogen will react with 32 g of oxygen to form 36 g of water

which is, of course, the same as you worked out in Section 17.1.

So we can summarise the different information the equation gives us like this.

$2H_2(g)$	+	$O_2(g)$	→	$2H_2O(l)$
hydrogen		oxygen		water
2 molecules hydrogen		1 molecule oxygen		2 molecules water
2 moles hydrogen molecules		1 mole oxygen molecules		2 moles water molecules
4 g hydrogen		32 g oxygen		36 g water

The equations in the box below show the relationship between number of moles, mass and relative atomic (or molecular) mass.

$$\text{number of moles} = \frac{\text{mass}}{\text{relative atomic (molecular) mass}}$$

$$\text{mass} = \text{number of moles} \times \text{relative atomic (molecular) mass}$$

$$\text{relative atomic (molecular) mass} = \frac{\text{mass}}{\text{number of moles}}$$

These help us calculate quantitative information about chemicals that we use. The examples below show how.

WORKED EXAMPLES

3 How many moles of calcium carbonate ($CaCO_3$) are used in a reaction if 10 g of the solid is used?

$$\text{Number of moles} = \frac{\text{mass}}{\text{relative molecular mass}}$$

Molecular mass of $CaCO_3$ is 40 + 12 + 3 × 16 = 100

$$\text{Number of moles} = \frac{10}{100}$$

$$= 0.1 \text{ moles}$$

4 To make 10 moles of water by burning hydrogen we must burn 10 moles of hydrogen. What mass of hydrogen is this?

Mass = number of moles × relative molecular mass

Molecular mass of H_2 is 2 × 1 = 2

Mass = 10 × 2 g

= 20 g

How much?

5 0.2 moles of magnesium oxide are formed when 0.2 moles of magnesium burns. The mass of the oxide formed is 8 g. What is the relative molecular mass of magnesium oxide?

$$\text{Relative molecular mass} = \frac{\text{mass}}{\text{number of moles}}$$

$$\text{Relative molecular mass} = \frac{8}{0.2}$$

$$= 40$$

We are now in a position to answer some of the important 'how much?' questions that chemists might ask, like:
- how much iron will I get from a kilogram of pure iron ore?
- how much sulfur will be needed to make a kilogram of sulfuric acid?
- how much hydrogen will be produced if 10 g magnesium completely reacts with acid?

In order to answer these questions we need two pieces of information. Firstly, we need a full knowledge of the reaction, including the formulae of the compounds involved. Secondly, we need the relative molecular masses of all the compounds used.

Consider these three questions one by one.

WORKED EXAMPLES

6 How much iron will I get from a kilogram of pure iron ore?

Iron ore is iron oxide, formula Fe_2O_3. From one molecule of this oxide we should be able to obtain two atoms of iron. Therefore from 1 mole of the oxide we should get 2 moles of iron. From tables we can find the relative atomic masses of iron and oxygen (Fe = 56, O = 16) and then we can calculate the relative molecular mass of iron oxide.

Fe_2O_3 relative molecular mass = $(2 \times 56) + (3 \times 16)$
$= 160$

We can then perform a proportion sum as follows.

From the formula of iron oxide, Fe_2O_3:

1 mole Fe_2O_3 will give 2 moles Fe

In grams, this will mean:

160 g Fe_2O_3 will give 2×56 g Fe

$= 112$ g Fe

Therefore 1 g Fe_2O_3 will give $\frac{112}{130}$ grams Fe

Therefore 1000 g Fe_2O_3 will give $\frac{112 \times 1000}{160}$ grams Fe

$= $ **700 g Fe** (to 2 significant figures)

7. How much sulfur will be needed to make a kilogram of sulfuric acid?

Sulfuric acid has the formula H_2SO_4. This contains one sulfur atom. We need not know the full details of how sulfur is turned into sulfuric acid. Clearly one atom of sulfur will make one molecule of sulfuric acid. Therefore 1 mole of sulfur atoms will make 1 mole of sulfuric acid molecules.

Relative atomic masses, H = 1, S = 32, O = 16

H_2SO_4 molecular mass = $(2 \times 1) + 32 + (4 \times 16)$
= 98

From the formula of sulfuric acid, H_2SO_4:

1 mole sulfuric acid can be made from 1 mole sulfur

In grams this will be:

98 g sulfuric acid can be made from 32 g sulfur

Therefore 1 g sulfuric acid can be made from $\frac{32}{98}$ grams sulfur

Therefore 1000 g sulfuric acid can be made from $\frac{32 \times 1000}{98}$ grams sulfur

= **330 g sulfur** (to 2 significant figures)

8. How much hydrogen will be produced if 10 g magnesium completely reacts with acid?

Before this question can be done, the equation for the reaction must be known. Here are two equations, one with sulfuric acid and one with hydrochloric acid.

$Mg(s) + H_2SO_4(aq) \rightarrow MgSO_4(aq) + H_2(g)$

$Mg(s) + 2HCl(aq) \rightarrow MgCl_2(aq) + H_2(g)$

In both equations one atom of magnesium liberates one molecule of hydrogen. This does not alter if a different acid is used. So we can use this fact in our calculation.

Relative atomic masses, Mg = 24, H = 1, Therefore H_2 = (1 + 1) = 2

1 mole of magnesium can liberate 1 mole of hydrogen molecules

In grams: 24 g magnesium can liberate 2 g hydrogen

Therefore 1 g magnesium can liberate $\frac{2}{24}$ g hydrogen

Therefore 10 g magnesium will liberate $\frac{2 \times 10}{24}$ g hydrogen

= **0.83 g hydrogen** (to 2 significant figures)

QUESTIONS

17.1 Calculate the mass of the following.
  a) 3 moles of aluminium atoms (Al = 27)
  b) 5 moles of magnesium atoms (Mg = 24)
  c) 4 moles of sulfur atoms (S = 32)
  d) 10 moles of carbon atoms (C = 12)
  e) 0.2 moles of calcium atoms (Ca = 40)
  f) 0.01 moles of iron atoms (Fe = 56)
  g) 0.08 moles of sodium atoms (Na = 23)

17.2 Calculate the mass of the following.
  a) 3 moles of water (H_2O) molecules (H = 1, O = 16)
  b) 2 moles of sulfur dioxide (SO_2) molecules (S = 32, O = 16)
  c) 8 moles of carbon dioxide (CO_2) molecules (C = 1, O = 16)
  d) 10 moles of sodium chloride (NaCl) ions (Na = 23, Cl = 35.5)
  e) 3 moles of calcium carbonate ($CaCO_3$) ions (Ca = 40, C = 12, O = 16)
  f) 0.1 moles of ethane (C_2H_6) molecules (C = 12, H = 1)
  g) 0.02 moles of ammonia (NH_4) molecules (N = 14, H = 1)
  h) 3 moles of oxygen molecules (O = 16)

17.3 How many moles of atoms (or molecules) are there in the following?
  a) 14 g silicon (Si = 28)
  b) 5.6 g iron (Fe = 56)
  c) 88 g carbon dioxide, CO_2 (C = 12, O = 16)
  d) 4 kg helium (He = 4)
  e) 19.6 g sulfuric acid, H_2SO_4 (H = 1 S = 32, O = 16)
  f) 3.7 g calcium hydroxide, $Ca(OH)_2$ (H = 1, Ca = 40, O = 16)
  g) 66 g copper sulfate crystals, $CuSO_4.5H_2O$ (H = 1, Cu = 64, S = 32, O = 16)
  h) 0.32 g methane, CH_4 (H = 1, C = 12)

17.4 Write the equation showing the burning of calcium to give calcium oxide (CaO).
  a) How many moles of calcium oxide can be made from 1 mole of calcium atoms?
  b) How many grams of calcium oxide can be obtained from burning 4 g calcium? (Ca = 40, O = 16)

17.5 The equation for the reduction of iron ore by carbon monoxide is:
$$Fe_2O_3 + 3CO \rightarrow 2Fe + 3CO_2$$
  a) How many moles of iron can be obtained if 1 mole of carbon monoxide is used?
  b) How many grams of iron can be extracted using 1 mole of carbon monoxide?
  c) How many grams of iron can be extracted using 1 tonne (1000 kg) of carbon monoxide? (Fe = 56, C = 12)

17.6 How much water is produced when 100 g of hydrogen is burnt? (H = 1, O = 16)

17.7 The concentration of sulfur in a sample of coal is 2%. How much sulfur dioxide is produced when 1 tonne of coal is burnt? If a power station burns 4 tonnes of coal per hour, how much sulfur dioxide is put into the atmosphere in a week? (S = 32, O = 16)

17.3 Formulae of compounds

Many formulae are used in this book. Some are simple, like water (H_2O); others are more complex, like glucose ($C_6H_{12}O_6$). All of these formulae have been discovered at some time by experiment. These are often not easy experiments to do. For example, scientists have found by experiment that when 1 g of hydrogen gas is burnt, 9 g of water is produced. Hydrogen is a light gas and it is not easy to weigh it. When it burns it produces water vapour, which must all be condensed and weighed.

The results from this experiment on the burning of hydrogen can tell us the formula of water. To find the formula of water we need to know how many molecules of hydrogen combine with one molecule of oxygen. This will be the same as the number of moles of atoms of hydrogen that combine with one mole of atoms of oxygen. The relative atomic mass of oxygen is 16. Therefore we want to know:
- how many grams of hydrogen combine with 1 mole (16 g) of oxygen
- how many moles of atoms of hydrogen this is (the relative atomic mass of hydrogen is 1).

WORKED EXAMPLES

9 *Calculation a)*

From the experimental results we have:

1 g of hydrogen produces 9 g water

Therefore 1 g of hydrogen must combine with 8 g of oxygen to give the 9 g of water.

So 8 g oxygen reacts with 1 g hydrogen to give water

Therefore 1 g oxygen reacts with $\frac{1}{8}$ grams hydrogen to give water

Therefore 16 g oxygen reacts with $\frac{1 \times 16}{8}$ grams hydrogen to give water

= **2.0 g hydrogen** (to 2 significant figures)

Calculation b)

If the relative atomic mass of hydrogen is 1, then 2 g hydrogen is 2 moles of hydrogen atoms.

So from this calculation we find that 1 mole of oxygen atoms combine with 2 moles of hydrogen atoms. Therefore 1 atom of oxygen combines with 2 atoms of hydrogen to give water. This tells us the formula of water must be H_2O.

We are not quite there however. If the formula of water were H_4O_2 or H_6O_3, we would still find that 1 mole of oxygen atoms would combine with two moles of hydrogen atoms! What we have found is the simplest formula for water. We call this the **empirical** formula.

In order to find which is the actual formula for water, we need more information. We need to know the relative molecular mass of water. The relative molecular masses for some of the possible formulae of water are shown in Table 17.1

Formula	Relative molecular mass
H_2O	18
H_4O_2	36
H_6O_3	54

◀ Table 17.1
Possible molecular masses for some formulae of water.

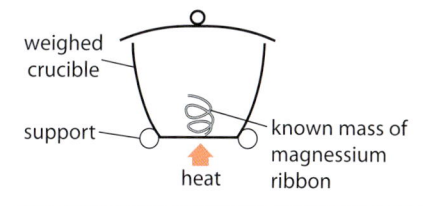

To find which one of these is the actual relative molecular mass of water, the mass of one mole of water molecules must be found in a separate experiment. Such an experiment gives the mass of one mole of water molecules as 18. This is called the molecular formula and therefore the molecular formula of water is H_2O, the same as the empirical formula.

Experiments to find empirical formulae of compounds

We can use experiments like the one below to tell us empirical formulae of compounds. This one gives us the formula of magnesium oxide.

A crucible plus its lid is carefully weighed when empty and again with about 5 cm of carefully cleaned magnesium ribbon in it. It is then heated strongly to burn the magnesium. This is not as easy as it may seem because air cannot get in easily past the lid. The lid has to be lifted a little from time to time to let in air but this must be done very carefully because magnesium oxide smoke must not be allowed to escape.

▲ Figure 17.1
Apparatus for finding the formula of magnesium oxide.

When all the magnesium has burnt, the crucible is allowed to cool and reweighed. From the results we can:
- calculate the mass of the magnesium used, and
- calculate the mass of the magnesium oxide produced, and so
- calculate the mass of oxygen used in the reaction, and finally
- given that Mg = 24 and O = 16, we can calculate the number of moles of oxygen atoms that combine with 1 mole of magnesium atoms.

Activity 17.1
Finding the formula of magnesium oxide

The reaction that takes place in the crucible is as follows and some sample results are shown in the boxes.

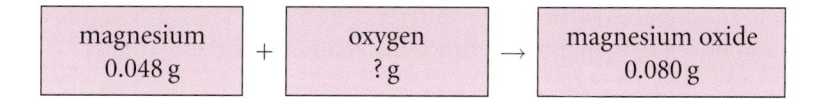

magnesium 0.048 g + oxygen ? g → magnesium oxide 0.080 g

> ## WORKED EXAMPLES
>
> **10** *Calculation (using the sample results)*
>
> To find the mass of oxygen that will combine with one mole (24 g) of magnesium:
>
> Mass of oxygen used is 0.080 − 0.048 g
>
> = 0.032 g
>
> Therefore we have:
>
> 0.048 g magnesium combine with 0.032 g oxygen
>
> Therefore 1 g magnesium combines with $\frac{0.032}{0.048}$ g oxygen
>
> Therefore 24 g magnesium combine with $\frac{0.032 \times 24}{0.048}$ g oxygen
>
> = **16 g oxygen** (to 2 significant figures)
>
> But 16 g oxygen is 1 mole of oxygen atoms. Therefore 1 mole of magnesium atoms combines with 1 mole of oxygen atoms. The empirical formula for magnesium oxide is therefore MgO.

Another experiment that can help us find the formula of a compound is the reduction of copper oxide. In this case, oxygen is removed from a metal oxide to give the metal, the opposite reaction from the one with magnesium above. The apparatus is shown in Figure 17.2.

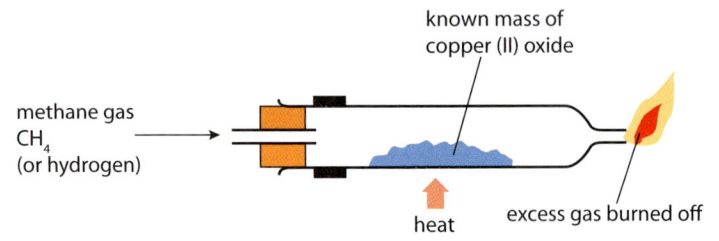

▶ **Figure 17.2**
Apparatus for reducing copper oxide.

When the copper oxide is heated in a stream of either hydrogen or methane, the oxide is reduced to copper. The reaction that happens is:

(if hydrogen is used)

copper oxide + hydrogen → copper + water

(if methane is used)

copper oxide + methane → copper + carbon dioxide + water

The oxide is weighed before the experiment and the copper that is produced is weighed after it. The difference between these two weights is the amount of oxygen that was originally combined with the copper.

Examples of results

Mass of copper oxide = 2.0 g

Mass of copper left at the end of the experiment = 1.6 g

Cu = 64, O = 16

> **WORKED EXAMPLE**
>
> 11 *Calculation*
>
> To find the mass of oxygen originally combined with 1 mole (64 g) of copper:
>
> Mass of oxygen originally combined with the copper
>
> $2.0 - 1.6 = 0.40\,g$
>
> From the experiment
>
> 1.6 g copper combines with 0.40 g oxygen
>
> Therefore 1 g copper combines with $\frac{0.40}{1.6}$ g oxygen
>
> Therefore 64 g copper combines with $\frac{0.40 \times 64}{1.6}$ g oxygen
>
> $= \mathbf{16\,g\ oxygen}$ (to 2 significant figures)
>
> 16 g oxygen is 1 mole of oxygen. 1 mole of copper is combined with 1 mole of oxygen and therefore the empirical formula of copper oxide is CuO.

Experiments to find the molecular formula of compounds

Sometimes the molecular formula is different from the empirical formula. Think about this example.

> **WORKED EXAMPLE**
>
> 12 10 g of a hydrocarbon is found to contain 8 g carbon and 2 g hydrogen. Its relative molecular mass is 30. What is its empirical formula and its molecular formula? (C = 12, H = 1)
>
> 8 g carbon combines with 2 g hydrogen
>
> Therefore 1 g carbon combines with $\frac{2}{8}$ g hydrogen
>
> Therefore 12 g carbon (1 mole) combines with $2 \times \frac{12}{8}$ g hydrogen
>
> $= 3\,g$ hydrogen
>
> $= 3$ moles hydrogen atoms
>
> Therefore the empirical formula of the hydrocarbon is CH_3.
>
> This cannot be the actual formula because carbon always has four bonds and in CH_3 it is only combined with three other atoms. The compound CH_3 cannot exist (M_r would equal 15).
>
> The actual relative molecular mass is 30, which is twice the empirical formula mass. Therefore the formula must have twice the number of each atom at the empirical formula.
>
> **The molecular formula is therefore C_2H_6.**

Finding the actual molecular formula is often quite a difficult experiment and involves finding the density of a substance if it is a gas like this. The process is beyond the scope of this book.

QUESTIONS

17.8 5.6 g iron was found to combine with 2.4 g oxygen. How much oxygen would combine with one mole of iron? What is the simplest formula for the iron oxide? (Fe = 56, O = 16)

17.9 6 g sodium combines with chlorine to give 11.7 g of sodium chloride. How much chlorine was used in the reaction? What is the formula of sodium chloride? (Na = 23, Cl = 35.5)

17.10 In an experiment to electrolyse molten lead bromide, 74.6 g lead bromide was weighed and electrolysed. At the end of the experiment a bead of lead weighing 10.4 g was obtained from the bottom of the crucible and the mass of the lead bromide unused was found to be 56.2 g. Calculate: a) how much lead bromide was electrolysed and b) how much bromine was lost during the electrolysis. Calculate the molecular formula of lead bromide. (Pb = 207, Br = 80)

17.4 The volume of a mole of gas

As long as three hundred years ago, scientists such as Dalton (Section 4.2) were making observations that could only be explained by the rather strange conclusion that a mole of all gas molecules always occupied the same volume (as long as pressure and temperature were constant). This is so for all gases, no matter how big or small the molecules are. So one mole of carbon dioxide molecules (mass 44 g), occupies the same volume as one mole of helium atoms (mass 4 g).

It was Avogadro who finally stated this and he worked out the volume of a mole of a gas (at 1 atmosphere pressure, 100 kPa, and room temperature, 20 °C) was 24.0 dm^3 (or 24 000 cm^3 or 24.0 litres). We call this volume the **molar volume**.

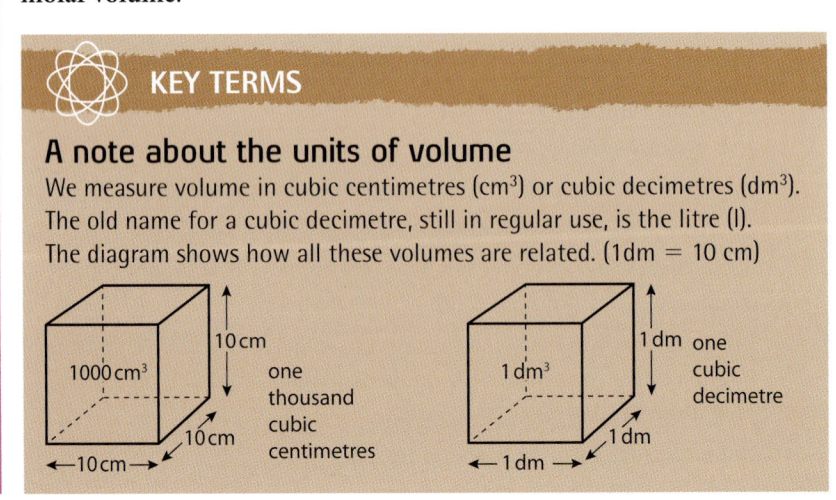

KEY TERMS

A note about the units of volume
We measure volume in cubic centimetres (cm^3) or cubic decimetres (dm^3). The old name for a cubic decimetre, still in regular use, is the litre (l). The diagram shows how all these volumes are related. (1dm = 10 cm)

1000 cm^3 — 10 cm — one thousand cubic centimetres

1 dm^3 — 1 dm — one cubic decimetre

How much?

A mole of particles is 6.02 × 10²³ particles. This means the molar volume of any gas contains this number of molecules. This means therefore that the gas molecules are *always the same average distance apart*, no matter how big the molecules are.

Figure 17.3
Molar volumes of oxygen, ammonia and neon.

One mole of various gases at 0 °C and 1 atmosphere pressure

1 mole of oxygen molecules

$$24 \text{ litres } O_2$$

24 000 cm³ oxygen contains 6.02 × 10²³ molecules of oxygen.
Mass of this oxygen (O_2) 32 g

1 mole of ammonia molecules

$$24 \text{ litres } NH_3$$

24 000 cm³ ammonia contains 6.02 × 10²³ molecules of ammonia.
Mass of this ammonia (NH_3) 17 g

1 mole of neon atoms

$$24 \text{ litres } Ne$$

24 000 cm³ neon contains 6.02 × 10²³ atoms of neon.
Mass of this neon (Ne) 20 g

This observation of Avogadro and others is very useful because it is quite difficult to measure the mass of a gas but it is much easier to measure its volume. If we know the volume of a gas (at 1 atmosphere and 20 °C) we can very quickly work out how many moles it contains.

KEY TERMS

Rules for relating the volume of a gas to the number of moles it contains

- Volume of gas (dm³) = number of moles × 24.0 dm³
- Number of moles of gas = $\dfrac{\text{volume of gas (dm}^3)}{24.0 \text{ dm}^3}$

WORKED EXAMPLE

Examples of gas volume calculations

13 The action of some acid on a carbonate produced 7.2 dm³ of carbon dioxide (measured at 1 atmosphere and 20 °C). How many moles of carbon dioxide is this? What is the mass of this gas? (C = 12, O = 16)

Calculating the number of moles of carbon dioxide

Number of moles of carbon dioxide = $\dfrac{\text{volume (dm}^3)}{24.0}$

= $\dfrac{7.2}{24.0}$ moles of a gas

= **0.30 moles** (correct to 2 significant figures)

Calculating the mass of carbon dioxide

The mass of 1 mole of carbon dioxide (CO_2) is 12 + 16 + 16 = 44 g

Therefore the mass of 0.30 moles carbon dioxide is 0.30 × 44 g

= **13.2 g**

241

▶ **Figure 17.4**
Apparatus to collect a measured quantity of hydrogen over water in an inverted burette.

Activity 17.2
How many grams of magnesium are used to produce a measured quantity of hydrogen?

Measuring the volume of a gas produced in a reaction

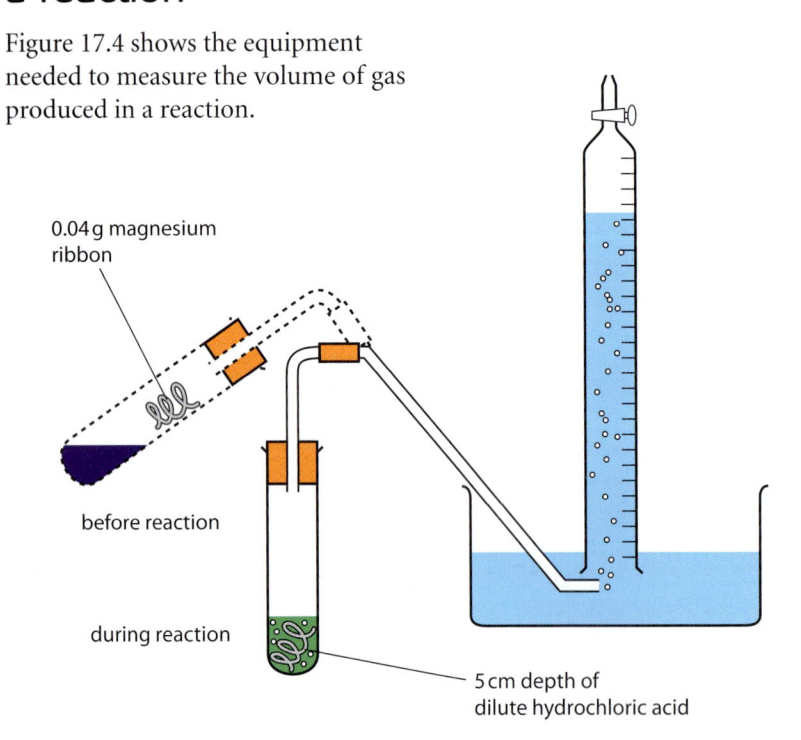

Figure 17.4 shows the equipment needed to measure the volume of gas produced in a reaction.

0.04 g magnesium ribbon

before reaction

during reaction

5 cm depth of dilute hydrochloric acid

The test tube contains about 5 cm depth of dilute hydrochloric acid (enough to react with all the magnesium). A weighed piece of magnesium (about 0.04 g) is placed higher in the test tube so that it does not come into contact with the acid. When the equipment is connected and the burette is full of water the magnesium is shaken down into the acid. The bubbles of hydrogen are collected in the burette and the total volume of hydrogen produced is measured (in dm^3).

(The water levels inside and outside the burette should be equalised to make the pressure on the gas inside and outside the same.)

The equation for the reaction is this:

Mg(s) + 2HCl(aq) → MgCl$_2$(aq) + H$_2$(g)

Suppose the volume of hydrogen produced is 60 cm^3 (0.060 dm^3).

WORKED EXAMPLES

14 *To find how many moles of hydrogen were produced*

$$\text{Number of moles of hydrogen} = \frac{\text{volume of hydrogen}}{24 \text{ dm}^3}$$

$$= \frac{0.060}{24}$$

$$= 0.0025 \text{ moles (correct to 2 significant figures)}$$

The equation shows that 1 mole of magnesium atoms react with the acid to form 1 mole of hydrogen molecules.

Therefore the number of moles of magnesium atoms used is also 0.0025 moles.

To find out the number of grams of magnesium used to make 60 cm³ hydrogen

(Mg = 24)

Mass of magnesium used = number of moles × relative molecular mass

= 0.0025 × 24 g

= **0.060 g** (correct to 2 significant figures)

So we calculate that 0.060 g of magnesium will make 60 cm³ of hydrogen (measured at 20 °C and 1 atmosphere pressure).

Temperature and pressure affect the volume of a mole of gas

The molar volume of a gas is 24 dm³ at 20 °C and 1 atmosphere (100 kPa) pressure. At any other temperature or pressure the volume will be different. If the pressure is higher then the volume will decrease. If the temperature rises the volume will increase; for example, the volume of a mole of gas at 100 °C is 30.6 dm³.

QUESTIONS

17.11 How many moles of gas are there in the following (all measured at 20°C and 1 atmosphere pressure)?

a) 120 cm³ chlorine

b) 2000 cm³ hydrogen

c) 480 cm³ carbon dioxide

d) 1120 cm³ methane.

17.12 What is the volume (at 20 °C and 1 atmosphere pressure) of the following gases?

a) 0.1 moles fluorine molecules

b) 10 moles hydrogen molecules

c) 0.5 moles argon atoms

d) 0.01 moles carbon dioxide molecules.

> **17.13** When acid is added to sodium carbonate, carbon dioxide is evolved. The reaction is as follows:
>
> $Na_2CO_3(s) + 2HCl(aq) \rightarrow 2NaCl(aq) + H_2O(l) + CO_2(g)$
>
> a) What volume of carbon dioxide (at 20 °C and 1 atmosphere) is produced from one mole of sodium carbonate?
> b) What volume of carbon dioxide (at 20 °C and 1 atmosphere) is produced from 6.3 g sodium carbonate? (Na = 23, C = 12, O = 16)
>
> **17.14** What volume of sulfur dioxide (at 20 °C and 1 atmosphere) is produced from the coal burnt in Question 17.7 on page 236?

17.5 Moles in solutions

Chemists very often use chemicals in solution in water. For example, dilute sulfuric acid is a solution of concentrated sulfuric acid in water and hydrochloric acid is a solution of the gas hydrogen chloride in water. It is often very important to know the **concentration** of the solution. We can measure the concentration of a solute in two different ways. We could measure the number of grams of the solute there are in each dm^3, or we could measure the number of molecules (or moles of molecules) there are in each dm^3. It is more useful to know the concentration in moles per dm^3. We often call this the **molarity** of the solution and we use the 'M' to describe the concentration of the solution in moles per dm^3.

So:

a 1M solution is a solution that contains 1 mole of solute per dm^3 (1 mol/dm^3)

a 2M solution contains two moles per dm^3 (2 mol/dm^3)

a 0.1M solution contains 0.1 moles per dm^3 (0.1 mol/dm^3).

Also:

1 dm^3 of a 1M solution contains 1 mole of solute

0.5 dm^3 of a 2M solution contains 1 mole of solute

10 dm^3 of a 0.1M solution contains 1 mole of solute

KEY TERMS

Rules for relating the number of moles in a solution to the volume of a solution and to the concentration (in moles per dm^3)

- Number of moles in solution
  = volume of solution (in dm^3) × concentration

- Concentration = $\dfrac{\text{number of moles}}{\text{volume of solution in } dm^3}$

- Volume of solution in dm^3 = $\dfrac{\text{number of moles}}{\text{concentration}}$

How much?

WORKED EXAMPLE

What we can find out using these equations?

We can use these equations to solve a number of problems like these:

15 a) What is the concentration of a solution of sodium chloride that contains 0.5 moles in 200 cm³?
   b) What volume of a 1 M solution of hydrochloric acid will contain 10 moles?
   c) How much sodium hydrogen carbonate ($NaHCO_3$) will be needed to make up 500 cm³ of a 4 M solution? (Na = 23, H = 1, C = 12, O = 16)

a) Concentration $= \dfrac{\text{number of moles}}{\text{volume of solution in dm}^3}$

$= \dfrac{0.5}{0.2}$

$= 2.5\,M$

b) Volume of solution in dm³ $= \dfrac{\text{number of moles}}{\text{molarity}}$

$= \dfrac{10}{1}$

$= 10\,dm^3$

c) Number of moles in solution = volume of solution (in dm³) × molarity

$= 0.5 \times 4$

$= 2.0\text{ moles}$

The relative molecular mass of $NaHCO_3$ is 23 + 1 + 12 + (3 × 16) = 84

One mole of sodium hydrogen carbonate has a mass of 84 g

Therefore mass of sodium hydrogen carbonate = 2 × 84 g

$= 168\,g$

Reacting volumes

When hydrochloric acid is neutralised by sodium hydroxide, the reaction that occurs is shown by this equation.

$HCl(aq) + NaOH(aq) \rightarrow NaCl(aq) + H_2O(l)$

From the equation we can see that one mole of the acid is neutralised exactly by one mole of the alkali. We know therefore that 1 dm³ of 1M alkali will neutralise:
- 1 dm³ of 1 M acid, or
- 500 cm³ of 2 M acid, or
- 10 dm³ of 0.1 M acid

because all these volumes contain 1 mole of the acid.

The reaction between sulfuric acid and sodium hydroxide is a little different.

$H_2SO_4(aq) + 2NaOH(aq) \rightarrow Na_2SO_4(aq) + H_2O(l)$

Activity 17.3
Finding the percentage purity of a sample of sodium hydroxide

In this case 2 moles of the alkali are needed to neutralise 1 mole of the acid. Can you work out what volumes of 1 M acid, 2 M acid and 0.1 M acid will be needed to neutralise 1 dm^3 of 1 M alkali in this case?

Titrations

When reactions in solution like these neutralisations are being investigated, we need to have ways of measuring volumes accurately. This requires several pieces of special apparatus for measuring the volumes.

A **pipette** is used for measuring out accurately a known volume of solution. The liquid is sucked up into the pipette using a **pipette filler** until the bottom of the meniscus is level with the line on the stem of the pipette. (The meniscus is the name given to the top of the liquid; it is not horizontal but raised slightly at the edges where the liquid is attracted to the glass.) Your eye should be on the same level as the meniscus.

A **burette** is used for measuring accurately a volume that we do not know in advance. The volume is read at the beginning. We can then run out as much of the solution as we want and then read the burette again. The difference between the two readings tells us how much we have run out. Again, to read it we look at the graduation at the bottom of the meniscus

An important point to note when you are using both the pipette and the burette is that they must both be washed out before use, first with distilled water and then (more than once) with the solution you are going to measure. Can you think of reasons for this?

The **volumetric flask** is used to make a solution of accurately known concentration. How this is done is shown in Figure 17.7.

The steps below show how this apparatus is used and the kind of work they are used for. The sequence shows how to find out how pure a sample of sodium hydroxide is. This kind of work is called **quantitative analysis**.

Sodium hydroxide reacts with the carbon dioxide in the air and so it is never 100% pure. In this experiment a sample of sodium hydroxide is weighed accurately and made into a solution in a volumetric flask so that the solution is around 0.1 M. It is then neutralised with sulfuric acid that is exactly

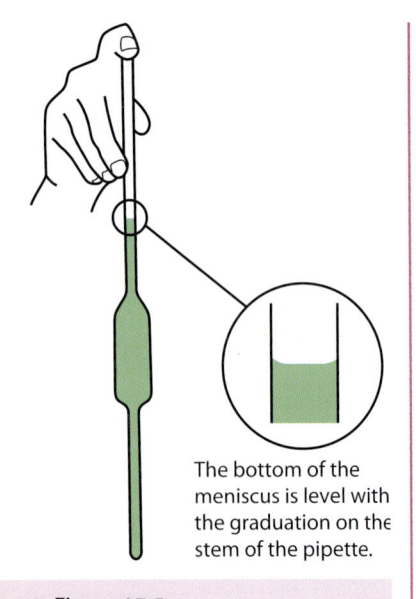

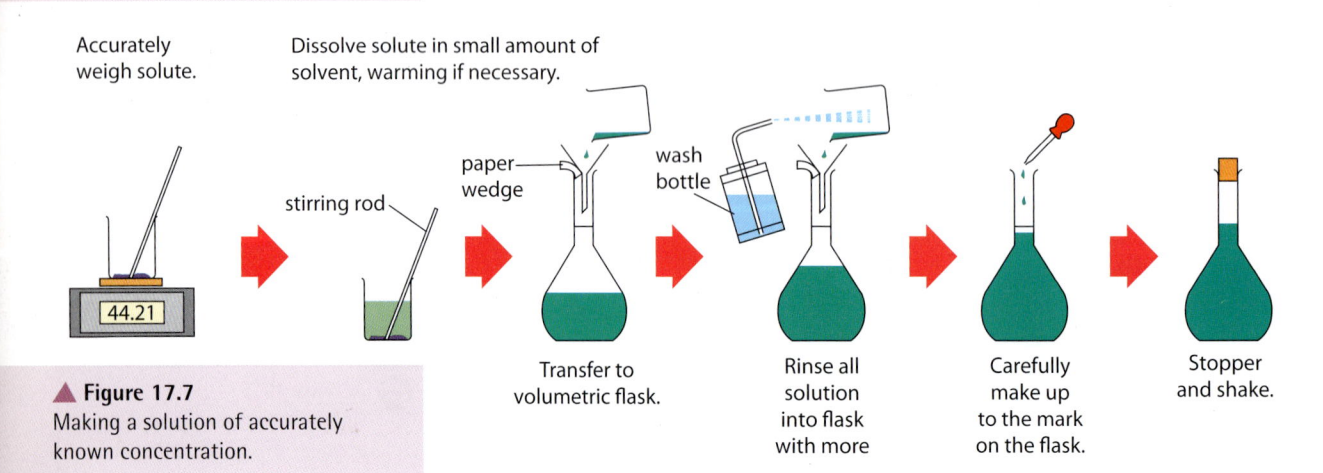

▲ **Figure 17.5**
Pipette with inset showing meniscus when pipette is full.
The bottom of the meniscus is level with the graduation on the stem of the pipette.

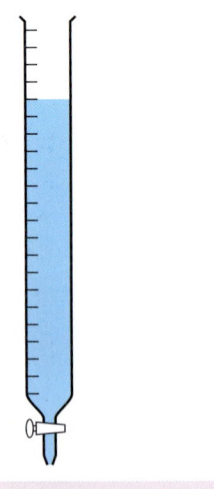

▲ **Figure 17.6**
Burette.

▲ **Figure 17.7**
Making a solution of accurately known concentration.

Accurately weigh solute. → Dissolve solute in small amount of solvent, warming if necessary. (stirring rod) → Transfer to volumetric flask. (paper wedge) → Rinse all solution into flask with more (wash bottle) → Carefully make up to the mark on the flask. → Stopper and shake.

246

0.1 M. This acid is called a **standard solution** and it is usually made up very accurately by the manufacturer. When the acid is added we need to know when the point has been reached when the solution has been neutralised exactly (to the nearest drop!). To find this, litmus solution is added to the alkali and when the neutralisation point is reached it will be neither blue nor red but a purple colour. This point in the titration is called the **end-point**. The whole process is called a **titration;** we are *titrating* the alkali with acid.

Steps in the titration

All the glassware must be very clean.

1. Weigh out accurately (to the nearest milligram) 4 g of sodium hydroxide. This is the right amount to make a solution of about 0.1 M when it is dissolved in distilled water and made up to 1 dm^3.
2. Dissolve the sodium hydroxide in distilled water in a volumetric flask and make the volume up to 1 dm^3. This procedure is shown in Figure 17.7. Stopper the flask and invert it several times to mix it thoroughly.
3. Wash the burette with the standard acid and then fill it. It should be filled almost to the top but it is not sensible to try and fill it exactly to the top.
4. Wash a conical flask with distilled water.
5. Wash the pipette with the alkali and fill it to the mark using a pipette filler. Empty the alkali into the conical flask.
6. Add one or two drops (only) of litmus solution to the flask. Note that the solution turns blue.
7. All the equipment for carrying out the titration is shown in Figure 17.8. First carry out an approximate titration. Read the initial level of the acid in the burette. Run 1 cm^3 of acid into the flask. Swirl it to ensure mixing. Note the indicator colour. Repeat this process until the indicator colour changes permanently. You will then know, to the nearest 1 cm^3, how much acid you must add to reach the end-point.
8. Carry out an accurate titration by repeating steps 5 and 6 and then adding acid until it is within 1 cm^3 of the end-point. Swirl the flask to make sure it is mixed. Then add the acid a drop at a time, swirling the flask after each drop. Note the volume in the burette after each drop. Eventually the litmus will change to purple. After the next drop it will change to red. Record the level of the acid *after the drop that made the colour change to purple*. This is the exact end-point.
9. Repeat step 8 until two values for the amount of acid added agree to within 0.1 cm^3.
10. Calculate the:
    - number of moles of sulfuric acid used
    - number of moles of sodium hydroxide in the pipette
    - number of moles of sodium hydroxide in the sample weighed
    - number of grams of pure sodium hydroxide in the sample weighed
    - percentage purity of the sodium hydroxide.

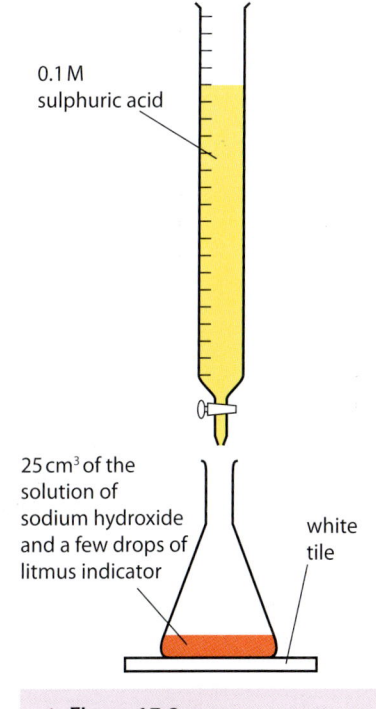

▲ **Figure 17.8** Carrying out a titration.

Table 17.2 shows some specimen results for this investigation. These five calculations are carried out below using the specimen results.

	Rough titration (cm³)	Titration 1 (cm³)	Titration 2 (cm³)
Initial reading	0.03	13.8	26.3
Final reading	13.8	26.3	38.9
Volume of acid used	13.5	12.5	12.6

Average of the two titrations: 12.55 cm³ acid used

▲ Table 17.2 Specimen titration results.

The equation for the reaction is:

$$H_2SO_4(aq) + 2NaOH(aq) \rightarrow Na_2SO_4(aq) + 2H_2O(l)$$
  1 mole   2 moles   1 mole   2 moles

Calculating the number of moles of sulfuric acid used

Volume of sulfuric acid used (see results table) is 12.55 cm³ (0.01255 dm³)

Number of moles = volume (in dm³) × concentration (in mol/dm³)

= 0.01255 × 0.1

= **0.001255 moles**

Calculating the number of moles of sodium hydroxide in the pipette

From the equation one mole of the acid reacted with two moles of the alkali. Therefore the number of moles in the pipette sample is:
2 × 0.001255 = **0.00251 moles**

Calculating the number of moles of sodium hydroxide in the sample weighed

The pipette holds 25 cm³ of solution. The flask holds 1000 cm³

25 cm³ of sodium hydroxide solution contains 0.00251 moles

Therefore 1 cm³ of solution contains $\frac{0.00251}{25}$ moles

Therefore 1000 cm³ of solution contains $\frac{0.00251 \times 1000}{25}$ moles

= **0.1004 moles**

Calculating the number of grams of pure sodium hydroxide in the sample weighed

Calculating the relative molecular mass of sodium hydroxide, Na = 23, O = 16, H = 1. Therefore NaOH = 23 + 16 + 1 = 40

The number of grams in the flask = number of moles × relative molecular mass

= 0.1004 × 40 g

= **4.016g**

Calculating the percentage purity of the sodium hydroxide

The number of grams weighed out originally was 4.12 g. The number of grams of pure sodium hydroxide that this contains was found by the titration to be 4.016 g:

The percentage purity of a substance can be calculated using the formula:

$$\text{Percentage purity} = \frac{\text{mass of pure material} \times 100}{\text{total mass of material}}$$

$$= 4.016 \times \frac{100}{4.12}$$

$$= \mathbf{97\%} \text{ (correct to 2 significant figures)}$$

A note on accuracy – why give the answer to two significant figures?

It is possible to carry out very accurate titrations but only with accurately made apparatus and with very pure chemicals. If you work carefully it is possible to get two results for the acid added which agree with each other to within 0.1 cm³. The total amount added in this titration is around 12 cm³ so your accuracy is ± 0.1 in 12 which is a little better than 1%. This means that any answer you give at the end of your calculations should be corrected to two significant figures, which means an accuracy of 1 part in 100.
If you give the answer to the calculation to three significant figures it would be 10 times greater than the accuracy of your practical work. So your answer should be given to two significant figures only.

QUESTIONS

17.15 What is the concentration of the following solutions?
   a) 1000 cm³ sodium chloride solution containing 2 moles
   b) 500 cm³ hydrochloric acid containing 2 moles
   c) 100 cm³ copper sulfate solution containing 0.1 moles
   d) 10 dm³ sodium carbonate solution containing 1 mole
   e) 10 dm³ sodium chloride solution containing 0.1 moles
   f) 2 dm³ sulfuric acid containing 0.5 mole
   g) 50 cm³ ammonia solution containing 0.01 moles
   h) 1 cm³ sodium chloride solution containing 0.003 moles

17.16 How many moles are there in each of the following solutions?
   a) 1000 cm³ of 0.5 M copper sulfate solution
   b) 2000 cm³ of 2 M sulfuric acid
   c) 100 cm³ of 0.2 M sodium sulfate solution
   d) 1 cm³ of 0.5 M hydrochloric acid
   e) 10 dm³ of 0.5 M copper sulfate solution
   f) 5 dm³ of 0.01 M sodium sulfate solution
   g) 10 cm³ of 0.05 M ammonia solution
   h) 5 dm³ of 2 M nitric acid

17.17 What is the concentration (in mol/dm³) of the following solutions?
   a) 1 dm³ of solution containing 73 g hydrogen chloride, HCl
      (H = 1, Cl = 35.5)
   b) 1 dm³ of solution containing 4 g sodium hydroxide, NaOH
      (H = 1, O = 16, Na = 23)
   c) 100 cm³ of solution containing 19 g magnesium chloride, $MgCl_2$ (Mg = 24, Cl = 35.5)
   d) 10 dm³ of solution containing 9.8 g sulfuric acid, H_2SO_4
      (H = 1, S = 32, O = 16)
   e) 10 cm³ of solution containing 0.8 g copper sulfate, $CuSO_4$
      (Cu = 64, S = 32, O = 16)
   f) 1 dm³ of solution containing 0.4 g copper sulfate, $CuSO_4$
      (Cu = 64, S = 32, O = 16)
   g) 5 dm³ of solution containing 34 g ammonia, NH^3
      (H = 1, N = 14)
   h) 200 cm³ of solution containing 2.1 g nitric acid, HNO_3
      (H = 1, N = 14, O = 16)

17.18 Excess of calcium carbonate was added to 200 cm³ of 2 M hydrochloric acid.
  a) Write an equation for the reaction.
  b) How many moles of carbon dioxide were produced?
  c) What volume of carbon dioxide was produced (measured at 20 °C and 1 atmosphere pressure)?
  d) What mass of calcium carbonate was used in the reaction?
  (Ca = 40, C = 12, O = 16)

17.19 a) What volume of 2 M copper sulfate would be needed to react with 13 g zinc according to the equation:

$$Zn(s) + CuSO_4(aq, 2M) \rightarrow ZnSO_4(aq) + Cu(s)$$

  b) What mass of copper is produced in the reaction?
  (Cu = 64, Zn = 65)

17.20 In an experiment to determine the concentration of a solution of potassium hydroxide, 25 cm³ of it was titrated with 0.1 M hydrochloric acid. 16.2 cm³ of the acid was required. What is the concentration (in mol/dm³) of the potassium hydroxide?

17.21 Baking powder is a mixture of sodium hydrogen carbonate and flour. In an experiment to work out the proportion of sodium hydrogen carbonate in the mixture, 10.20 g of the powder was mixed with water and made up to 1 dm³ in a volumetric flask. 25 cm³ of this was then titrated against exactly 0.10 M hydrochloric acid. It was found that 22.2 cm³ of acid was needed to neutralise the baking powder. What percentage of the baking powder was sodium hydrogen carbonate? (Na = 23, H = 1, C = 12, O = 16)

Summary

Now that you have completed this chapter, you should be able to:

- define, understand and use in calculations, relative atomic mass, relative molecular mass and relative formula mass
- use balanced equations to calculate reacting quantities
- define, understand and use the mole in calculations on reacting quantities
- distinguish between empirical and molecular formulae of compounds and describe simple ways of finding empirical formulae
- know that a mole of any gas occupies 24 dm³ at room temperature and pressure, and be able to use this in calculations involving reacting gas volumes
- define the concentration of an aqueous solution in terms of moles per dm³ and use this in calculations involving reactions in solution
- know how to make up solutions of accurately known concentration and how to use them in titrations involving the use of pipettes and burettes

Index

A

acacia tree 215
acetic acid (see ethanoic acid)
acetyl salicylic acid (aspirin) 198
acidic oxides 82
acids 74, 75–81, 85
    reactions with metals 76, 115–16
actinides 59
activation energy 127
addition polymers 205
addition reactions 193
alchemists 35
alcohol (see ethanol)
alcohols (generic) 194–6, 199, 206
alkali industry 211, 222–4
alkali metals 57, 59–62
alkaline earth metals 57
alkalis 74, 77–81, 85, 199
    uses 211
alkanes 189–90
alkenes 191–4, 205
allotropes 52–3
alloy steels 154
alloys 110, 153–4
alpha particles 31
aluminium 23, 84, 114, 116
    extraction 146, 149–50
    ions 89
    physical properties 110, 111
    uses 151–2, 156
aluminium chloride 24
aluminium hydroxide 82–3, 91
aluminium oxide 24, 70, 149, 151–2
americium 40, 59
amines 206
amino acids 18, 207–8
ammonia (nitrogen hydride) 24, 91, 183
    manufacture 69
    test 92
    uses 80, 217
ammonium chloride 24, 183
ammonium ions 89, 91
amphoteric oxides 83–4
amyl acetate 186, 200
analysis 18, 87, 88
anhydrous copper sulfate 132, 181
anhydrous crystals 86
anions 89, 90, 102
anodes 100, 102, 103, 136
antioxidants 94

B

aqueous solutions 77–8
argon 23, 67, 70, 161, 162
    uses 214
aspirin (see acetyl salicylic acid)
atmosphere 159–68
    pollution of 164–8
atomic mass units 33
atomic numbers 33
atomic theories 30–1
atoms 28, 29, 30–4
Avogadro, Amadeo 231, 240–1

bacteria 28, 62, 80, 197
Baekeland, Leo 207
Baghdad battery 138
bakelite 207
baking soda 80
barium 23
barium chloride 24
barium sulfate 24, 91
bases 77, 84
basic oxides 82
batteries (cells) 137–9
bauxite 143, 149
Becquerel, Henri 39–40
beryllium 23
Bessemer converters 149
bitumen 226
blast furnaces 148
blood 69, 80
Bohr, Niels 31, 37–8
boiling points 48, 69
boron 23
branched chain hydrocarbons 190
brass 152, 153
breathalysers 97
Bristol 107
bromide ions 65
bromine 9, 23, 62, 64–6, 192, 193
bromine water 65
bronze 143, 153, 155
Brownian movement 10
Buchner, Eduard 179
buckyballs 53, 203
burettes 87, 246
butane 188, 189
butanoic acid 197
butene 191

C

caesium 28, 40, 59, 61
calcium 23, 113, 114, 115, 116
    ions 89
calcium carbonate 24, 76, 81
    uses 118–19
calcium chloride 24
calcium hydroxide (slaked lime) 24, 76, 81, 91, 220–1
calcium nitrate 24
calcium oxide (quicklime) 24, 119, 145, 220–1
calcium silicate (slag) 145
calcium sulfate 221
candle wax 22, 48, 189
carbohydrates 207–8
carbon 23, 34, 145, 187–8, 239
    allotropes 52–3
    atomic structure 38
    isotopes 40
carbon dioxide 6, 24, 32, 79, 161
    atmosphere 161, 165, 167
    molecular structure 47
    test 75, 76, 92
    uses 214
carbon monoxide 24, 82, 95, 133, 145, 148, 150
    pollution by 165
carbon nanotubes 53, 203
carbon steels 154
carbonate ions 90, 91
carbonates 75–6, 91, 120, 199
carbonic acid 79, 80
carboxylic acids 197–200
case hardening 154
catalysts 69, 178–9
catalytic converters 69, 166, 179
cathodes 100, 102, 103, 136
cations 89, 90, 102
caustic soda (see sodium hydroxide)
caustic substances 79
Cavendish, Henry 162, 163
cells (batteries) 137–9
cellulose 204, 208, 209
cement 220
CFCs (chlorofluorocarbons) 165, 168
Chadwick, James 31
chalk 220
charcoal 145, 154
chemical properties 109

251

chemical reactions 20–2
chloride ions 49, 64, 65, 97
    test 90, 91
chlorine 23, 62, 63, 64–6
    atomic structure 48–9
    isotopes 34
    manufacture 64, 223
    molecular structure 45
    test 92, 100
    uses 223, 224
chlorine oxide 70
chlorine water 65
chloroethene 205
chlorofluorocarbons (CFCs) 165, 168
chromatograms 17
chromatography 17–19, 20
chromium 23, 68, 105
chromium (III) oxide 24
chromium steel 154
citric acid 80, 198
civetone 186, 187
cleaning liquids 80
Cleopatra 74, 76
coal 126, 130, 131, 132–3, 225
Coalbrookdale 145, 155
cobalt 23, 68
cobalt (II) chloride 24, 182
cobalt chloride paper 132
cobalt steel 154
coke (fuel) 131, 145, 150
column chromatography 17
compounds 20, 21, 24–5
concentration, solutions 79, 244
concrete 220
condensation polymers 206–7
condensation reactions 181, 200
conductivity, electricity 111, 203
conductivity, heat 112
conservation of energy 126
contact processes 218
cooking 129
cooking oil 192
copper 23, 76, 113, 114, 115, 116, 117, 118
    alloys 153
    extraction 104, 145
    ions 89, 97, 116, 117
    physical properties 68, 111
    uses 152
copper (I) oxide 24, 96
copper (II) chloride 24, 100
copper (II) hydroxide 90
copper (II) nitrate 24, 119
copper (II) oxide 24, 85, 96, 114
copper (II) sulfate 24, 69, 77, 86, 100, 103, 132, 181–2
copper (II) sulfide 145
copper–zinc cell 137
corrosion, metals 121–2
covalent bonds 45–8
cracking, hydrocarbons 192
crude oil 2, 133, 225–7
cryolite (sodium aluminium fluoride) 149
crystal lattices 50, 51
crystallisation 15, 86
crystals 48, 50–1, 86, 154
cupro-nickel 153
Curie, Marie 3, 39

D

Dalton, John 30, 32, 240
Darby, Abraham 145, 155
Davy, Humphrey 151
dehydrating agents 217
Democritus 7, 30
density, elements 68, 70, 109, 110
di-esters 206
diamonds 52–3
dicarboxylic acids 206
diesel oil 226
diffusion 8–10
2,2-dimethylpropane 190
dinitrogen monoxide 82
diols 206
dissociation, acids 198
distillation 15, 16
Döbereiner, Johann 35
doped silicon 112
double bonds 47, 191, 192
Drax power station 135, 221
ductility 112
duralumin 153

E

Einstein, Albert 10
electric arc furnaces 148
electric current 109
electrolysis 98–105, 146, 147, 151, 223
electrolytes 136
electrolytic processes 122
electromagnets 16
electrons 30, 31, 33, 37–8, 96, 100, 116
electrophoresis 19
electroplating 105
elements 21, 22, 23
empirical formulae 237
endothermic reactions 127
energy changes 21, 126–8
enzymes 164, 179, 207, 208, 209
equations (reactions) 230
essential oils (see terpenes)
esters 186, 199–200, 210
ethane 189
ethane diol 206
ethanoic acid (acetic acid) 80, 197, 198–200
ethanol (alcohol) 48, 97, 98, 188, 194, 197
    manufacture 195–6
    uses 131, 134, 196
ethene 48, 191–2, 205
ethyl ethanoate 199
eutrophication 170
exothermic reactions 115, 127, 129

F

Faraday, Michael 101
fats 209–10
fatty acids 193
filaments 110
filtering 14
filtrates 14
flint 54
fluoride ions 66
fluorine 23, 62, 63, 66, 139, 150
food 128–9

formic acid (see methanoic acid)
formulae (compounds) 32, 46, 48, 236
fossil fuels 131, 225–7
fractional distillation 16, 214–15, 225–7
fractionating columns 16
froth flotation 144
fruit juices 80
fuel cells 139
fuels 130–5
fullerenes 53, 203

G

galena 143
gallium 23
galvanised iron 109
gas (fuel) 130, 133, 225, 226
gas syringes 159
gases (state of matter) 6, 7
germanium 23, 37
glass 111
glucose 32, 129, 180, 181, 204, 207, 209
glycerine 209
glycerol 209
gold 23, 105, 111, 113, 115, 116
    extraction 144
    physical properties 110
graphene 203
graphite 52–3, 145
greenhouse effect 167–8
Grove, William 139
guano 213

H

Haber process 215–17
haematite 143
haemoglobin 69
hair colour 69
halide ions 63, 65
halides 64–5
Halifax Island 213
Hall–Héroult process 150
halocarbons 190
halogens 45, 62–6
    reactions with alkanes 190
hayboxes 129
helium 23, 38, 44, 67, 162
Higgs boson 31
Hindenburg (airship) 135
Hodgkin, Dorothy 3, 207
homologous series 189
hydrated copper sulfate 132, 181–2
hydrated crystals 182
hydrobromic acid 64
hydrocarbons 131–2, 133, 189–94
hydrochloric acid 64
hydrogen 23, 38
    atomic structure 38, 44
    ions 85
    isotopes 40
    molecular structure 45
    test 75, 76, 92
    uses 134–5
hydrogen bromide 24, 64
hydrogen chloride 24, 64, 183
hydrogen fluoride 24
hydrogen iodide 24, 64

Index

hydrogen oxide (see water)
hydrogen peroxide 24
hydrogen sulfide 24
hydroiodic acid 64
hydrolysis 181, 207–8, 210
hydroxides 77, 83, 120
hydroxyl group 194

I

impurities 14, 19
indicators 75, 78, 87
inert gases 44, 58, 66–7, 161–2
insoluble substances 13, 14
insulin 207
iodide ions 64, 65, 90, 91
iodine 6, 23, 62, 63, 64–5
    isotopes 40
ionic compounds 48–51, 98, 100, 229
ionic crystals 50
ionic solutions 51, 101
ions 49, 50, 88–91, 116
iron 23, 95, 113, 114, 115, 116, 117
    corrosion 122
    extraction 145, 147–9
    history 155
    ions 89, 90, 91, 96, 97, 117
    physical properties 68, 110, 111
    uses 69
iron (II) chloride 24, 69
iron (II) hydroxide 90
iron (II) sulfate 24, 96
iron (II) sulfide 24
iron (III) chloride 24, 63, 69, 97
iron (III) hydroxide 90
iron (III) iodide 63
iron (III) oxide 24, 95, 96, 97, 145
iron (III) sulfate 96
Ironbridge 58, 145
irreversible reactions 21
isotopes 34

K

khaki dye 69
kinetic particle theory 7–10
krypton 23, 67, 162

L

lactic acid 79, 80, 198
lanthanides 59
lard 192
Lavoisier, Antoine 162
lead 23, 58, 84, 113, 115, 116
    extraction 151
    pollution by 165
lead (II) bromide 24, 98
lead (II) chloride 24
lead (II) iodide 64, 88, 91
lead (II) nitrate 24
lead (II) oxide 24
lead (IV) oxide 24
Leclanché, Georges 138–9
lemon juice 75
lemons 136
Liebig, Justus 15
Liebig condensers 15
light 180–1

lime (see also calcium hydroxide, calcium oxide) 118, 220–1
limelight 221
limestone 81, 145, 148, 220–1
limewater 76
limonene 186
Lindow man 39
liquid helium 67
liquids 6, 7–8
lithium 23, 59, 60, 139
    atomic structure 61–2
litmus 75
locating agents 18, 208
lubricating oils 226

M

macromolecules 51–4, 203–11
magnesium 21, 23, 113, 114, 115, 116, 127, 128
    atomic structure 38
    extraction 146
    ions 49
    physical properties 110
magnesium chloride 24
magnesium ethanoate 198–9
magnesium nitrate 24
magnesium oxide 21, 24, 51, 70
malic acid 198
malleability 112
maltose 196
manganese 23, 68
manganese (IV) oxide 24
manganate (VII) ions 96, 101
marble 76, 220
margarine 69, 192, 193
Mars 19, 158
marshmallows 128
melting points 48, 69, 109, 110
memory metals 107, 154
Mendeleev, Dmitri 35
menisci 246
mercury (element) 23, 144
Mercury (planet) 164
mercury (II) chloride 24
mercury (II) oxide 24
mercury (II) sulphide (cinnabar) 144
metalloid elements 70
metals 22, 57–8, 107–22
    alloys 110, 153–4
    extraction 143–51, 155
    history 154–6
    reactions with acids 76, 115–16
    uses 151–2
metamorphic rock 220
meteorites 5, 155
methane 46, 133, 188, 189
methanoic acid (formic acid) 197, 198
methanol 48, 194
methylated spirits 195
2-methylbutane 190
3-methylbutanoic acid 186
mho (unit) 111
microscopes 28
minerals 143
molar volumes 240–1, 243
molarities, solutions 244
molecules 29–30, 32, 229

moles 231, 240–1, 244, 248
molybdenum steel 154
monomers 205
Moon 4, 5
muskone 187

N

names, compounds 120
nanotubes 53, 203
naphtha 226
natural gas (see gas)
natural polymers 207–9
Nauru 213
neon 23, 67, 162
neutral oxides 82
neutralisation reactions 77, 84–5, 245–6
neutrons 31, 33
Newlands, John 35
nichrome 111
nickel 23, 68
    uses 69, 105
nitrate fertilisers 215, 217
nitrate ions 90, 91
nitrates 119, 170–1
nitric acid 24
    manufacture 69
nitrogen 23
    atmosphere 160
    molecular structure 47, 48
    uses 214, 215–17
nitrogen dioxide 25, 165
nitrogen hydride (see ammonia)
nitrogen monoxide 24, 165
Nobel, Alfred 3
Nobel Prizes 3, 39, 179, 205
noble gases (see inert gases)
non-renewable fuels 130, 131, 225
nuclear reactions 40
nuclei (atoms) 31, 33
nucleon numbers 33
nylon 204, 206, 207

O

octane 188
oil (fuel) 130, 133, 225
oleum 218
ores 143–6
organic acids 79, 197–200, 206
organic chemistry 187
organic compounds 187–8
Orion nebula 4, 5
osmium 56
oxidation 95, 96–7
oxidation states 96, 120
oxidative damage 94
oxide displacement reactions 118
oxide ions 49, 97
oxides 70, 77, 81–4
oxygen 23
    atmosphere 159, 160–1
    atomic structure 45, 47
    discovery 162
    molecular structure 47
    solution in water 168
    test 92
    uses 214
ozone 168

P

paper 224
paper chromatography 17
paraffin 226
Pasteur, Louis 179
pectinase 179
pentane 190
percentage purities 249
periodic properties, elements 68
periodic table 35–9, 56–70
petrol (gasoline) 189, 226
petroleum 133, 225
pH scale 78, 79, 80, 85
phelonic acids 80
phlogiston theory 162, 163
phosphates 170–1
phosphoric acids 80
phosphorus 23
phosphorus pentachloride 25
phosphorus pentoxide 25, 70
phosphorus trichloride 25
photochemical reactions 166
photograph 180
photosynthesis 129, 160–1, 180
physical processes 20
physical properties 108
pig iron 148, 149
pipettes 246
Plante, Gaston 139
plants 181, 215
plastics 1
platinum 23, 69, 178–9
pollution 143, 155, 164–8, 170–1
polyamides 206
polyesters 206
polymerisation 205
polymers 51, 205–9
polypropylene 205
polytetrafluoroethylene 205
polythene 52, 69, 188, 204, 205
polyvinyl chloride (PVC) 205, 223
potassium 23, 59, 60, 113, 114, 115, 116
  atomic structure 61–2
  discovery 151
potassium bromide 25, 100
potassium chloride 25
potassium chromate (VI) 69
potassium hydroxide 25
potassium iodide 25
potassium manganate (VII) 8–9, 25, 69, 96, 101, 192, 193
potassium nitrate 25
potential energy 127
precipitates 88
products (chemical reactions) 21
propane 189
propanoic acid 197
propanol 194
propene 191, 205
proteins 18, 207–8
proton transfer reactions 85
protons 31, 33, 85
ptyalin 179, 181, 209

Q

qualitative analysis 88
quantitative analysis 88, 246
quarks 31
quartz 54
quicklime (see calcium oxide)

R

radioactivity 39–40, 67
radiocarbon dating 39
radon 67
rainwater 79
Ramsay, William 162
rates of reaction 175–9
Rayleigh, Lord 162
reactants 21
reactivity series, metals 116, 117–18, 147
rechargeable cells 137, 139
recycling 16, 156
redox reactions 95
reducing agents 95, 97, 145
reduction 95, 96–7, 145
relative atomic masses 34, 229, 231–2
relative formula masses 229
relative molecular masses 34, 229, 231–2, 237, 248
renewable fuels 130, 131, 133–4, 225
residues 14
respiration 129, 160–1
reversible reactions 181–3
Rf values 17
rock salt 15, 130, 222
rubidium 59
rust 69, 122
Rutherford, Ernest 31
Ruzicka, Leopold 187

S

sacrificial protection 122
saliva 80, 179, 181, 209
salt (see sodium chloride)
salts (generic) 77, 84–9
sand 53, 54, 91
saturated fats 210
saturated hydrocarbons 193
saturated solutions 13
scandium 68
scanning tunnelling microscopes (STMs) 28–9
sea salt 15
sedimentary rock 220
selenium 56, 94
semiconductors 112
sewage 169
shells (electrons) 38, 44–5
silicon 23, 58, 70, 111
silicon dioxide 25, 53–4, 70
silver 23, 105, 111, 115, 116
silver bromide 25
silver chloride 25, 64, 91
silver hydroxide 25
silver nitrate 25
silver sulfate 91
slag (see calcium silicate)
slaked lime (see calcium hydroxide)
smelting 143
smoke cells 10
soap 204, 210–11, 222
sodium 23, 59, 60, 113, 114, 115, 116
  atomic structure 48–9
  discovery 151
  extraction 146
  ions 49, 89
  physical properties 110
sodium bromide 25, 65
sodium carbonate 25, 222
sodium chloride (salt) 25, 48–9, 65, 98, 100
  extraction 61, 222
  uses 222–3
sodium ethanoate 199
sodium hydrogen carbonate 199
sodium hydroxide (caustic soda) 25, 79, 199, 222, 223, 224, 246, 248
sodium iodide 65
sodium nitrate 25, 119
sodium oxide 25, 70
sodium sulfate 25
soil 81
solar prominences 4
solder 153
solids 6, 7
solubility 13
soluble substances 13, 14
solutes 14
solutions 13, 14
Solvay process 222–3
solvent extraction 144
solvents 13, 14
SS Great Britain 125–6, 130
stainless steel 154
standard solutions 247
starch 181, 204, 208–9
states of matter 6
stearic acid 198
steel 147, 149, 154
strength, acids 79
structural formulae 46, 48
structural isomers 190
sublimation 6–7
sugars 181
sulfate ions 90, 91
sulfide ores 146
sulfur 23, 139
sulfur dioxide 16–17, 25, 70, 146
  pollution by 143, 146, 165, 221
  uses 219
sulfur trioxide 25, 218
sulfuric acid 25, 32, 80, 99
  manufacture 69, 217–18
  uses 219
Sun 4, 158, 164, 167
superconductivity 203
superfluids 67
sustainability 134
symbols 32
synthetic elements 59
synthetic polymers 205

T

tartaric acid 198
temperature 177–8
temperature inversion 165
terephthalic acid 206
terpenes (essential oils) 186
terylene 204, 206, 207
tetrachloroethane 190
tetrafluoroethene 205

Index

thermal decomposition 183
thermal displacement reactions 118–20
thermit mixture 118
Thomas, John 145
Thomson, John Joseph 30, 31
tin 23, 57
titanium 68, 69
titanium alloy 153
titration 87, 88, 247
tooth decay 62
toothpaste 80
trace elements 94
transition metals 56–7, 68–9, 96
    purification 103
triple bonds 47
tritium 40
tungsten 110
tungsten steel 154
Tutankhamun 112, 113

U

Universe 22, 40, 158
unsaturated fats 210
unsaturated fatty acids 210
unsaturated hydrocarbons 193
uranium 23, 59, 143

V

vanadium 68, 69
vanadium steel 154
Venus 158, 164
Victoria Falls Bridge 1, 107
vinegar 75, 76, 98, 197
Volta, Alessandro 138
voltaic piles 138
volume
    gases 240–1, 242, 243
    solutions 244
volumetric flasks 246

W

water (hydrogen oxide) 22, 24, 32, 80
    electrolysis 98, 99
    molecular structure 46, 188
    pollution of 170–1
    uses 168–70
water cycle 169
water of crystallisation 220
wood (fuel) 134, 225

X

xenon 23, 67, 162

Y

yeast 179, 196

Z

Ziegler, Karl 205
zinc 23, 84, 113, 114, 115, 116, 118
    extraction 150–1
    ions 89, 97, 116
    physical properties 68, 110
    uses 152
zinc chloride 25
zinc hydroxide 91
zinc oxide 25, 114, 150, 151
zinc sulfate 25, 100, 151
zinc sulfide 150
zymase 179